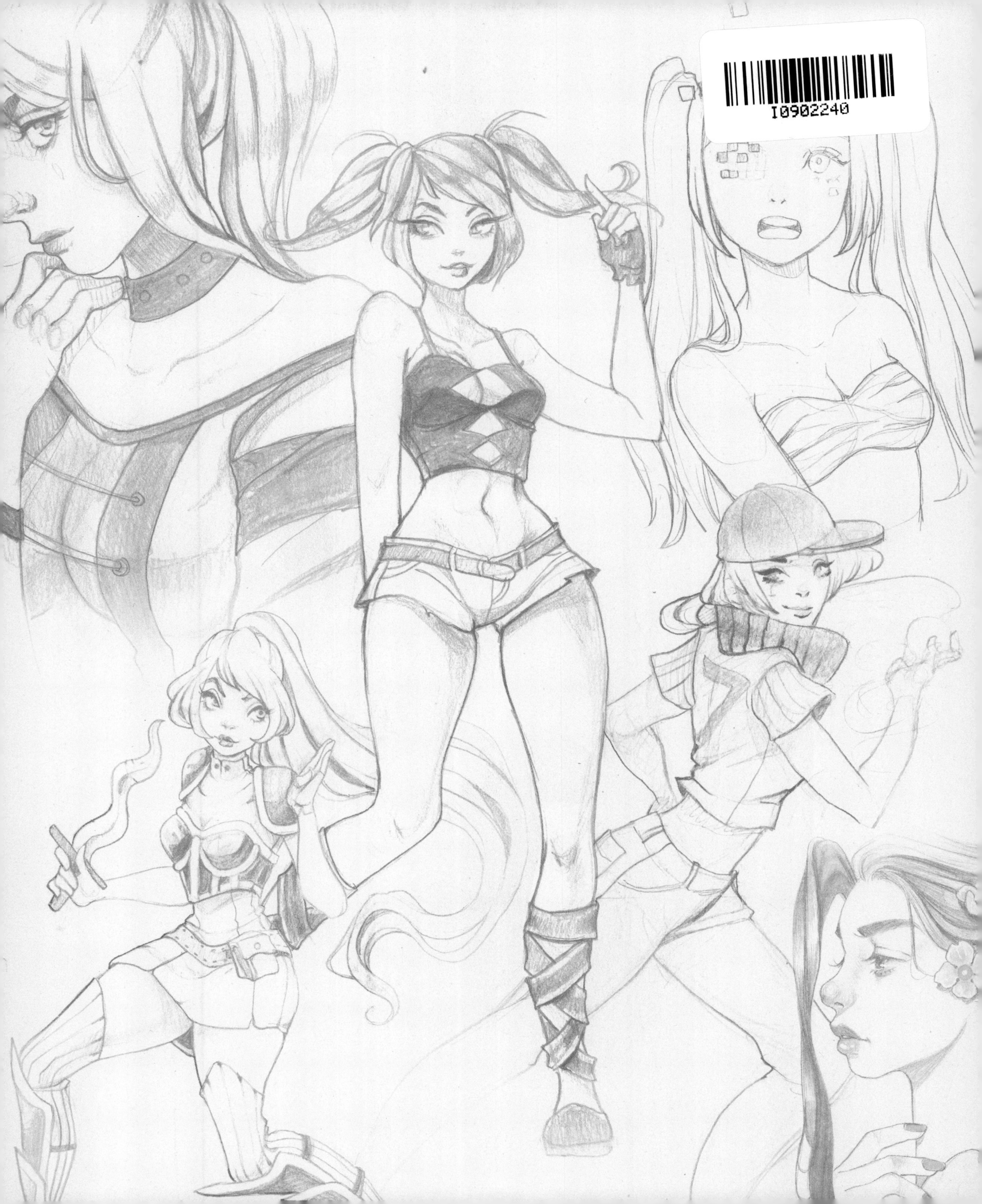

I0902240

# THE ART JOURNEY OF
# LORD GRIS

**3dtotal**Publishing

Correspondence: publishing@3dtotal.com
Website: www.3dtotal.com

*The Art Journey of Lord Gris* © 2022 3dtotal Publishing. All rights reserved. No part of this book can be reproduced in any form or by any means, without the prior written consent of the publisher. All artwork, unless stated otherwise, is copyright © 2022 Lord Gris. All artwork that is not copyright of Lord Gris is marked accordingly.

Every effort has been made to ensure the credits and contact information listed are present and correct. In the case of any errors that have occurred, the publisher respectfully directs readers to the www.3dtotalpublishing.com website for any updated information and/or corrections.

First published in the United Kingdom, 2022, by 3dtotal Publishing.

Address: 3dtotal.com Ltd,
29 Foregate Street, Worcester
WR1 1DS, United Kingdom.

Hard cover ISBN: 978-1-912843-53-4

Printing and binding: Gutenberg Press Ltd (Malta)
www.gutenberg.com.mt

Visit www.3dtotalpublishing.com for a complete list of available book titles.

Managing Director: Tom Greenway
Studio Manager: Simon Morse
Lead Editor: Samantha Rigby
Lead Designer: Fiona Tarbet
Editorial Project Manager: Sophie Symes
Editor: Jenny Fox-Proverbs

MIX
Paper from responsible sources
FSC® C022612

## One tree planted for every book sold

We at 3dtotal Publishing donate 50% of our profits to charity. For every book sold, we give to reforesting charities to plant new trees. This is just one part of our annual donation to a large number of the most effective charities, covering causes such as humanitarian work, animal welfare, and the protection of existing rainforests. We also aim to be a carbon-neutral publisher with carbon-neutral products, which means that by buying from 3dtotal Publishing, you are helping to balance the environmental damage caused by the publishing, shipping, and retail industries, as well as supporting many other causes. See 3dtotal.com/charity for full details.

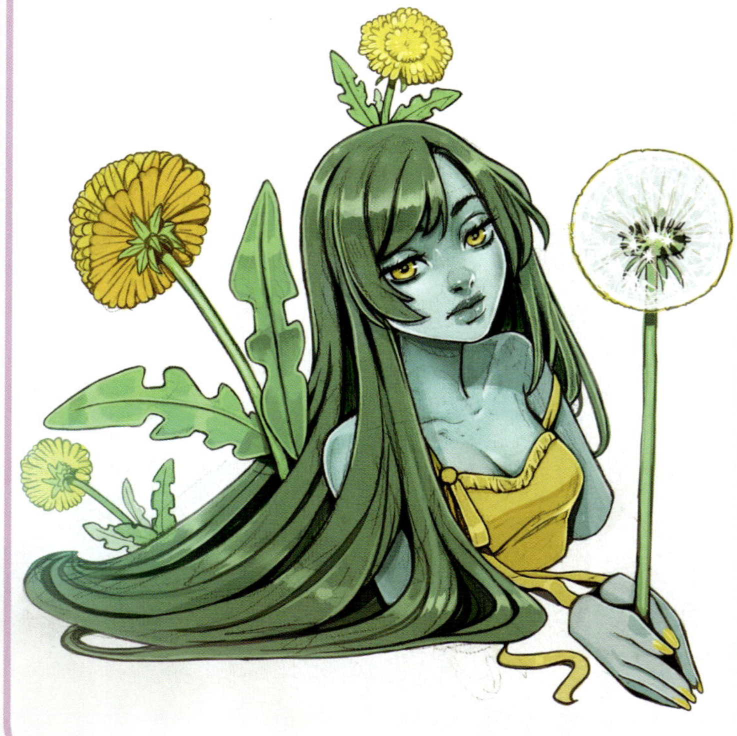

# contents



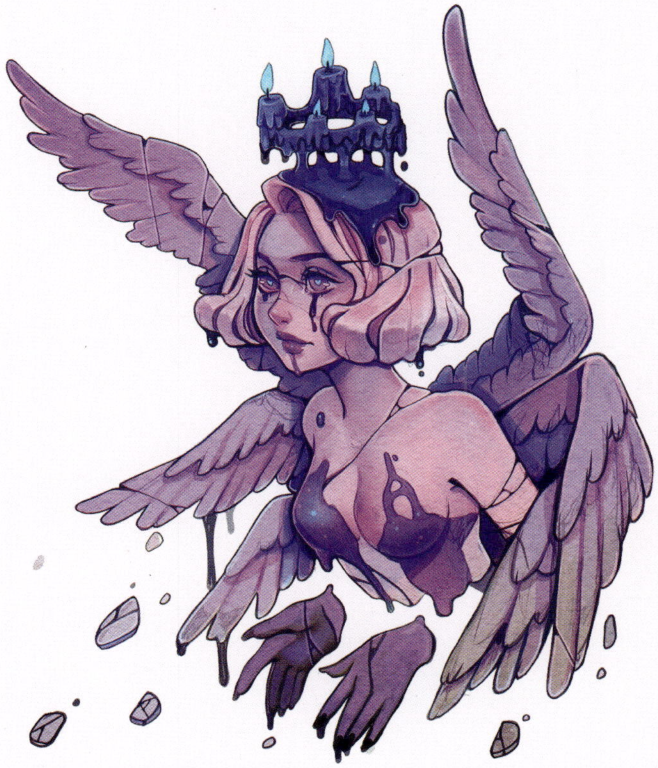

# foreword

Most of my artistic background has involved creating traditional paintings and working with galleries, but I've always had a strong appreciation for digital artwork. Wanting to connect with more digital artists, I went in search of people in the gaming industry to learn from and collaborate with.

Gris and I first met online in an art group for local artists looking to connect and potentially work on projects together. We loved each other's artwork and clicked from the very beginning. Gris eventually reached out to me and asked if I'd be able to teach her a few techniques with acrylic paint, since she was primarily working in a digital format. I happily invited her to my art studio and we began to paint clouds and objects that have a glowing effect. I immediately realized that she was also eager to learn and showed a lot of potential in acrylic painting. Before long we were meeting regularly, talking about art and our inspirations, and bonding over good and bad pizza. We do not recommend turnips on pizza.

One of the first things I noticed about her artwork was the vibrant and exciting feeling to it. I felt that she was definitely creating something that people would enjoy and be inspired by. After many studio visits, Gris officially moved into our art studio and began painting and creating work there. She wasn't sure if she would be able to have a career as an artist, as she lacked the confidence she needed to make that leap. I knew this phase would quickly pass as she realized her own abilities and found the boost to move forward. She worked hard on her craft and constantly improved while creating and molding a unique style of her own. This led to the well-deserved recognition she has in the art community today, and she shares her experience with other artists in need of confidence.

Having a massive international following comes with a sense of responsibility and isn't always easy to navigate. But Gris has gracefully made it just a part of who she is, and happily reaches out to young artists who look up to her and make a huge impression. She has navigated the ups and downs of being an icon and continues to handle every situation with charm and style. It's no surprise that Gris has become such a popular and sought-after artist. Not only is she incredibly creatively talented, but she's also a loving, funny, and kind person, making her art just a little bonus to who she is.

The artwork of Lord Gris has always been able to speak for itself. In the art world there is an abundance of figurative drawings and paintings. Gris has always had the ability to set her work apart from others by setting a wonderfully unique style of her own.

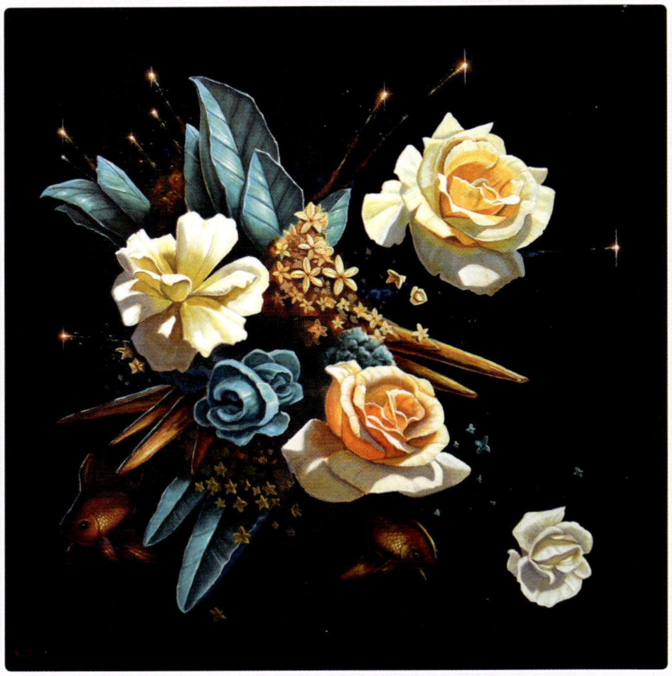

*Barrage* by Matt Linares. Created in 2021 in acrylic on wood panel.

From hypnotically beautiful facial expressions to masterfully posed figures, Gris's artwork is always something to look forward to. She depicts a whimsical world that reaches her audience in a comfortable and familiar way. Her fun and playful elements have always kept the viewers excited to see what she will create next. Her work is hugely inspiring and often used as references for other aspiring artists, as seen in her "draw this in your style" series. I can only imagine what to expect as her work and upcoming projects continue to evolve.

As the years have passed since our first meeting, I've been lucky enough to watch Gris's art journey consistently grow and bloom. Seeing her take on multiple projects and successfully reaching goals she set long ago has only confirmed the confidence I've had in her from the beginning. I have been very much looking forward to this book and seeing my friend achieve another one of her dreams.

**MATT LINARES**

Painter & Illustrator

*mattlinares.com*

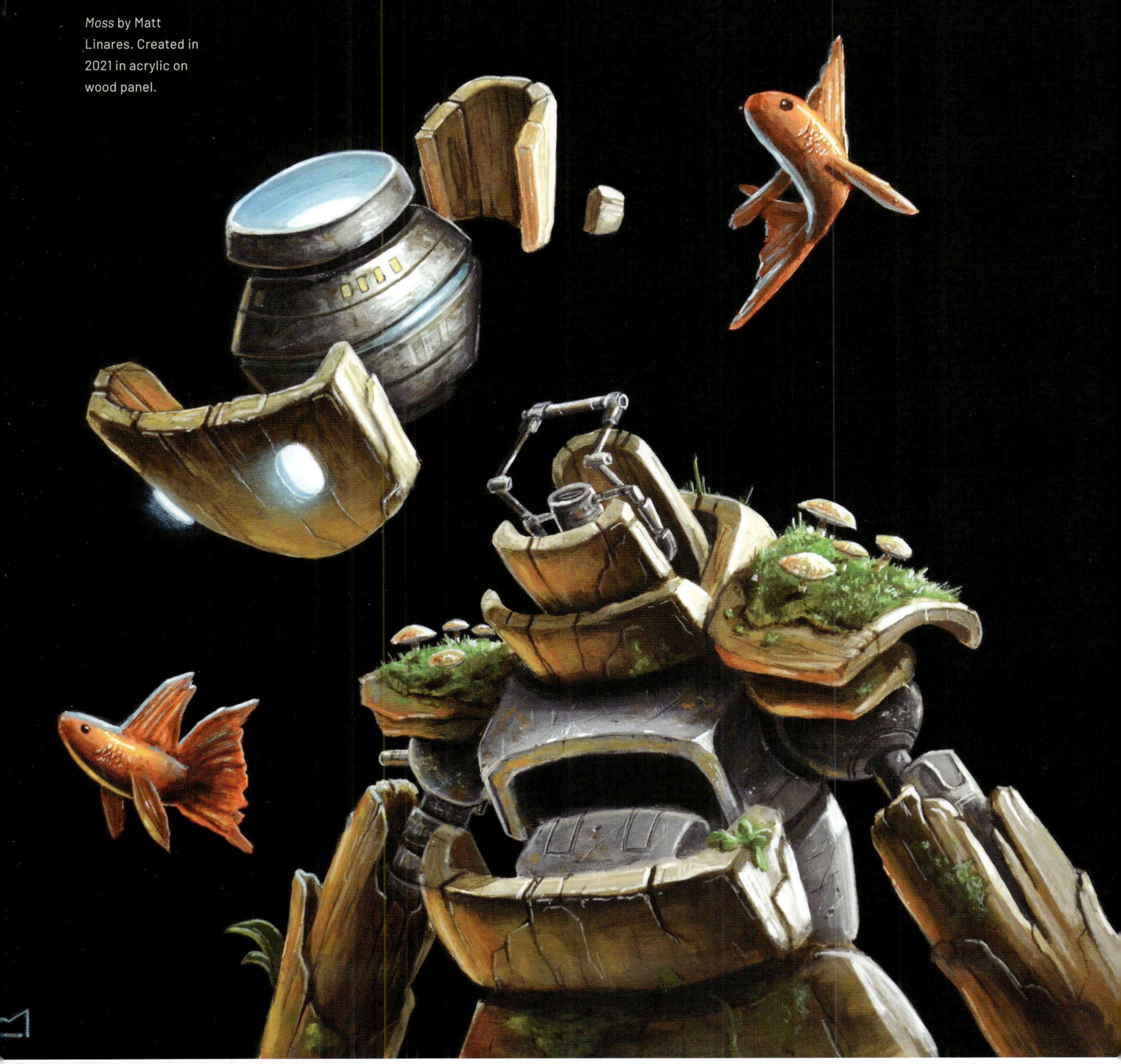

*Moss* by Matt Linares. Created in 2021 in acrylic on wood panel.

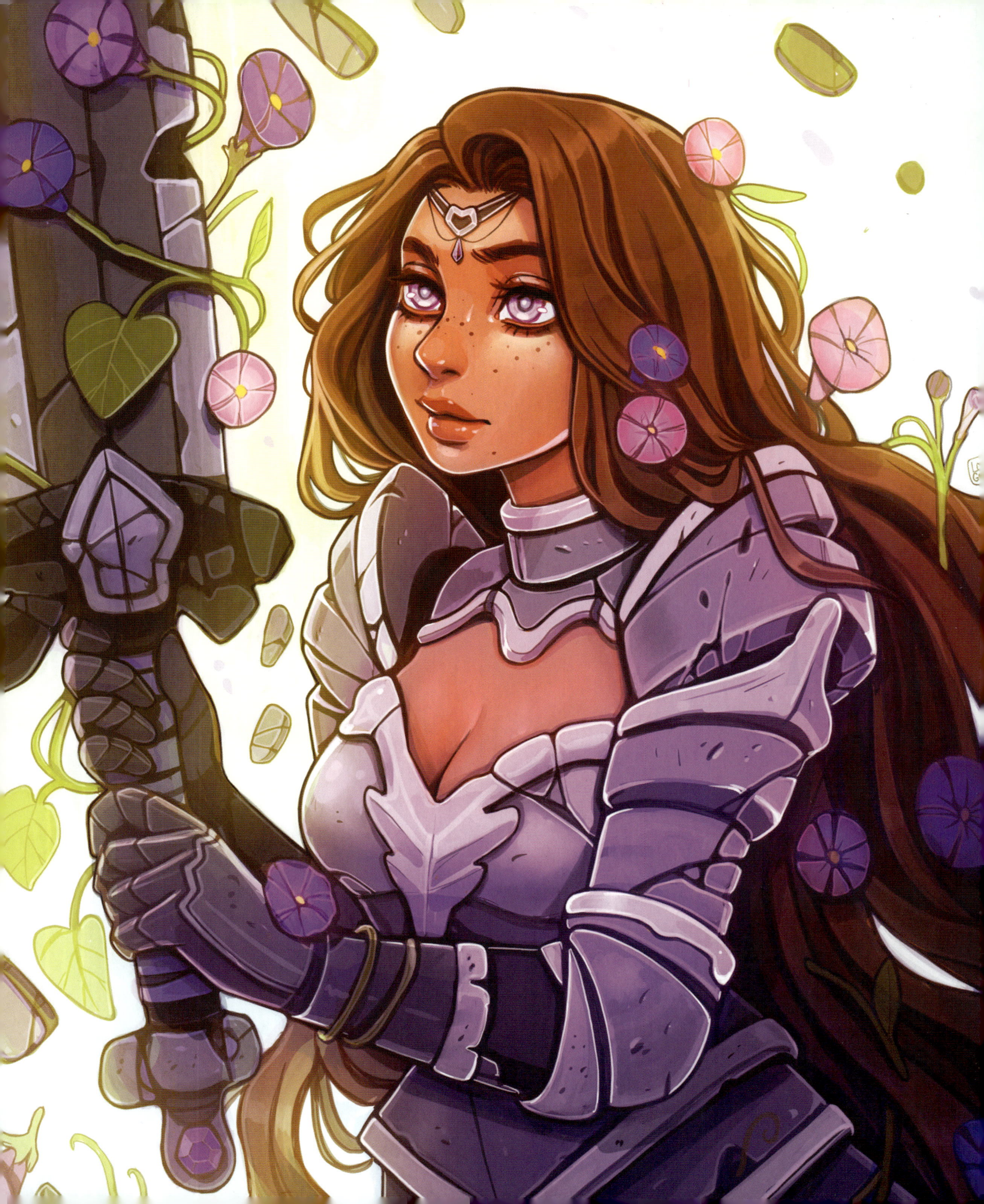

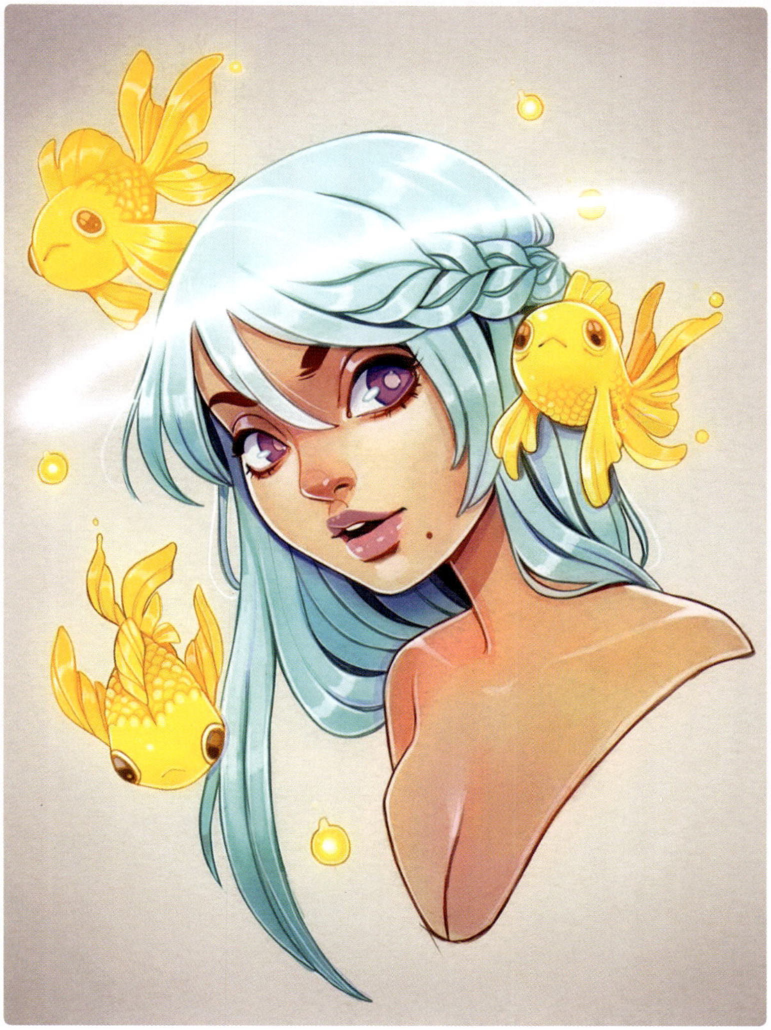

# introduction

I can't remember a time in my life when I wasn't drawing. Children start off with this beautiful unashamed enthusiasm to create, but over time, many pull away from the arts. While for some it's a lack of interest in art and a new interest in other things, for many more we stop drawing because we have become discouraged. Either the talents of our peers have soared far beyond our own and we begin to question the validity of our worth as artists, or even worse, the people in our lives – friends, family members, teachers begin to denigrate what we do, discouraging us from even trying.

In the end, we build walls to protect ourselves from the harsh words we speak to ourselves and the harsh outlooks of our social circles, until finally we cut off art altogether. I believe that creation is part of us – it is intrinsic to who we are, and when we amputate that core part of ourselves, we end up feeling less than whole. It eats away at us.

This is certainly what happened to me, the culmination of many things that resulted in me burying my art for many years saying it simply wasn't for me: I wasn't good enough and I wasn't a "true artist." I spent a lot of time searching in those years for a new place to belong, but nothing ever sat with me like art did. I wish I could show my younger self what I create now, and let her know it's going to be OK; everything will work out. I think she would be impressed by what she saw and would say, "I never thought I'd be able to make something like that." Ultimately though I am happy with my journey because I know it represents the experiences that so many other artists go through. I hope that this book can plant hope and encouragement for all who are feeling discouraged or lost on their own journey.

Gris

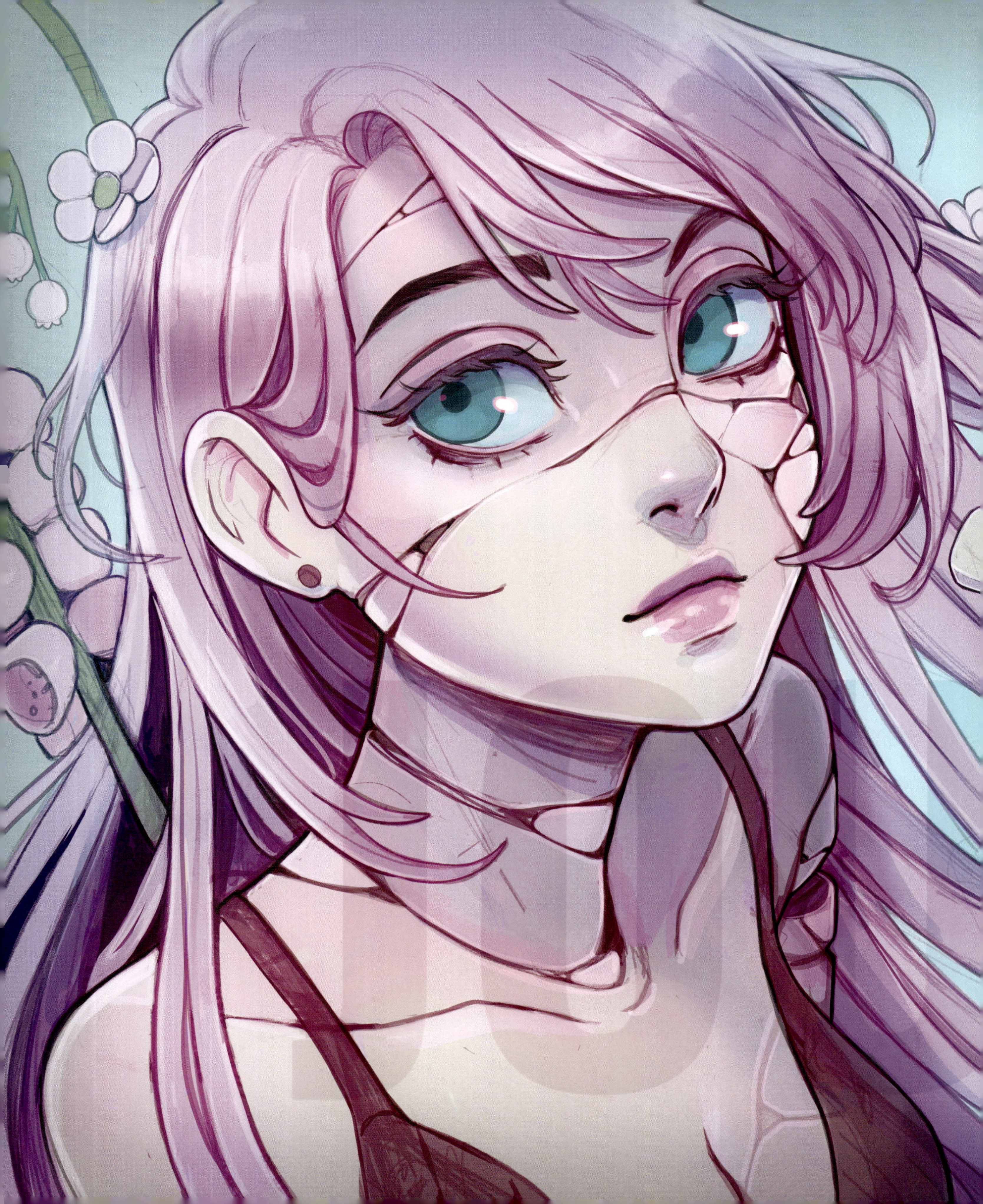

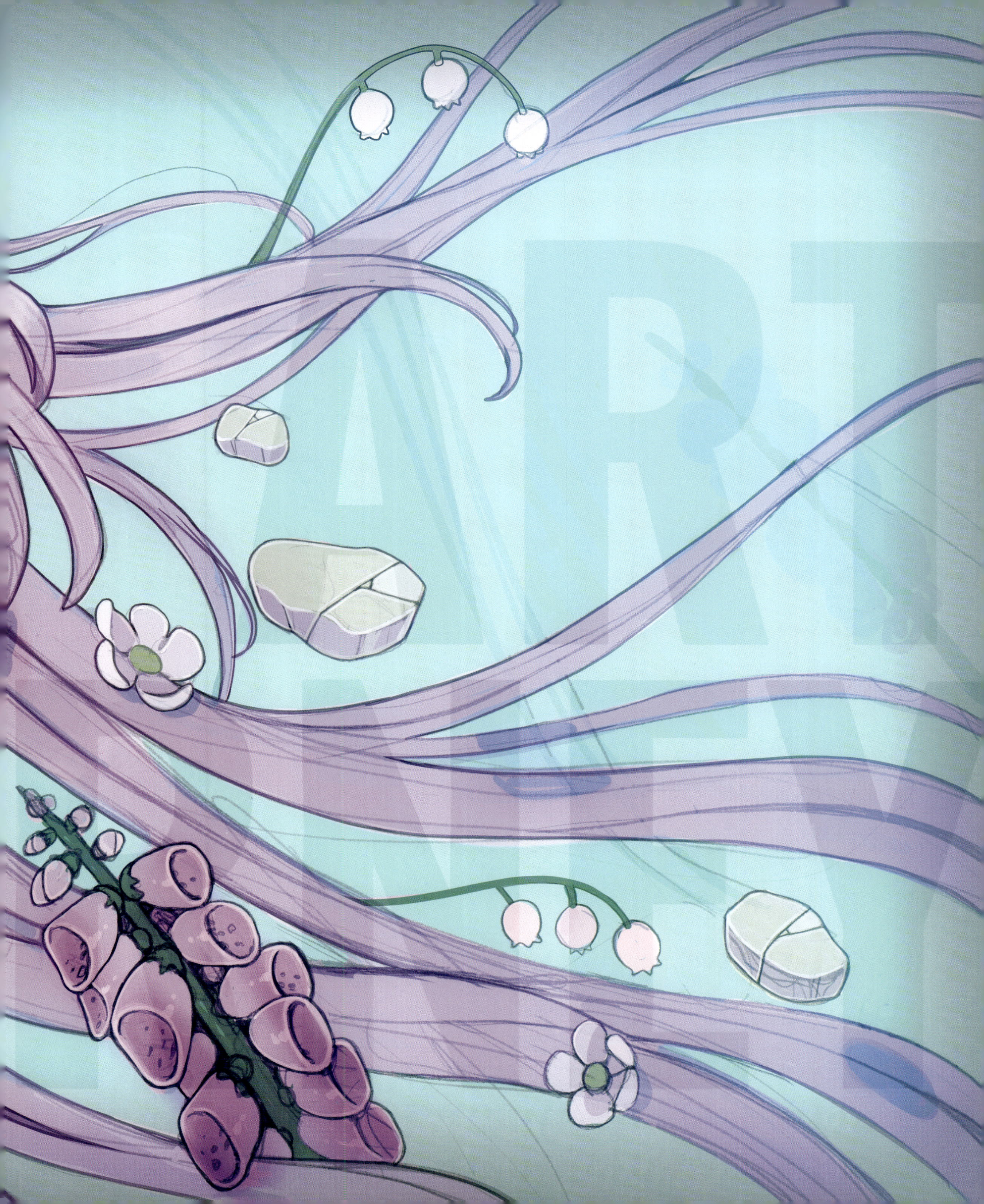

# education

## elementary school

I've always been inspired by magical women and fantasy worlds. Even the art I created during elementary school reflected my interest in the fantastical. I drew witches and fairies, angels and oracles, mermaids and mages, unicorns and dragons, and so on. I don't think by any stretch of the imagination I was particularly skilled at drawing, I just really enjoyed doing it, and that's what made it magical to me. My deepest source of inspiration at this time was the media that surrounded me — mainly video games and the art on trading cards. My brother subscribed to a magazine called *Nintendo Power* and I was obsessed with the concept art within it. I would see it and think to myself, "I'm going to be an artist some day and make art just like this." Any time I saw something in the magazine that inspired me, I cut it out and glued it onto the posterboard I had hanging in my room — I fell asleep looking at it most nights. The characters, poses, outfits, and stories behind the pieces fascinated me and I filled my sketchbooks dreamily with creations of my own. At the time, although I knew the kinds of concepts I wanted to use in my creations, I struggled with finding the style that suited my art.

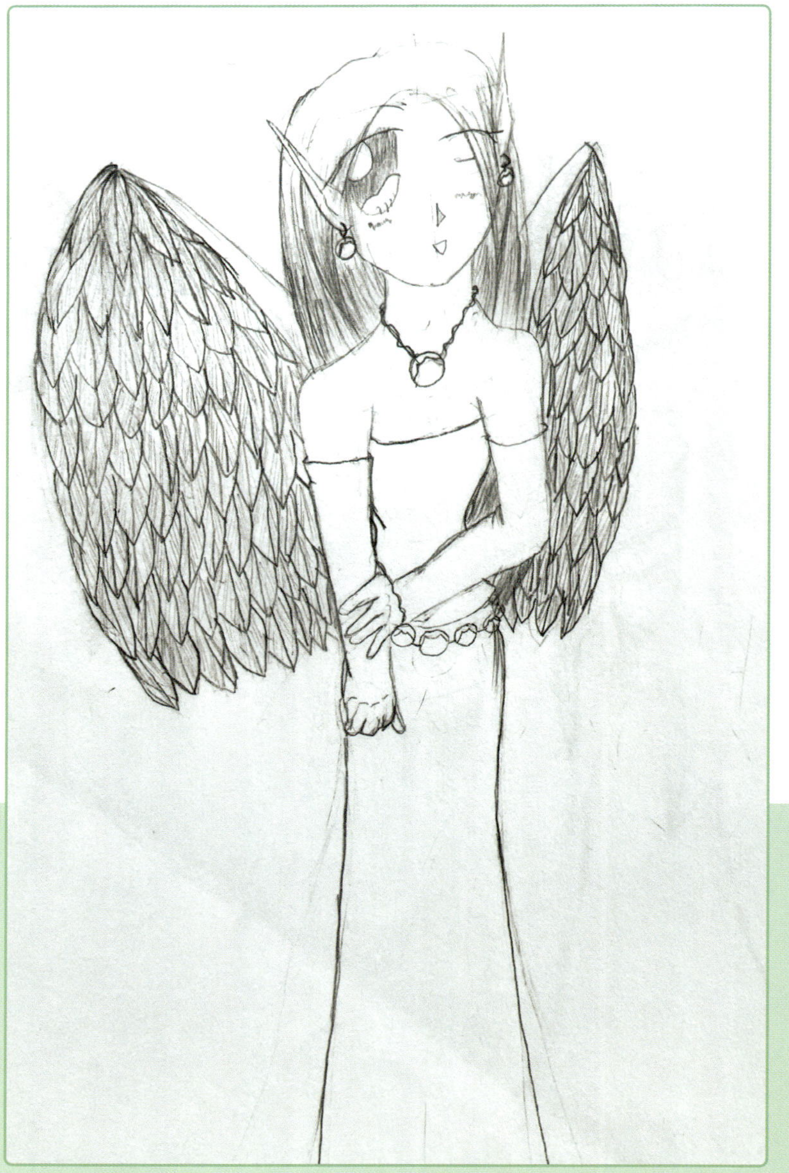

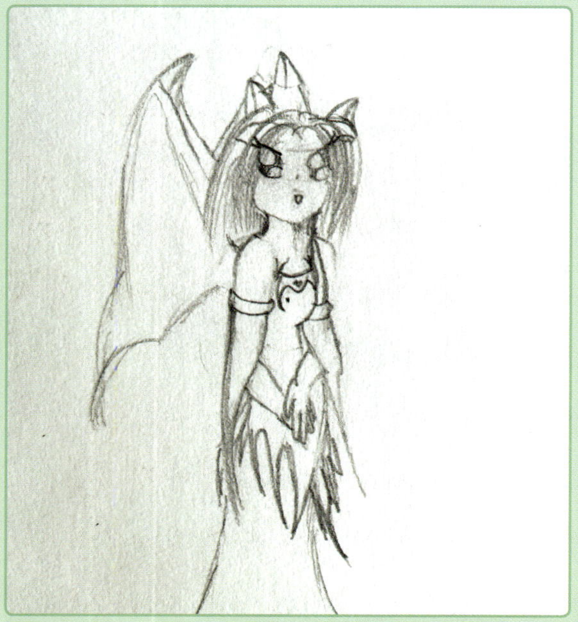

My deepest source of inspiration at this time was the media that surrounded me...

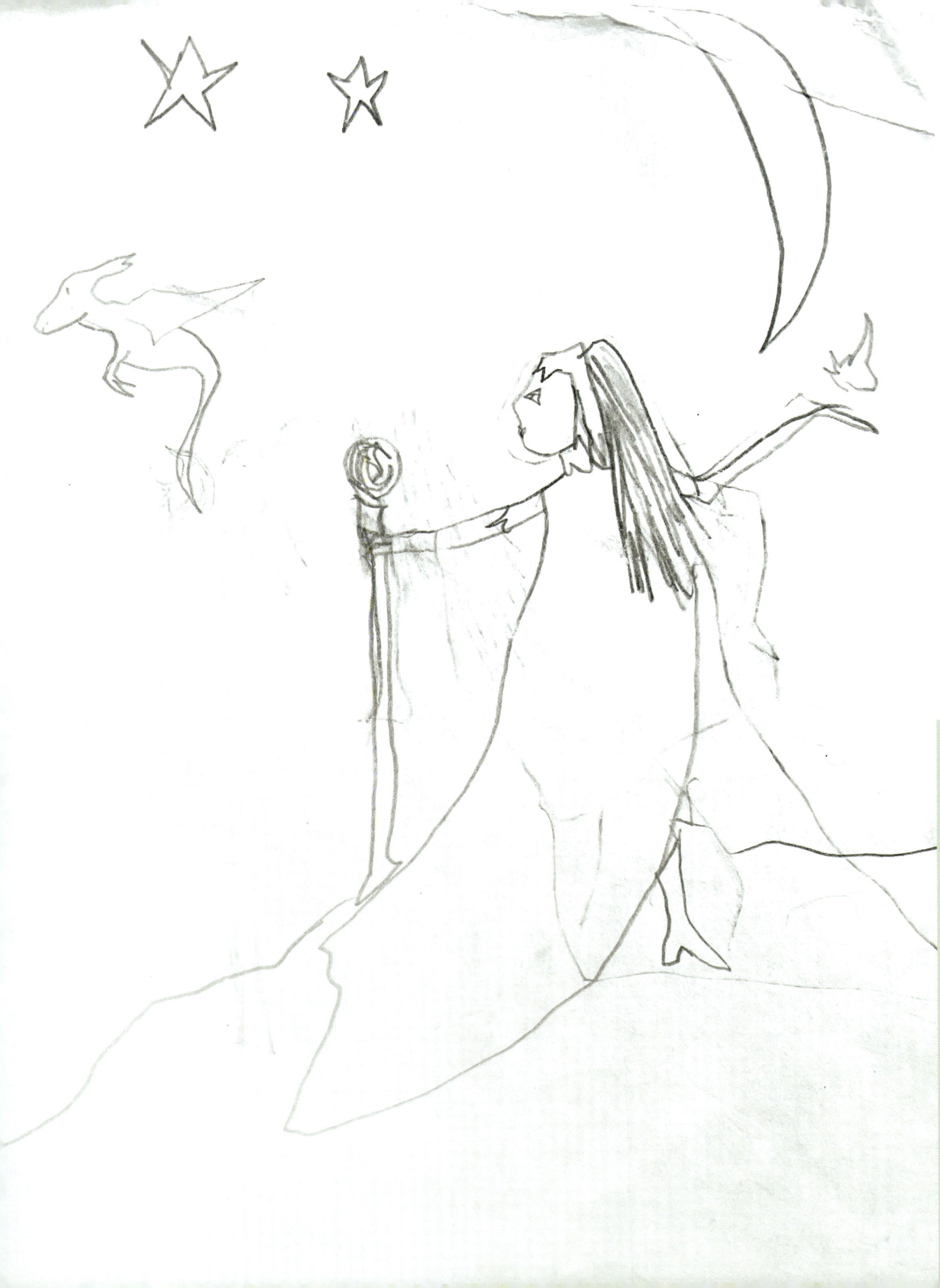

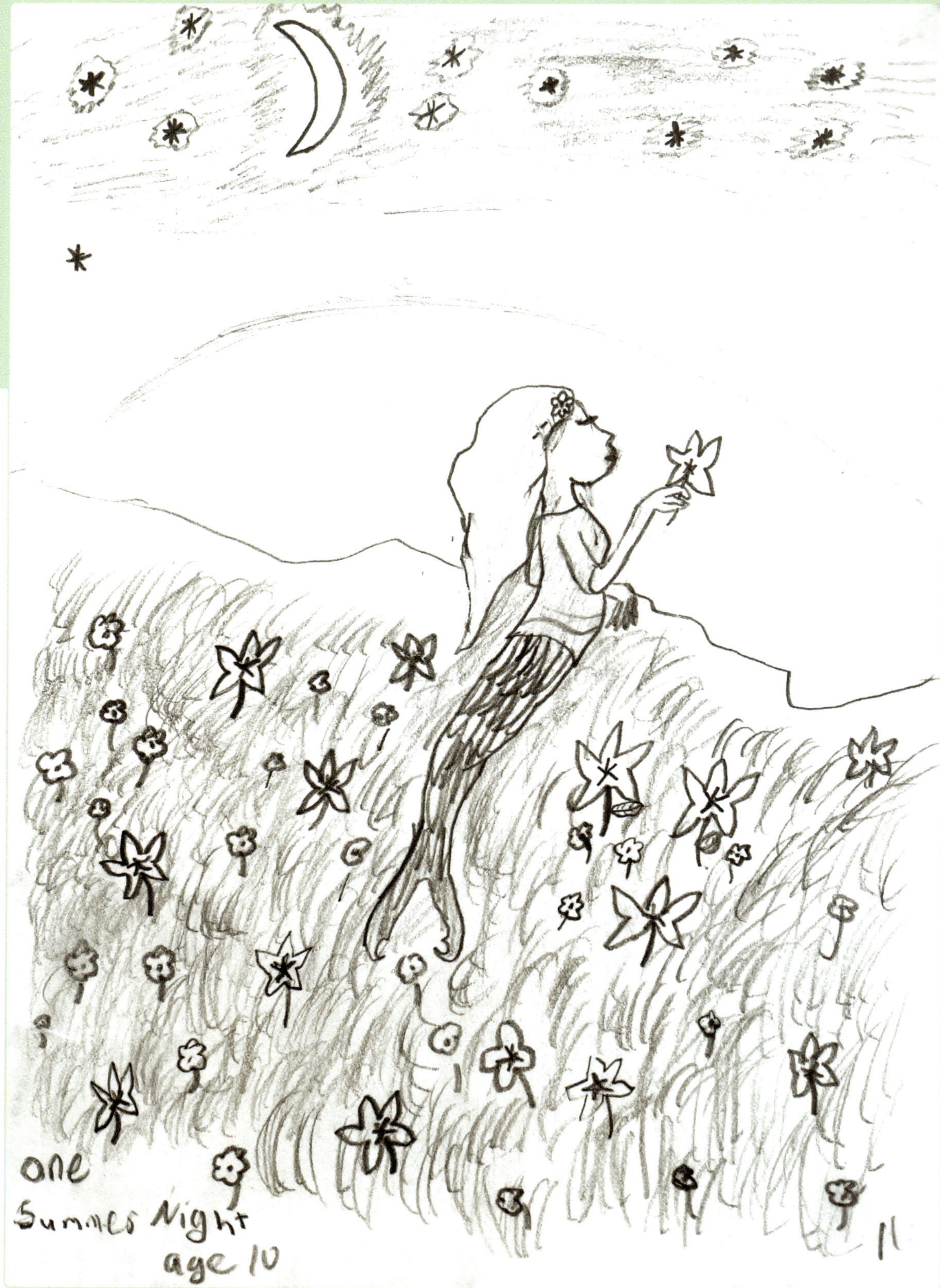
one
Summer Night
age 10
11

## In the moment when I saw that little sketch, I felt like it was exactly the style I had been looking for.

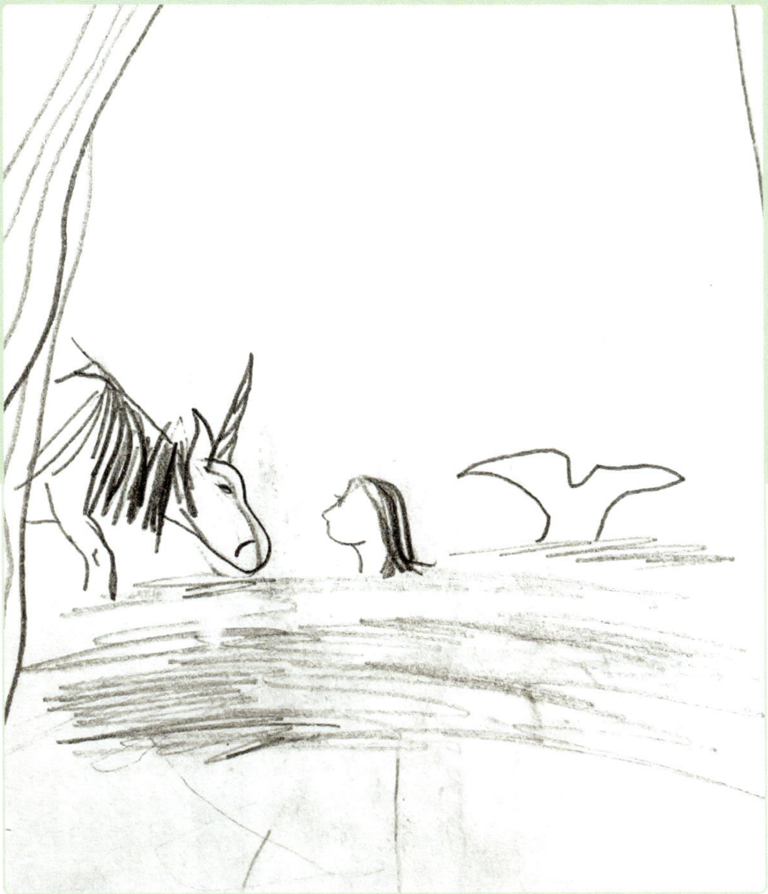

However, I very distinctly recall one day in fifth grade when I saw a piece of paper on my peer's desk. The paper had a drawing on it — anime style. Anime and manga were not as accessible as they are now, so it was the first time I had seen anyone draw like that. In the moment I saw the sketch, I felt like it was exactly the style I had been looking for. I asked my classmate who made the drawing and later at lunch he pointed out a girl drawing alone on a bench. I asked the girl if I could sit with her and watch her draw, and it quickly became a daily habit to sit with her and draw. I'm not sure why, but we didn't bother to learn each other's names for a long time. We called each other "Person" — it was our little thing. Each day at lunch I would sit down near her on a bench under a great big tree and say "Hello Person" and she would say "Hello Person" back, and we would laugh about it as our own silly joke. I don't remember having many conversations with her, we would simply draw side-by-side and sometimes she would create a drawing in my sketchbook or give me drawings she didn't like very much, which I stapled into my sketchbook. I treasured those drawings, I thought she was the most amazing artist I'd ever met, and to this day I honestly still look back on her drawings and can't believe a fifth grader made them. She was incredible.

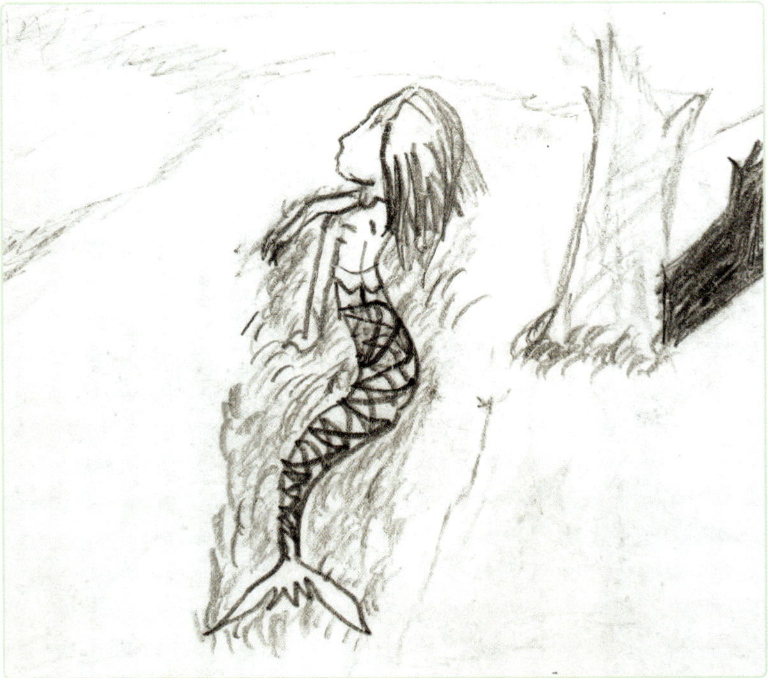

As a kid who was bullied and often alone, I was so grateful for a safe space to sit and just be. I never felt like I had to be any particular way around her, and I learned so much about art simply by watching her work. When we entered middle school, she gave me a little froggy keychain and then moved away. I never saw or heard from her again but I often think of her with so much gratitude. I would not be the artist I am today without her kindness.

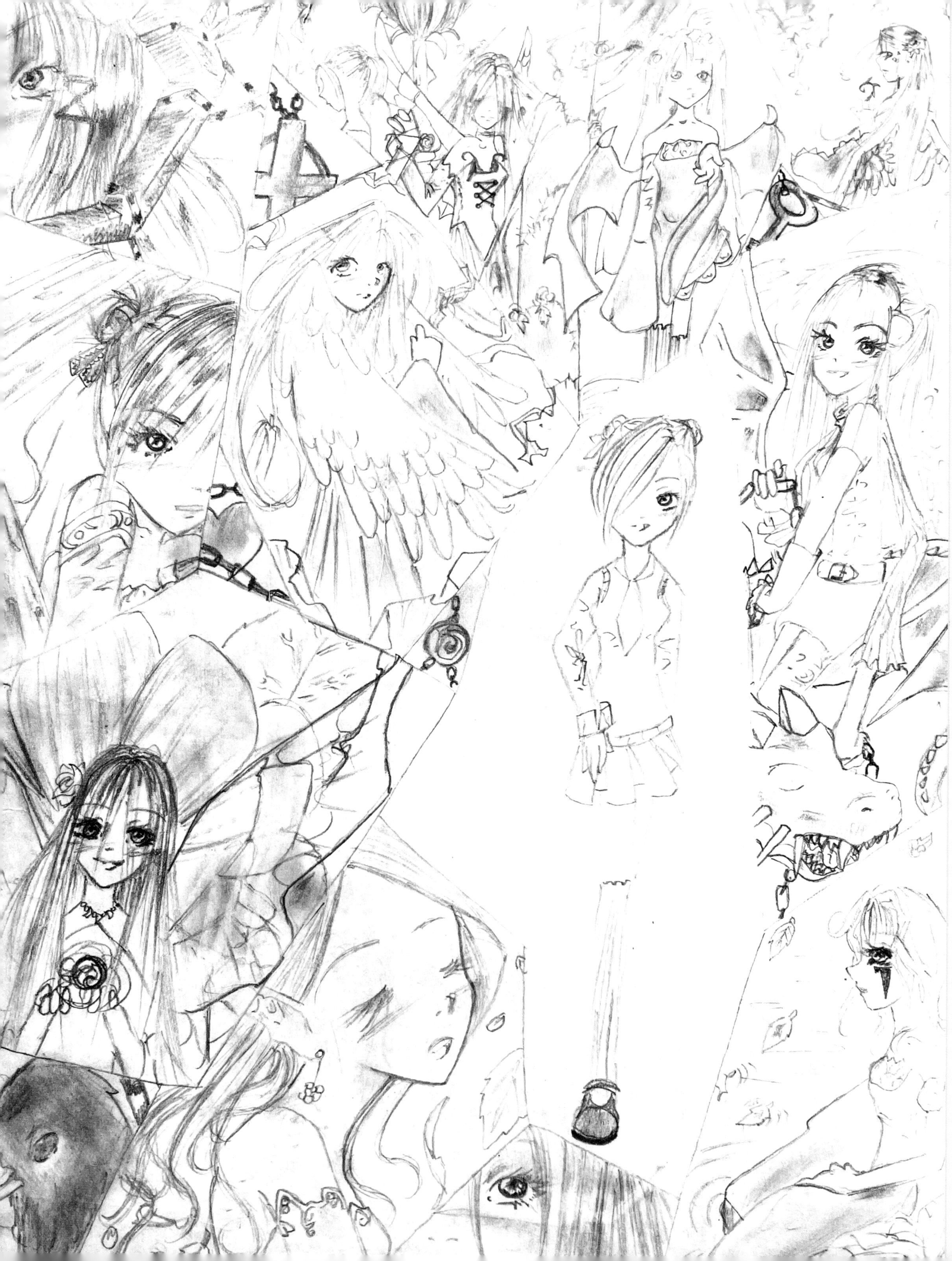

## middle school

During my time in middle school, I really grew into my art. In fact, the art I made in middle school is still my favorite art. If my house was burning and I could only save art from one period of my life it would be my middle school art. It's perfect to me, because it's the art I earnestly wanted to make. My skill level was starting to catch up enough that I could actually put what I imagined down on paper and make something I felt proud of. It was around this time that I was introduced to my first manga books. They were in hot demand and short supply with my friends, so they would get passed around from person to person, each of us eagerly awaiting our turn to read the next instalment of the story. But what I loved most was the art. It was the prettiest thing I'd ever seen.

I drew voraciously, often during class. I had undiagnosed ADHD and so I struggled to pay attention unless I was doing something with my hands. Drawing helped me to stay focused, much to the chagrin of many of my frustrated teachers who insisted that drawing meant I wasn't paying attention. I feel so grateful that I had the inclination toward art because I don't think I would have passed school without it. It also meant that nearly every day, eight hours a day, I was filling my sketchbooks, my friends' sketchbooks, the backs of homework assignments, and any random piece of paper, with art. My friends and I drew each other as magical girls with weapons, powers, and cool outfits and I wrote my own manga chapters. I was always dreaming of the next thing. This period of my art journey was exhilarating, but began to change as I got older.

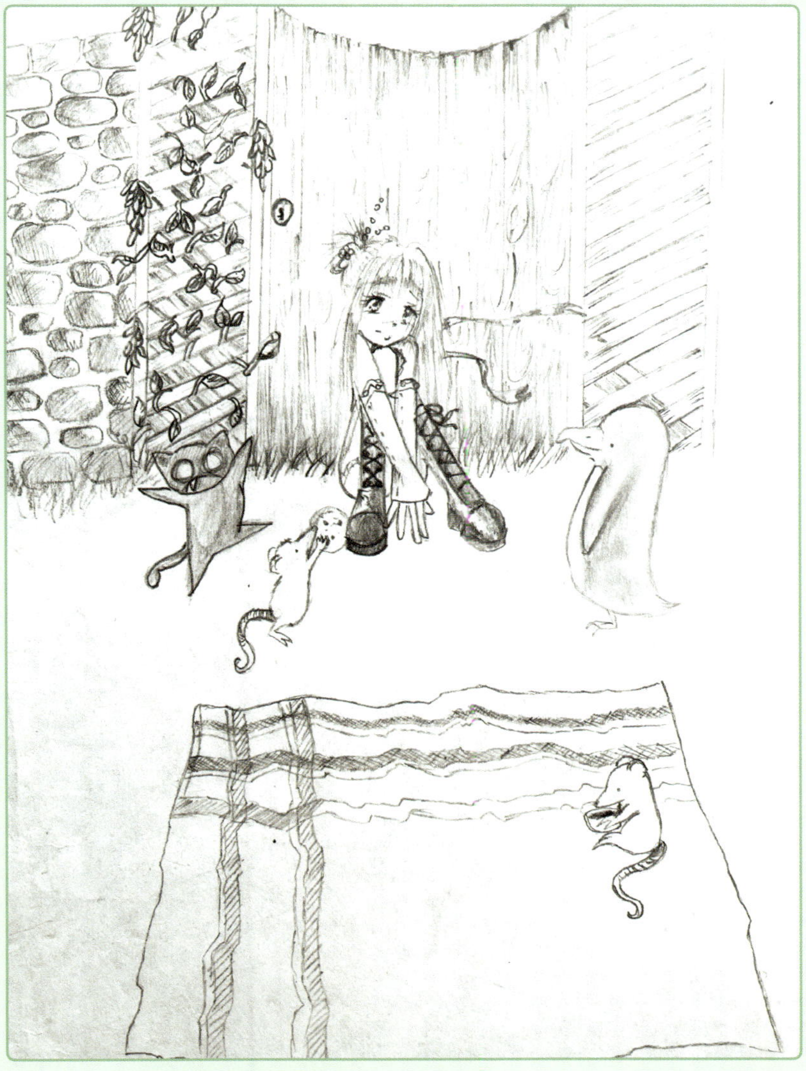

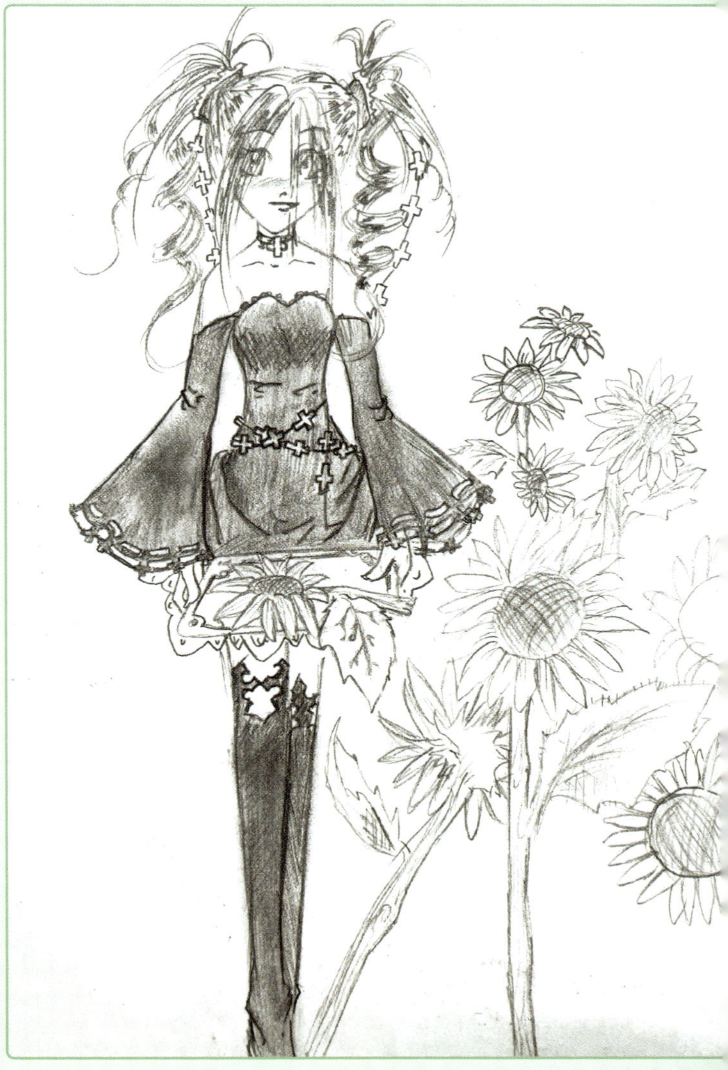

## high school

High school was when art became different for me. It was the first time I had an actual art class. It was just a basic class so we weren't given any instruction or training on technique, but stylistically we were pushed toward the fine-art world, studying the works of Salvador Dalí, M.C. Escher, and the Old Masters, with an emphasis on realistic rendering styles, or at the very least, surrealism.

I was discouraged from creating the cute character-based art I'd been making in class and for the first time I started to feel embarrassed about my natural art style. Compared to the great master artists I had studied, my art felt so silly and trite. Even more so though, I recognized that it wasn't practical. In high school, questions of the future are laid out before you: where will you go to college, what will you do, how will you get scholarships? Making the art I wanted was fun but was there any place for it in the real world? I thought perhaps a job in video games or animation may allow me to continue designing pretty characters. At this point in time, technology had improved; we had just moved on from dial-up internet at home and I was starting to have unlimited access to the online world. I saw the endless ocean of artists, leagues beyond my skill set, and I learned just how competitive those job markets are. It appeared to me that only the best of the best are hired, which wasn't me, not by a long shot, so I changed my style.

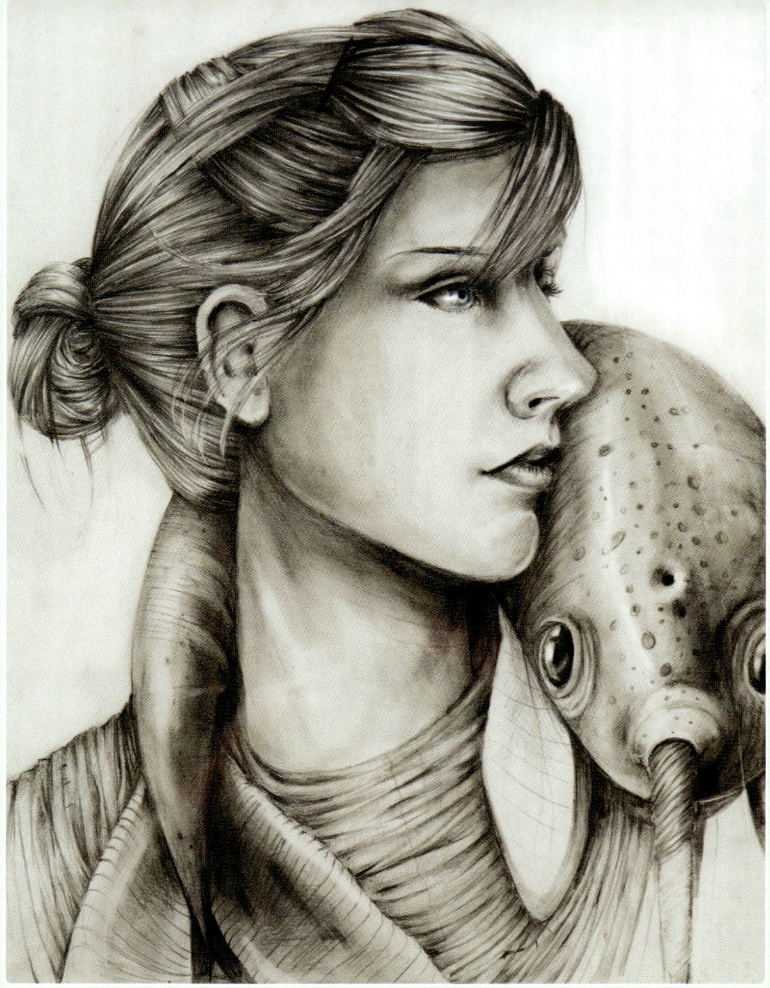

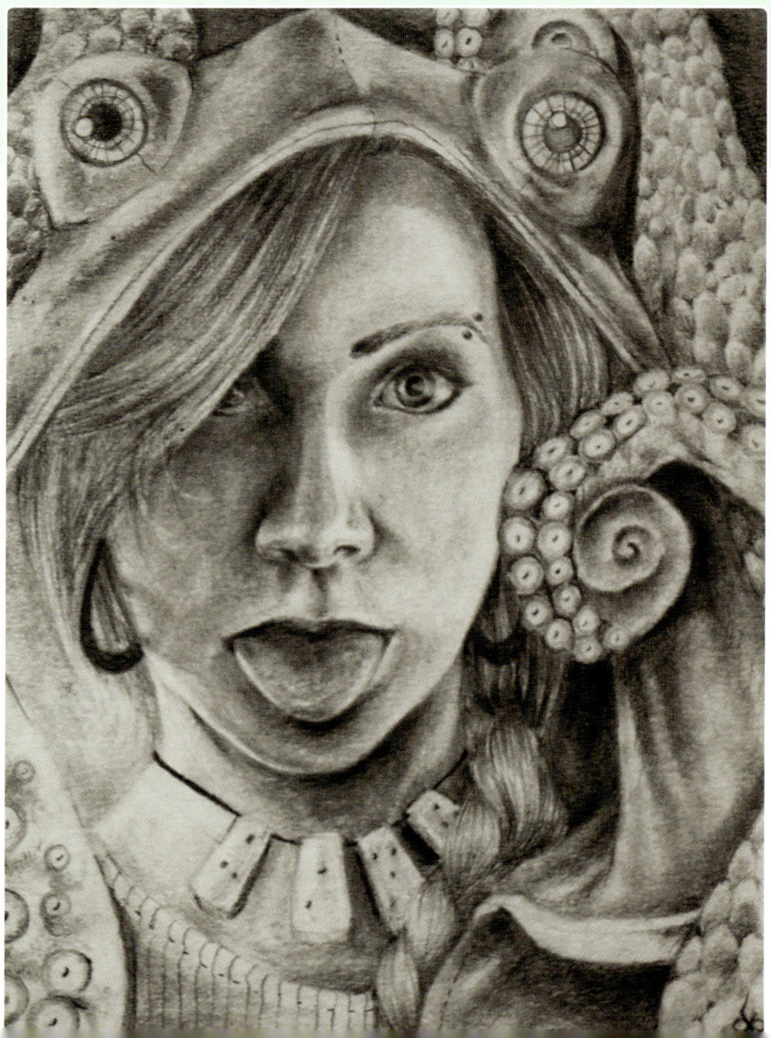

I saw the endless ocean of artists, leagues beyond my skill set, and I learned just how competitive those job markets are.

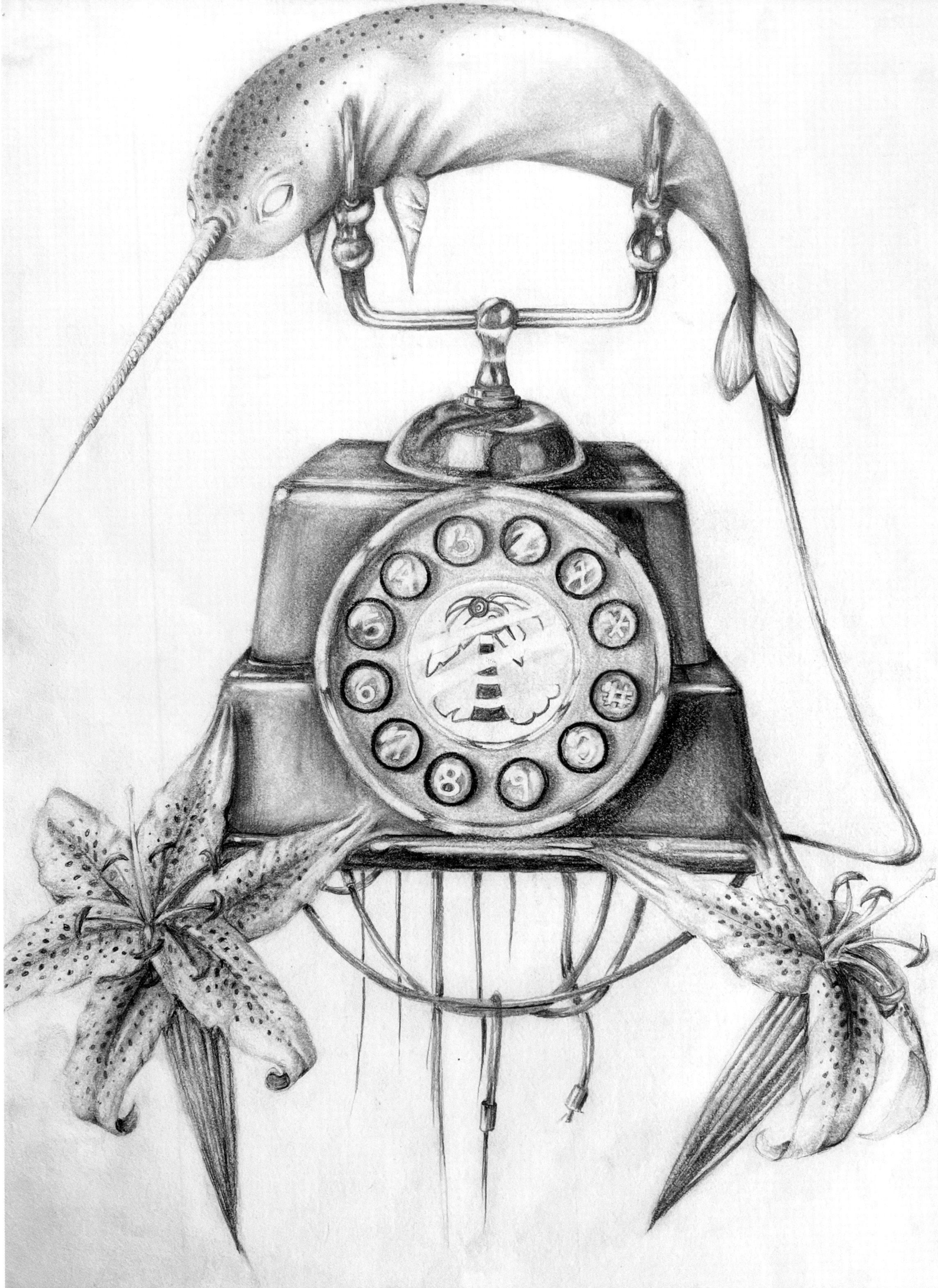

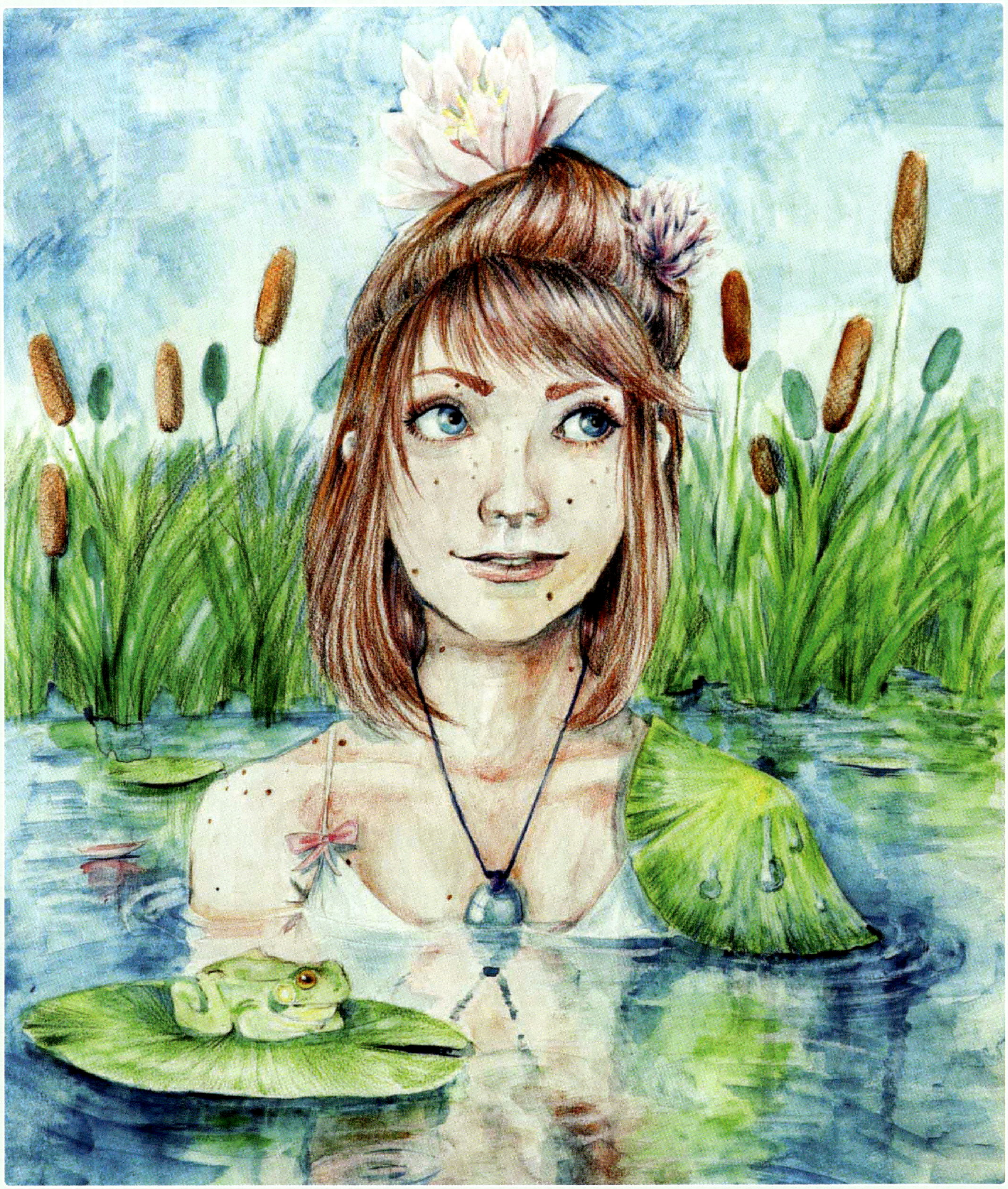

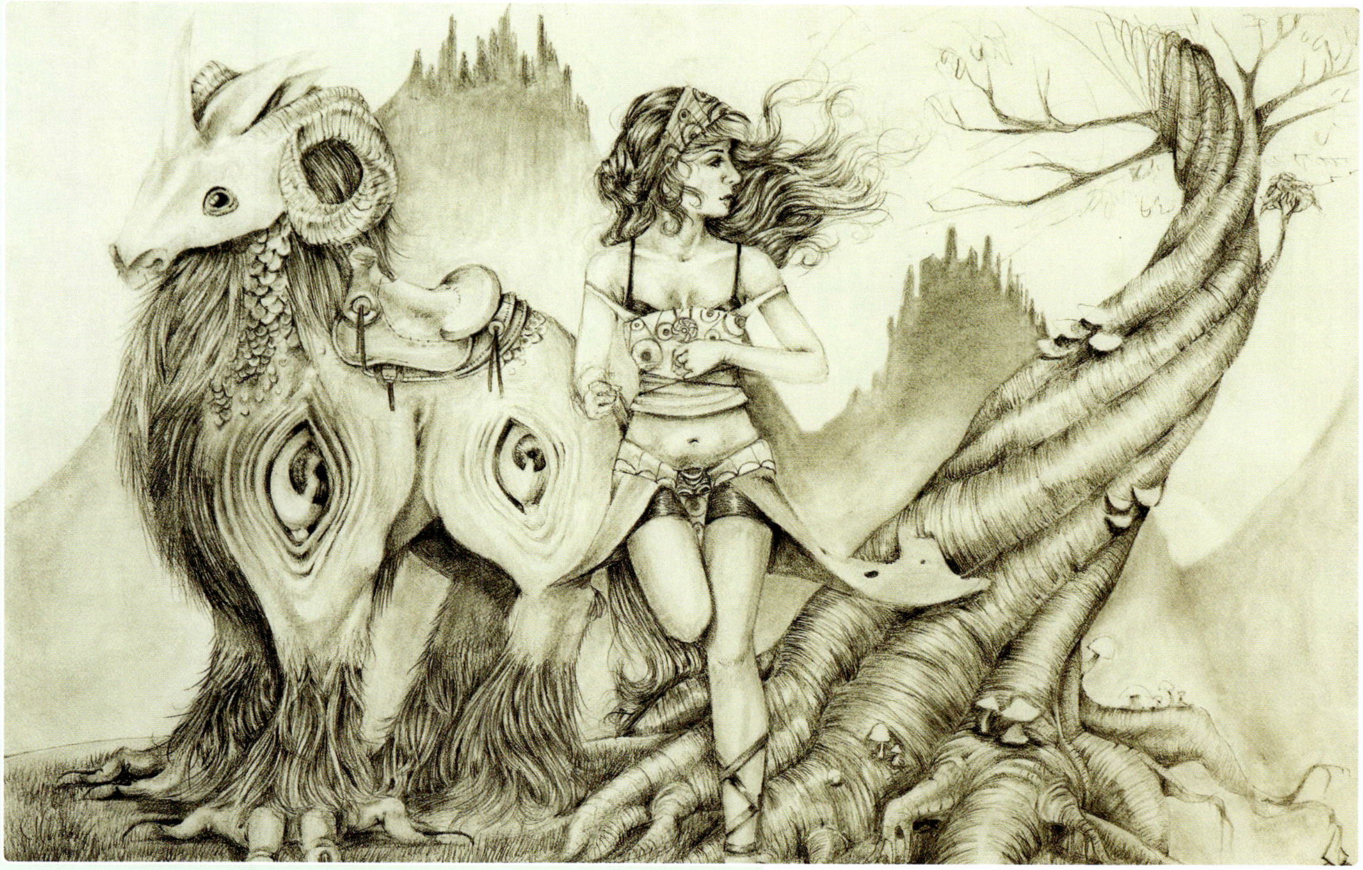

I spent my lunches in the art room and lost track of time so often that my art teacher gave me a stack of pre-signed late passes to save him filling them out every day.

My new art style was more realistic, refined, sophisticated. It wasn't exactly what I liked or wanted but I believed it was a smart decision if I was ever going to be respected or successful. Generally speaking, it worked. I got a lot of praise about this change, and even now people sometimes see these old realistic styles I drew in and ask, "Why don't you draw like that anymore?". I never stopped enjoying creating, but it wasn't the same feeling I had in middle school. Still, I spent my lunches in the art room and lost track of time so often that my art teacher gave me a stack of pre-signed late passes to save him filling them out every day. The thing was though, when summer rolled around and I didn't have assignments to complete and grades to earn, I stopped creating. I'd tell myself I'd get around to all these big ideas once I had free time, but those two and a half months would roll on by and I'd get nothing done. At the time I thought I was lazy but now I understand it was something different. My soul wasn't in that art. I made it to the end of high school and was ready for the next phase of my life — art college.

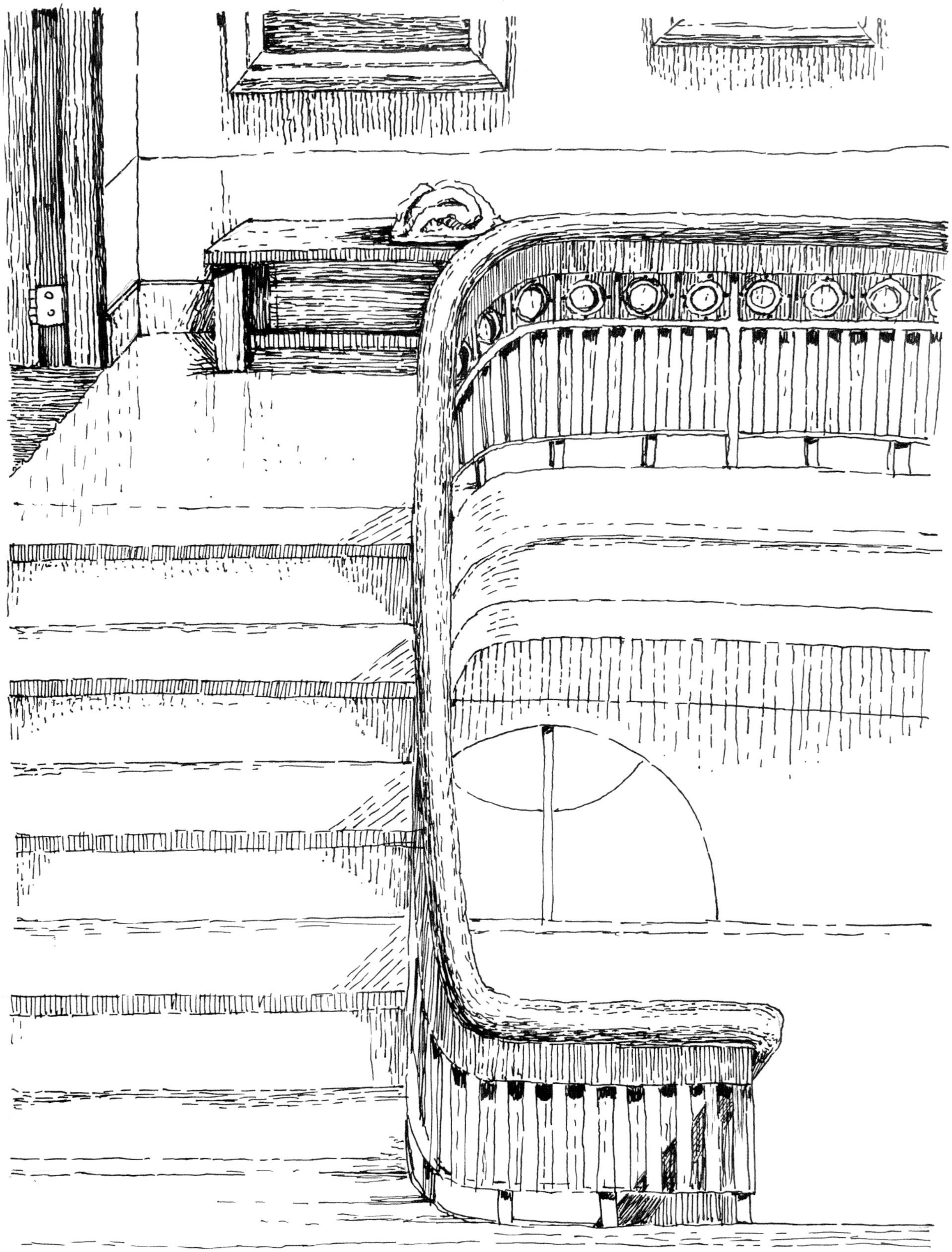

## college

What I expected from college and what I got were very different. I expected to *finally* receive some art instruction for the first time in my life as well as to meet fellow artists and feel a long-awaited sense of belonging. Instead, what I got was a realization that I was behind my peers technically and a sense of utter isolation. I had naively thought that everyone going to college, except maybe a few outliers, was like me: self-taught and given little instruction and experience with different mediums (my most familiar tool was still the yellow school pencil and I'd never even touched digital tools). As soon as I got there, I realized that kids had been mastering these tools for years, been mentored from a young age, and everything I was hoping to learn was considered foundational knowledge upon entry. I was leagues behind everyone else.

More so, I felt deeply out of place. All of the other students felt to me like "real artists," they were refined and sophisticated, they'd been to museums, and even been to Europe. They had big plans for deeply conceptual art and none of them seemed to want to draw pretty girls and silly cartoons. In fact the kind of art I loved was actively sneered upon by them. Even though I'd long since abandoned drawing like that, I felt mortified that they might find out it had once been my dream, so I kept it to myself. Instead of feeling camaraderie with fellow artists, I ended up feeling like an out-of-place child.

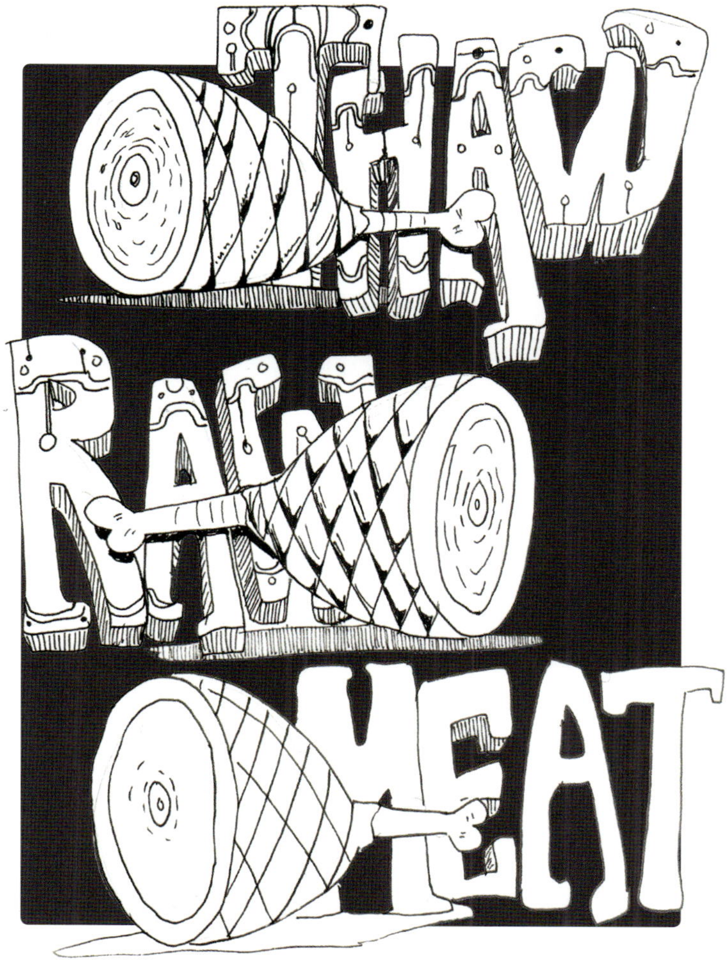


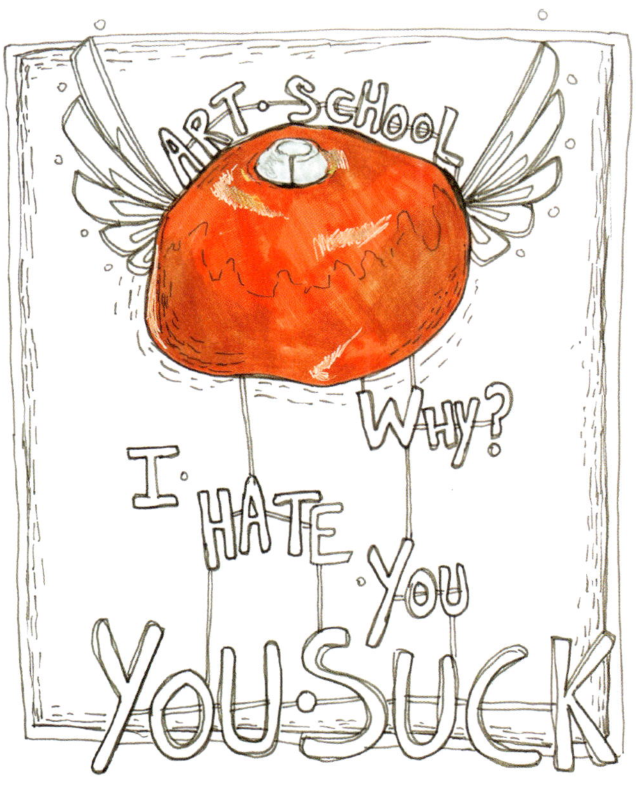


In class we were reminded constantly of competitive markets, how hard it is to get hired or end up in a gallery. We were pushed in the directions that were the most "hirable," which meant editorial styles. While the art I made in high school wasn't my dream art, I still think I could have happily drawn in that style if it meant I had a job, but in art college I was suddenly making endless piles of quirky stylized ink drawings and caricatures – things that magazines might need as illustrations alongside their articles. I hated every second of it. I kept trying to tell myself that as long as I could get a job drawing, even if it wasn't the art I wanted to make, I'd be OK. But it wasn't OK. Not only did I feel like it was sucking out any creativity I had left, I wasn't even any good at it.

Everyone else seemed perfectly happy to make art this way. This further fed my inner monologue that I wasn't a real artist, because a real artist would be happy creating no matter what the subject matter was. I remember feeling deeply despondent one day and saying to my friend, "I just want to draw art that looks pretty, is that OK?". I felt like an impostor every day I was there.

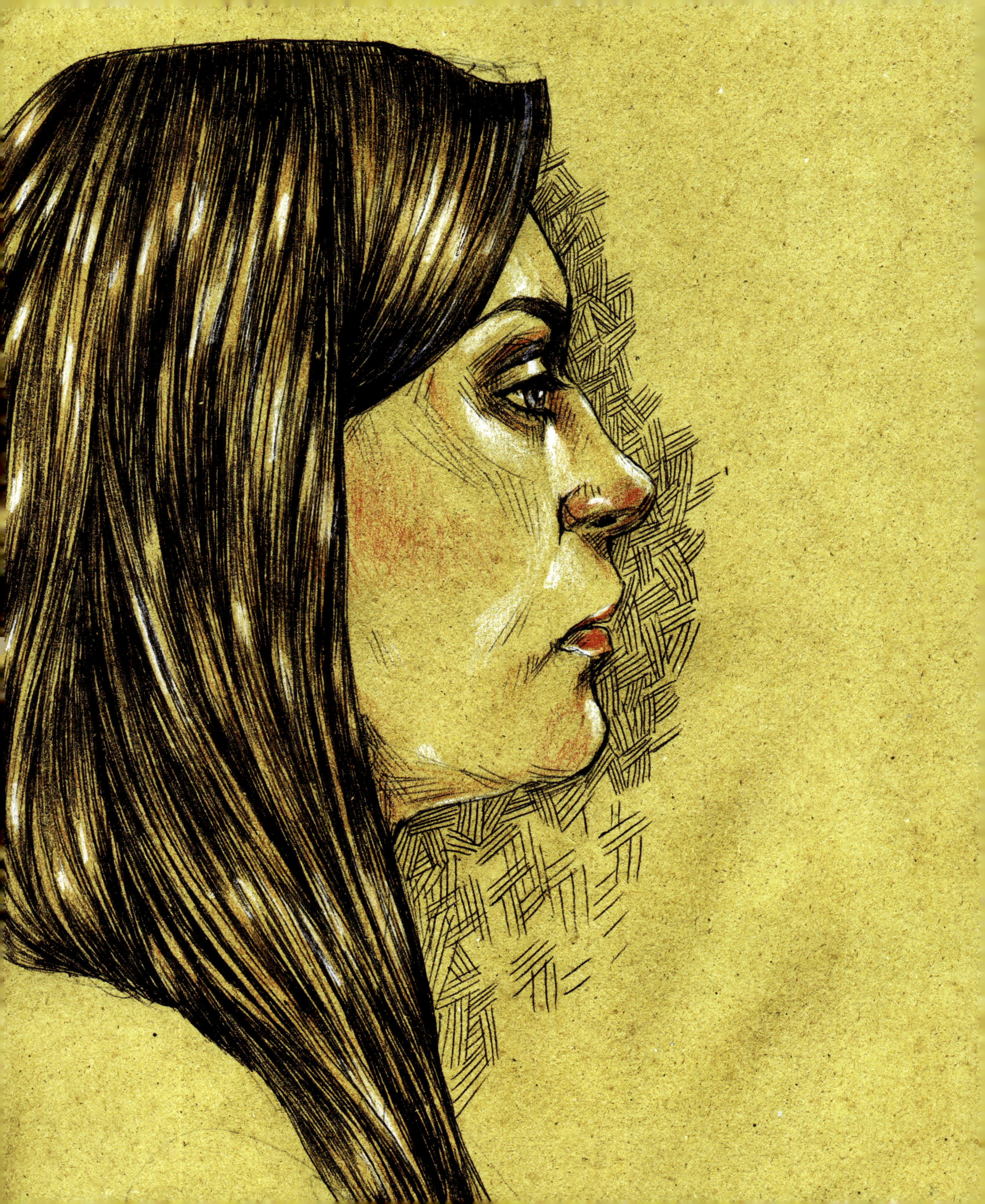

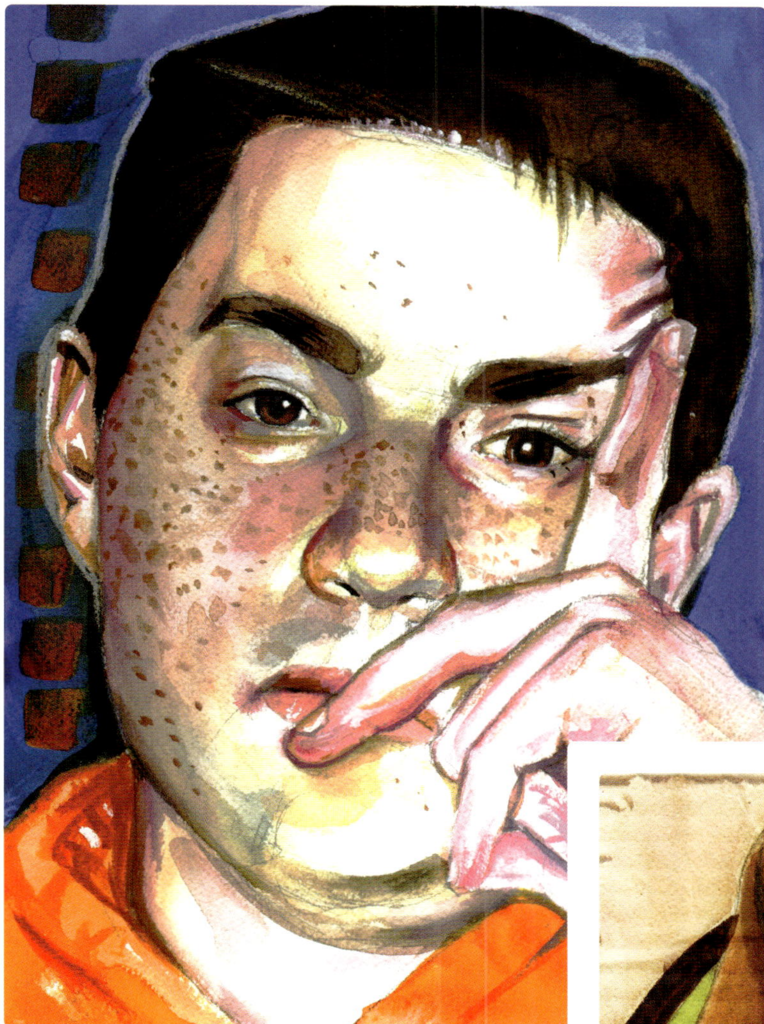

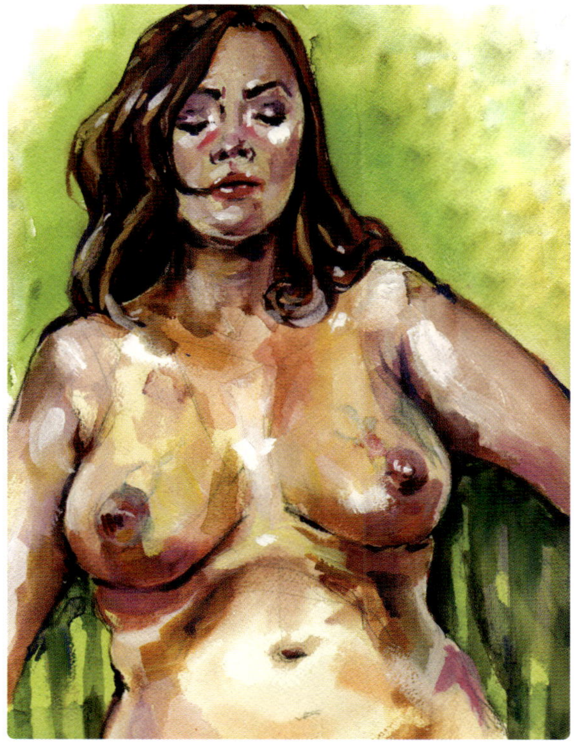

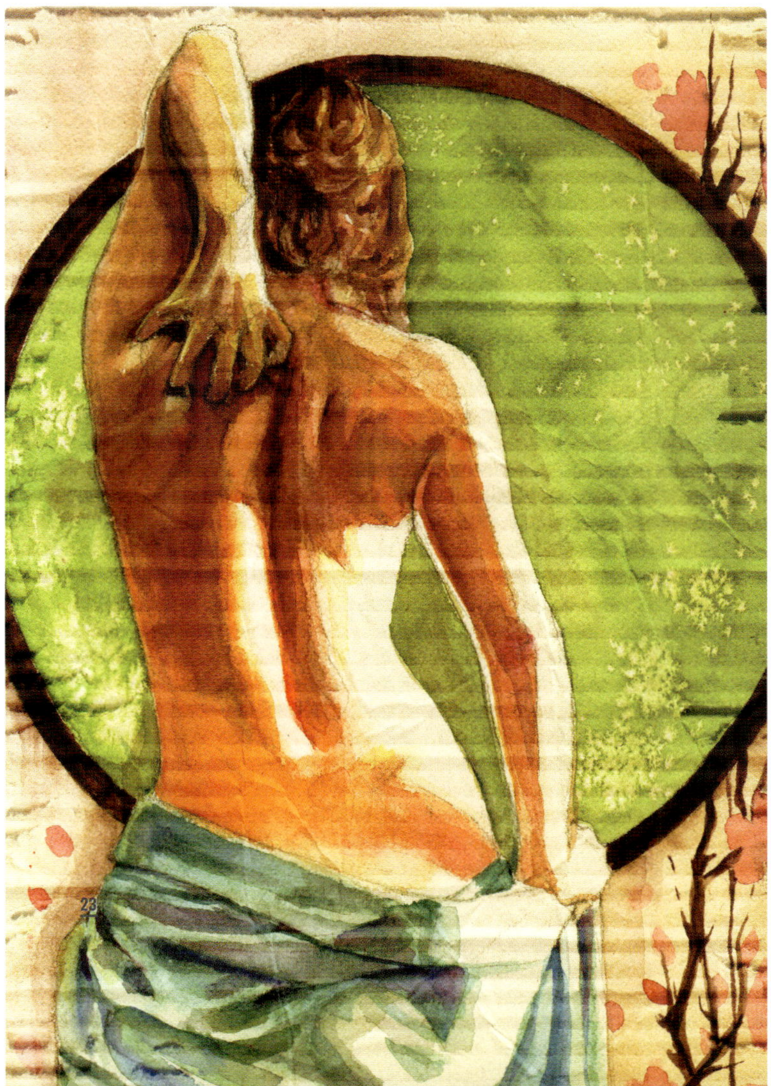

Near the end of my time at that school, a teacher I deeply admired shouted at me in the middle of class, saying that I would never go anywhere, I wasn't creative like my peers were, and I was wasting his time and my money by being at that school. It was such a horrific moment, to not only be told that, but to have everyone there, staring awkwardly at their feet. I remember being so humiliated and excusing myself to go to the bathroom. I locked myself in a stall and just sobbed. Art was not what I had expected. It wasn't beautiful or magical or fun. It was so far from the dream I had when I was a kid and spent every night falling asleep staring at the poster on my wall. It wasn't inspiring, it was an expensive grind and a shot in the dark at a job. At the end of my third semester, I concluded I definitely wasn't a real artist and I dropped out with the intention to quit art forever.

## after college

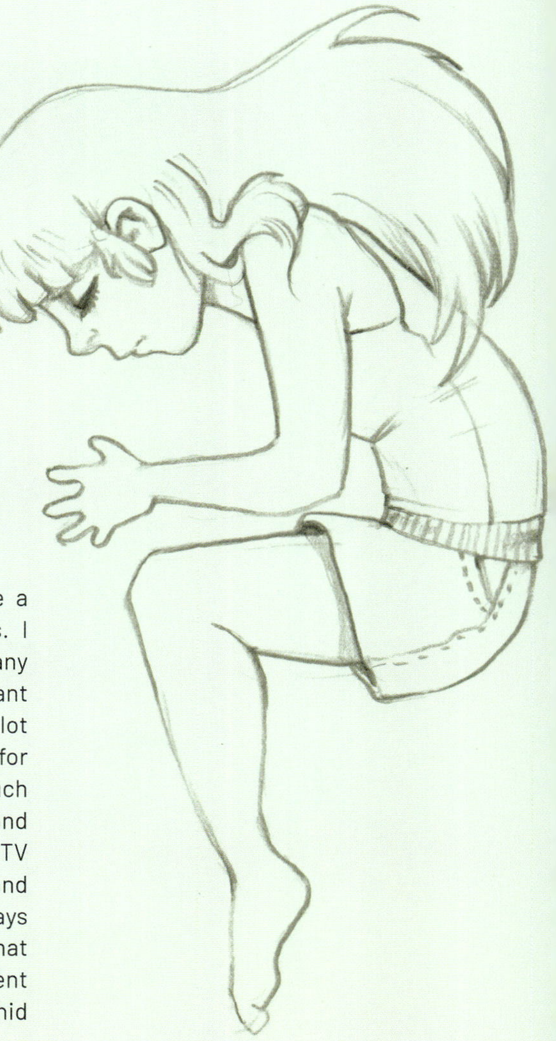

After quitting school, I felt lost. Art had always been what I was going to do my whole life and I had no plan B. I wasn't sure what to do, or even who I was anymore without it, I just knew I felt very bitter toward art and that I was quitting. I got a retail job and started trying to forge a new path for myself. In this time of searching, I tried many different routes: making headbands and selling them on Etsy, being a private tutor, starting a fashion blog, undertaking writing courses at a community college and writing books, and trying to make a video game, but nothing took off.

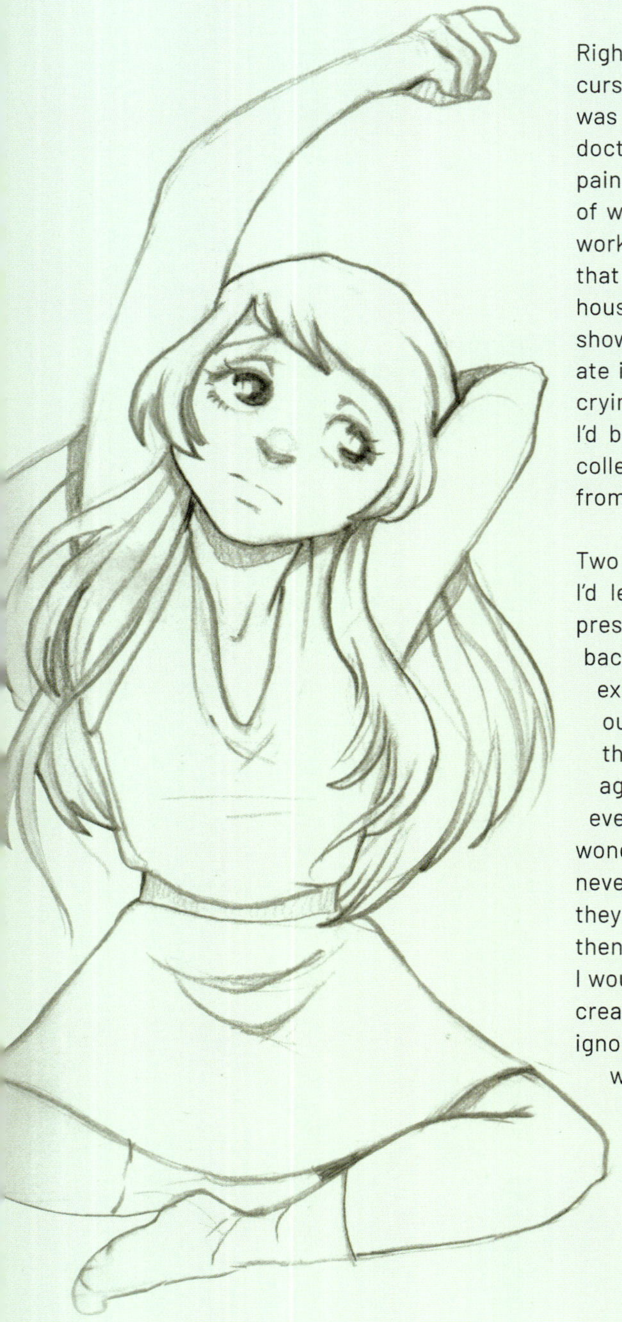

Right around the time I quit school, almost like a curse for leaving, I developed a chronic illness. I was never given a name for it, no matter how many doctors and specialists I went to, but I was in constant pain and could hardly eat anything at all. I lost a lot of weight and stopped leaving my house except for work. Eventually the sickness progressed so much that I had to quit my job, too. I was bedridden and housebound with nothing to do but binge-watch TV shows and play video games, which got old fast, and ate into any savings I had faster. I spent many days crying and felt deep shame about myself and what I'd become: an unemployed, sickly, behind-on-rent college dropout. I felt like a blight on society and hid from everyone, even my family.

Two and a half years after I dropped out, the friends I'd left behind at art school were graduating and presenting their thesis projects. I decided to go back to see their projects and it was a bittersweet experience. I was so proud of them for sticking it out — they did it, they finished. Standing in front of them I felt a lot of shame. I had left over two years ago and had very little to show for myself — I couldn't even figure out which direction I was going in. I kept wondering whether I'd made a mistake — maybe I never should have quit college. But I concluded that they were real artists and I was not. Every now and then I'd read a comic or see a beautiful drawing and I would feel something within me that said "I want to create" but I would shove that feeling back down and ignore it. The only thing I created during this time was the occasional noodly character, a cartoon version of myself that represented my sadness.

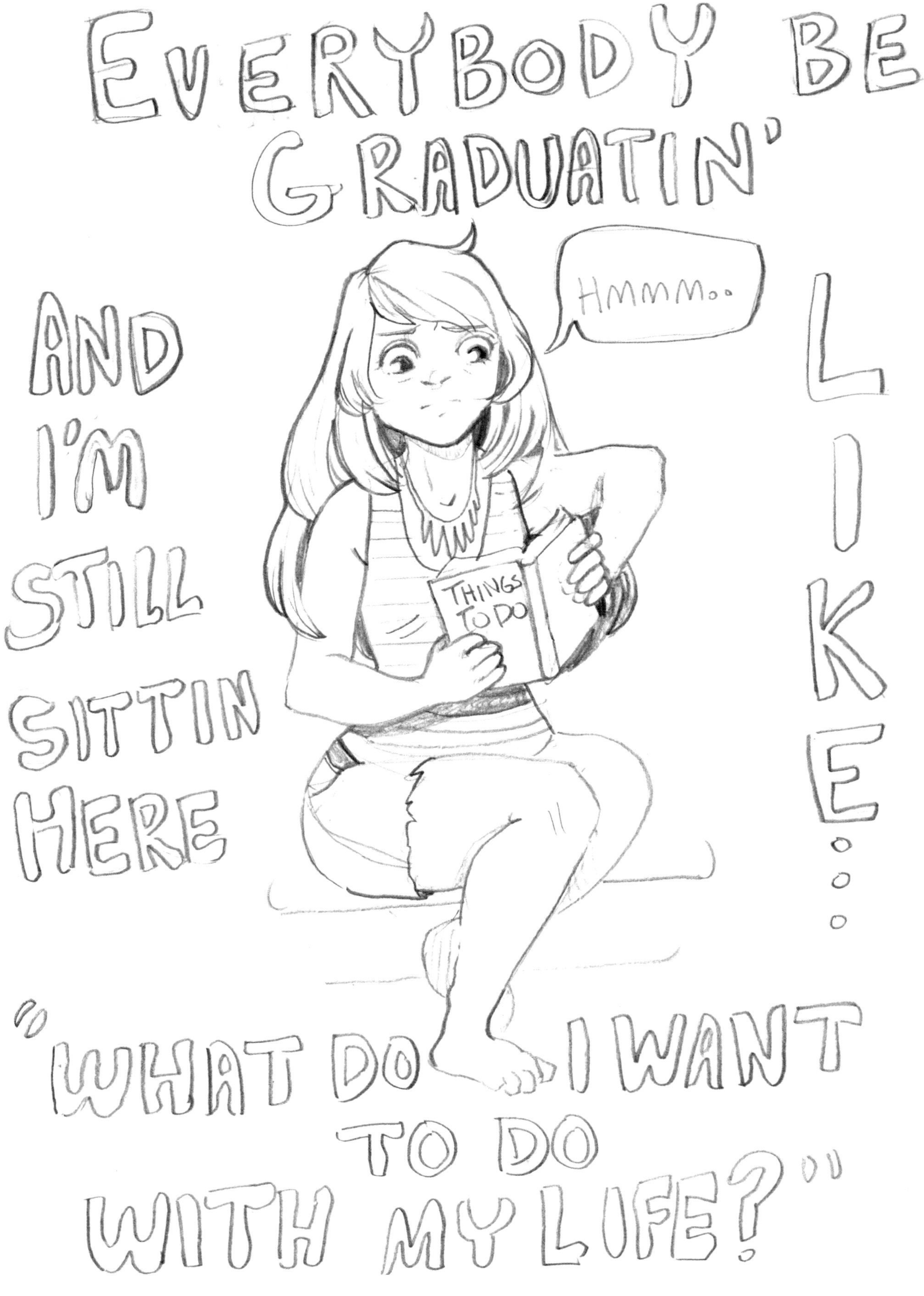
EVERYBODY BE GRADUATIN'
AND I'M STILL SITTIN HERE
HMMM..
THINGS TO DO
LIKE...
"WHAT DO I WANT TO DO WITH MY LIFE?"

## starting an art career

I stopped making art for over four years. Three things happened that I think triggered me getting back into it. The first was my brother buying me a tablet. Not a true art tablet, but a little Samsung tablet that could run apps, including a very limited art app. It only allowed for six layers, had no blending or smudge tools, and crashed all the time – but I loved it. You could draw directly on the screen (something very novel at the time) and it was the first time I was truly able to explore color. Physical paints were expensive so I felt scared to use them, especially as it was easy to choose the wrong color and ruin a painting. But with digital art I could explore endless color options and try out how a piece looked in infinite color palettes and never worry about ruining anything, it was amazing. My first digital art was a mess, but I had so much fun making it.

The second thing that happened was that I saw another artist's success. A friend had told me about a girl he knew who recently quit her job to pursue art full time and told me that I should follow her, which I did, and I watched her following absolutely explode. The best part was: she was making the kind of art I wanted to make, painting pretty girls. I started to discover social media and the power it held for artists. It appeared that there was a massive ocean of people in the world that were hungry for exactly the art I wanted to make; art I was told could never be marketable. I started to think that if that girl could do it, maybe I could too, I finally felt validated to draw once again in the style I loved and had abandoned.

The third thing that happened was the true turning point. It wasn't an event but a deeply important mental pivot. I remember the day so clearly. I was sitting on my couch in a deep depression, which was the norm at this time. I was still sickly, lost in life, and unemployed. I had the art tablet, but still only created sporadically. On this day, I was playing the game *Dark Souls*, spending hours just grinding. If you don't play video games, that just means I was killing the same enemy over and over in order to level up. It was in every capacity of the word, boring. I remember sitting there thinking how bored I was, and that in the end this didn't feel like playing a game, it felt like work.

Up until this point in my life, I thought of myself as a very lazy person because when I had the free time to create I didn't, but I realized I had free time in this moment and I was using it to do... work. I asked myself why I was willing to do something I didn't enjoy in this game but struggled to create when I had free time to do so. I realized that the answer was very simple – in a video game, progress is guaranteed, as long as you do the work you will always level up, but I didn't feel that same guarantee in life. I realized I wasn't lazy; I was just scared of wasting my time. What if I put in the time and never improve? Then I realized how silly that was.

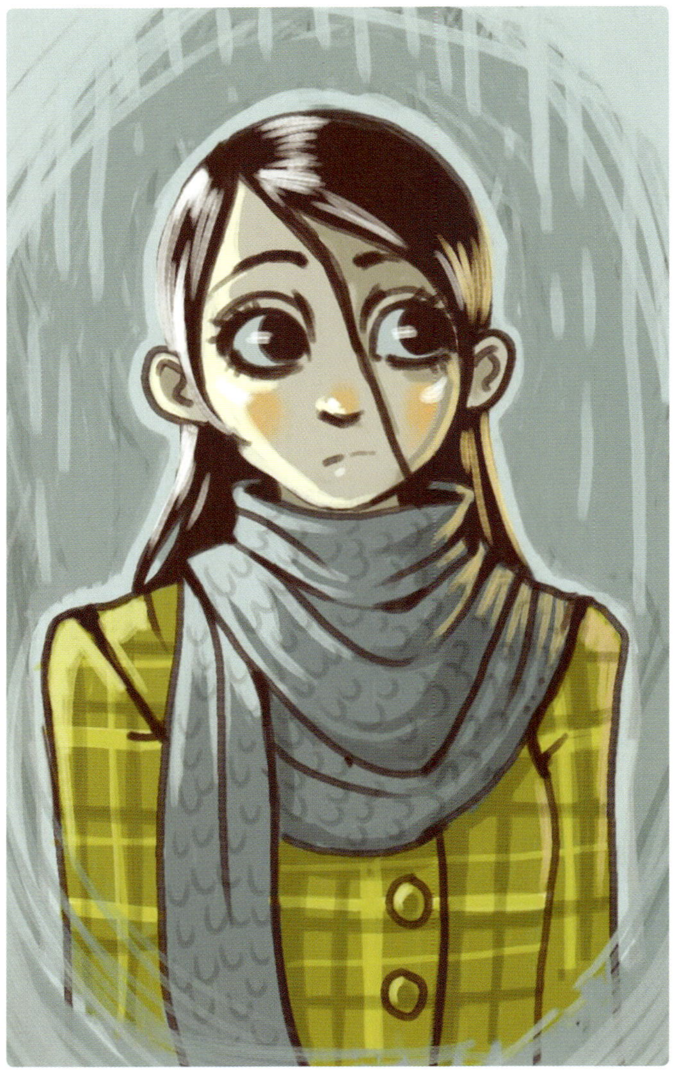

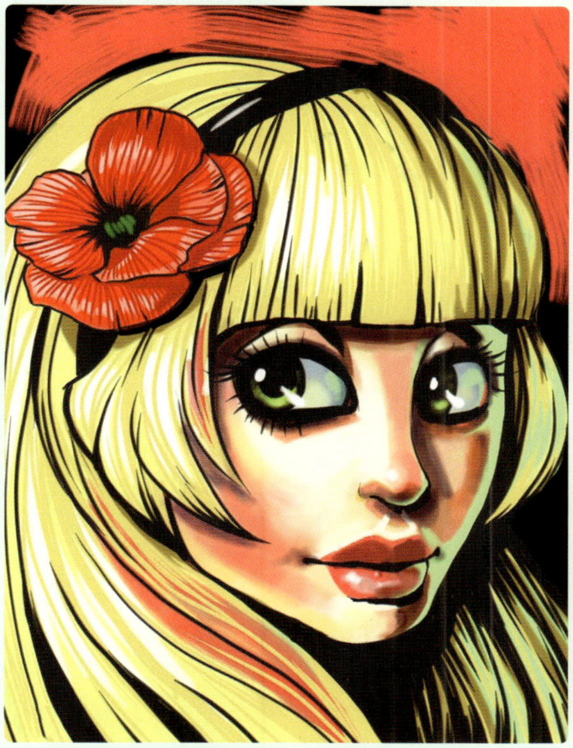

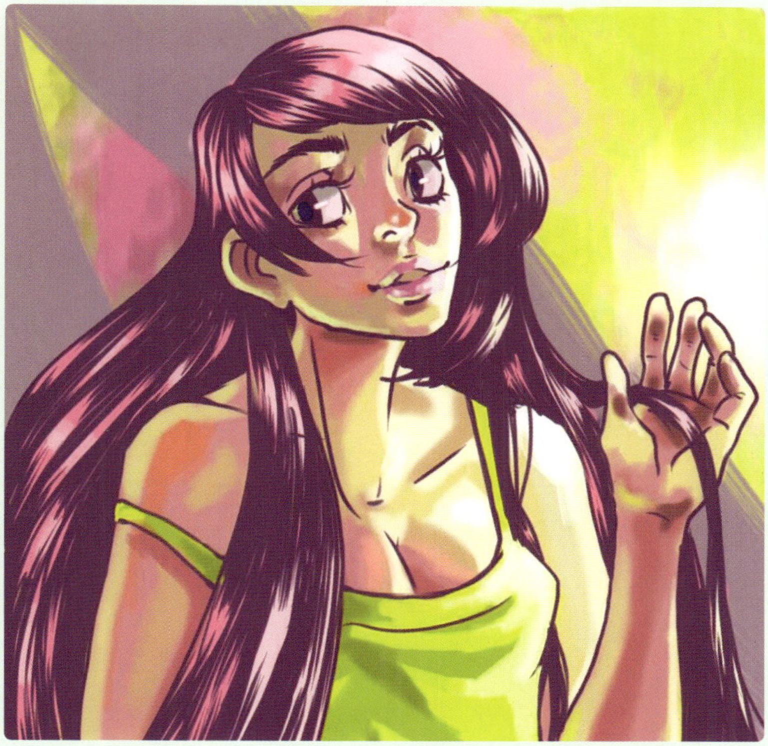

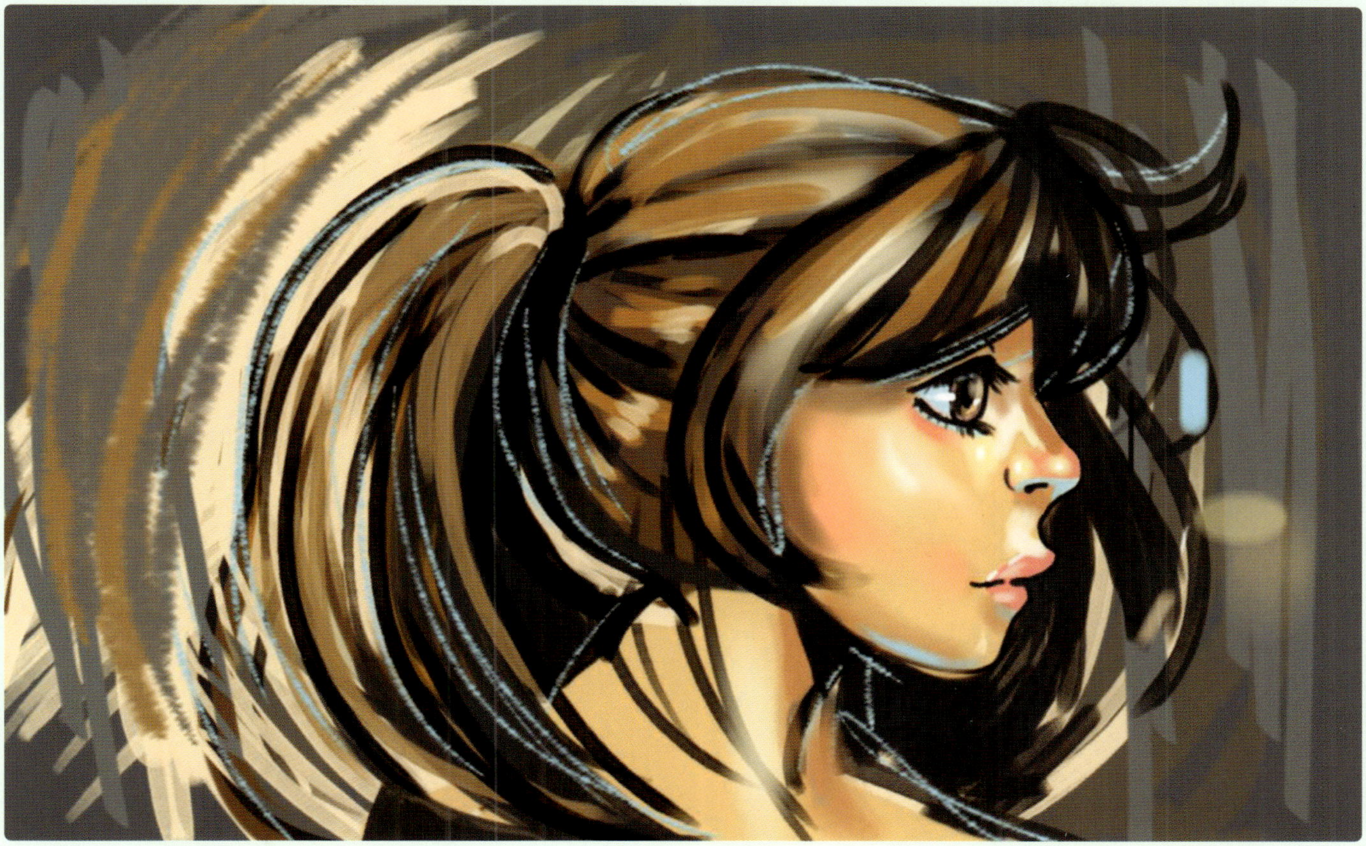

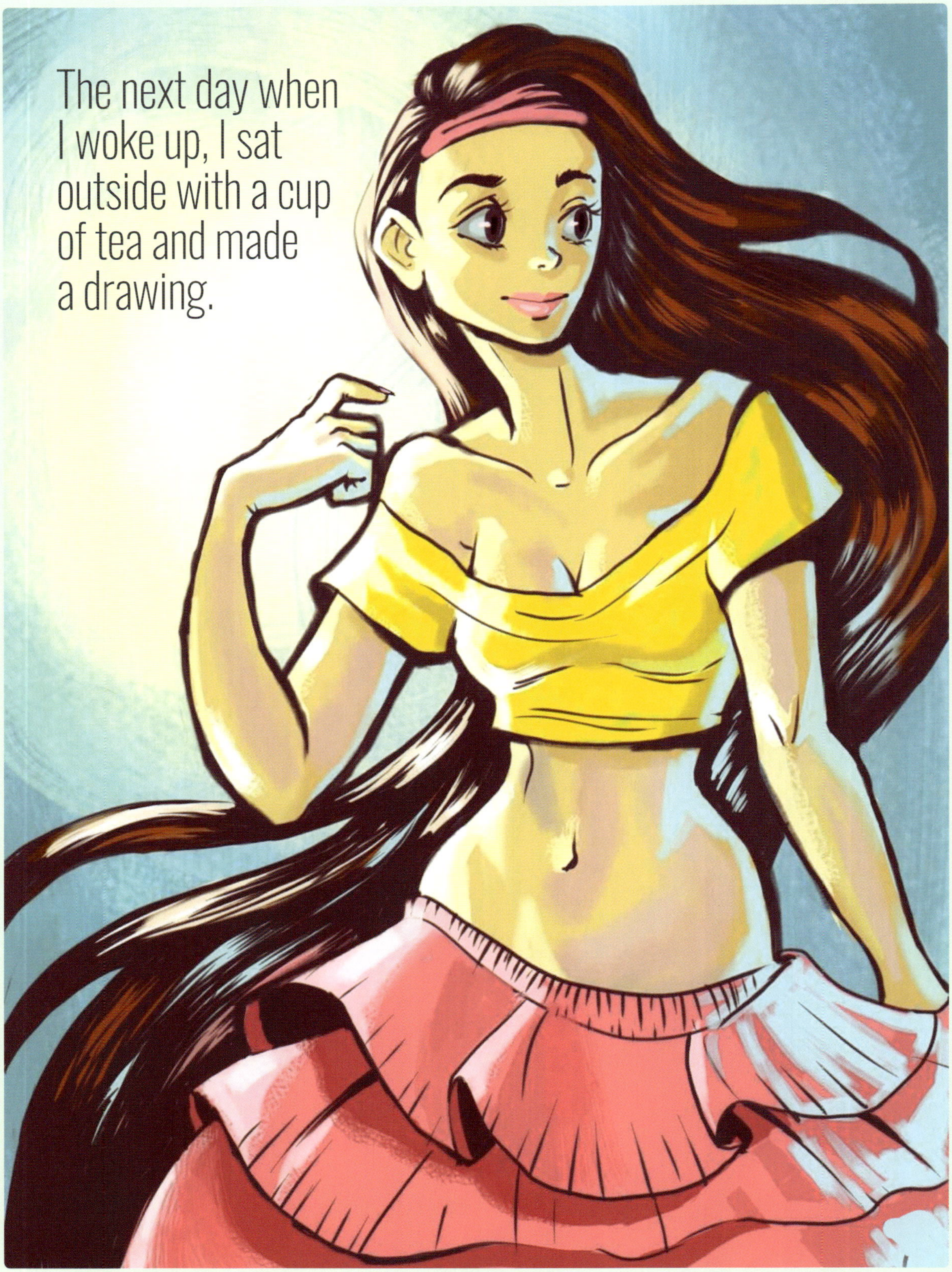
The next day when I woke up, I sat outside with a cup of tea and made a drawing.

I then thought about all the times I'd stopped myself throughout my entire life because I told myself I wasn't good enough. I'd never even given myself the chance; I'd quit before I even started because I told myself there was no point. I wondered at that moment, what if I approached my art in the same way I did a video game, if I took a leap of faith and trusted that if I did the work, I'd get the progress? I realized that improvement is rarely a risk – if I were to run every single day, it's not just a chance that I'd gain muscle and get fit, it's guaranteed, so if I draw every day, it must be the same, right? I don't know why it was just this simple exchange in my head, but I suddenly felt invigorated to try and see if I was right. The next day when I woke up, I sat outside with a cup of tea and made a drawing. And the next day I did it again. And again.

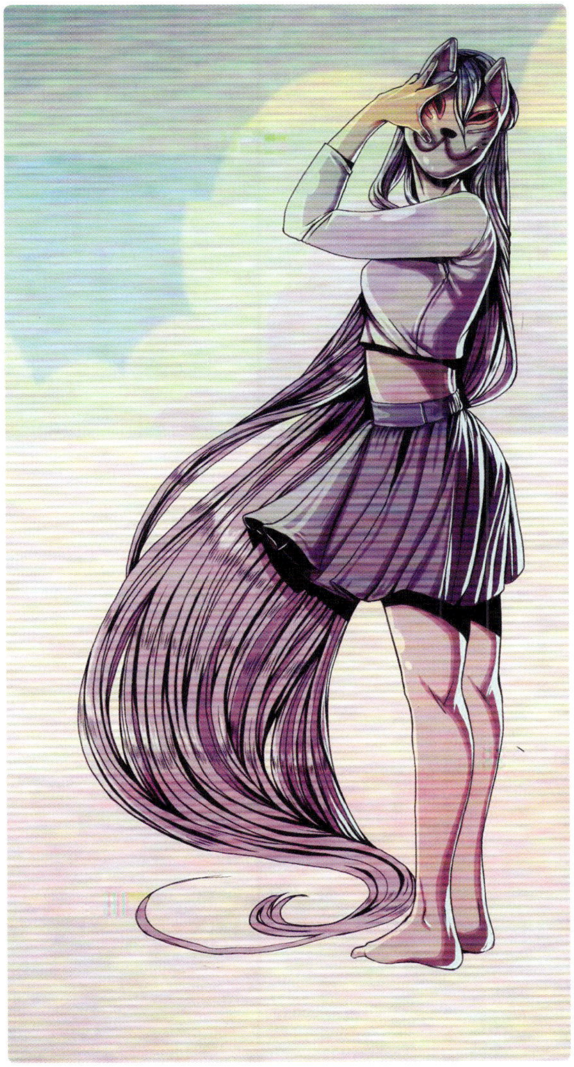

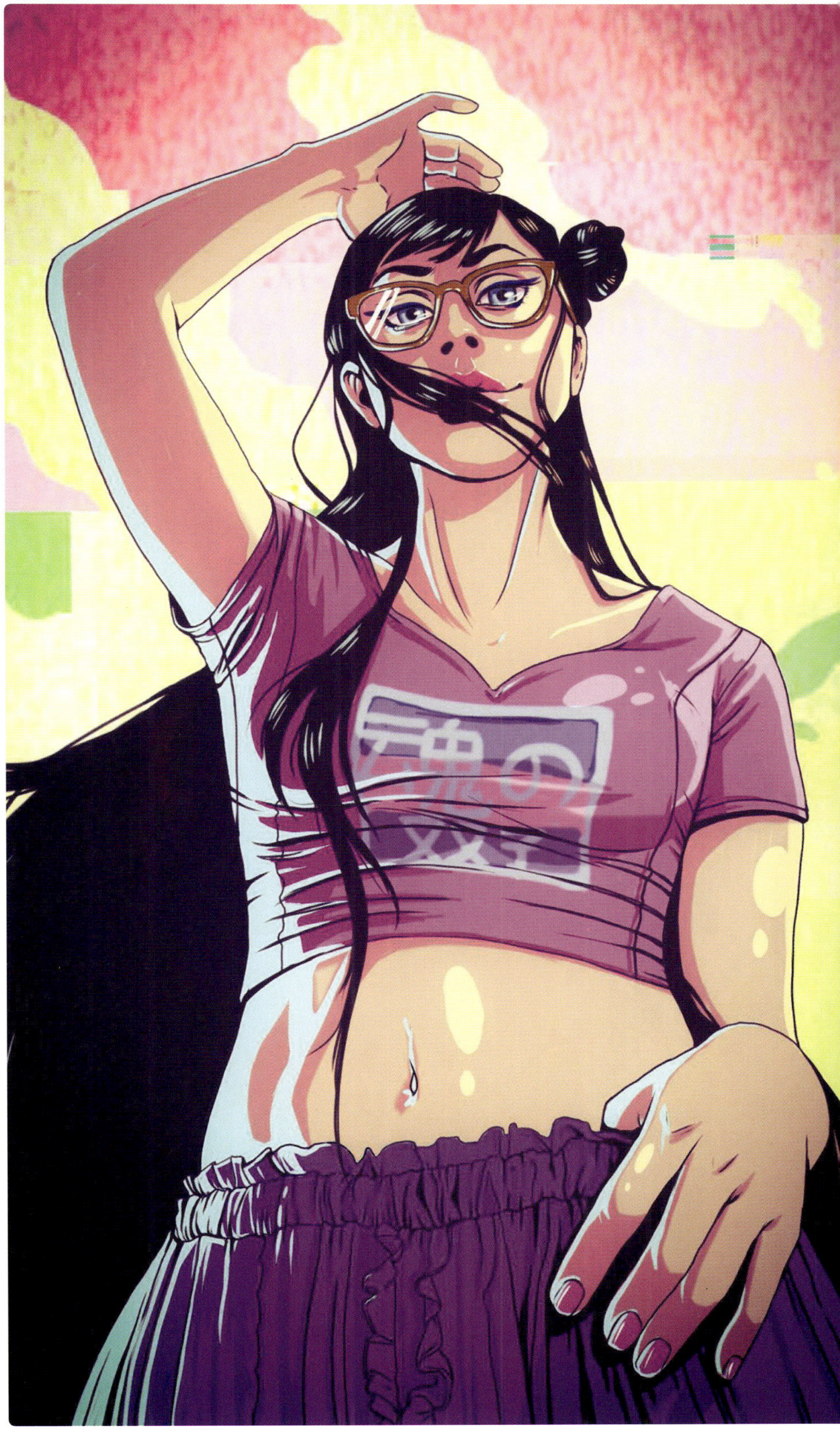

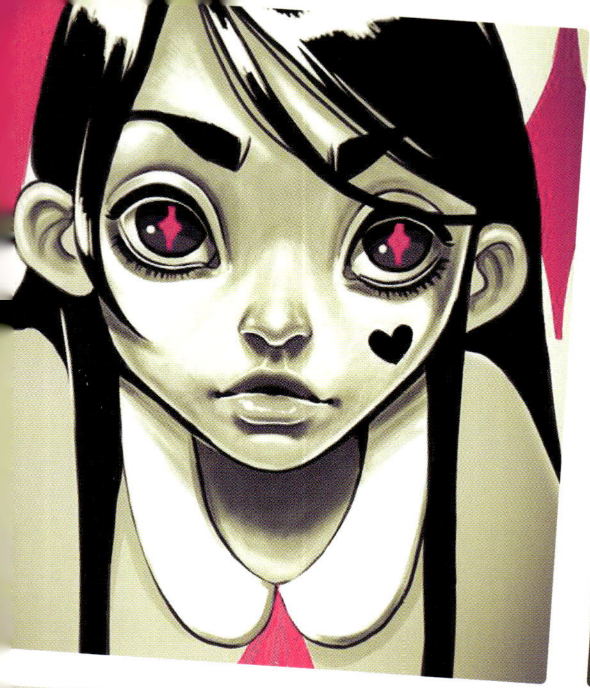

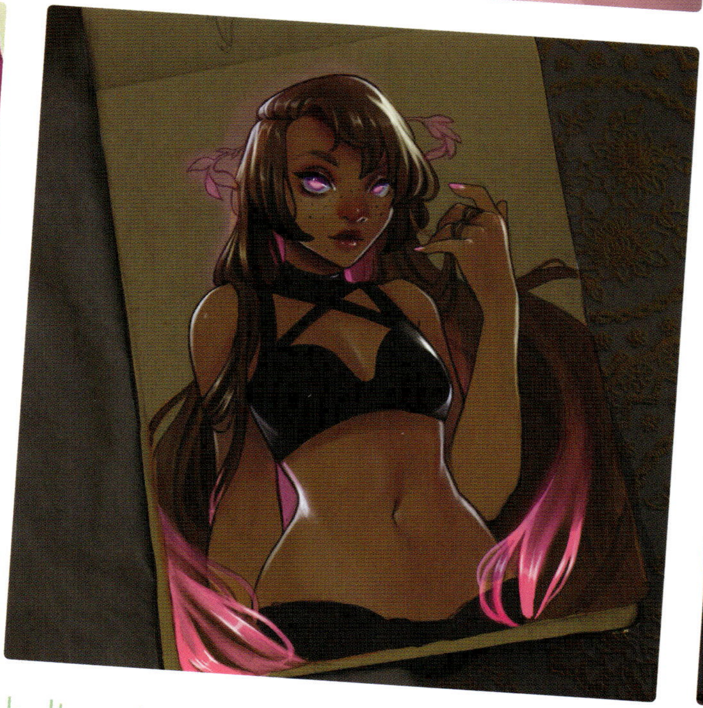

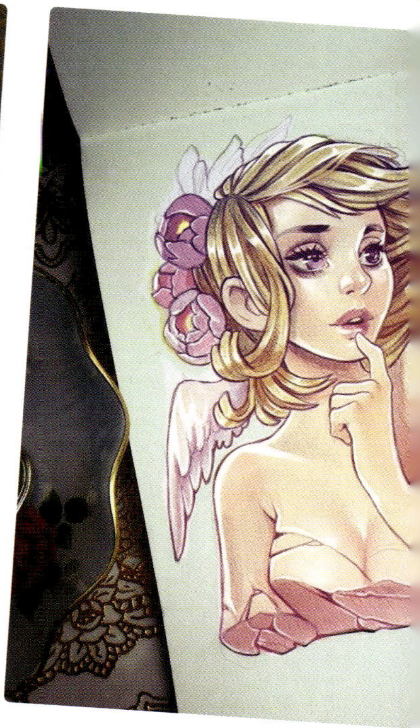

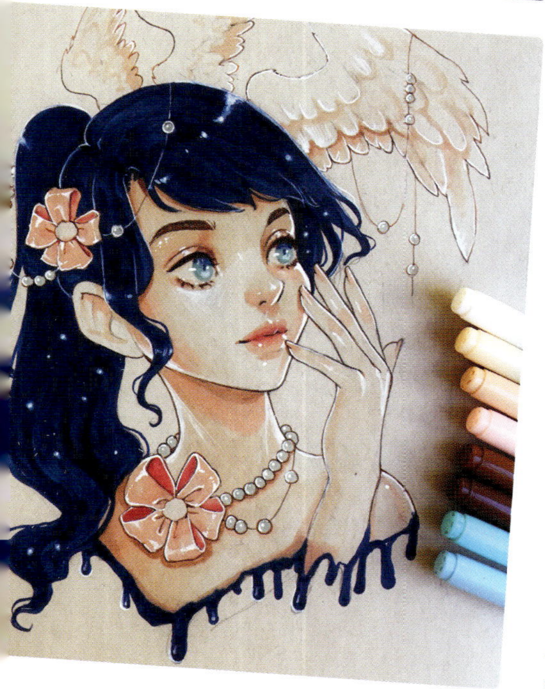

## believe in yourself

It's now six years later and I can't believe all the things that have happened because I decided to take that step. I built a social media following, I learned to paint, I worked on a video game, I've been in galleries, and I'm launching a book, all because I made the decision to just truly try. I think about that girl crying in the bathroom at art school, thinking she wasn't a real artist and I wish she could see all the things that are in her future. There are so many different ways to make art and so many paths that can be followed. Some styles are deeply technical, some are wild and evocative, some people start their journey young and some start halfway through life. All of these stories and styles matter, they're all valid, and they're all amazing. There's room for all of us.

To every person that feels art is a part of their soul, I say that burying it will never work. Embrace who you are and what you love and never let anyone take it from you. Believe in your ability to grow and see where life takes — that's what I want everyone to take away from this more than anything.

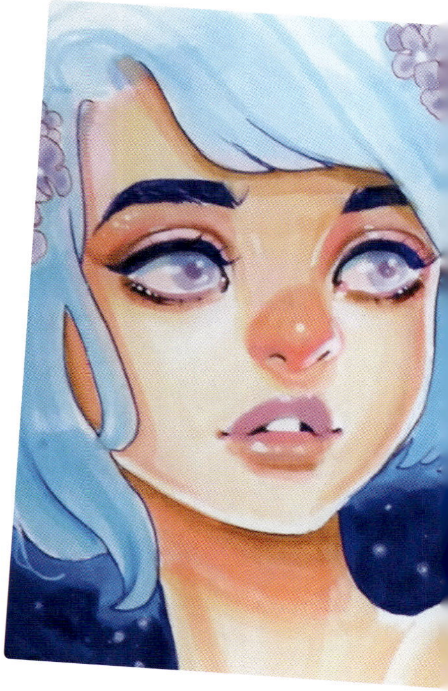

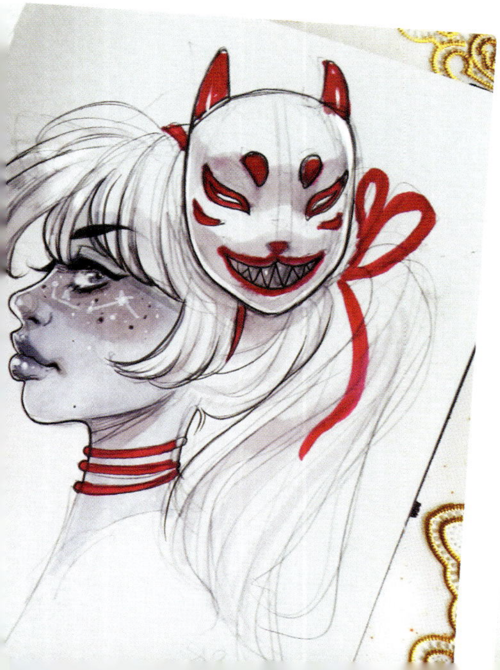

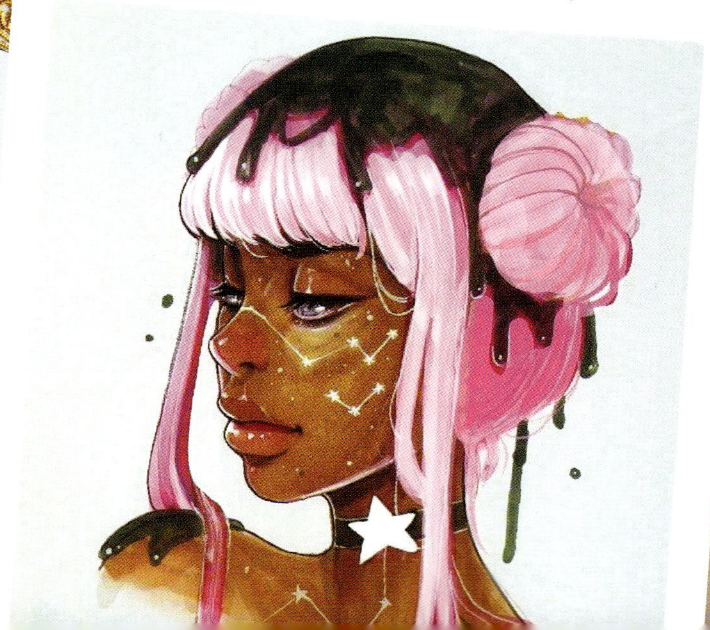

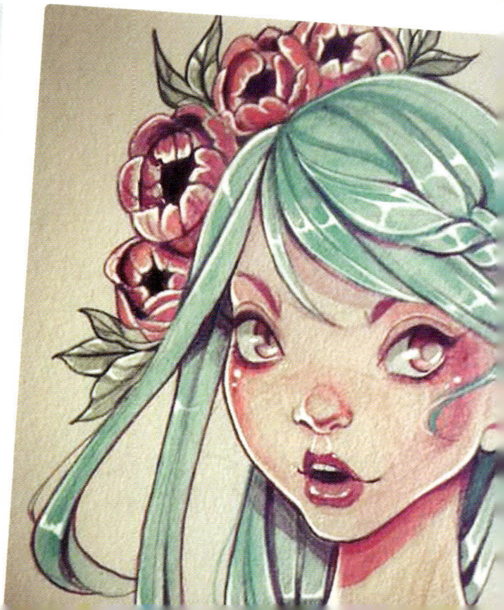

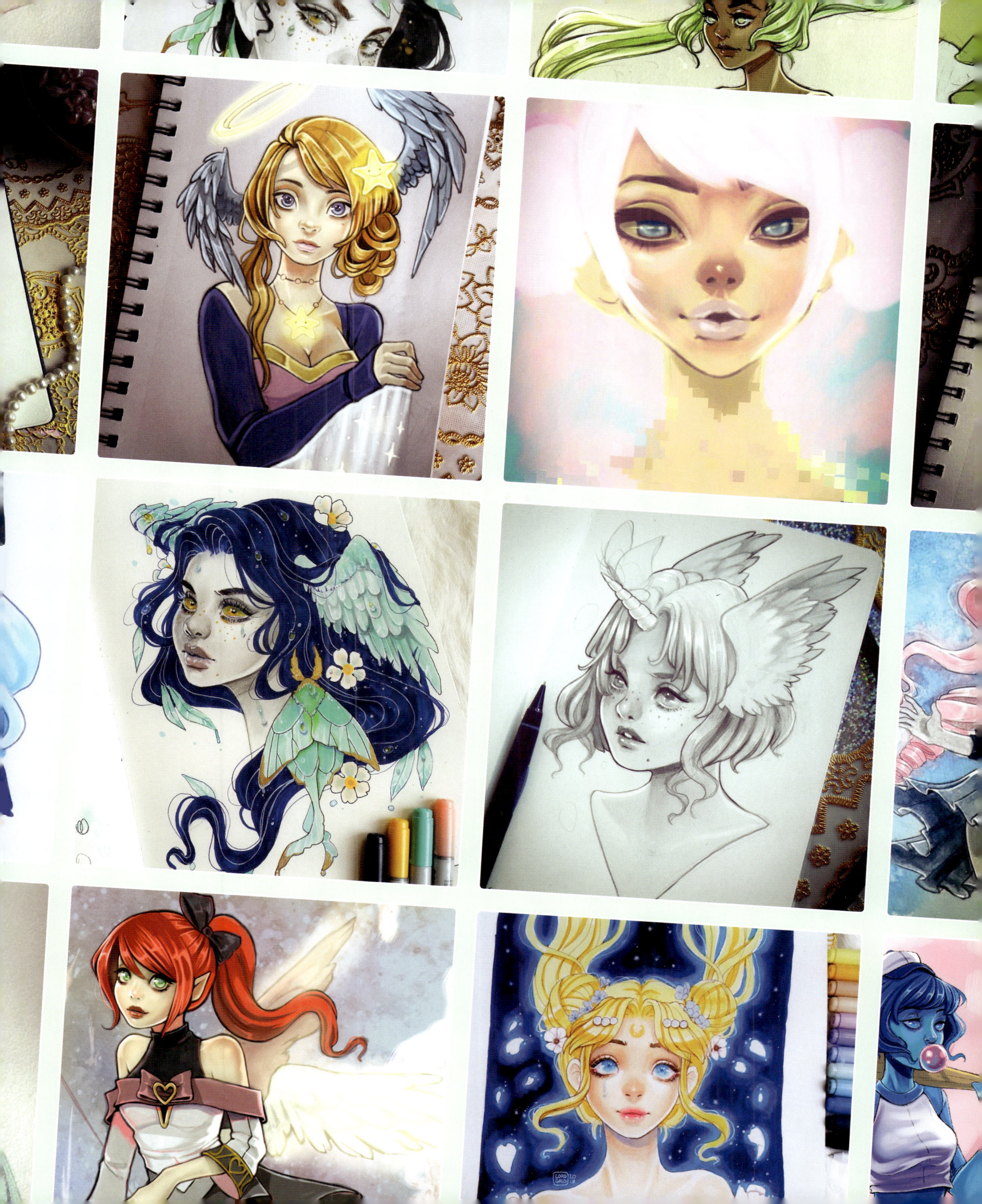

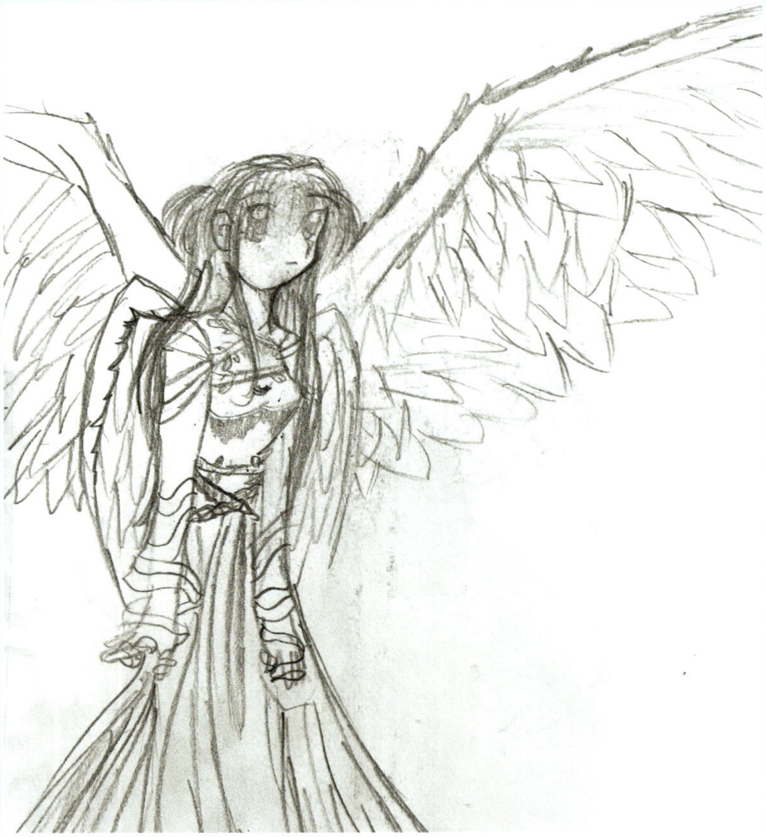

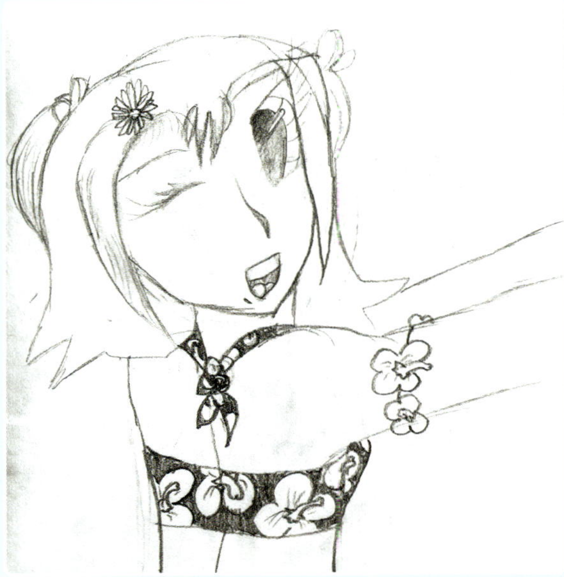

# inspiration

## encouragement at home

Growing up, I always loved to create. Any chance that I got to make something was a fond memory. While nobody else in my family ever drew like I did, I had the benefit of a mother who enjoyed getting messy and making crafts. She taught art literacy during my years at public school, which meant once a month, class was disrupted to make masks out of milk jugs, or put canvases on the bottom of our desks and lay on our backs to paint like Michelangelo (your arm gets tired very fast!). I was blessed in many ways to have the mother that I did. People often compared her to Ms. Frizzle – she even had the curly hair! She never discouraged me from being creative or pushing the boundaries. Instead, we got into all kinds of wonderful trouble with our projects together – we would put rocks in the oven to heat them up, then draw on them with crayons to watch the wax melt in beautiful patterns, or cover the table with shaving cream and draw shapes in the foam. She let me draw on my clothes with markers and dye my hair strange colors, and when I insisted I needed a poodle skirt with cats on it, she made it for me and I wore it nearly every day.

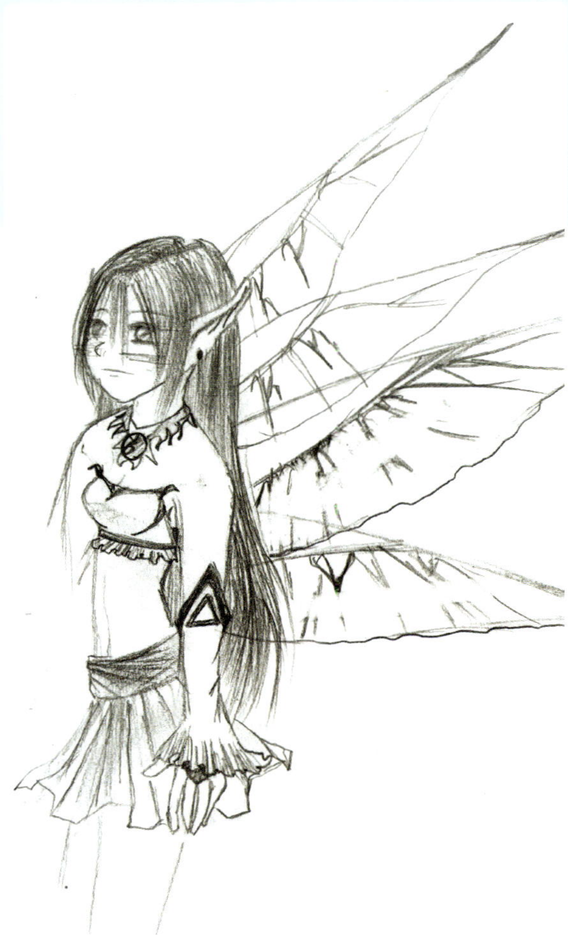

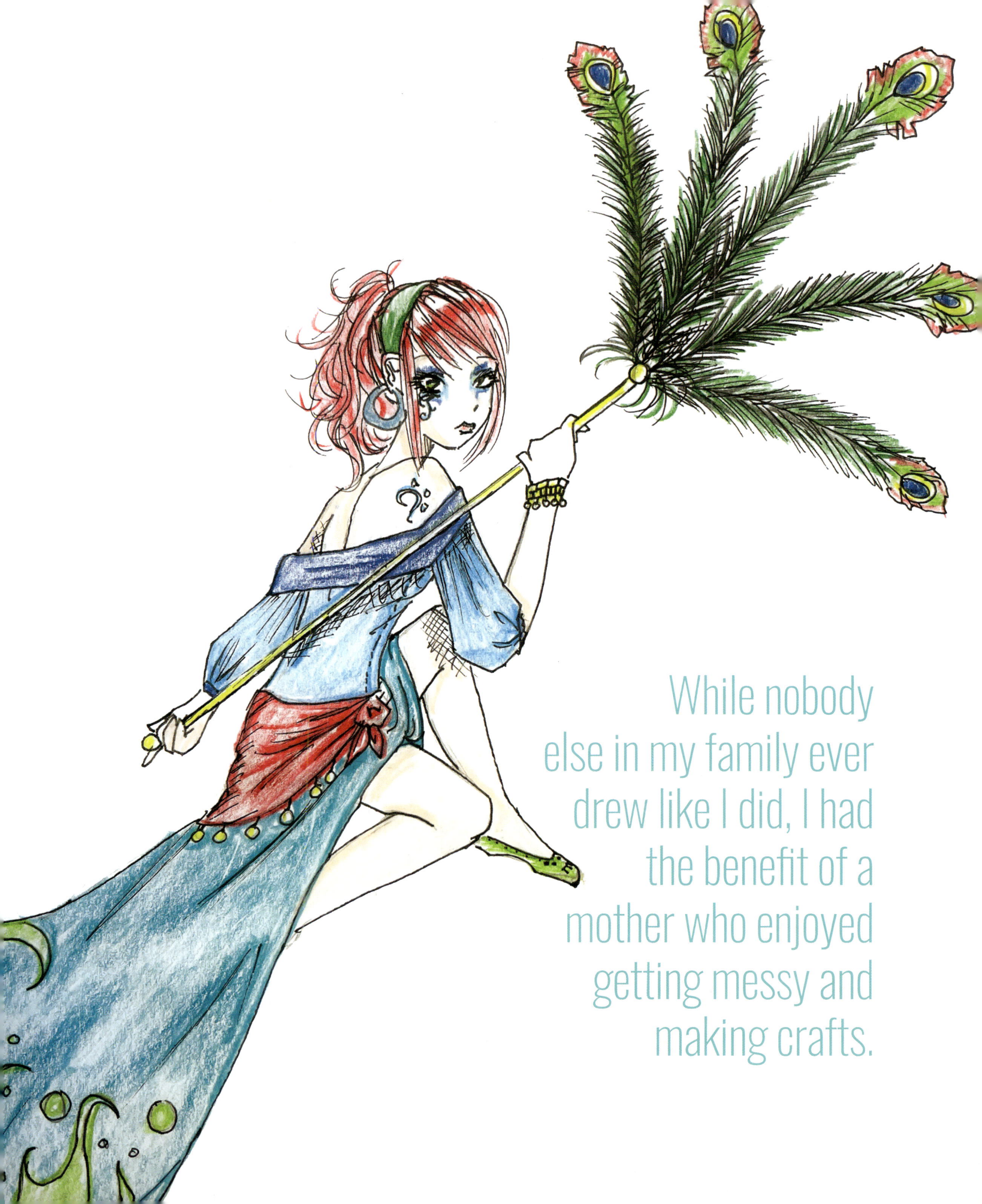

While nobody
else in my family ever
drew like I did, I had
the benefit of a
mother who enjoyed
getting messy and
making crafts.

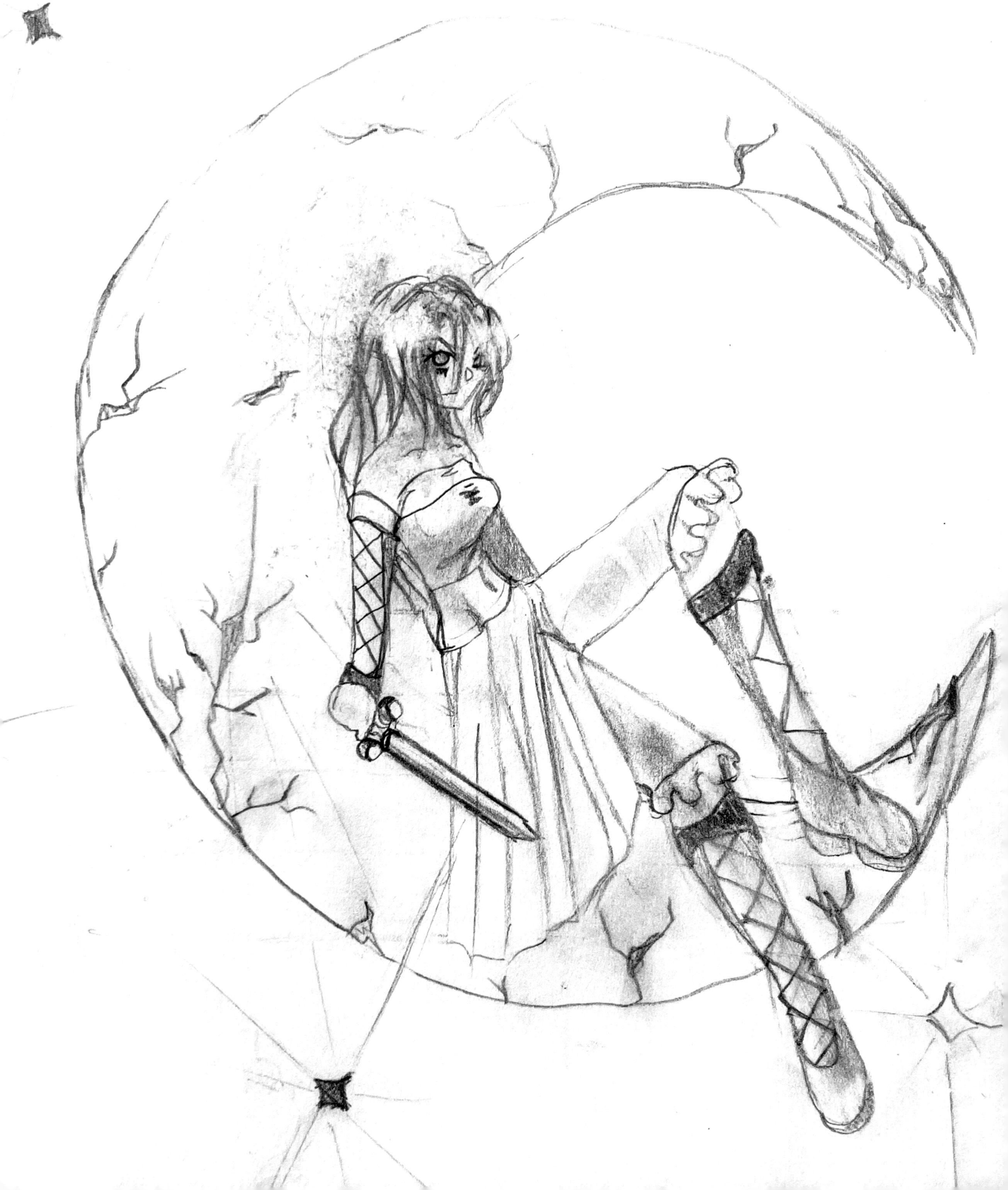

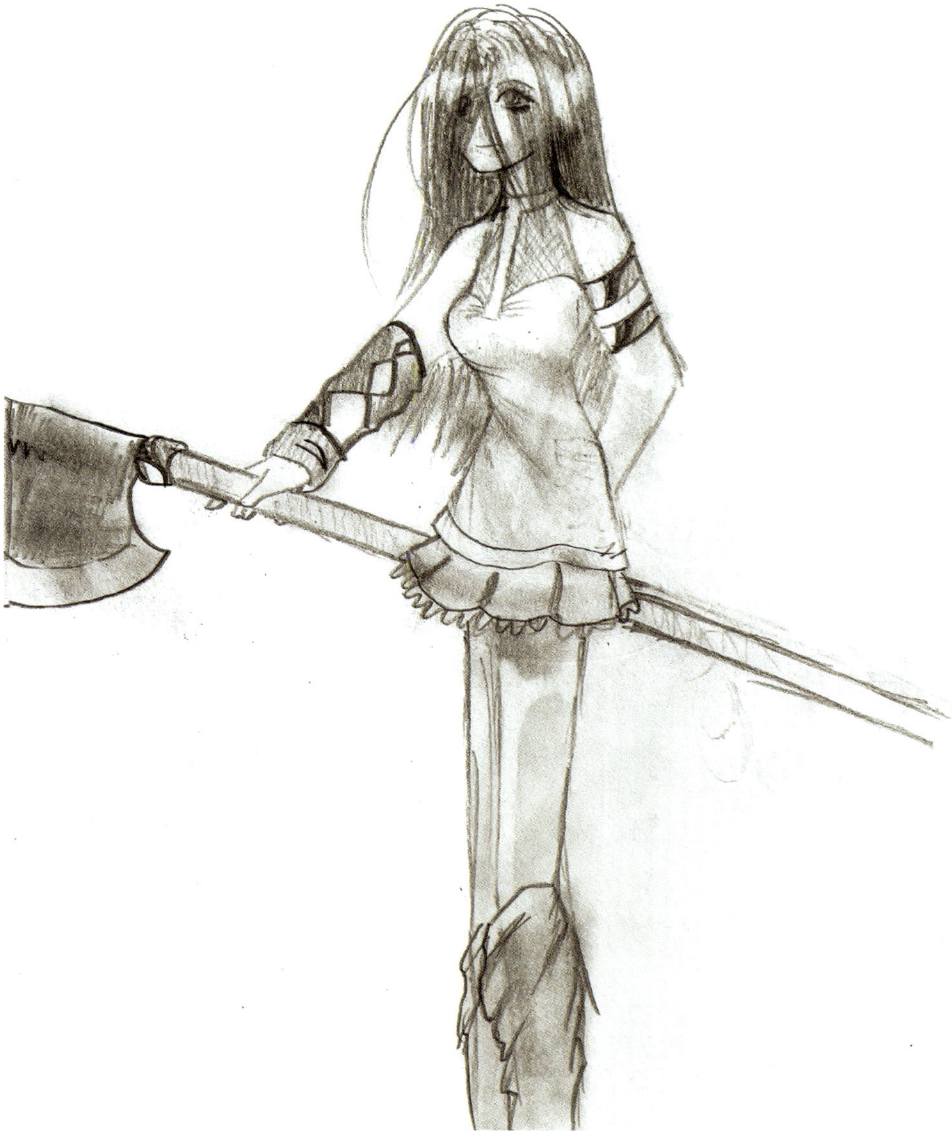

I fell in love with the beautiful fantasy women that I encountered in the games, cards, and concept and fan art.

## video games

As you might imagine, being the poodle-skirt-wearing-kid did not make me very popular. I was quite the target for bullying, which meant instead of having friends my own age, I found myself following my older brother around a lot, and much of my childhood was spent playing video games and trading cards with him and his friends. It was here that I fell in love with the beautiful fantasy women that I encountered in the games, cards, and concept and fan art sections of the gaming magazine we subscribed to. There was something incredibly enchanting about them. They had fierce outfits and big eyes, wings or horns or impossibly large weapons, they cast magic and flew, and their hair could be any color at all. When I saw these fantastical girls, all I wanted to do was draw them – both the characters I encountered as well as my own creations. I wanted to write their stories and dream of their adventures, which is exactly what I did.

Video games, by and large, played the biggest role in my early artistic inspiration. I can recall many games with character designs that made an impact on me – titles such as *Skies of Arcadia*, *Tales of Symphonia*, *Shining Force*, *The Legend of Zelda* series, *Phantasy Star Online*, *Final Fantasy*, *Capcom Vs. SNK*, the *Soulcalibur* games and *Fire Emblem*. Some games I never even played, but was still able to draw inspiration from the game art.

The *Phantasy Star Online* series was a huge source of inspiration for me. I first saw drawings of the characters in our *Nintendo Power* magazine before I encountered the game itself. There was this pretty mage girl gently holding a fireball and I thought it was the loveliest thing I'd ever laid eyes on. It was actually the first ever image I cut out of the magazine, and the inception of the inspiration board I kept in my room. That particular drawing was

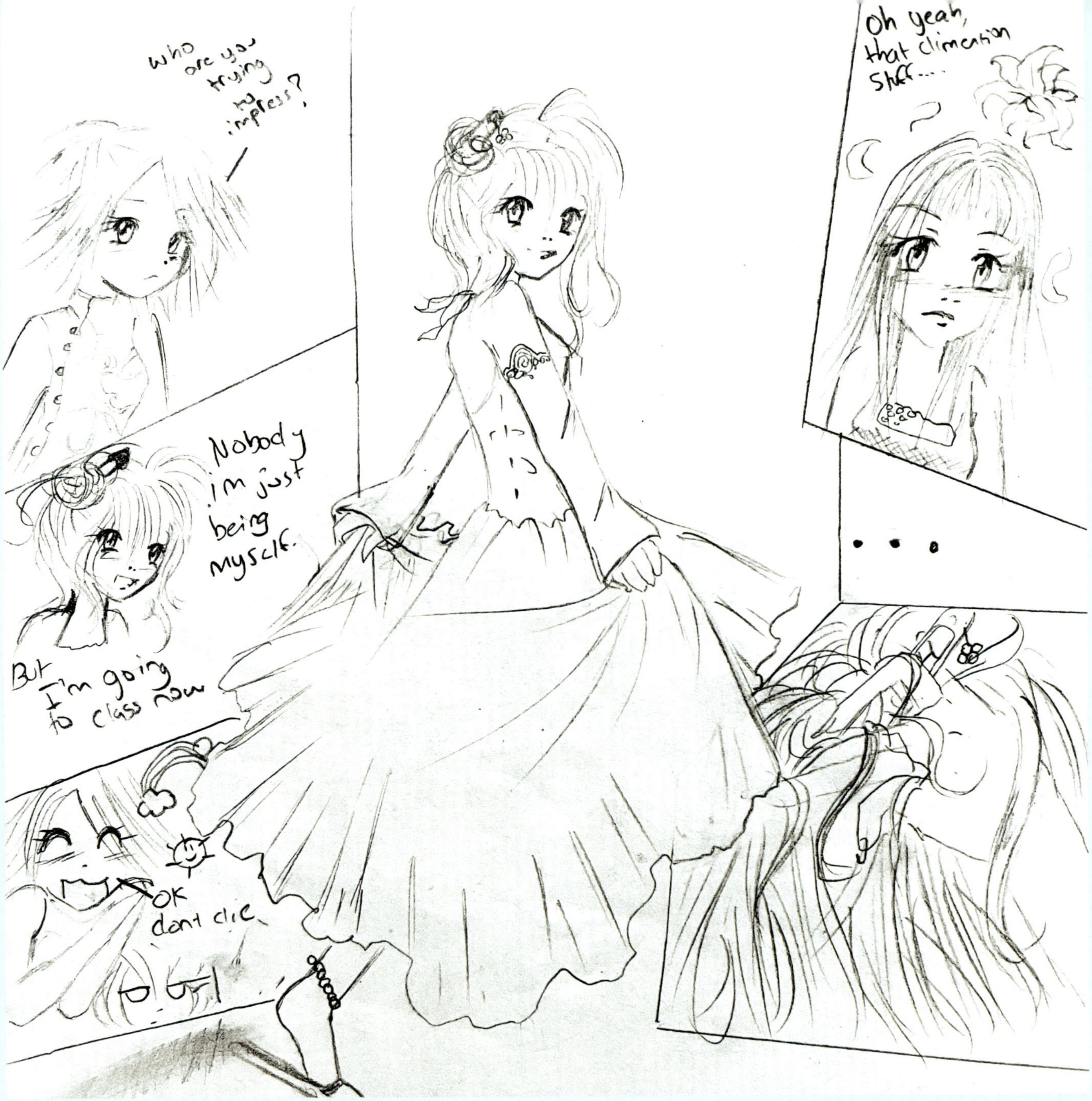


just so beautiful, I couldn't bear the thought of it getting thrown in the trash where I'd never see it again. I wasn't sure what I should do with it, so I glued it to a piece of extra posterboard I had in my room, and the inspiration board just grew from there. Whenever I saw *Phantasy Star* characters in an issue, I'd cut more of them out, and glue them on, and I eventually started gluing on characters from all sorts of games until I had a poster overflowing with amazing character designs. At the time, the characters and poses seemed so far beyond anything I could ever possibly make — the skill was pure wizardry to me. It amazes me that I can now finally look at the designs on that poster and say, "I could make something like this" — it's the most rewarding feeling.

I don't know what it was about *Phantasy Star*'s game aesthetic that I loved so much. It's not the most feminine game design, but the almost 1990s-futuristic/high-fantasy design that was just enchanting. I loved the mix of cute characters with machinery and high-tech weapons—a huge source of inspiration for the mechanical elements in my current designs. I assumed that I would never play the game; I was in elementary school so I didn't have much spare money for buying expensive games, and nobody in my life owned a copy. But by chance, the girl next door invited me over to play games one day and she pulled out *Phantasy Star Online*. I couldn't believe it. I'd never mentioned to anyone that I wanted to play it and yet here it was, the game whose art I'd been admiring for months!

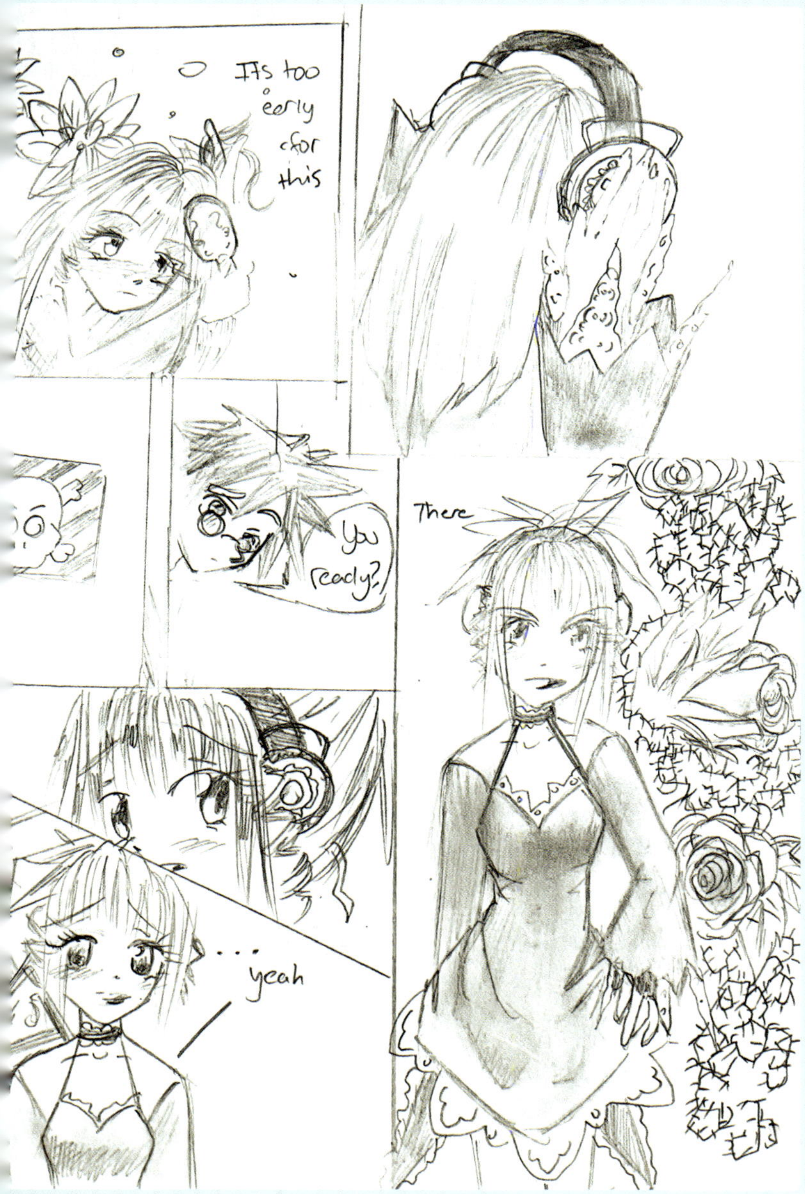


Playing it just once was enough for me to become obsessed. I went home and begged my parents to let me buy it. At first they were reluctant (there were pools of blood when the enemies died) but I wanted it so badly I wrote a paper on why I should be allowed to buy it. I even got my brother to go half in on it with me. When they agreed, I can't tell you how many hours I sunk into that game, sometimes just making characters in the character creator or running around in the beautiful game environments, not even playing the game. It was an invaluable source of inspiration for my art. I drew an embarrassing amount of fan art based on that game for many years, and even to this day I find myself referencing old *Phantasy Star* characters for inspiration and ideas.

## manga and anime

As I got older, manga books began to play a role in my life, especially around the time I was in eighth grade. They were hard to find because manga wasn't as common as it is now. I adored the art; not only were the characters fun and dynamic but the scenes flowed together, often with beautiful backgrounds of flowers or shimmering jewels or skyscapes. The black-and-white style worked well, as I was mostly only able to work with graphite at the time. I tried to write several of my own manga books, but discovered very quickly that it's a labor of love and never got very far with any of them. Titles I remember playing a role in the shaping of my style were *Fruits Basket*, *Alice 19th*, *Othello*, and the strange manga by Courtney Love, *Princess Ai*, which was the manga I learned to draw wings from.

The only anime I saw as a child was children's TV shows such as *Pokémon* and *Digimon*. I saw my first anime film when I was almost seventeen. *My Neighbor Totoro* was my first meaningful introduction to the genre. I watched it in Japanese class and I was struck by how stunning 2D animation could really be. The backgrounds and characters were enchanting – I'd never seen anything like it! I went through a phase where I couldn't get enough of Miyazaki movies. Every weekend I would rent a new film by him and invite all my friends over for viewing parties. We eventually watched every one of his films. Until I discovered Miyazaki movies, the only 2D animation I'd seen was Western animation such as Disney films, which have never been particularly compelling to me. I loved seeing that cartoons weren't just for sugary children's stories, that they could tell very dark and serious tales such as *Princess Mononoke*. I loved that I could have the delectable treat of beautiful art and a complex tale all in one package. I was sad when I ran out of films, I wanted more. Western animation still reserves animation for children's stories, unfortunately, which I hope will change some day. I believe animation and cartoons are not inherently childish; they are loved and appreciated by all ages.

At the time, the characters and poses seemed so far beyond anything I could ever possibly make, the skill was pure wizardry to me.

# emotional inspiration and recharging

I was born and raised in Portland, Oregon. I've tried to live in other places but nowhere else feels like home. If I'm away too long I start to miss the fir trees, the rain, the gray skies, the waterfalls, the hiking trails, and the lush greenery. One of the most frequent activities my family did together when I was growing up was hiking. We hiked in every weather, be it beautiful sun or heavy rain with ankle-deep mud, it didn't matter — we hiked through it. Nothing beats standing high in the Columbia gorge and looking down at the river that cuts below, at the hills full of trees and the rolling gray heavens up above. Oregon has a mystical quality and it feels as though it can't be tamed — it has always felt bigger than me, and in control. The skies deluge, the moss grows, and the pavement is cracked apart by ivy and ferns. It wants what it wants, and it wants to be green and alive.

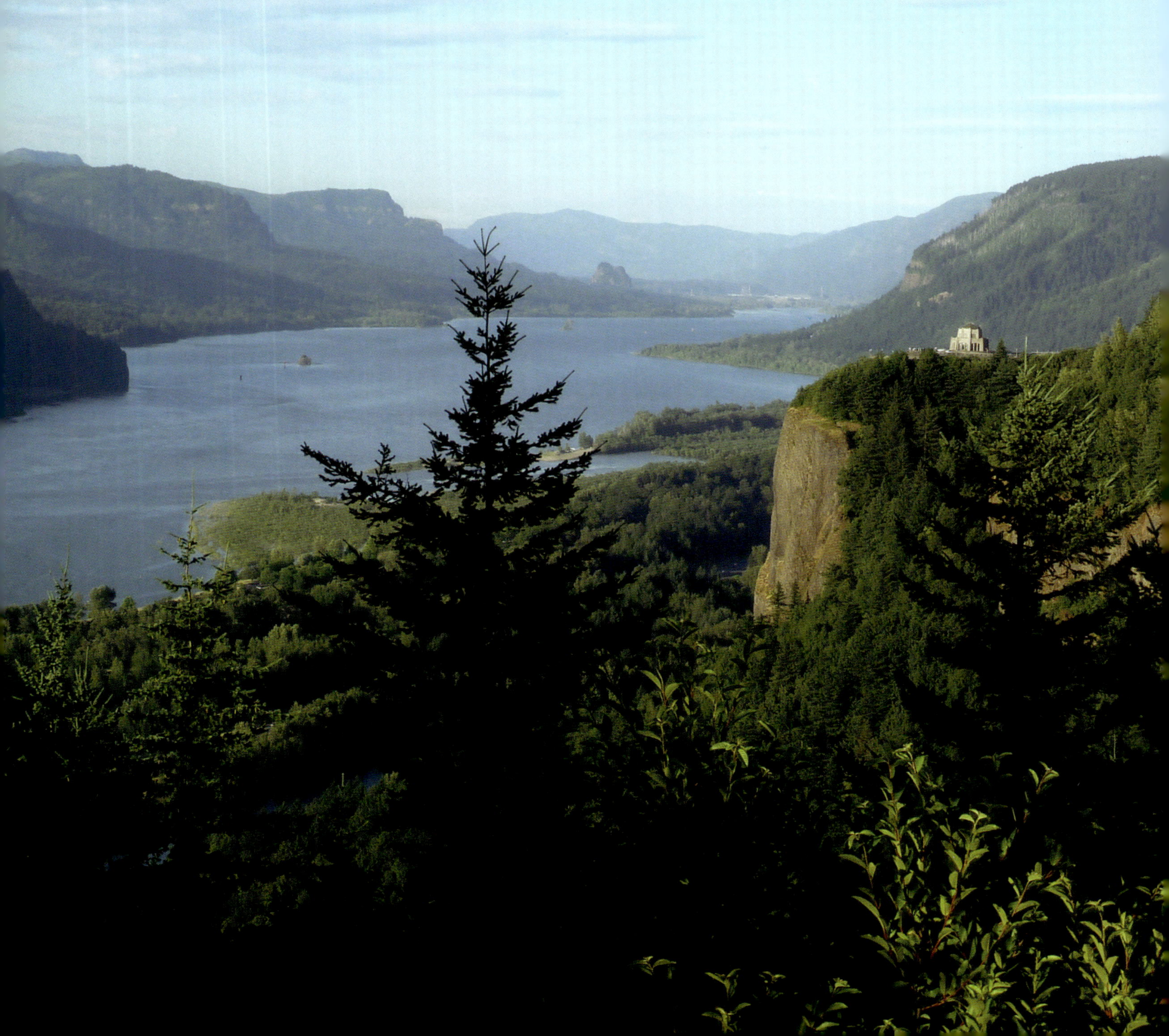

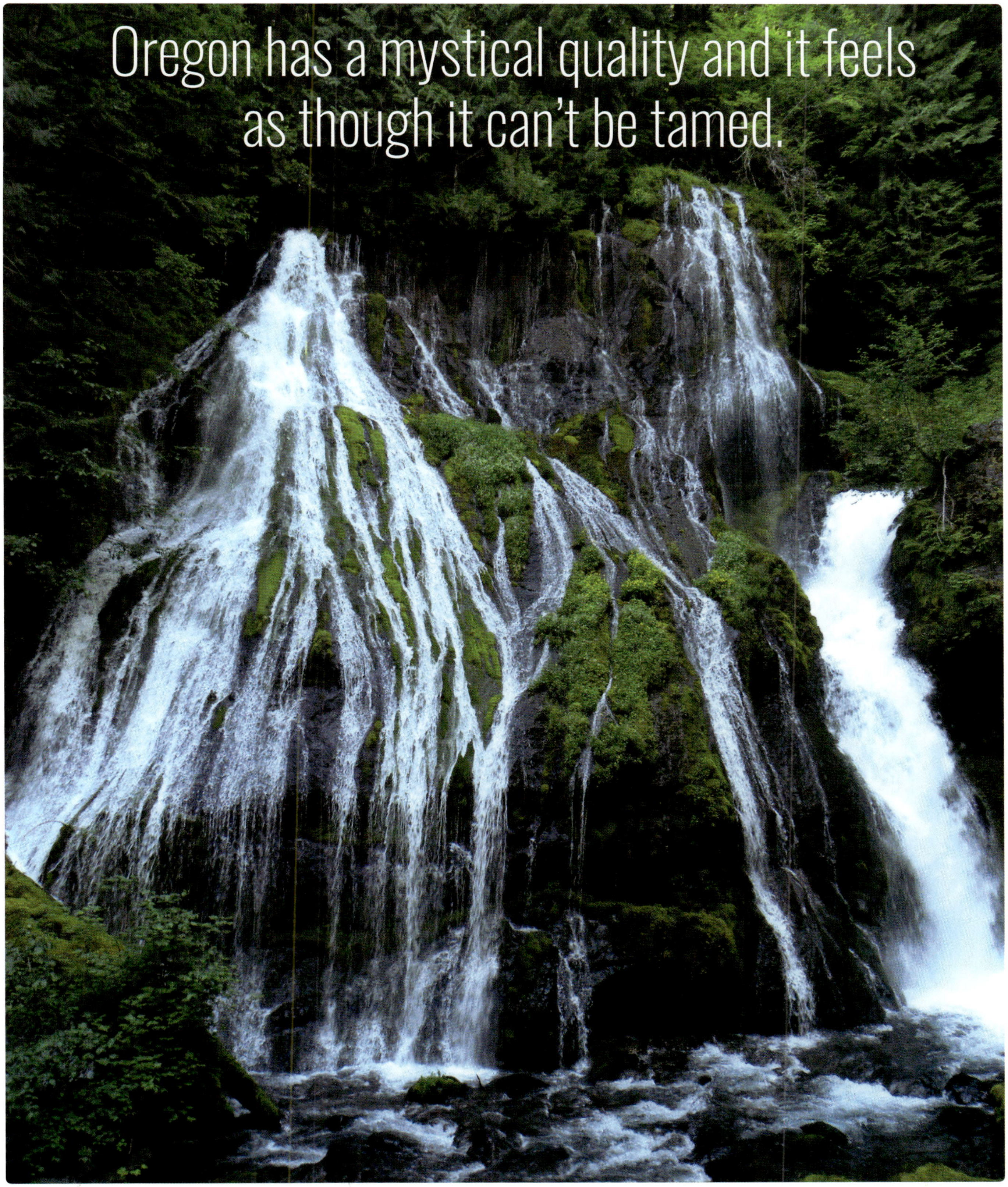
Oregon has a mystical quality and it feels
as though it can't be tamed.

My father is from a small village in New Brunswick, Canada. He moved to Oregon in his college years, so I spent many summers going back to Canada to visit family. Summers in New Brunswick were hot and humid and full of the cries of cicadas. There were rustling birch trees everywhere, endless seas of soft grass along the empty roads, and old covered bridges. We swam in natural ponds and rivers and caught frogs and salamanders. We would also drive to Prince Edward Island to sit on the iron-red beaches and spend the day filling bottles with found pieces of sea glass. I love the rugged beauty of Canada. Much of the surrounding area where we stayed was old, overgrown, and dilapidated. It was different from Oregon — softer and more subtle, but like Oregon, nature consumed it. It echoed stories of a more vibrant time, full of ghosts, rust, and abandoned train tracks. I spent much of my time just wandering around, admiring the strange beauty of the place. I would always come home and want to make something.

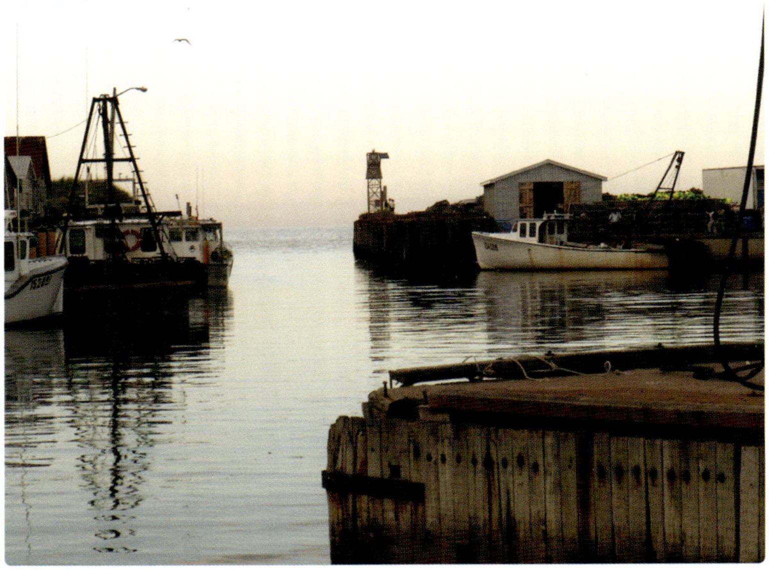

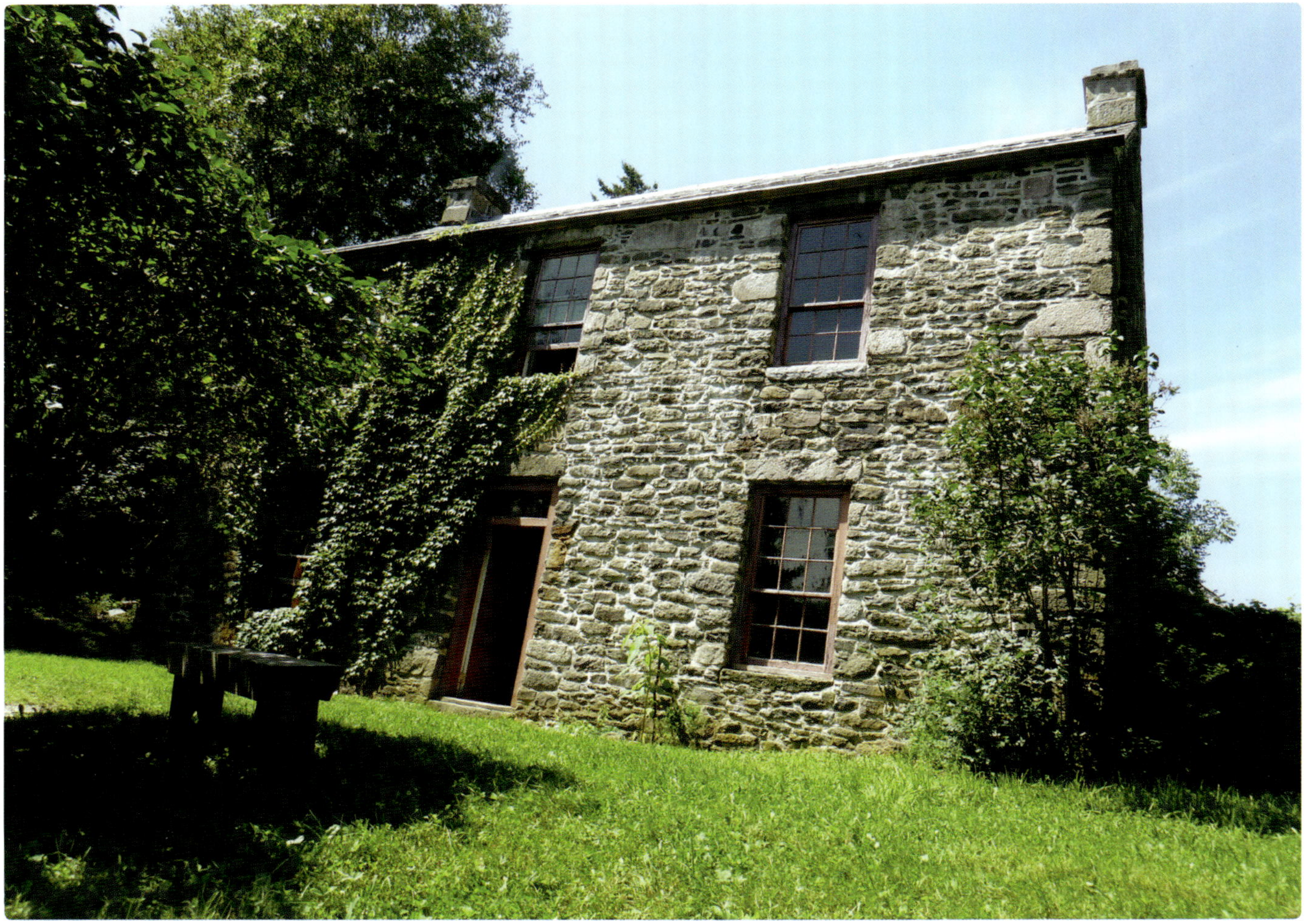

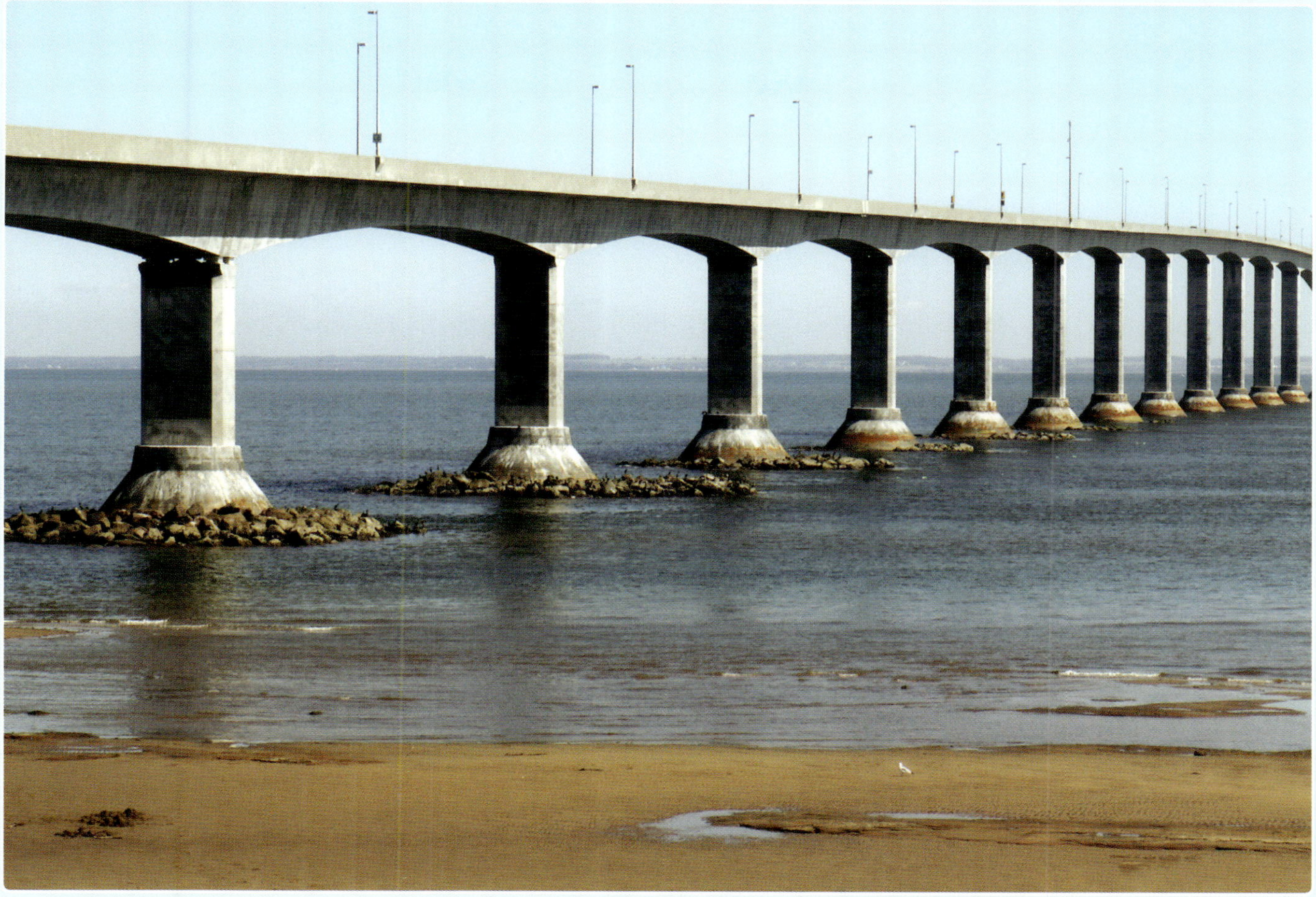

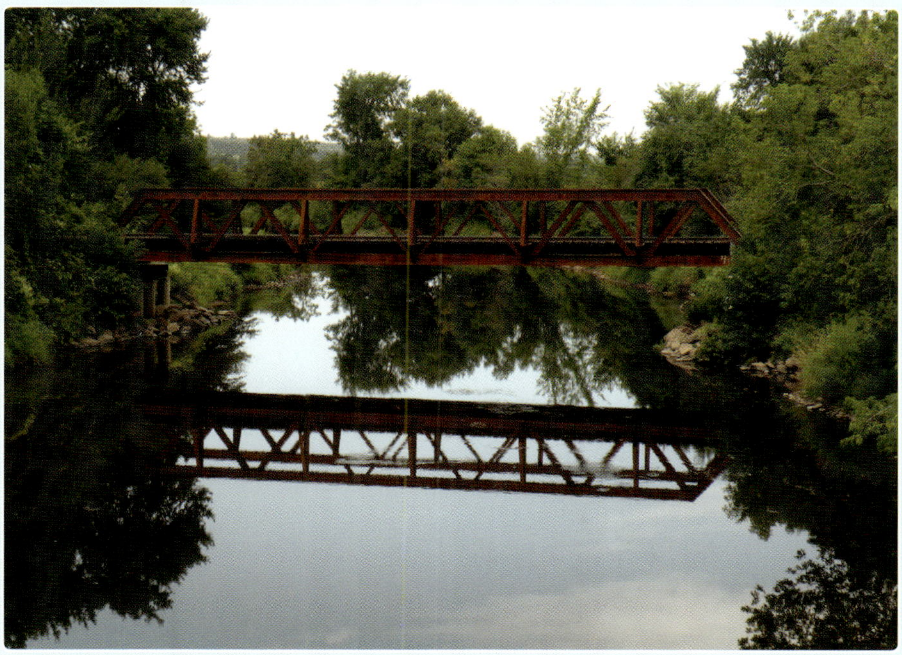

I spent much of my time just wandering around, admiring the strange beauty of the place.

Nature is hugely important to my art, as it feeds into my creative energy. It doesn't directly inspire me, in the sense that I want to draw it specifically, but being around it makes me want to draw, to write, to play music, to create in any form. If I am away from it for too long, I start to feel as though I've been unplugged from my power source. I find it's important to take beautiful moments to disconnect from the chaos of mundane life and feel a part of the cycle of this world, to see everything around you moving, growing, changing, rotting, and starting again. It rejuvenates me when I feel depleted. Sometimes when I'm very busy and feeling strained, I can forget to go out, and I lose myself in the cycle of seemingly endless emails and arbitrary tasks that need to be done. When I finally go out again, I remember myself. I believe it's important to find the things that inspire, but also rejuvenate you. When you create, you draw from a well inside yourself and it must be refilled somehow. Everyone's well is filled in a different way, but you cannot just endlessly create, you may as well try to endlessly exhale; you must inhale at some point. So, what do you find rejuvenating?

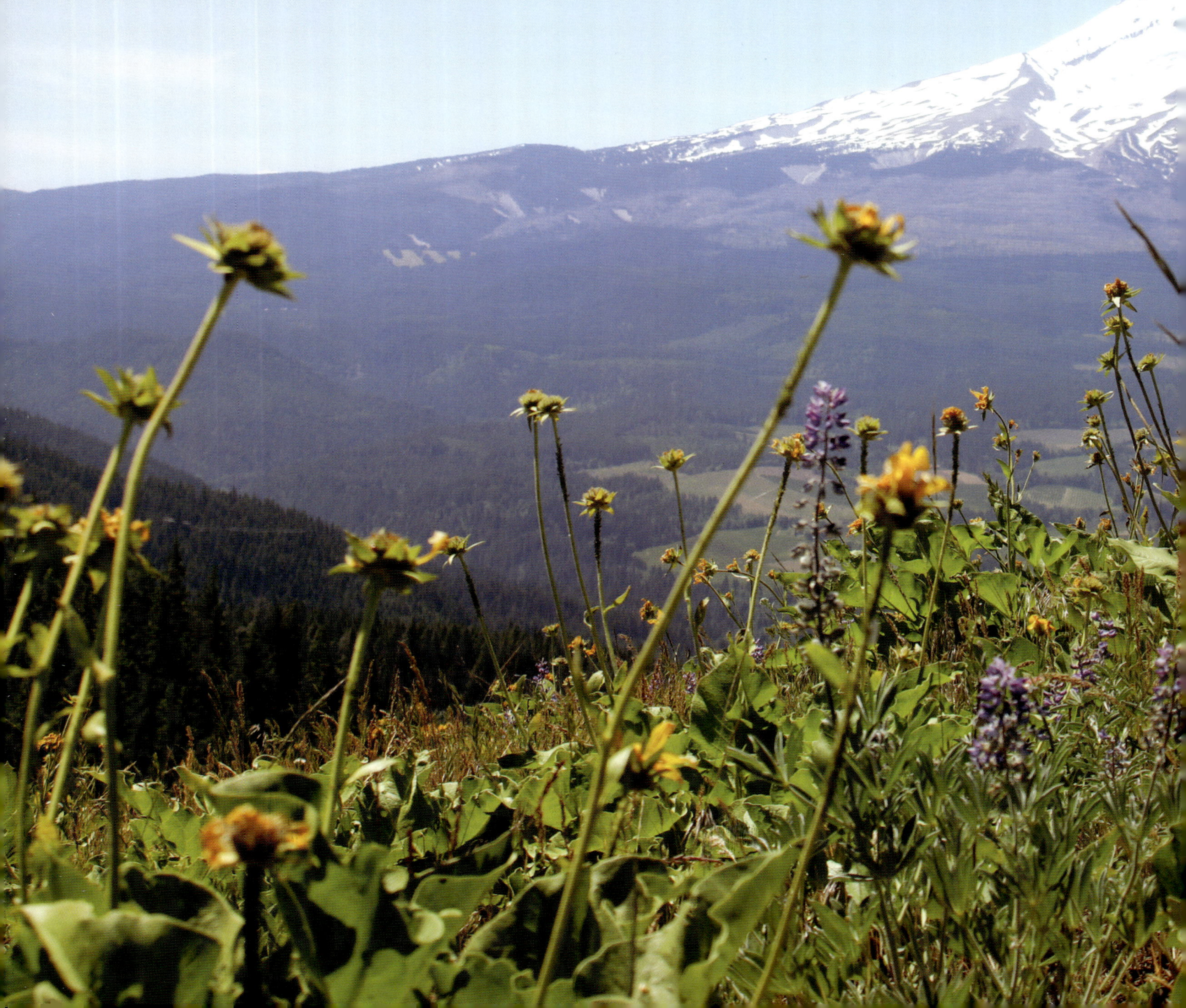

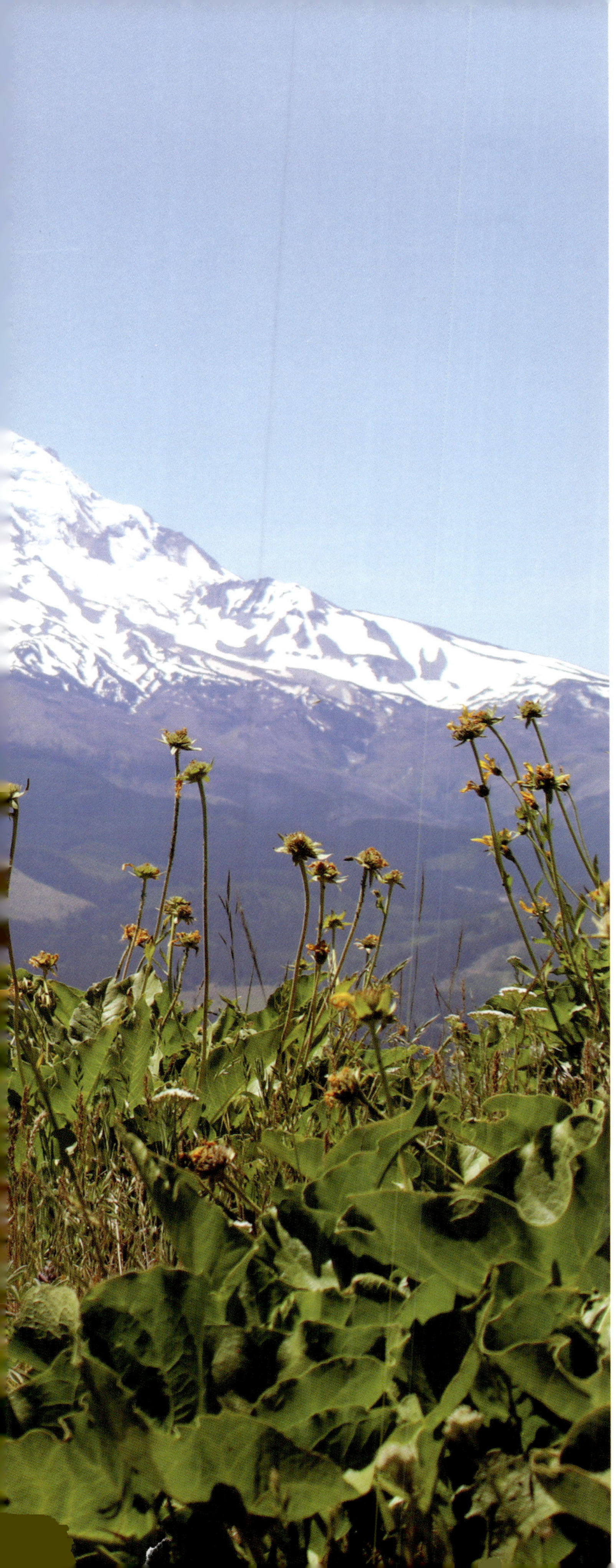

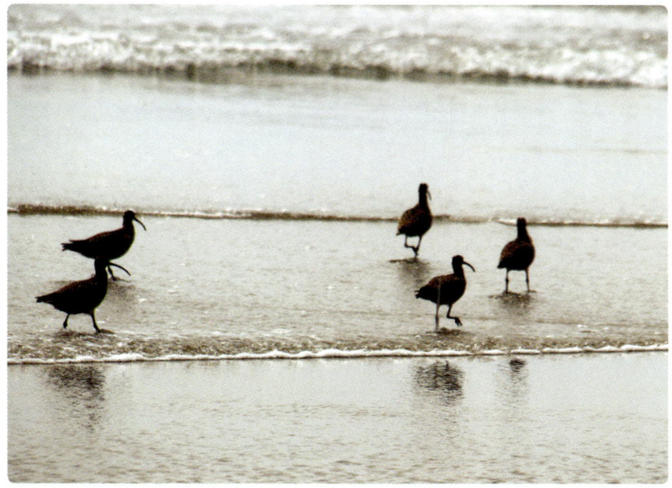

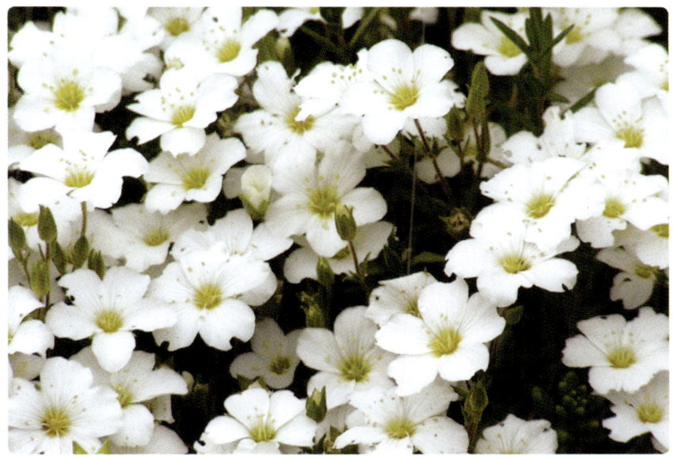

I find it's important to take beautiful moments to disconnect from the chaos of mundane life and feel a part of the cycle of this world...

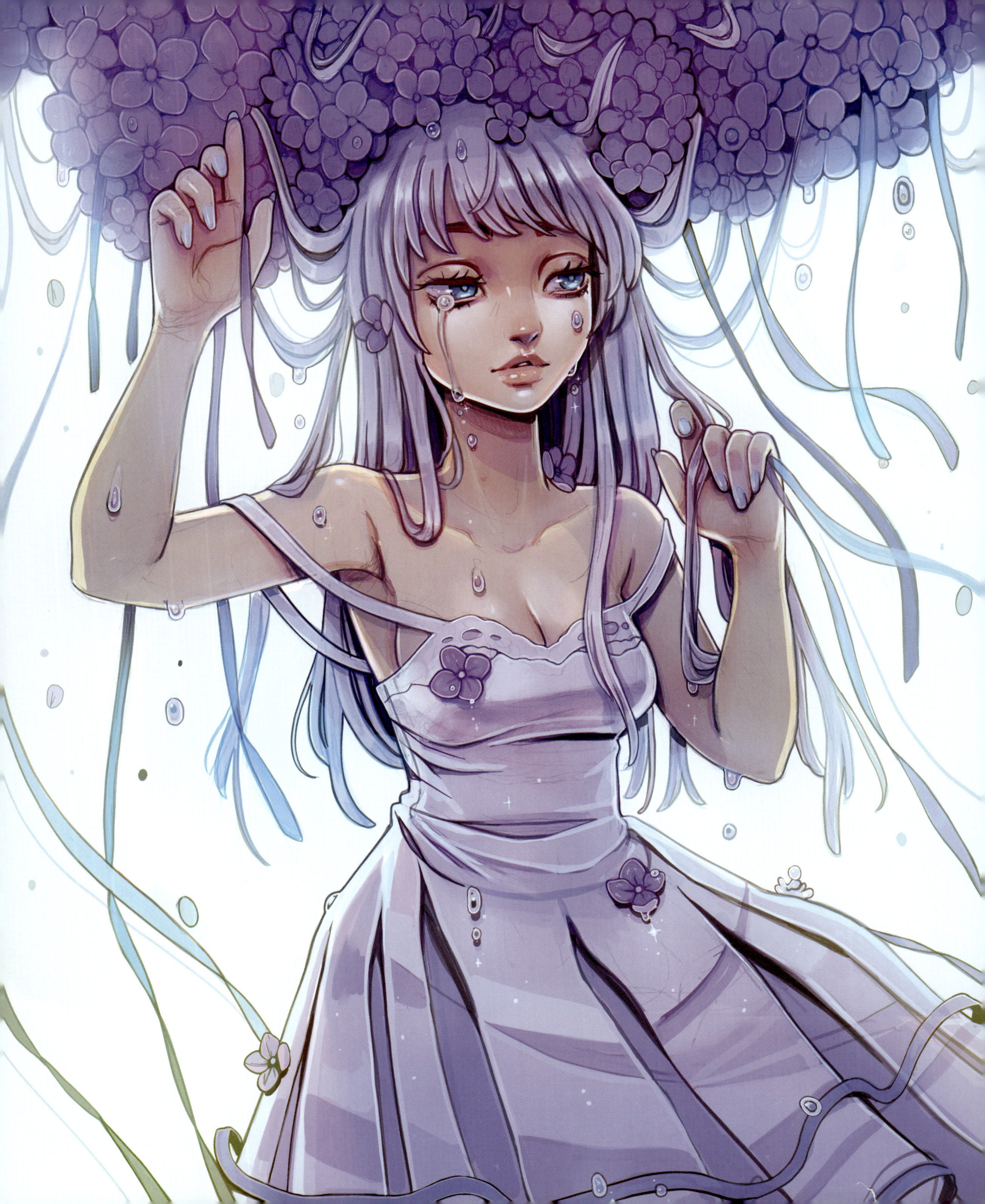

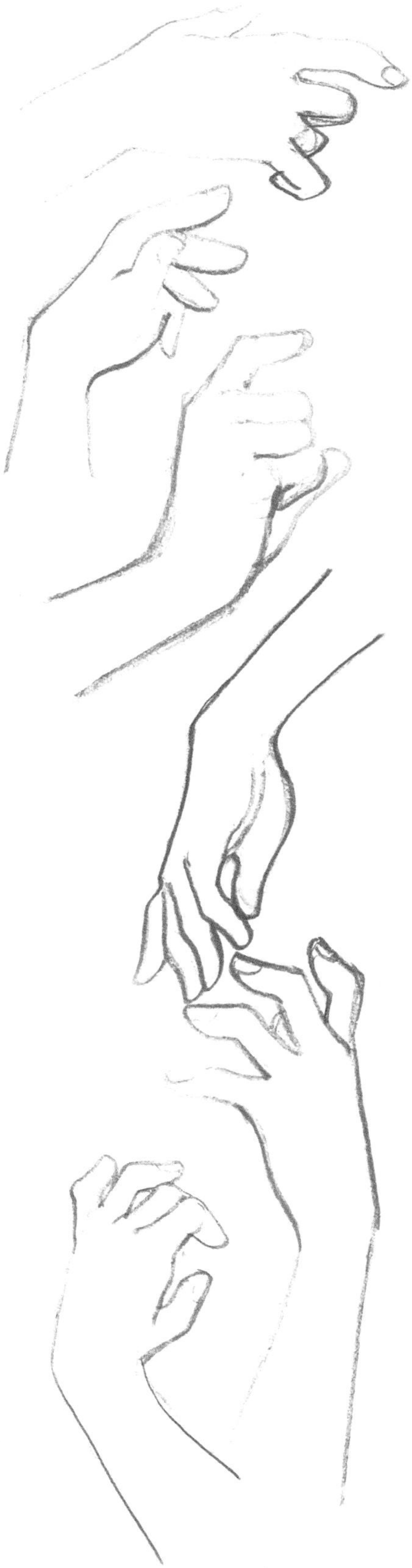

# finding a style

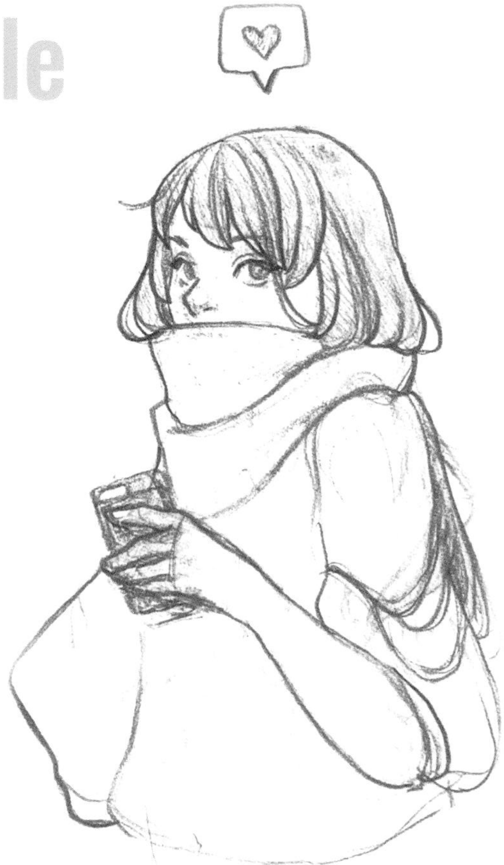

I often see people worrying about finding a unique art style and I remember feeling this stress, especially when I was in art school. I kept looking for "my style," a signature way of drawing that as soon as people saw my art, they would know it was mine. I believe style is a mix of two things: the way you want to work, and muscle memory. Once you find the way you want to work, the muscle memory will just come naturally from drawing those same shapes over and over and over again. Finding the way you want to work is a different story.

I believe that many people already know what their style is, they just don't think they're allowed to draw that way. I knew the way I wanted to draw in fifth grade, but as I got older, I felt like that style wasn't profitable, so my search for "style" became a search for: which way can I draw that will make me money? I tried realism for the fine-art galleries, cartoony styles for editorial, and I considered trying to make comics, which is where the noodly character came from during my time away from art. I went through dozens of styles but none of them were right because they weren't how I wanted to work; I was just looking to get a job. In the end it was the style I loved and adored, that my heart and soul went into, that got me any sort of traction online. Ask yourself, making money aside, what kind of art in your heart of hearts do you want to make? Whatever comes to mind, that's your style, and that's the path you should follow.

It is truly amazing how many doors are open now in this beautiful time we live in. In the past, artists were completely reliant on being hired by companies, or accepted by galleries, which meant only a tiny fraction of styles were ever explored or celebrated. But the rise of social media blew that world wide open. With the limitless, open quality of the online world, the artist now has control. It is possible to build any kind of niche following desired. I am so delighted every time I see how people have found ways to be creative and flourish with their own voices and styles – styles I know I would never have seen come to fruition when I was growing up.

If you feel truly lost and don't know the kind of style that speaks to you, try creating a compilation of inspirations. Every time you find a work of art that evokes an emotional response, keep it in a folder. As you build your folder, look for similarities. What do you notice? Are the images colorful, muted, or black and white? Do they feature people, animals, or landscapes? Is the lighting harsh or soft? Are the objects stylized or realistic? Once you identify the components that speak to you, try them out yourself! Anything new will always be awkward or clunky at first, but keep going and eventually you will develop the muscle memory that becomes indicative of your style.

# getting motivated

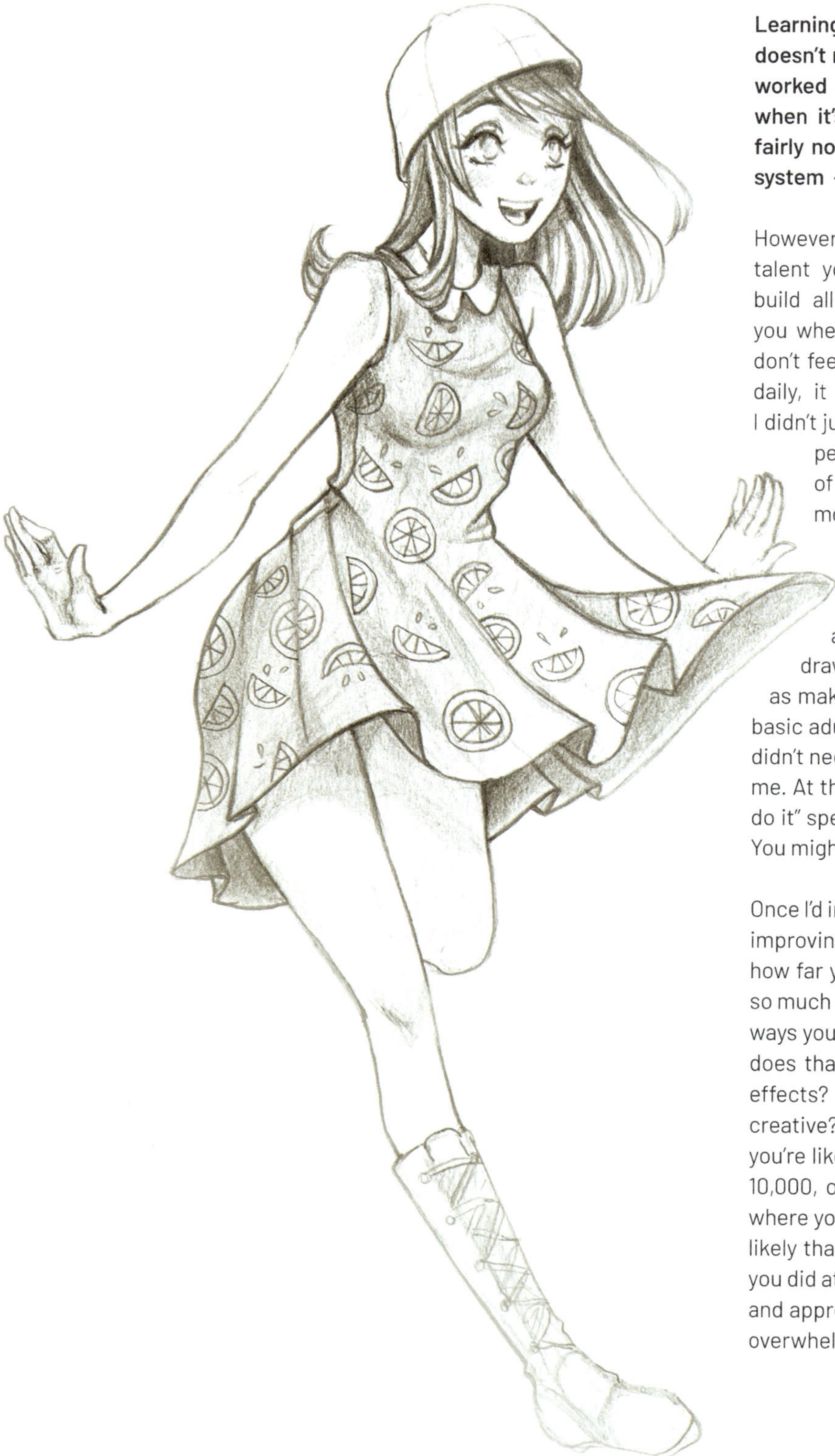

**Learning to be motivated is a skill. If you're not great at it that doesn't mean you're not an artist – it's just a muscle you haven't worked out yet! Many people tell me they struggle to create when it's not given to them as an assignment. I think this is fairly normal, especially if you're raised in the public education system – self-starting isn't a skill that is taught or rewarded.**

However, being motivated is by far the most important talent you can learn, because motivation alone will help you build all the other talents you need to succeed. It can take you wherever you want to go, even when (especially when) you don't feel like it. When I started out in my journey of creating art daily, it was sometimes hard to will myself to do something. I didn't just magically become the most motivated and consistent person ever; I struggled a lot. I ended up adopting all sorts of methods to get myself to stick to my commitment. One motivational exercise I invented involved origami stars. Every time I accomplished something, I wrote it down on a little strip of paper, folded it into an origami star, and put it in a fish-shaped jar, letting me watch my accomplishments build up over time. I didn't just reward drawing; I rewarded anything that was a good habit, such as making my bed or washing the dishes. Rewarding myself for basic adult skills felt silly at first but it did help, and after a while I didn't need it. I still have that fish jar on my mantelpiece to remind me. At the time I also had this weird remix of Shia LaBeouf's "just do it" speech that I found oddly motivating to play while I worked. You might find unusual things like that just work for you.

Once I'd instilled the habit of drawing daily, I wanted to work toward improving my skill. However, when trying to improve, looking at how far you have to go can be daunting, especially when there is so much amazing content online. You become very aware of all the ways you cannot create what you're looking at. You question: how does that artist do that line work, that rendering, those special effects? How do they draw so fluidly, or how are their ideas so creative? It can be overwhelming and discouraging. The problem is, you're likely comparing your 1,000 hours of practice to someone's 10,000, or even 100,000 hours of practice. But you have no idea where you'll be after 10,000 hours – you have to get there first. It's likely that the person whose art you're admiring drew exactly like you did at 1,000 hours. It's important to be patient, kind to yourself, and approach things with just one drawing at a time, or else you'll overwhelm yourself.

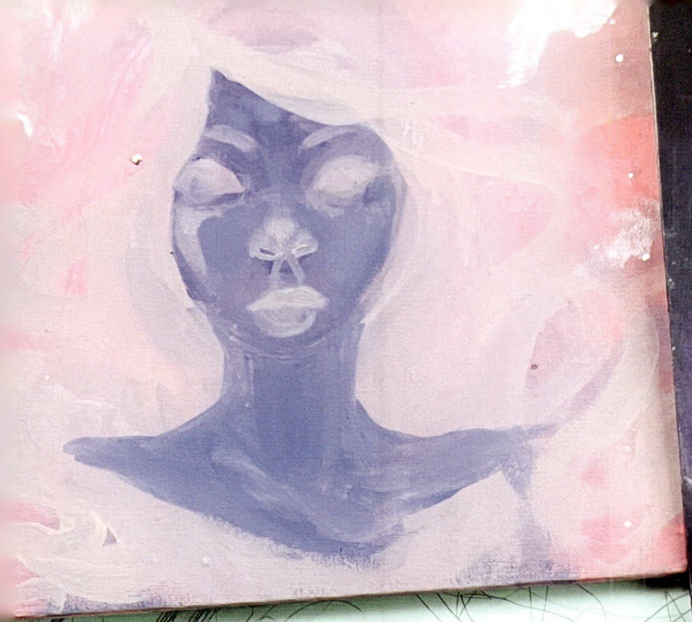

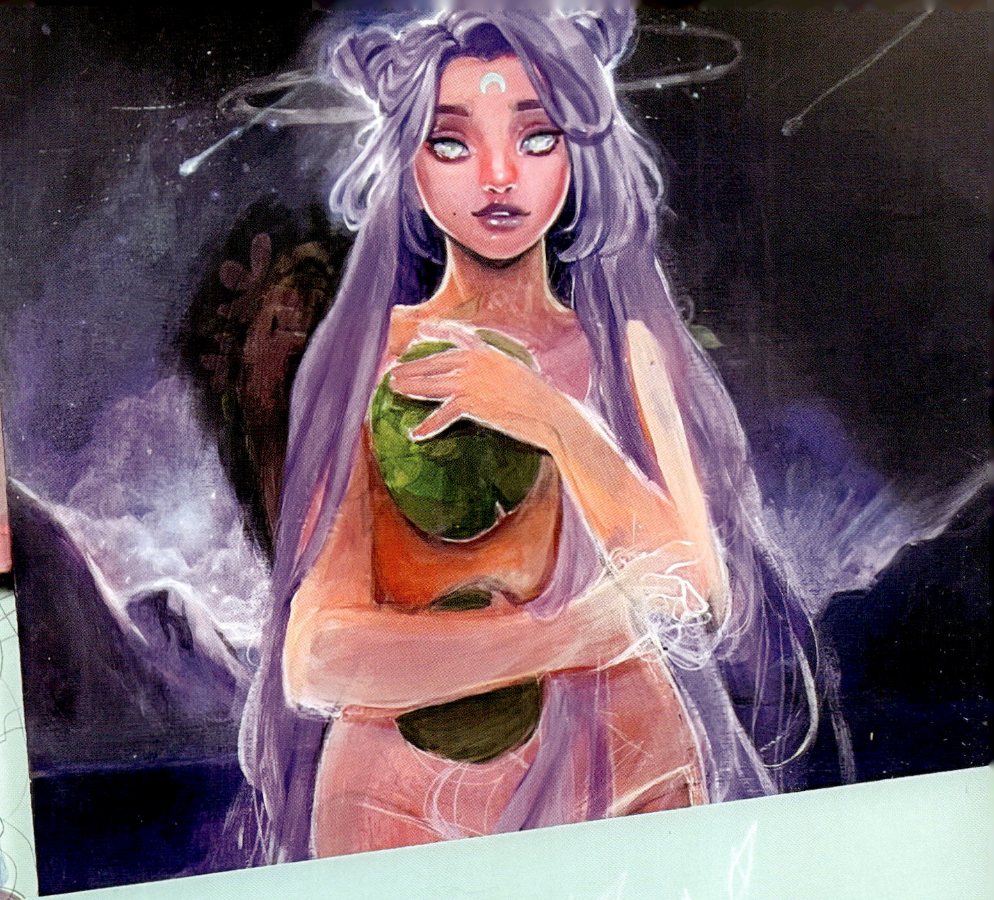

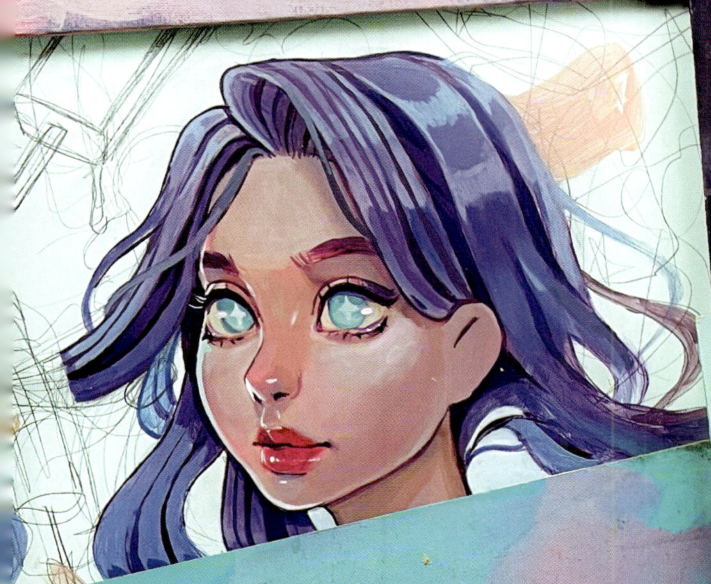

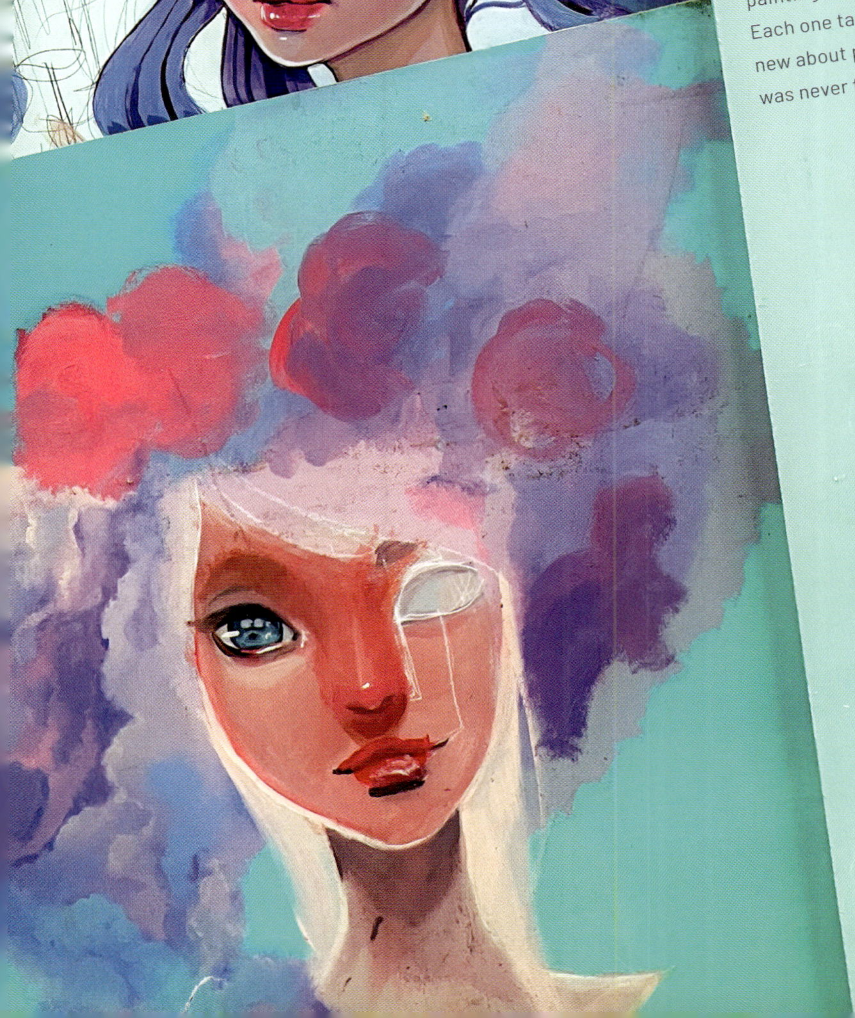

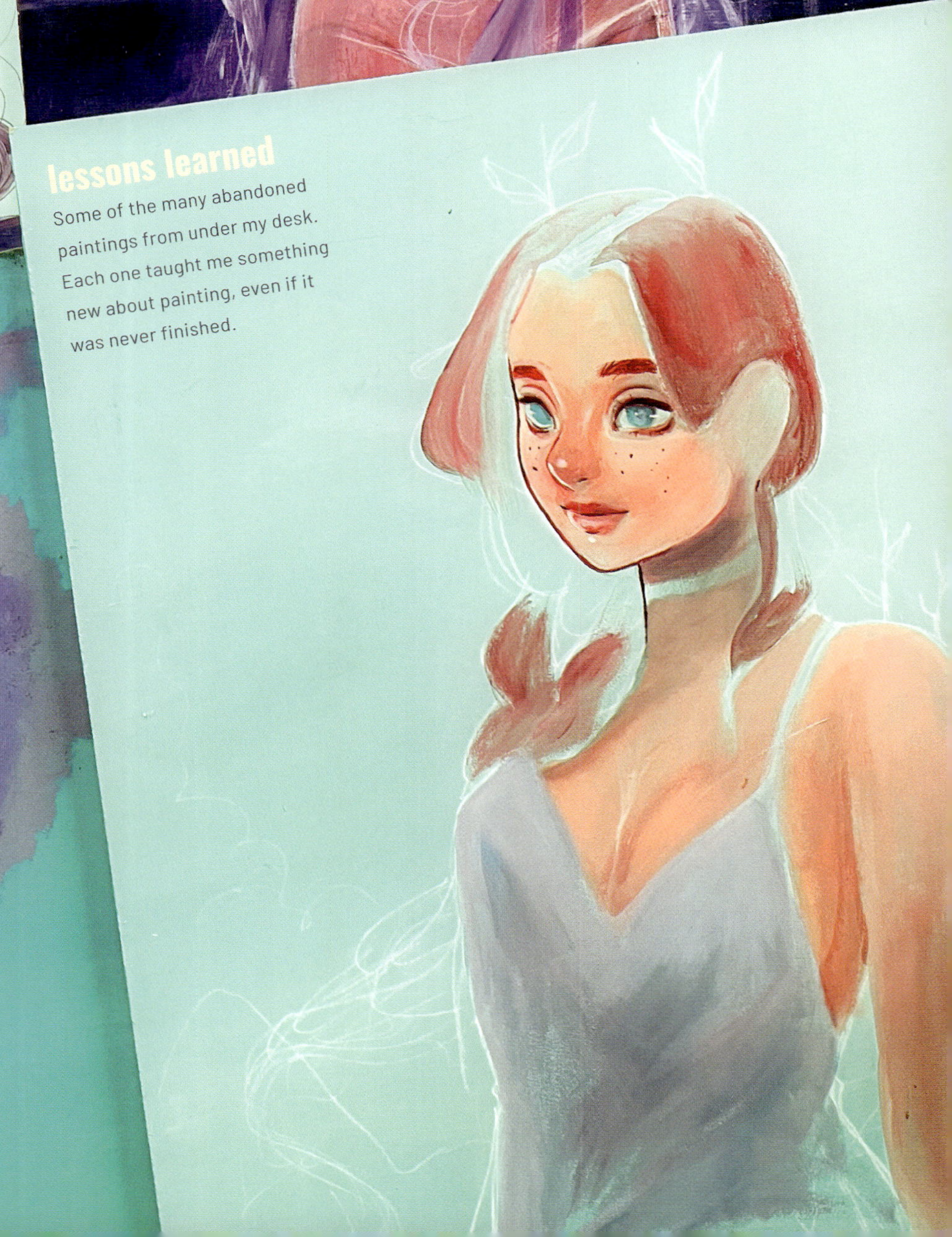

## lessons learned

Some of the many abandoned paintings from under my desk. Each one taught me something new about painting, even if it was never finished.

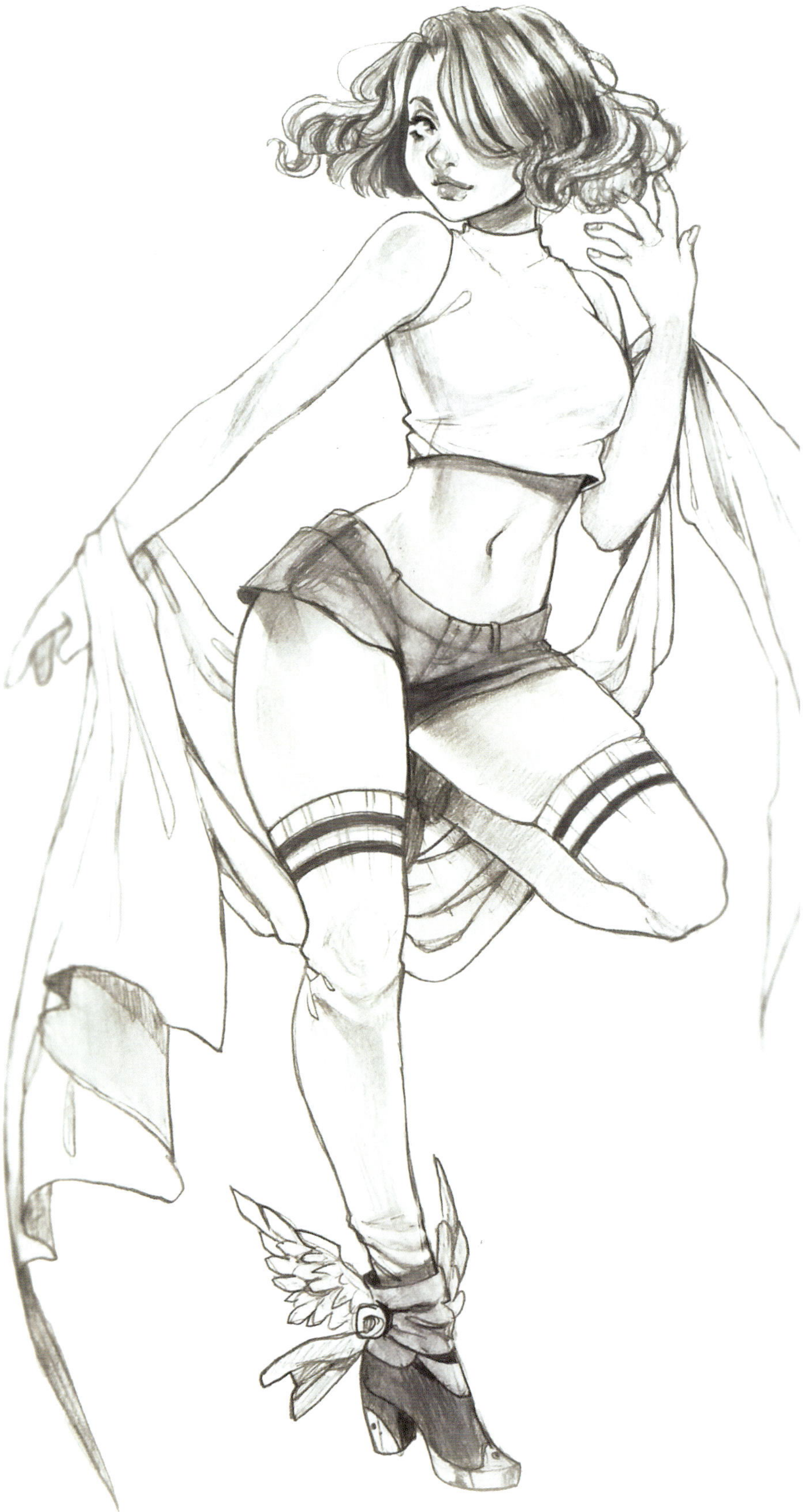

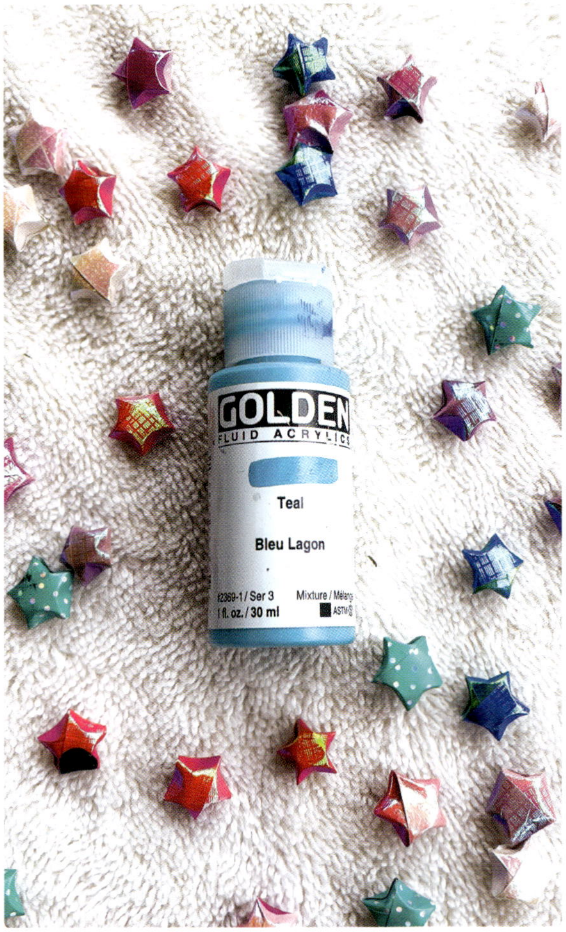


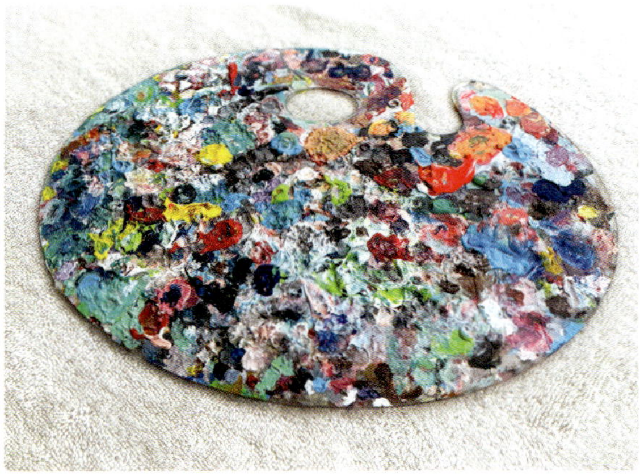

## inspired by the past

This paint palette was a gift from my parents – I was in high school and had started to experiment with acrylic paints. It's never been cleaned, so all the paint on it represents countless hours of work. Meanwhile, my motivational origami stars end up being used regularly in my product photography.

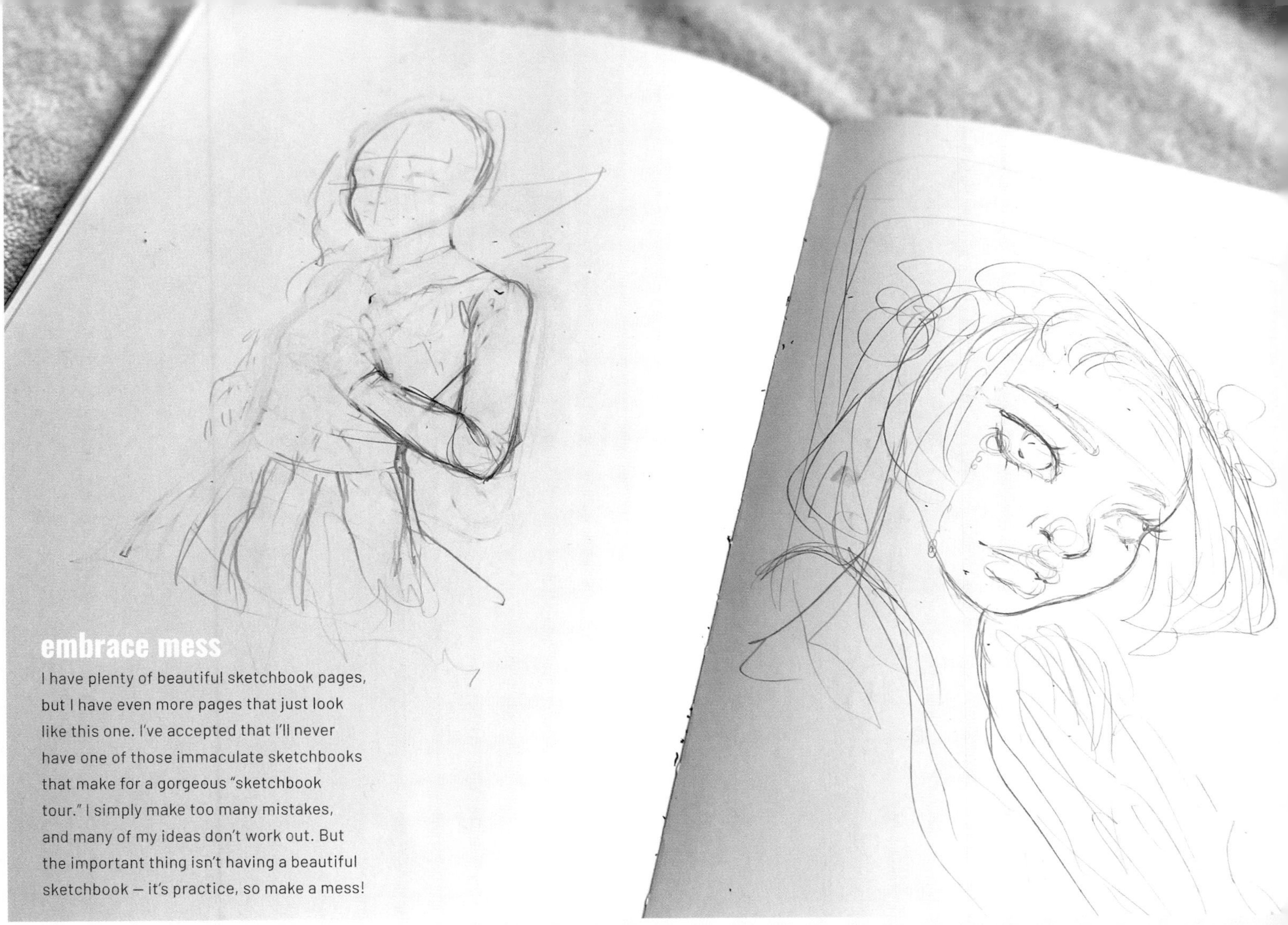

### embrace mess

I have plenty of beautiful sketchbook pages, but I have even more pages that just look like this one. I've accepted that I'll never have one of those immaculate sketchbooks that make for a gorgeous "sketchbook tour." I simply make too many mistakes, and many of my ideas don't work out. But the important thing isn't having a beautiful sketchbook — it's practice, so make a mess!

You alone will see all your mistakes, while online you will only see the polished art other creators allow to be posted. You won't see their mistakes or messes. Creating is not easy; it can be exhausting, laborious, and slow. Sometimes I post newly redrawn versions of my older art on Instagram. The two pieces may be 10, 12, 15 years apart, and someone always comments, "You've been drawing *that* long and you've only improved *that* much?" There's a common misconception that improvement will be just like a montage in a movie — after a few training sessions you're suddenly whipping out the Mona Lisa. But it doesn't work like that, so if you're in it for the long haul, it's important to have a healthy mindset and realistic expectations, or it's going to be a painful journey.

When I was studying writing at community college, I recall one professor talking about several novels he had written, and I was curious if they had ever been published. I stayed after class to ask him and he told me that none of his books had been published yet, but the newest one he was working on likely would be. I asked him how he handled that, pouring so many hours, even years into a book only to have it go nowhere. What he said really sat with me. He said he thought of each book that didn't get published as a very valuable stepping stone toward the one that does. That if he hadn't written those early books, he wouldn't have written the book he was writing now.

I think about that concept when I look at the piles of canvases under my desk that will never see the light of day, or the discarded drawings and scratched-out pages in my sketchbooks that didn't go well. Every line of pencil, every brushstroke, whether I remember it or not, has helped to propel me to where I am today. Even if a particular piece of art I made doesn't matter by itself, it was an important stepping stone in my growth. Sometimes it helps to look at the big picture — when you practice it may not go well in the moment but it's still progress, and that's what matters. Keep going and eventually, after endless piles of messy pages and trash cans full of discarded art, you'll find yourself making things that amaze you. You'll forget about all those frustrating days, and thank your younger self for enduring them.

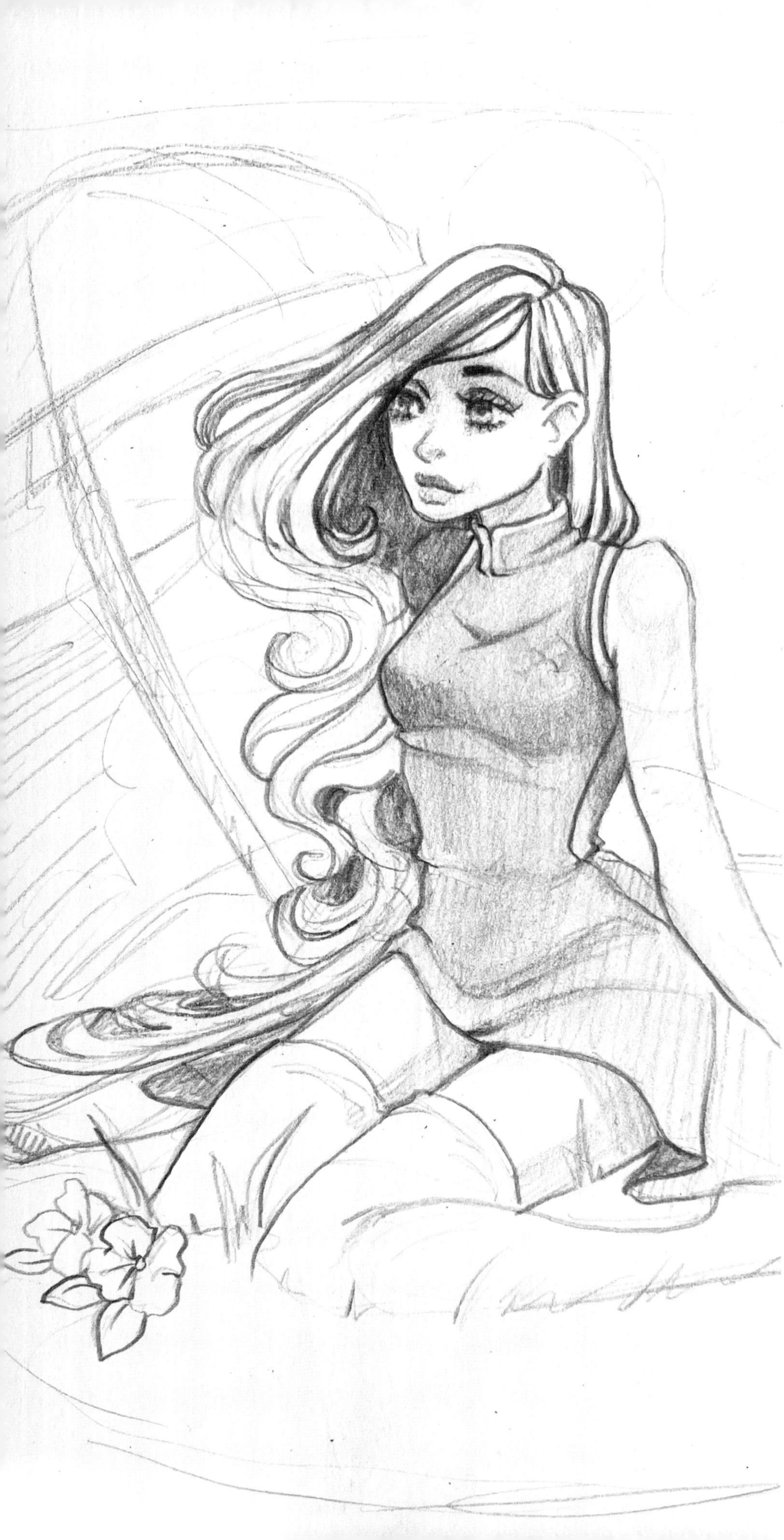

In truth, there were many times in the past when I felt sad or frustrated that I hadn't started pursuing drawing daily and improving my skill level sooner. If I had just believed in myself when I was in high school, I would be so much further along. Even now, I often feel behind my peers, not only people my own age but artists much younger than me who started drawing at an early age. I feel embarrassed sometimes when I see their skill level running laps around my own. I used to anguish, if I hadn't missed out on all that time, where would my skill level be now? This is the reason I try my best to encourage others to believe in themselves, to pursue their art now, because I know over time they will improve, and they will be so thankful to their younger selves that they did. The sooner you start, the sooner you can get to where you want to go!

The thing is though, even if you're starting "late" it doesn't matter, and it's certainly not something that should discourage you. I'm very glad I started at all — I've long forgotten all those frustrating days and difficult times I kept messing up. I know they were there, but they're muddled, fuzzy memories that I hardly think of at all anymore. Instead, I get to enjoy what I've built for myself, being an artist. Even if it's a bit later or I'm a bit behind, so what? I get to do what I love; I can look at the art I admired growing up and say, "I can do that now! I can make whatever I want!" And that is the most wonderful feeling.

It doesn't matter what age you are when you make a start, there are countless examples of famous authors, artists, and musicians who didn't find their art forms until their forties, fifties, or even sixties! If you've been telling yourself, it's too late to start, you're wrong! Right now is the best time to start, because you will love the end of the path you're walking down. It's not a race — your age will not stop you from being successful and it certainly won't stop you from enjoying creating. Focus on how much you will love being an artist — that should be the thought that guides and motivates you.

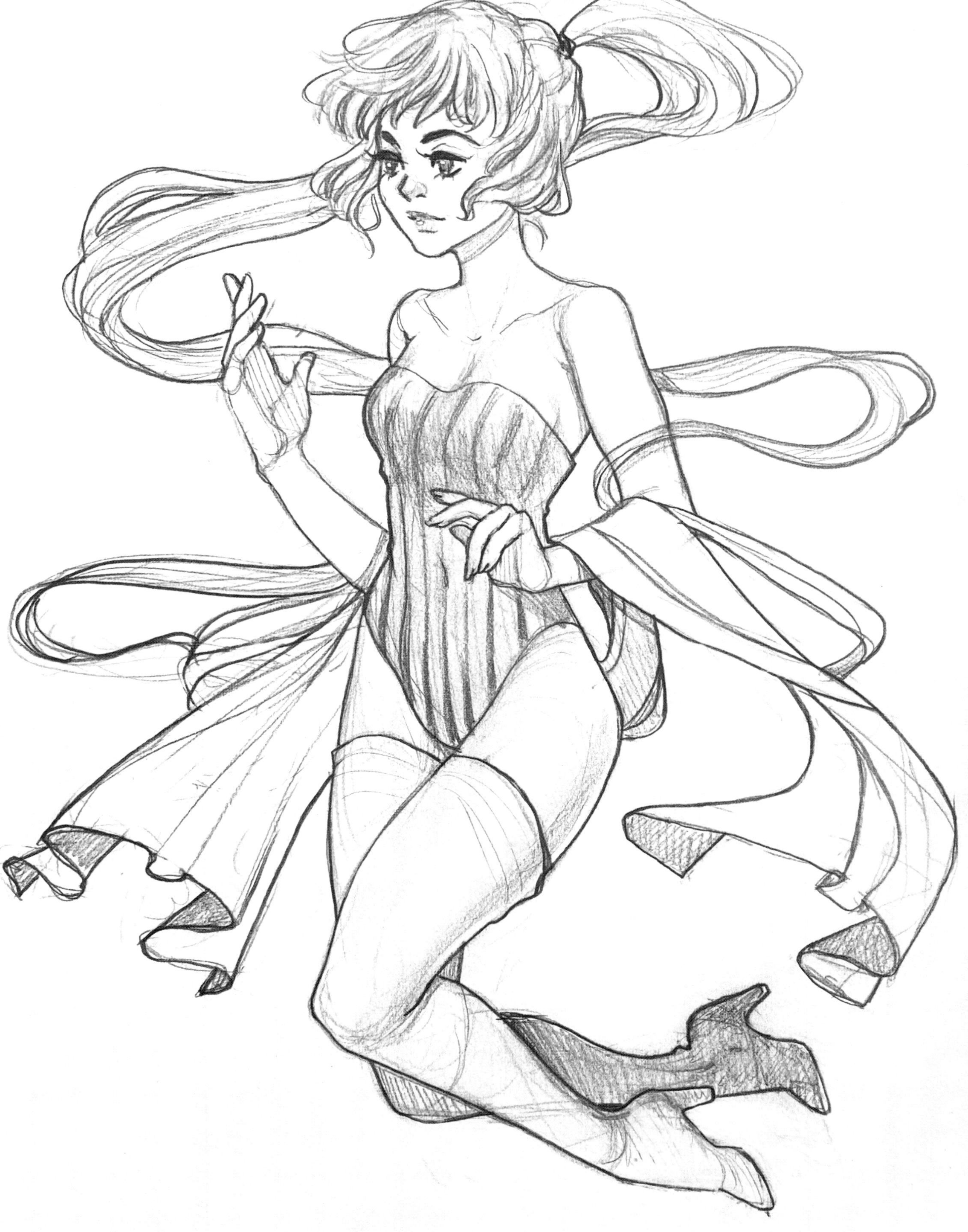

# tips for getting started

## Mindset

A valuable tool for me is getting into the right mindset. I often remind myself how much future me will be grateful that current me took the time to do the work. Working in the moment usually starts out exciting, but as the project continues, it can feel like a grind. While working on a project, especially a large one, I usually hit a point where I just want to quit. I become frustrated and tired of working on it and start to think the piece is an utter disaster and I'm a failure. But, when I have a painting hanging on the wall that I'm proud of, suddenly all that pain is forgotten. I look at it and feel glad I put in the work. I always say thank you to past me for sticking through the more anguishing parts of the process so that I can have that moment. So sometimes, when I'm struggling to push through or even get started, I think about future me, and how much she will appreciate that I did.

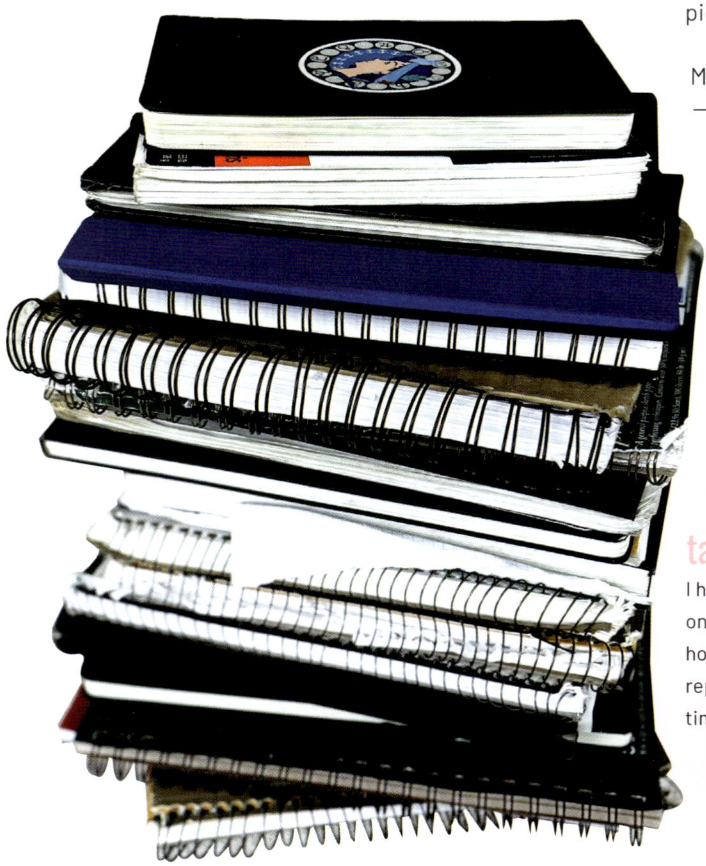

## Don't fear the blank, white page

The empty page is very intimidating. When starting a new sketchbook, I used to find it difficult to draw on the first page, so I would flip forward to start on another page. I felt that the first pages had to be just *perfect*. Most of my sketchbooks were totally blank for the first ten pages or so. I would get scared of ruining something that was supposed to be perfect and incredible from the start. People would gift me amazing high-quality sketchbooks, expensive watercolor paper, or a beautiful canvas to paint on, which would sit in my room for years, going to waste. Really, I was setting my standards way too high. I had to learn to push myself out of that discomfort and remember that a piece of paper is made to be created on. Whatever I added to it made it better than being blank, even if it's a bad drawing, even if I "ruin" the page. Taking a leap of faith and practicing is always more valuable than keeping a piece of paper pristine.

My advice is not to be too precious with your pages – ruin them, make them messy, it's the only way to progress as an artist. Draw on the first page of your sketchbook and lay paint on that big, beautiful empty canvas. Masterpieces happen at unexpected moments, so don't save your materials for when you get that big idea, just use whatever supplies you have, be kind to yourself, and remember that nothing can be perfect, but creating is always beautiful.

## taking time

I have bins of old sketchbooks in my house, this is just one of many stacks. When I look at this pile I think about how many hours even just one of these sketchbooks represents and I feel grateful that my past self took the time to get me here.

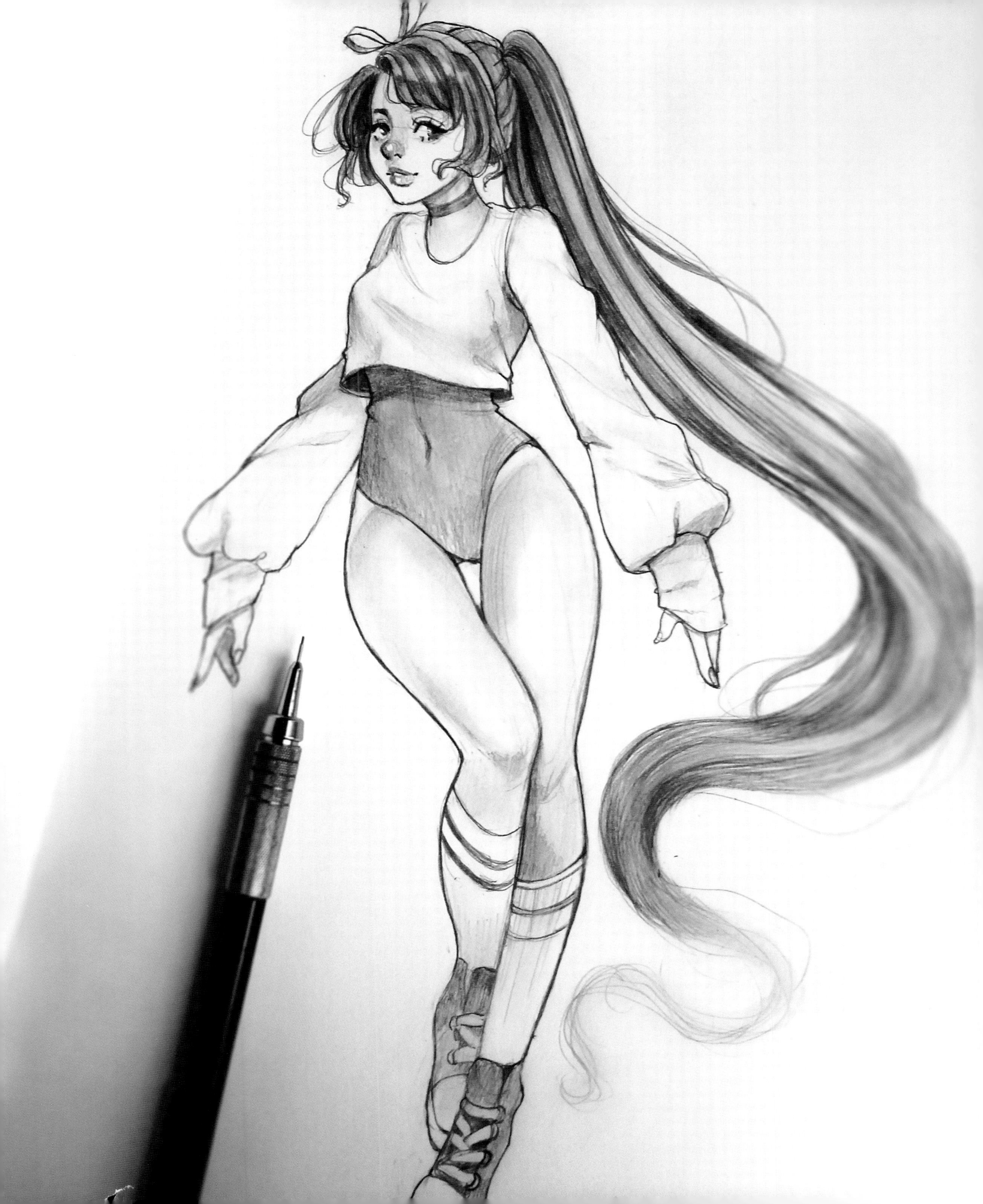

## Add a time limit

One great practical tip for getting started is to set a timer for a small amount of time, say, half an hour. Tell yourself you only have to draw for half an hour and once the time is up, if you want to stop, you can. Sometimes you really are done after thirty minutes, but often once you've started, you want to keep going. It's a great way to trick yourself into working.

## Start before you have the skill

Similar to being afraid of the blank white page, it can be easy to put off projects because you don't feel good enough yet. I used to have really big project ideas and I'd always put them aside for "when I was good enough," and by the time I felt I had the skillset to do the work, I'd forgotten what the projects were. But the truth is that you can only improve by practicing, so if you want to make comics but keep making paintings until you think you're capable of tackling comics, you'll find that you've become very skilled at painting but you've still gotten nowhere with creating comics. I grew up surrounded by comic books and I used to really love discovering a comic artist's very first book. The art within the first book seemed clunky and awkward, and it was clear that over time their style changed when they became more comfortable and their art transformed into the natural style everyone recognized it for. There's not a single comic artist I've ever seen whose first book looks the same as their last.

Start your projects before you have the skill to do them because that's the only way to make them a reality. I once heard someone say, "If someone ever offers you an opportunity and you don't have the skill set to do it, say yes, and learn along the way." As soon as I heard those words, it changed my life. I started saying yes to every opportunity that came my way that I wanted to do, and I grew so much. It was both wonderful and disastrous. I had no idea what I was doing but I just told myself, "Fake it until you make it", and that's exactly what I did. I managed to embarrass myself several times, but this was far outweighed by the skills I acquired and the experiences I had.

Just remember that every mistake is the shadow from the light of your progress.

## Learn to love failure

I don't agree with people saying, "It's fine to fail" or "You should forgive yourself for failing" because I believe it's the wrong message. It portrays failure as a negative thing, like an unfortunate but understandable offense. Failure is so much more important and wonderful than that, because when learning a skill, mistakes are guaranteed. You might make a mess, you may ruin designs, and you are going to mess up. You are not perfect, nor should you be. Failure is necessary and extremely valuable; you will fall a thousand times and at the end of those thousand times you will make something awesome. Failure isn't something to forgive, it's something to embrace. It's not "you might fail and that's OK," it's "you will fail and that's wonderful."

Failure is uncomfortable for most of us. We're taught that it's bad, to avoid it, and that if we're failing something clearly isn't for us, but that's the wrong message. You have to fail in order to get better, you just have to. When you take that leap into pursuing art you will not survive without a healthy respect for failure. Just remember that every mistake is the shadow from the light of your progress, the underside of your coin. With every failure comes new revelation, a new skill, a new way around what didn't work the last time. It's frustrating and it is beautiful. Make friends with failure, look at what your failure has taught you and use it to propel yourself forward, don't let it discourage you or convince you that you're not cut out for this. Growing is always a strain but the end results are stunning.

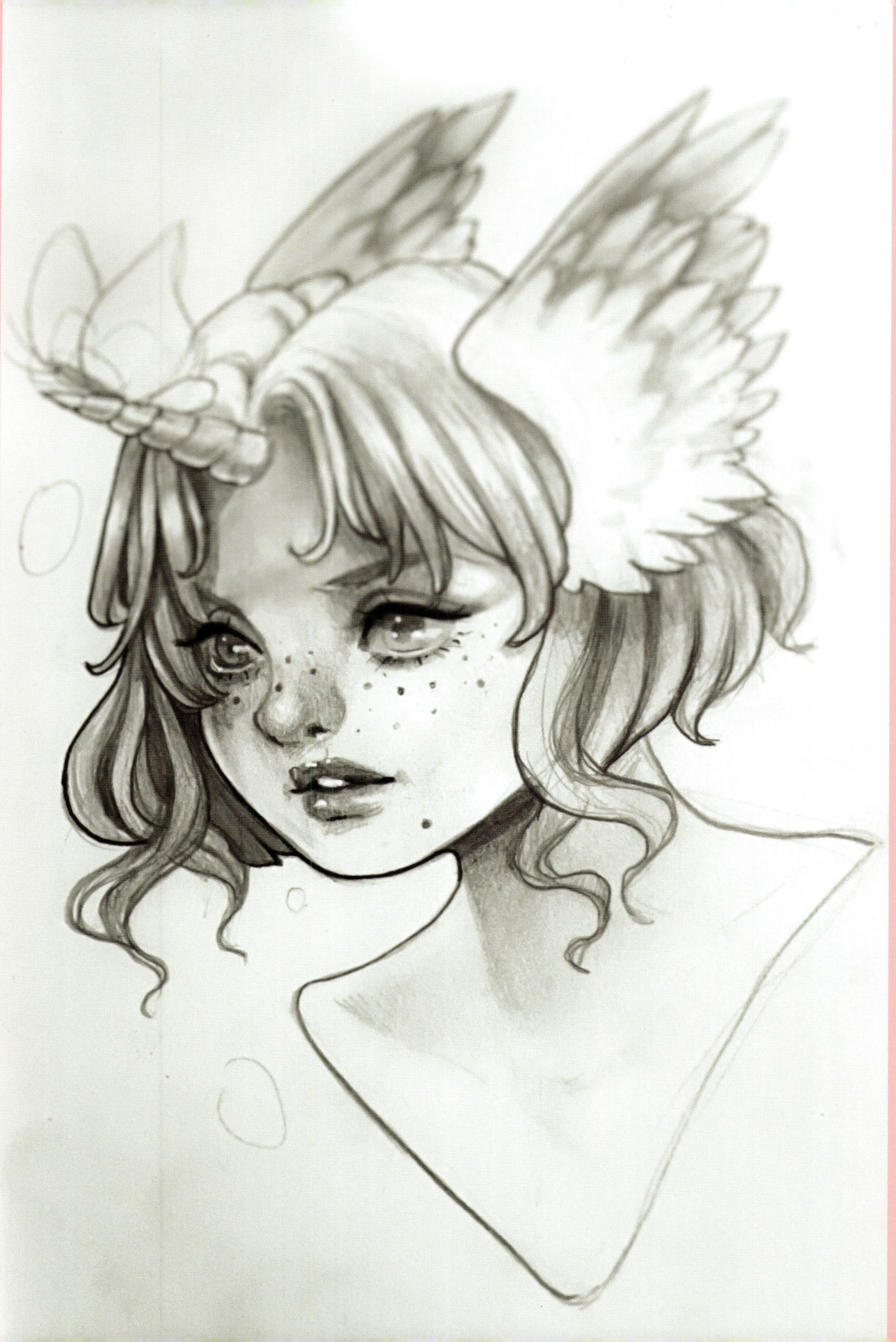

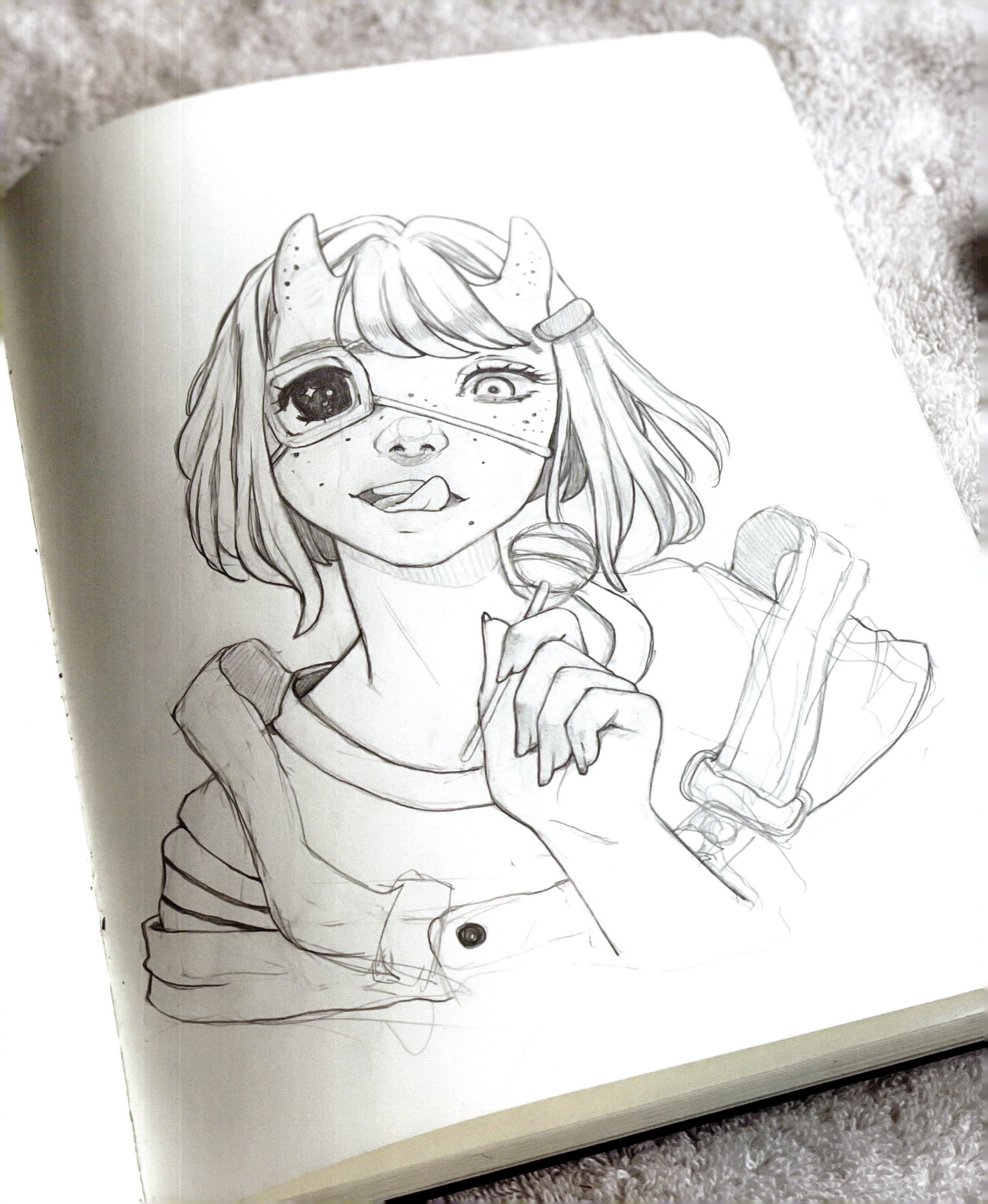

## Take breaks

Just as important as getting started is knowing when to stop. Once you master the art of good daily habits, it can be easy to tip the scale too far and produce too often. Burnout seems to be common among artists. It often originates from having lots of ideas but not enough time to tackle each idea before they pile up and become overwhelming. It can also come from perceived pressure – if you have built yourself an audience or a customer base waiting on commission pieces, you may feel obligated to produce at a certain speed or output. It may even come from watching another artist who is simply doing more than you – making art, posting daily, creating YouTube videos, launching new products, exhibiting at conventions – and you feel the need to keep up. Don't. Work at your own pace. You may be trying to copy someone who is overworking and producing an unsustainable level of work.

Ultimately, creativity is a pool to draw from, but it can be drained and it needs time to refill. It may not feel like it when you're under great pressure, but if you've become overburdened or burned-out, taking time to step away from work is the best thing you can do. I notice that when I'm in these times of burnout and I'm trying to produce anyway, my art suffers. It looks dull and sloppy and lifeless. When I take the time to relax, go somewhere peaceful, visit friends, or do something I find fun, I come back making some of my best pieces. When you're under pressure it can be hard to pull away, but it's necessary, not just for your mental health, but for the outcome of your art. Sometimes you may just need a bit of time, so you could simply step away for an hour, or take a day off; sometimes if you've been outputting a lot for a long time, you need a longer break. This is more than OK, it's necessary. This isn't something to be perceived as weakness, or anything to be ashamed of. It's human and it's healthy – you're not a machine that simply churns out content, you are a person with a life to live. As I mentioned previously, you cannot exhale forever, at some point you must inhale. Take the time to do the things you love, to surround yourself with things that give you joy.

## Be kind to yourself

Making sure you take good care of your mental space is invaluable to you as an artist. Confidence will keep you going when work seems tough, but it can be really easy to get discouraged. Art-making can be very lonely and isolating, and in that time, you're left alone with your thoughts. Many artists I've talked to note how mentally difficult it is. You'll find yourself saying all kinds of mean, critical things to yourself. But it's important when you notice yourself doing this to remember to speak kindly to yourself, and not to talk to yourself in a way you'd never speak to someone else. And, take note: what triggers this negative self-talk? Can anything be done to avoid the triggers?

For example, I used to find myself stopping halfway through works of art, not because it was going badly, but because it was going so well and I was afraid I would ruin it. This caused me to be self-critical, telling myself, "See? You're bad at being an artist, you never finish anything!" I ended up with piles of half-finished art that I never felt good about looking at or showing to anyone. When I noticed this, I started to make sure I always finished a piece. Even if it didn't look perfect, I still felt proud to have a finished piece instead of discouraged to have another piece I'd given up on.

Bravery is an important aspect of making art – doing things you're scared of and taking a leap of faith is necessary when making something new. There are times during the making of my paintings that something doesn't feel right, such as the face or the hand positioning, and it needs to be repainted entirely, but I get scared to do it as I worry that I might make it worse. But anytime I've tried to ignore glaring issues and finish the piece, I'm disappointed, and start to talk negatively to myself. I tell myself, "If only I hadn't been so scared and done something about that issue, I'd like this piece so much more." I've learned now to take that leap and repaint it – it's worth it to try. Doing things that make you feel confident at the end instead of discouraged is important, so identify where you're discouraging yourself and try to make those brave steps!

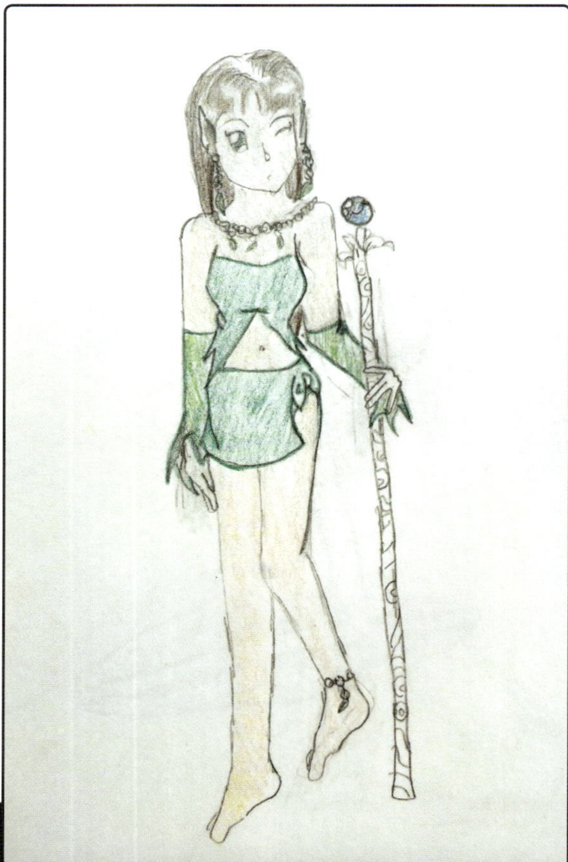

Original: ***Phoenix*** | 2003

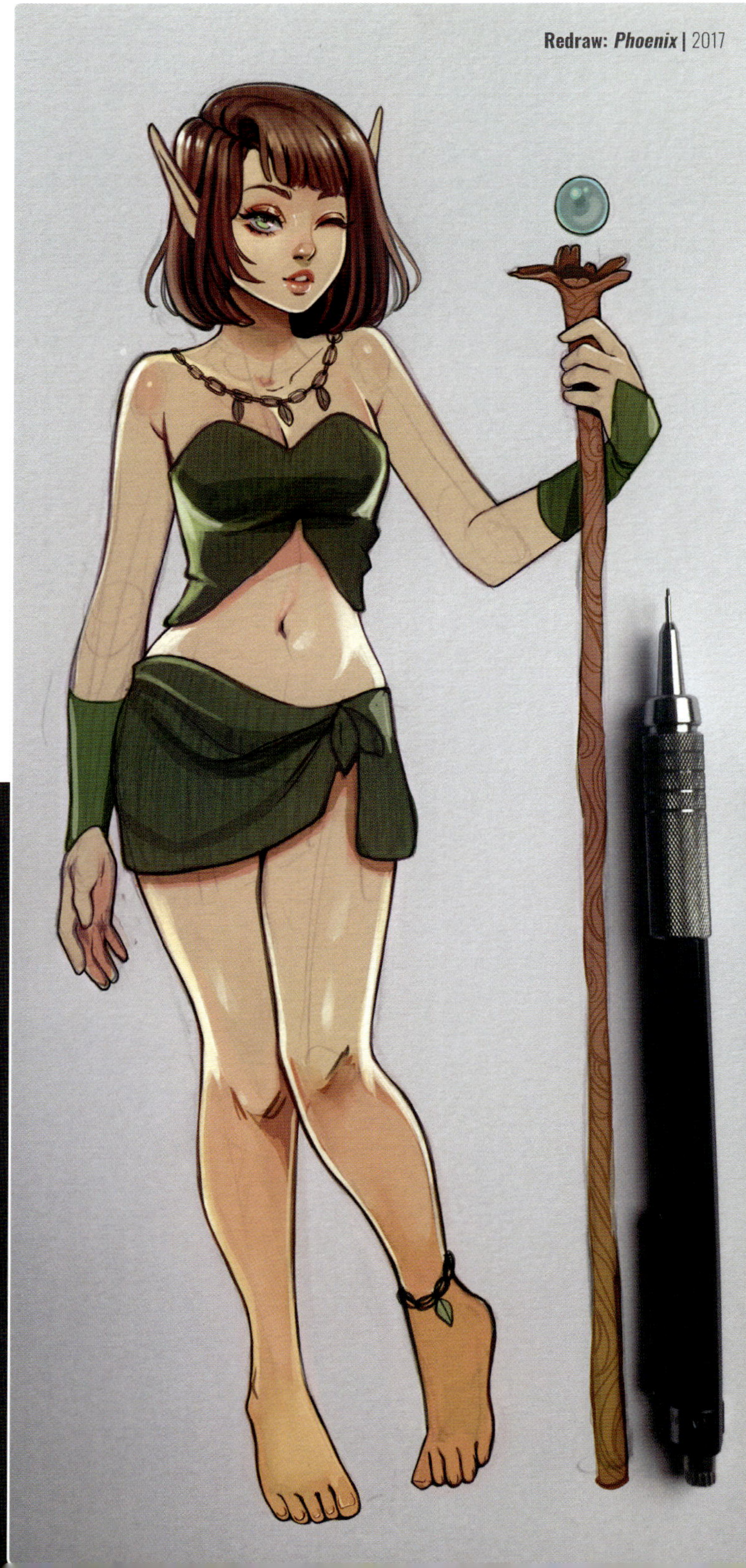

Redraw: ***Phoenix*** | 2017

GALLERY:

# redraws

**Redrawing old art is one of my favorite things to do. It's how I initially started building my following online and is a great little art exercise if you're feeling art blocked. You don't have to come up with a new idea – you can just focus on seeing how you've improved over time. As a warm-up, I often like to pull out my old sketchbooks from when I was a kid and recreate the characters that my younger self was trying to make but didn't have the skill for. It's a very rewarding and low-key way to make art; I always like to think I'm making my younger self happy when I do this. These are a few of my favorite redraws!**

## Get in character

I made these two drawings (this page and opposite page) in 5th grade. I remember asking my friend to make up a character that she wanted to be, and I'd make one up too. She said she wanted to be a cheerleader fairy named Tally, I wanted to be a magical forest elf named Phoenix, and these were the characters that came out. Recreating them as an adult was pretty fun because I still remember how proud I was of the original drawings when I was a kid. The redraws are fairly old now and I'm sure I could probably do even better if I drew them again.

**Original: *Tally* |** 2003

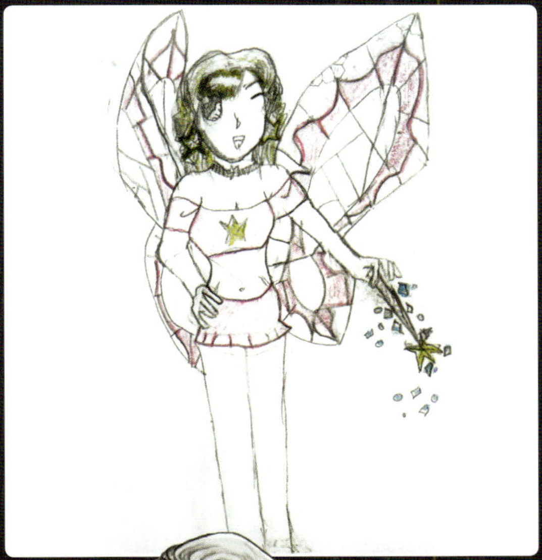

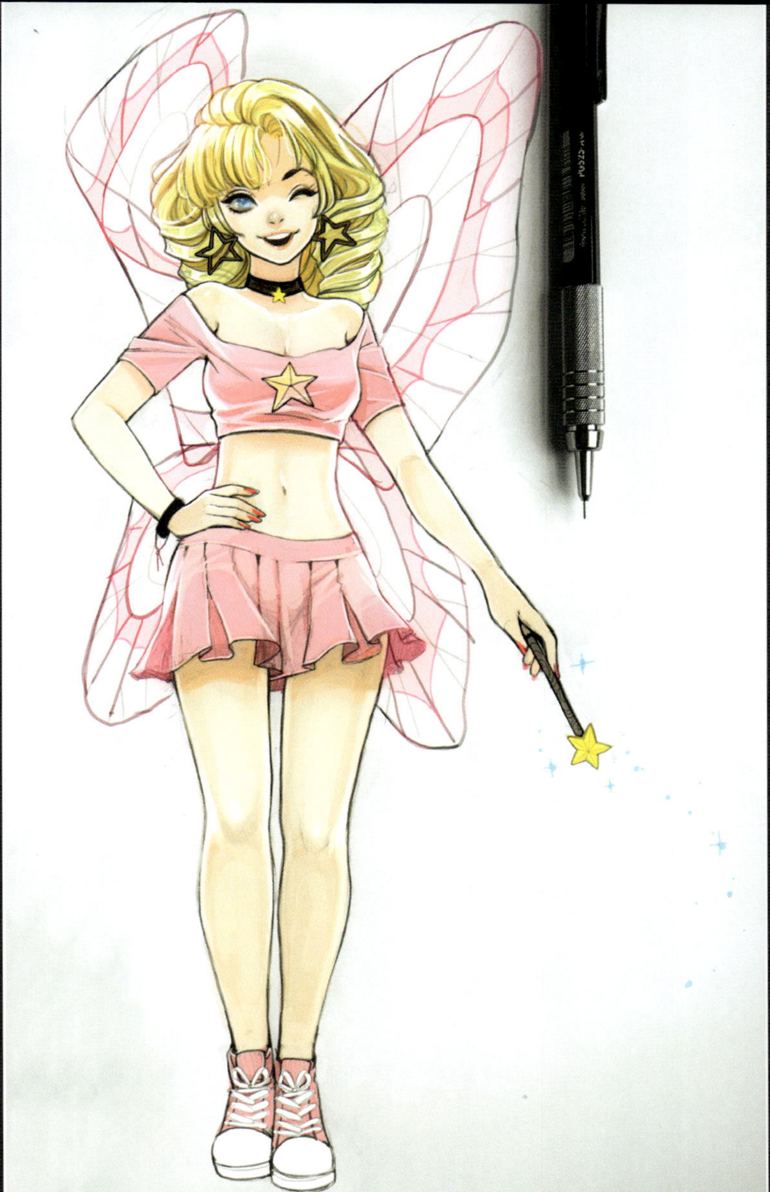

**Redraw: *Tally* |** 2017

**Redraw |** 2017

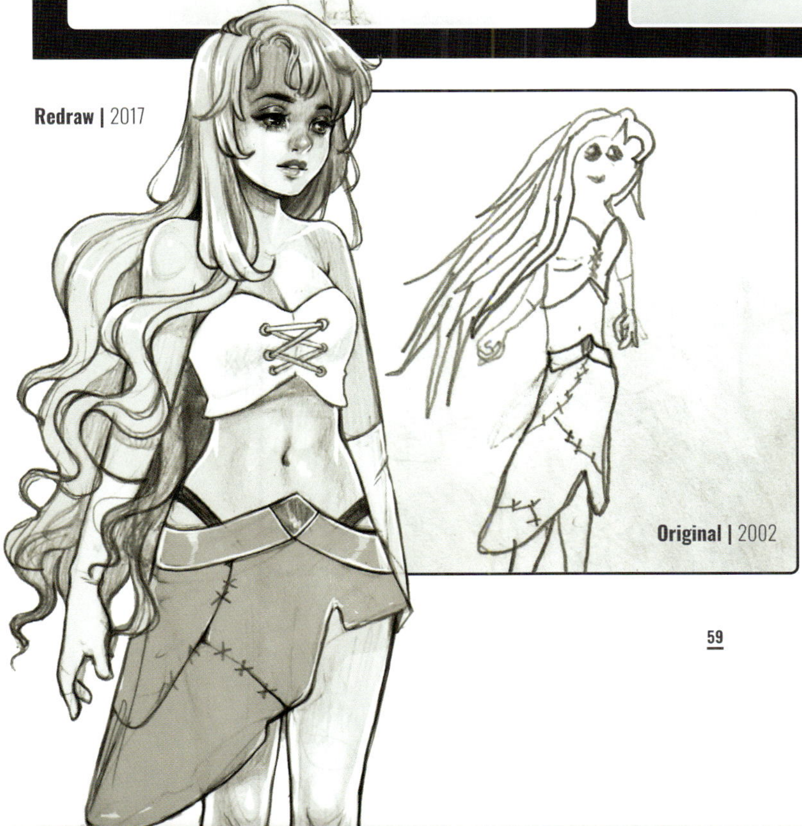

**Original |** 2002

## Early days

This was one of the first redraws I did in this style, from a drawing in my elementary-school sketch book. I don't have an exact date for the old drawing, but my best guess was when I was in 4th grade. When I made the redraw, it went pretty viral and got reposted to a lot of Instagram and Facebook pages; it was even featured on the Autodesk Sketchbook drawing app's intro. I was pretty new to having any sort of online following, so I wasn't accustomed to waves of criticism – I had many people saying that I faked the original picture. They essentially thought I quickly drew a really crappy drawing to claim I had improved... but nope, I really was just that bad at drawing when I was 11. It's definitely something I laugh about now!

## Overwhelmed

Titled *Anxiety*, the original drawing was made in 2017 in one of my small Moleskine sketchbooks to represent the overflowing thoughts of worry that build up in my head. Anxiety is something I've struggled with all my life. In some ways, it's a superpower that helps me stay on top of things, but in many other ways, it's a plague that keeps me from sleeping or being able to relax. There are times when I wish I could just open my head and let all the anxious thoughts pour out, so they'd just leave me alone. This drawing was supposed to represent that.

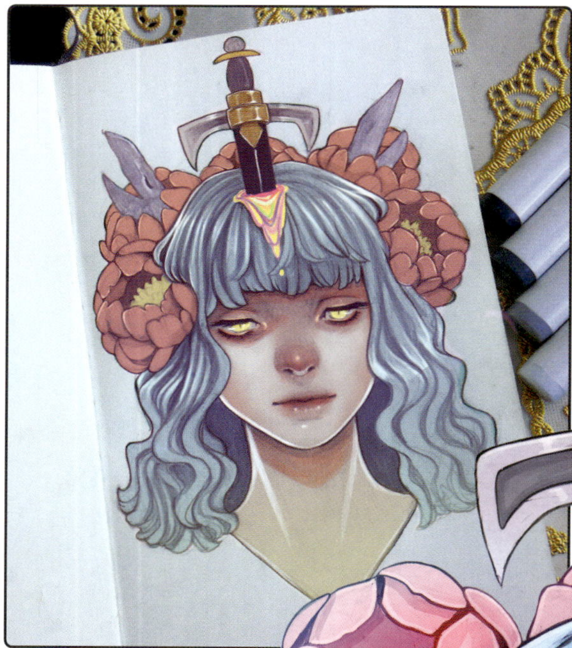

**Original: *Anxiety* |** 2017

**Redraw: *Anxiety* |** 2021

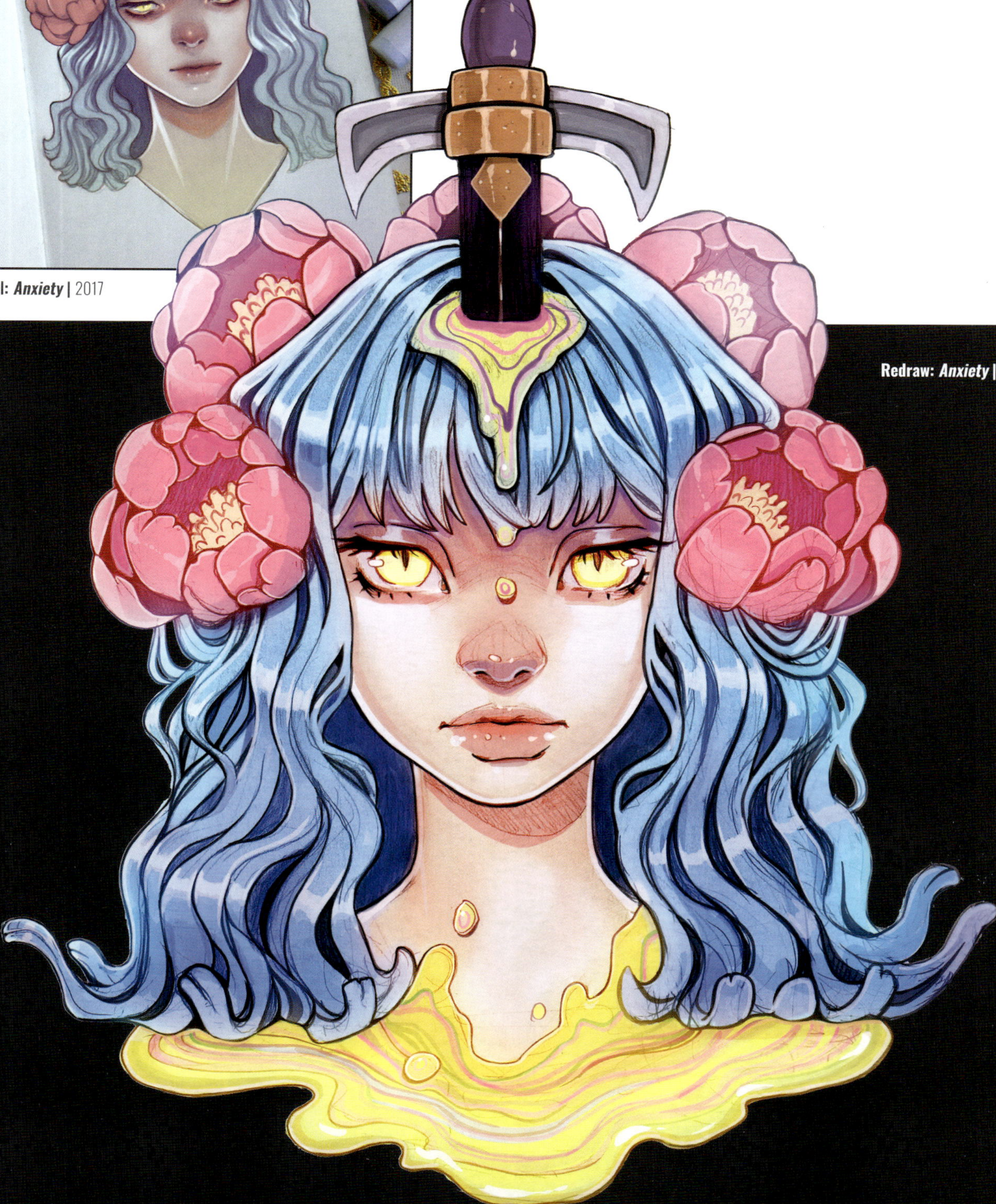

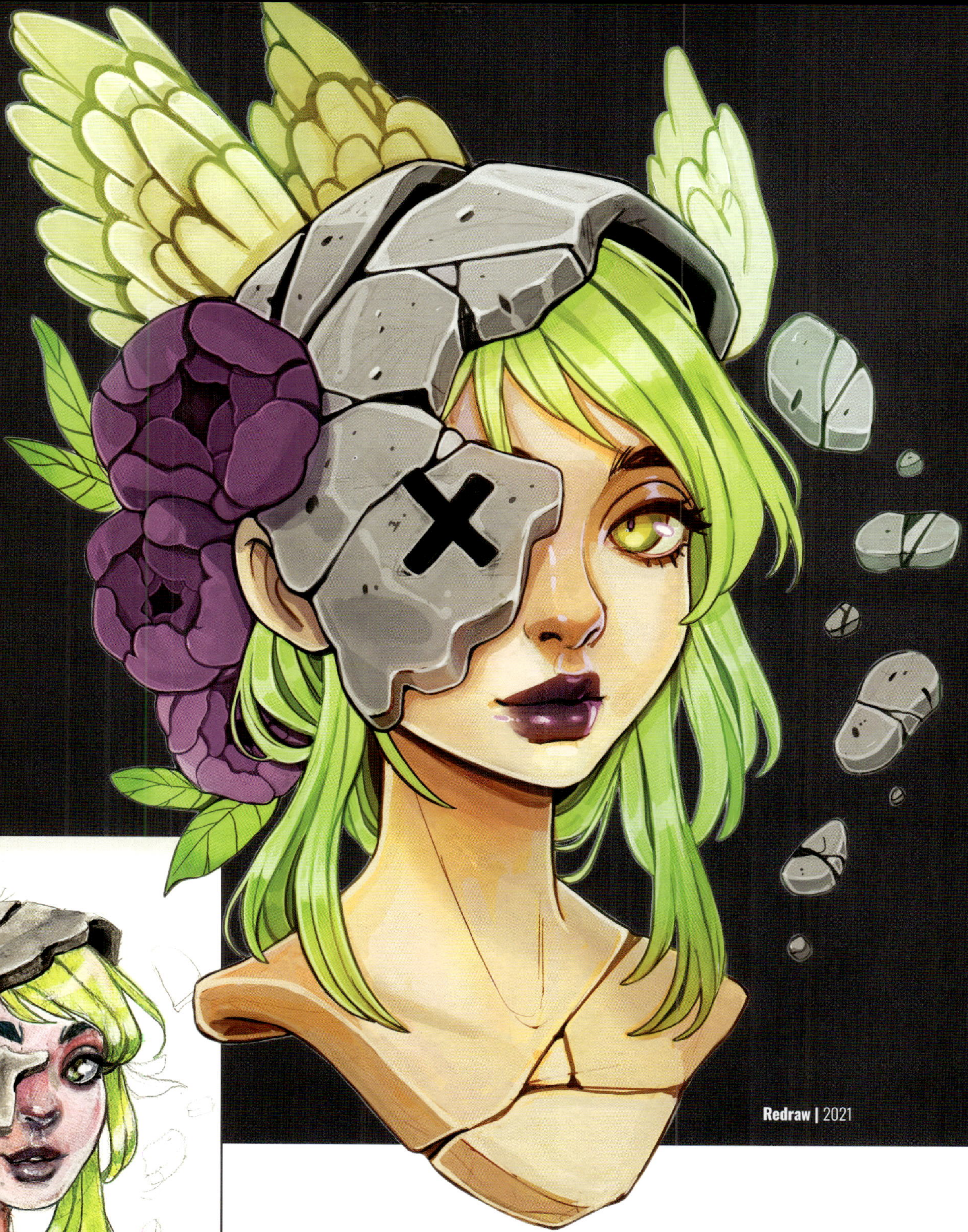

Redraw | 2021

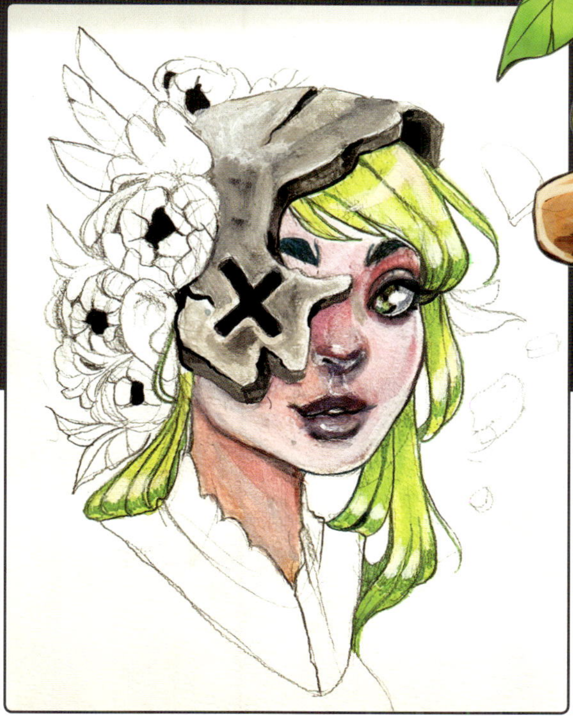

**Original** | 2016

## Learning curve

The original art is painted with acrylic paint before I understood how to use the medium very well. Her crumbling mask is inspired by the cover art for *Elfen Lied*.

## Regal inspiration

The original drawing for this one was done when I was in high school. At the time, a common manga that could be found at Hot Topic was *Princess Ai*, which I have a sneaking suspicion inspired this design with the tattered skirt.

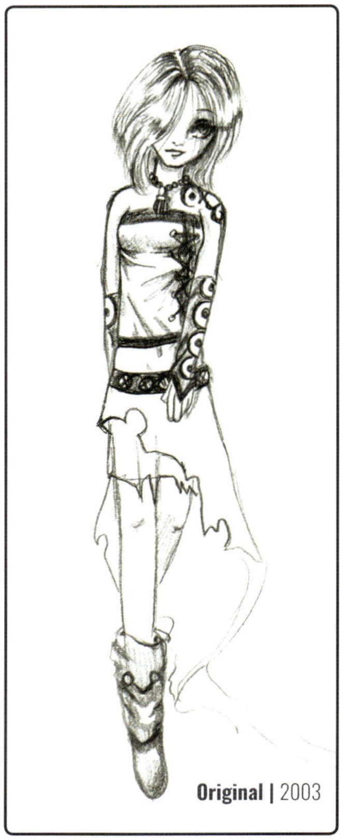

**Original** | 2003

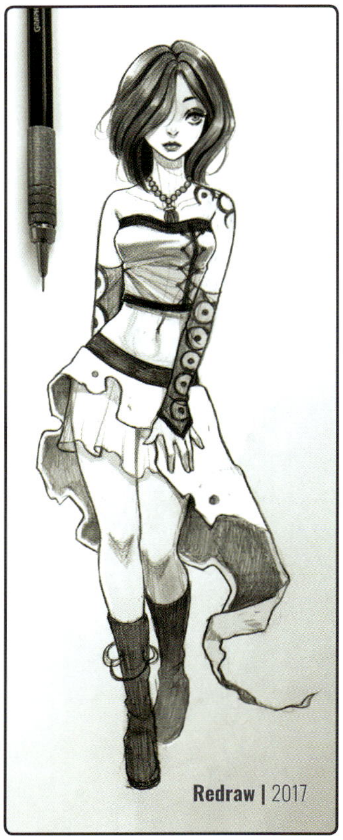

**Redraw** | 2017

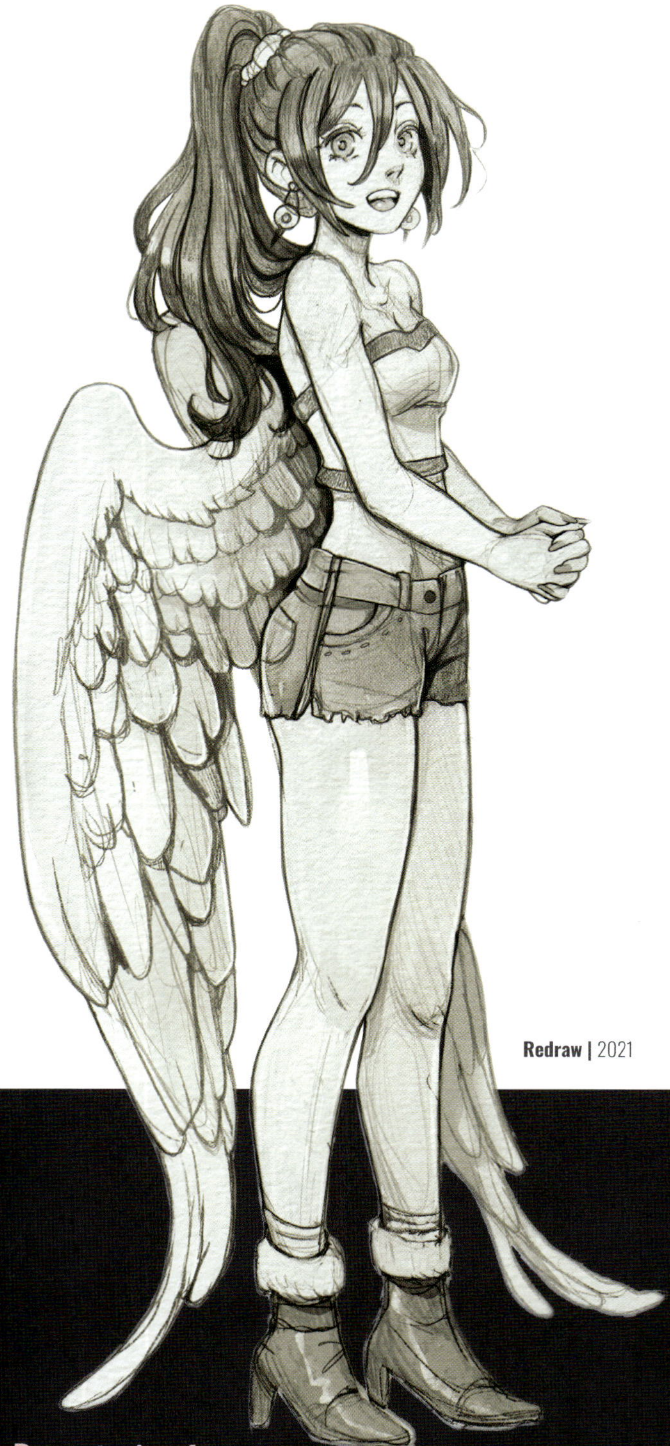

**Redraw** | 2021

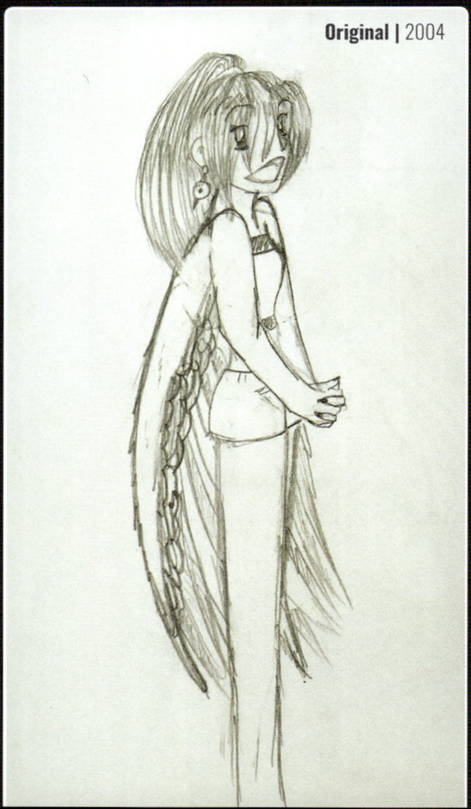

**Original** | 2004

## Recapturing fun

Something I really love about my younger drawings is that they were so expressive — every character felt unique, with a different mood and personality. I even see myself explore fun, unique poses to fit that mood and personality. I think that's a charm my art may have lost along the way, so I had a lot of fun remaking this one.

## Naturally better

This is one of the rare redraws I've made of art that was created after I started on Instagram. The redraw wasn't done all that long after the original was created. The original was made in 2018, and the redraw in 2020, both with the same digital-over-pencil method. This felt very refreshing to see, because this period in my life was really the first time I drew on a regular basis. Seeing such a big jump in improvement over those two years, with the pose and facial expression becoming much more natural, felt really encouraging. I've even made this design into a figurine prototype.

**Redraw** | 2020

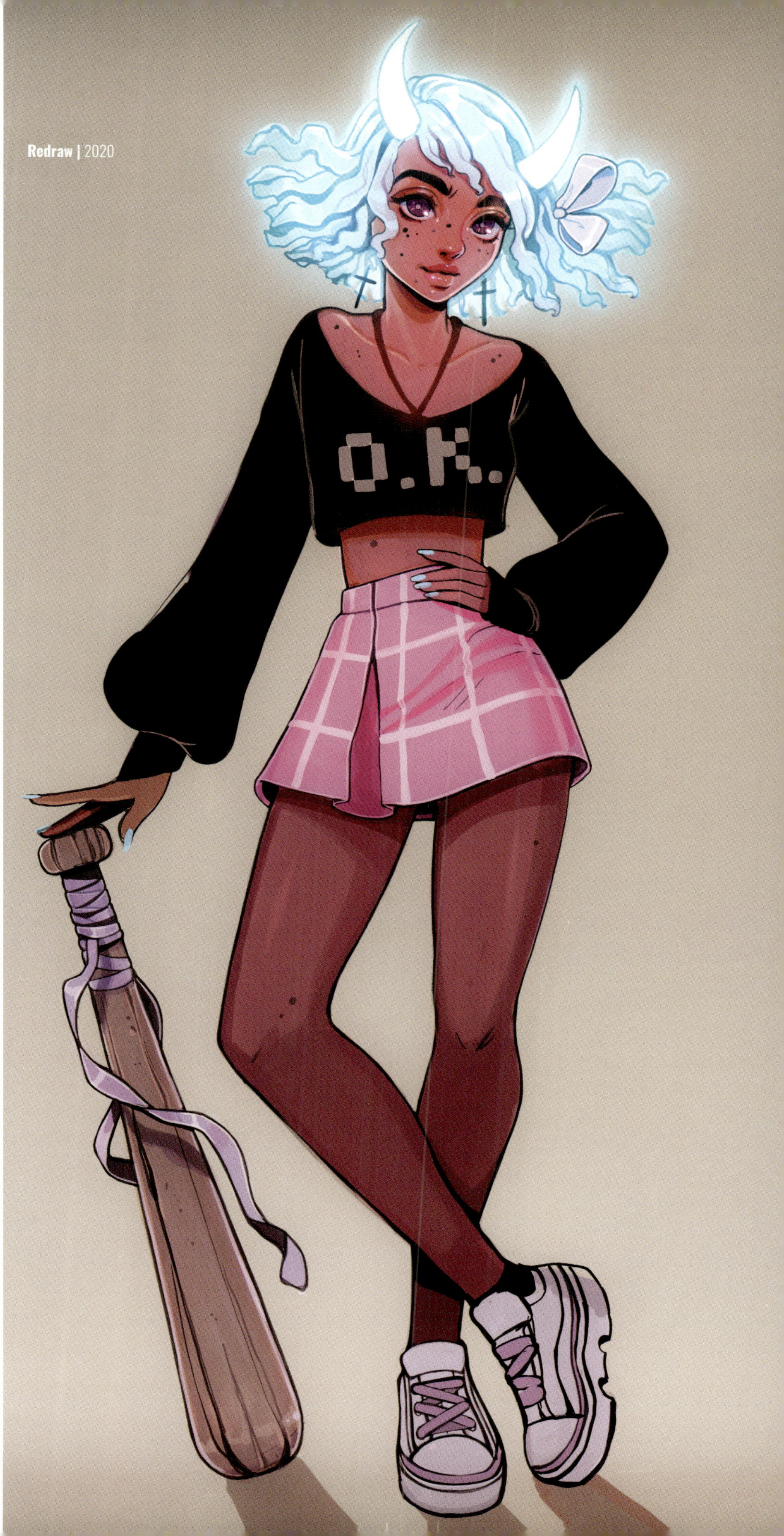


**Original** | 2018

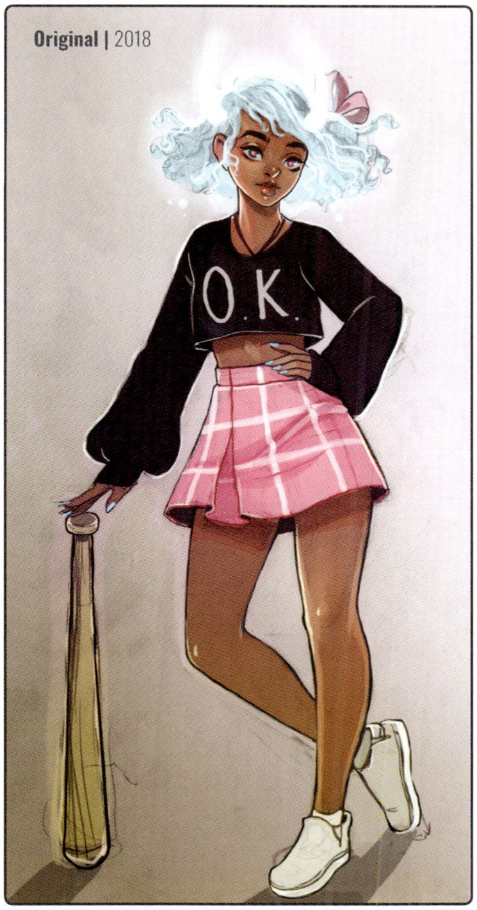

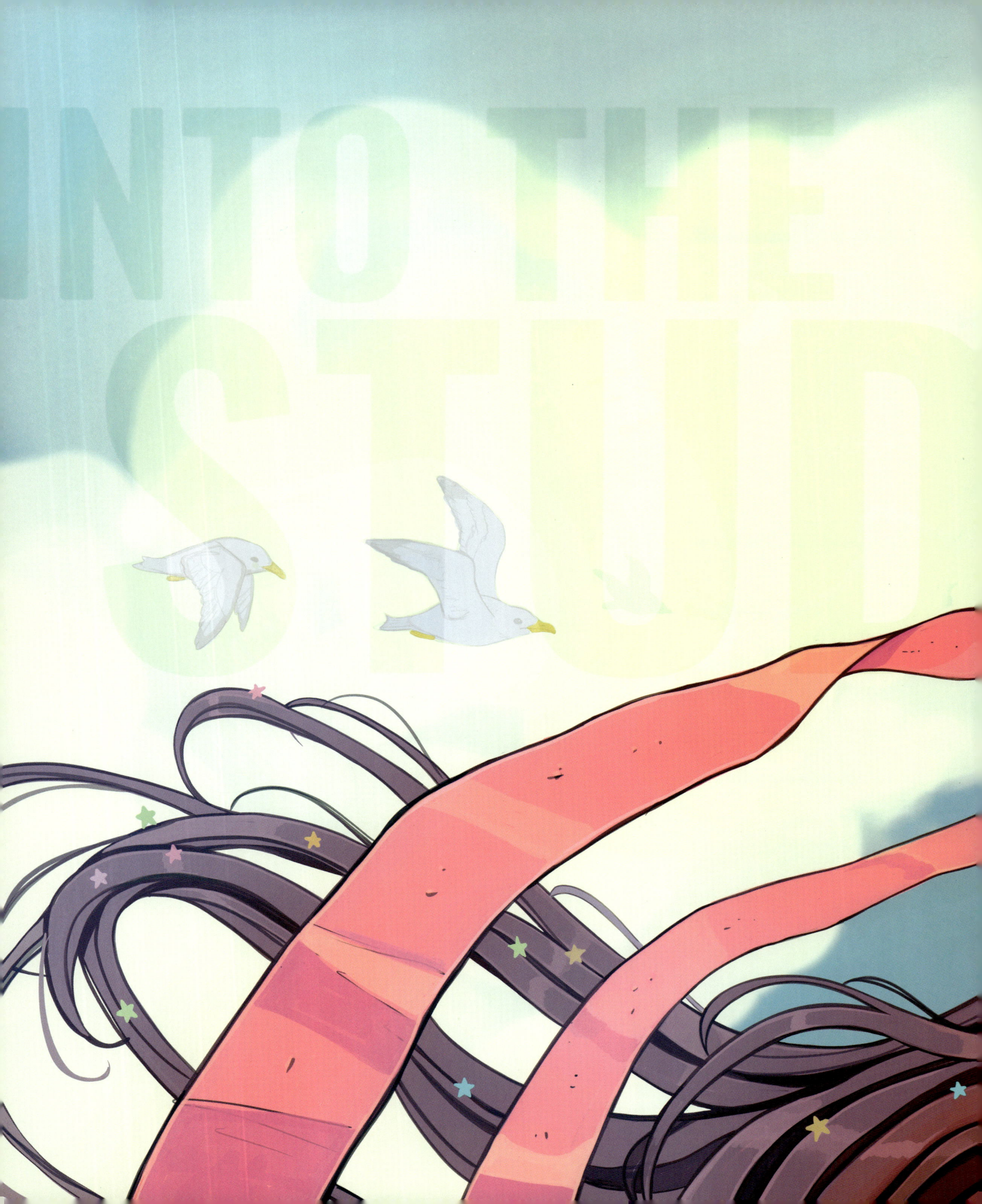
INTO THE
STUD

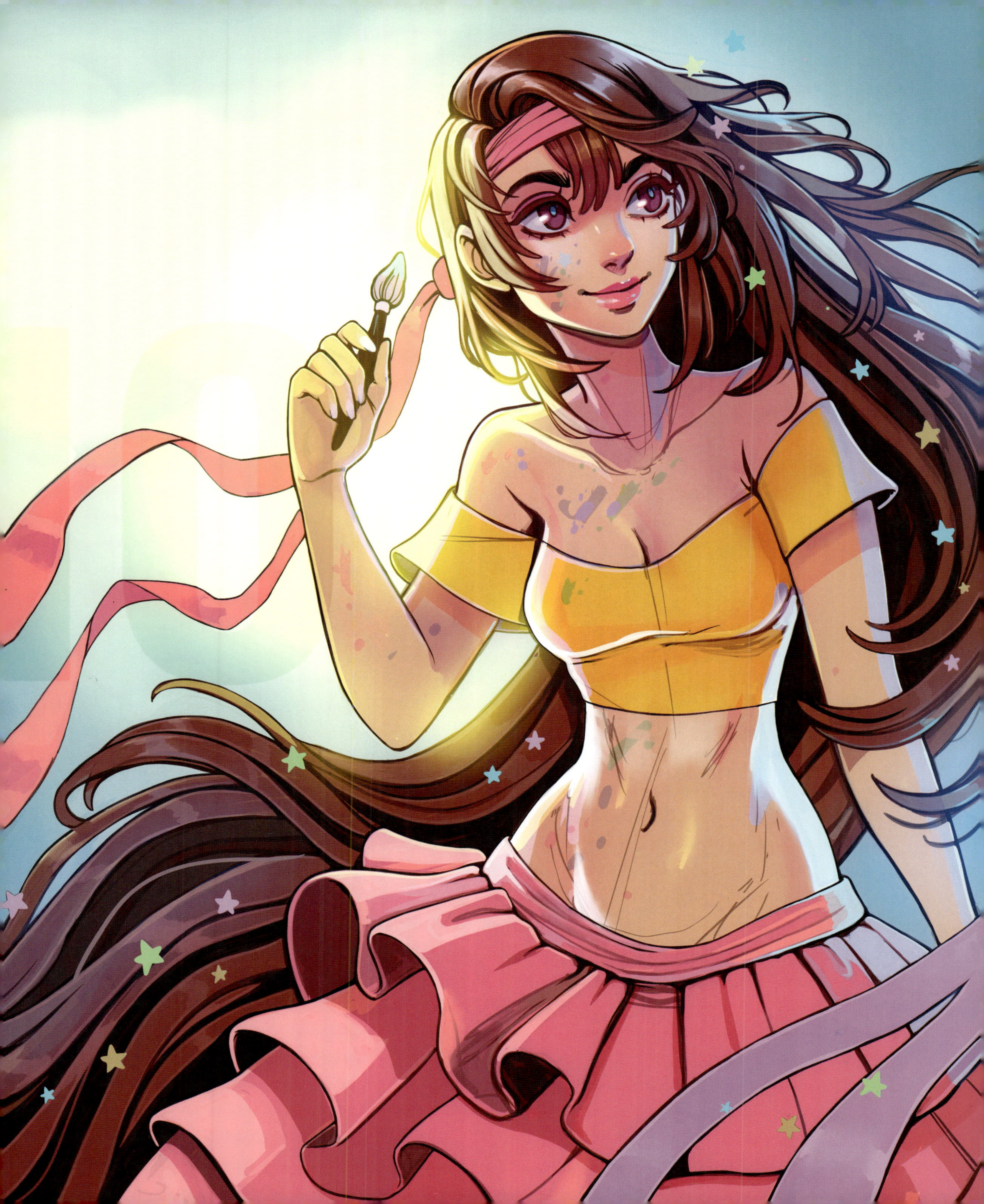

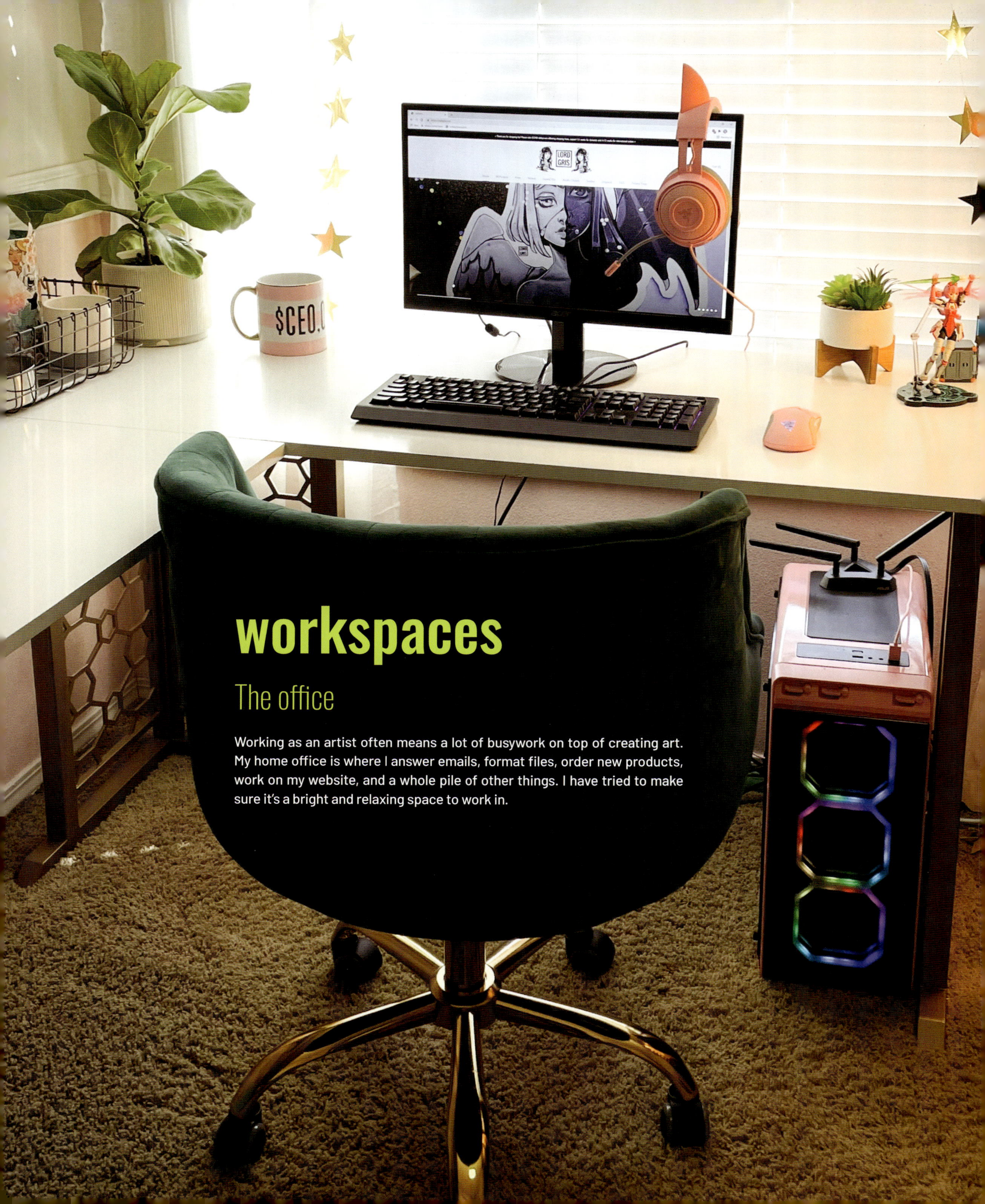


# workspaces

## The office

Working as an artist often means a lot of busywork on top of creating art. My home office is where I answer emails, format files, order new products, work on my website, and a whole pile of other things. I have tried to make sure it's a bright and relaxing space to work in.

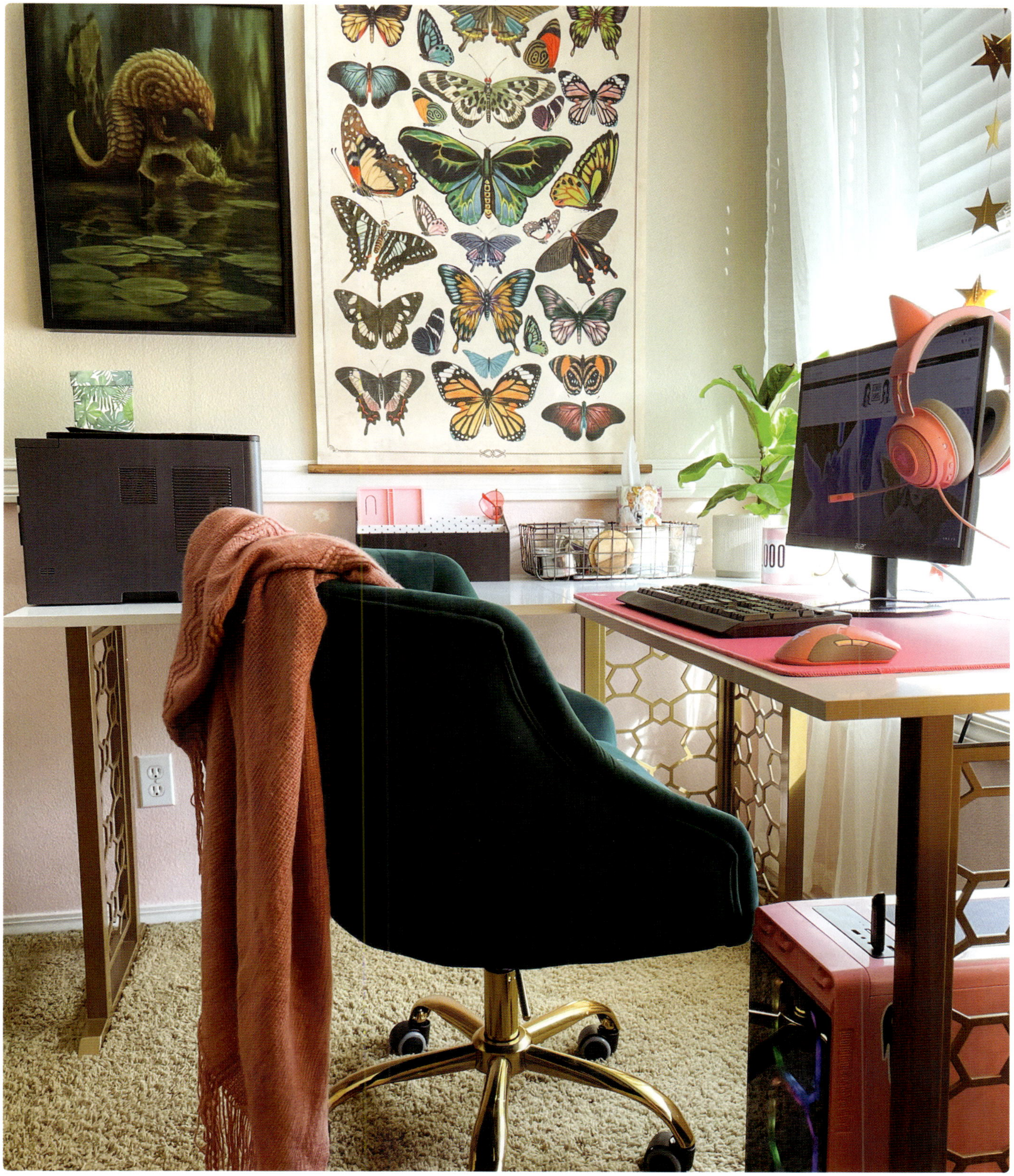

The pangolin oil painting seen in my workspace (top left) was created by Brin Levinson.

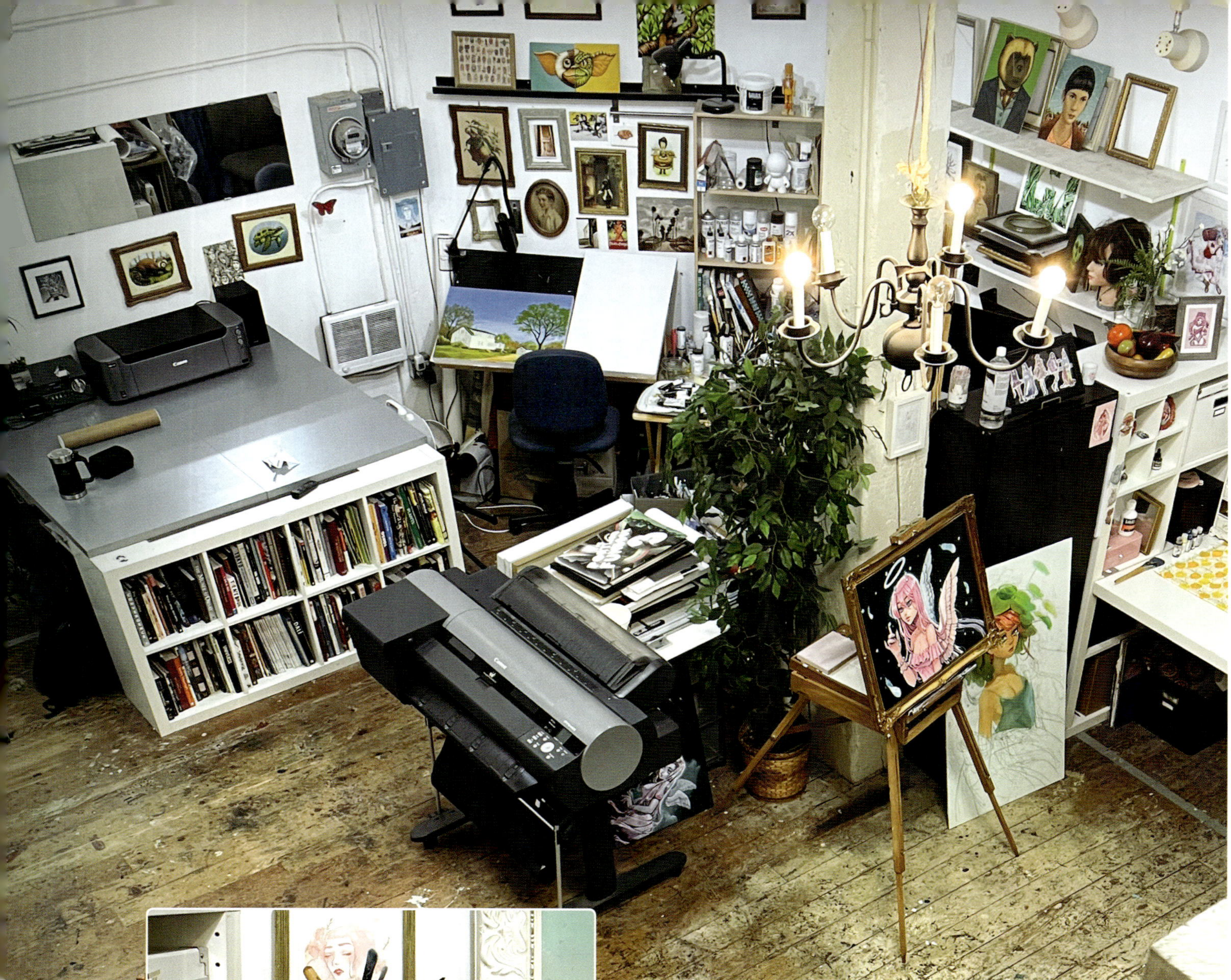

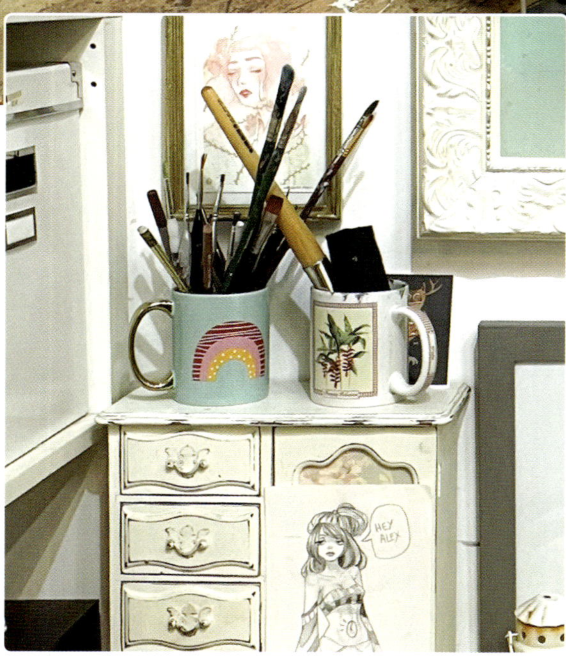

## The art studio

I share an art studio in Portland with fellow artists Matt Linares (who kindly wrote the foreword for this book) and Keith Carter. Our space is located in an enchanting old building that used to be a seed factory and still maintains many vestigial parts from its factory days. All the studio spaces in the building are packed full of talented artists that range from painters and sculptors to photographers and textile designers. It's a really inspiring place to be.

Having a dedicated art studio is great – you can throw paint around and get the floors dirty, and nobody complains! It's also nice to have a shared space with fellow artists because creating alone can ultimately be a very isolating job. Our studio space has two floors: the lower floor is broken down into our individual work areas and the upper floor is where we store frames and power tools for woodworking.

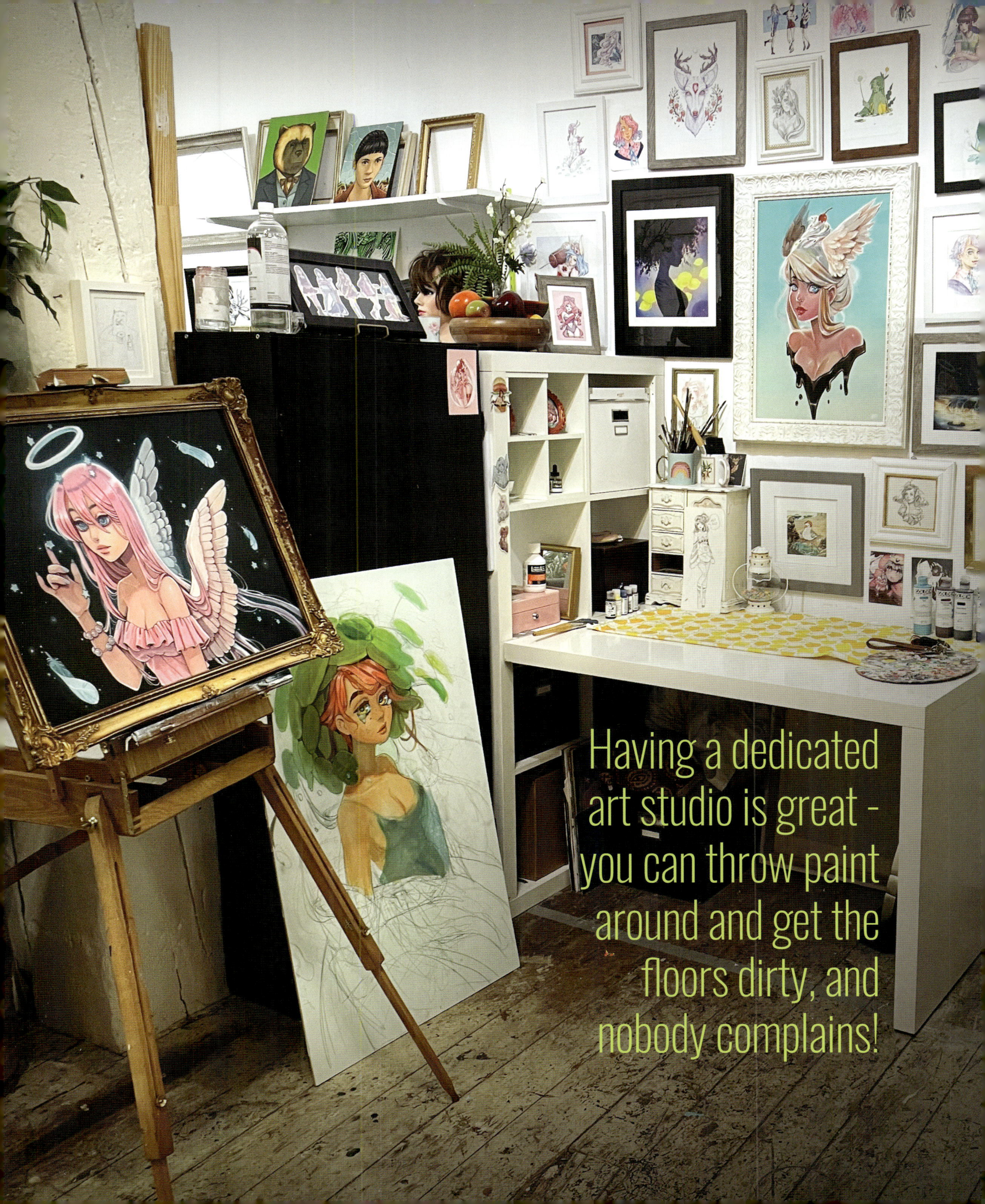

Having a dedicated art studio is great - you can throw paint around and get the floors dirty, and nobody complains!

# tools and materials

I truly believe you can make art from anything. For a long time, the only art supplies I had were basic pencils, printer paper, a beat-up children's Crayola watercolor set, and 70-cent craft store paints. However, I still managed to make art that I felt proud of. You should never let a lack of professional tools stop you from creating — innovate and have fun with what's available! That being said, having tools and materials that are suitable for the job can certainly make things much easier. The following pages feature some of the digital and traditional supplies that I've come to love when approaching the different ways I make art.

## DIGITAL SET-UP: Procreate

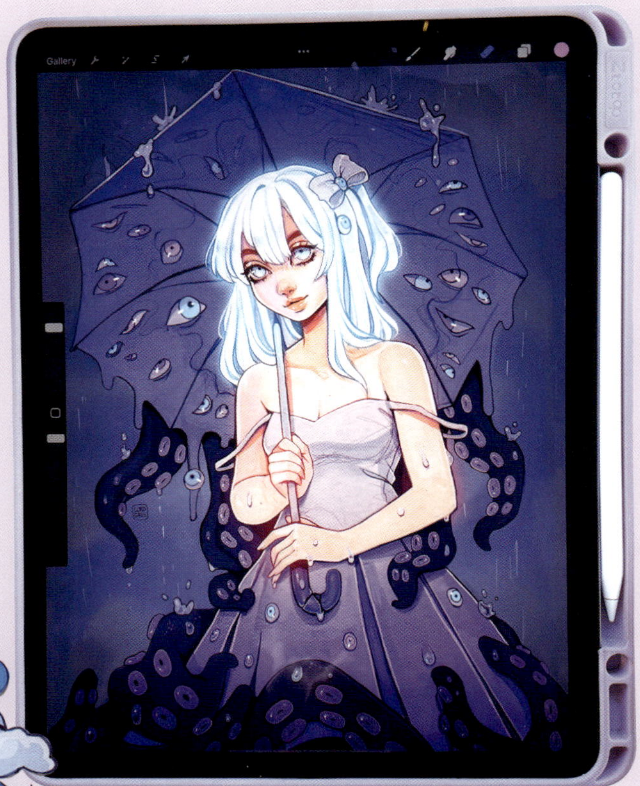

**iPad Pro** My favorite art tablet and application combination to use to create my digital art is the iPad Pro with Procreate. I personally prefer mobile tablets over wired tablets that connect to your computer because you have the freedom to make art from anywhere. I can take it with me to a coffee shop, to my art studio, or to the airport to work while I'm waiting.

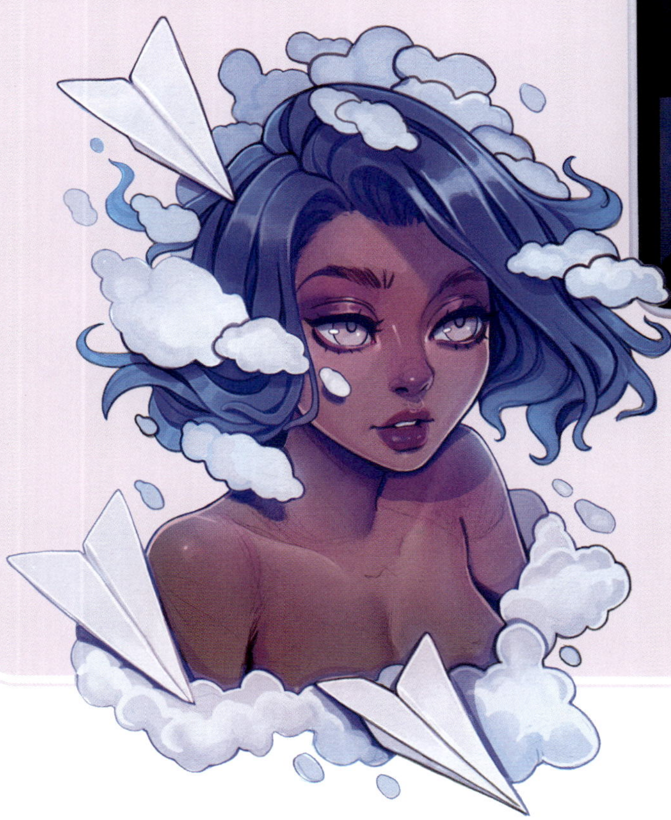

The mobility is hugely important to me because I don't like being stuck in my house all the time. As Procreate is an Apple-exclusive app, I use the Apple Pencil — it's a wonderful lightweight stylus that feels fairly natural, like a real pencil. Procreate is an exceptional drawing program, it's inexpensive and user-friendly but still manages to have a lot of complexity and versatility. I'd recommend it to anyone, beginner or professional.

TRADITIONAL SET-UP:

# sketching

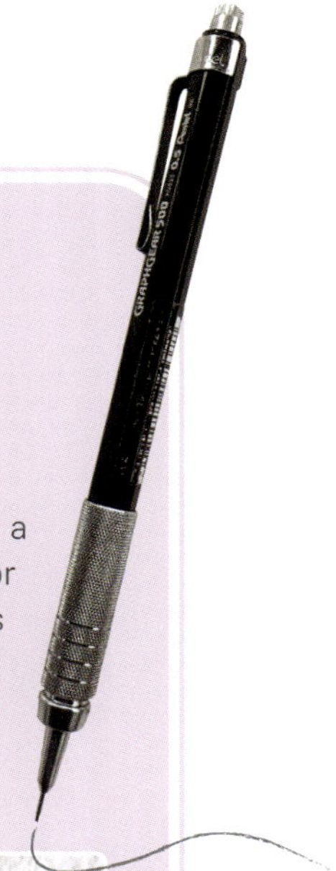

**Pencils** When sketching, I like to use a lighter sketching pencil for the initial sketch and then make the final lines with a mechanical pencil. For the light sketching, I find that any standard set of drawing pencils should do the trick, but for the mechanical pencil I swear by the Pentel Graphgear 500 with 0.5mm lead. Other mechanical pencils feel inferior in comparison. The Graphgear has a comfortable weight and offers amazing control for getting perfect lines. This is the pencil that shows up in a significant amount of my art posts — pretty much any time I'm displaying a pencil in my posts it's the Pentel Graphgear!

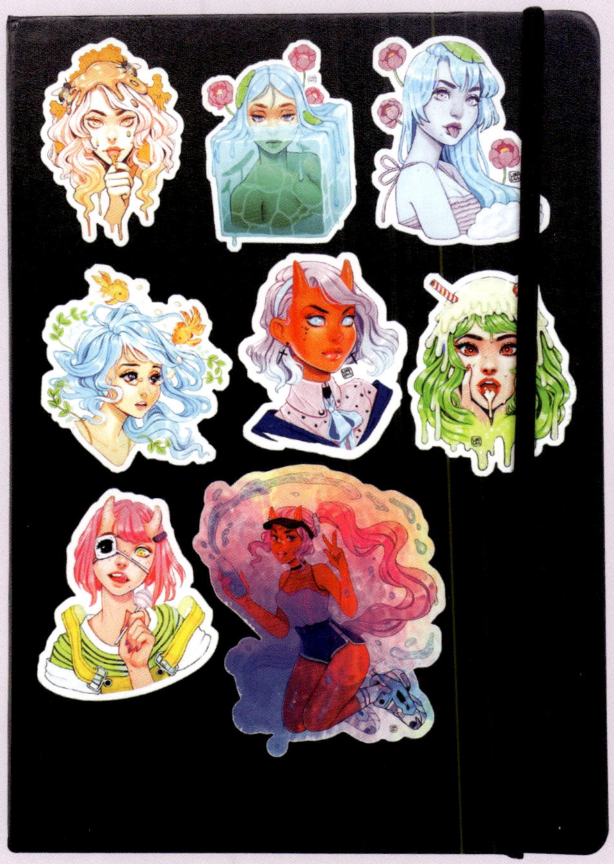

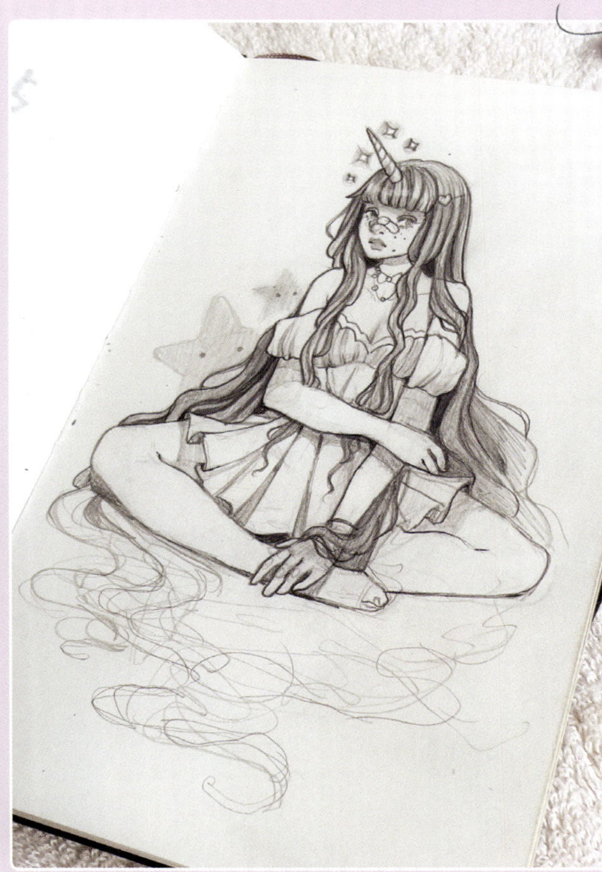

**Paper** I go back and forth between different kinds of sketchbooks because sometimes I crave more texture (Arteza) or blendability (Strathmore), but in the end I always come back to the Moleskine sketch pad as my one, true, favorite paper. Moleskine paper is flawlessly smooth and has a very nice thickness that can even hold marker ink. It has just the right amount of smudge for me — you can get a beautiful blend but the graphite will also stay in place, which allows you to create gorgeous line work.

TRADITIONAL SET-UP:

# mixed media

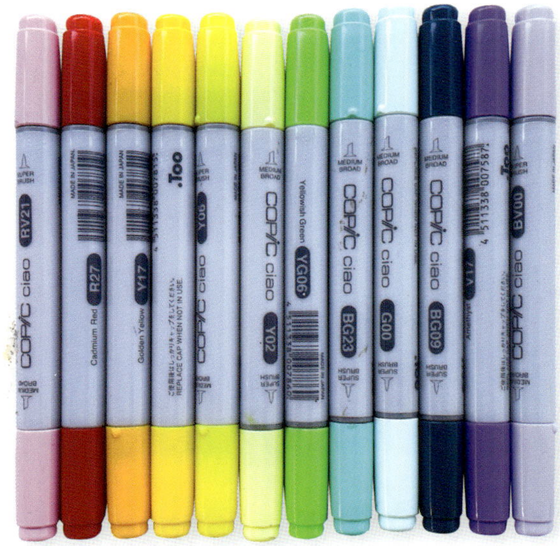


**Marker pens** I've tried an endless sea of different marker brands and I believe Copic is the leading brand for a reason – their markers are the best. Their ability to blend seamlessly with each other to get a smooth gradient is fantastic. Copics do have a higher price tag, but the Copic Ciao range offers a more affordable option. When I first invested in Copic pens I only bought the Copic Ciao skin tone set, and found I could do a lot with it, especially on a toned paper. I would recommend the skin tone set as a great place to start when working with markers, as all of the colors work harmoniously together.

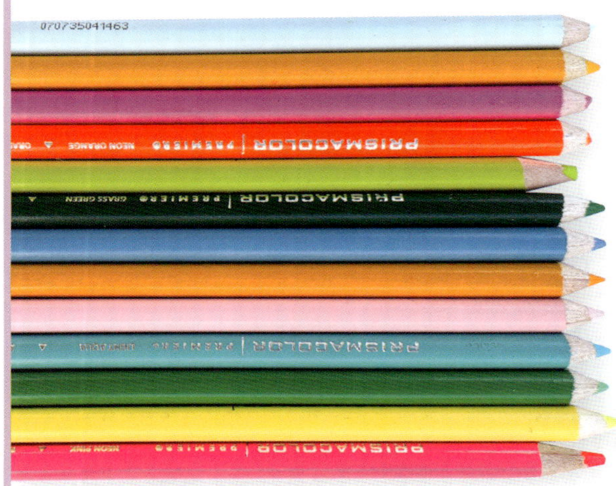


**Colored pencils** I almost never use markers alone when making art – I like to combine them with colored pencils. I use pencils for initial sketches and line art as well as introducing texture in areas such as the strands of hair. I am not particularly fussy about which type I use, but I enjoy working with Prismacolor pencils. They tend to be a little denser in color than your average colored pencil, and using them in conjunction with the colorless blender can get you a buttery smooth finish.

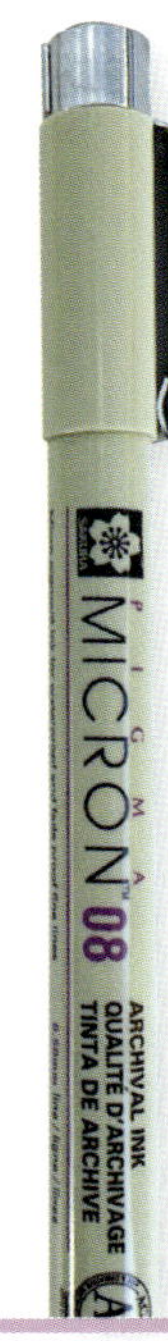


**Pens** When making dark outlines, such as those for eyelashes, fingers, or chunks of hair, I use Micron pens. I usually prefer a colored pen to a black. For example, when coloring skin, I find that a brown pen complements skin tones and makes the piece feel warmer. For hair, especially with cool tones, often I'll use a deep blue pen. Micron pens are great because they don't bleed when they come in contact with markers, which means you can make your line art first and color on top with markers worry free.

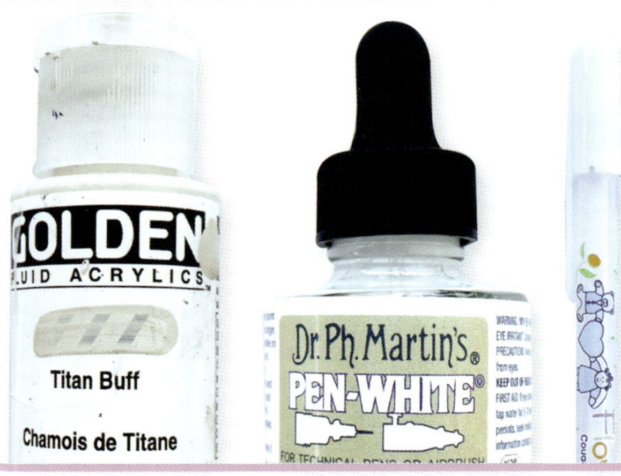


**Highlights** Depending on what's at hand, I'll use different mediums to add highlights. Gel pens are useful for adding a very dense, bright white as a pop here and there, but if I want to create larger white spaces, I use white paint (preferably Golden Fluid Acrylic paint) or a white ink.

**Paper** There are a few different papers I like to use depending on what I'm creating. Arteza Mixed Media paper is an effective option for practicing, as it holds ink fairly well, but the blend won't be as smooth as on a paper designed for marker pens. Strathmore marker paper is the best option for finished projects, because it's sleek, dense, and pristine white, allowing colors to vibrantly pop. For toned paper, which is great when you want to add beautiful white highlights (and which pairs brilliantly with the Copic Ciao skin tone set), I love Strathmore toned paper.

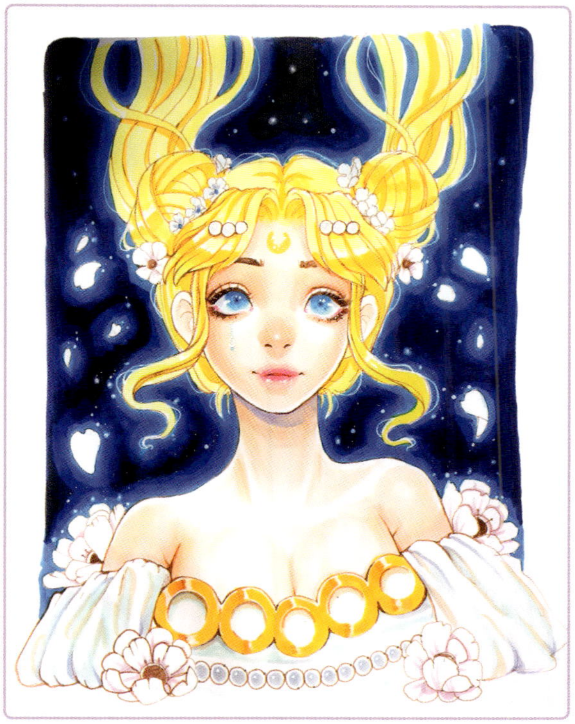

A marker pen portrait on Strathmore marker paper.

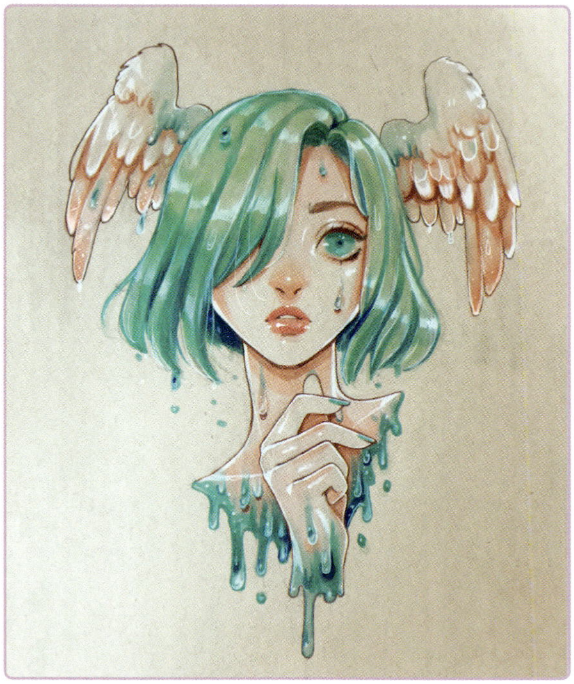

A marker pen portrait on Strathmore toned paper.

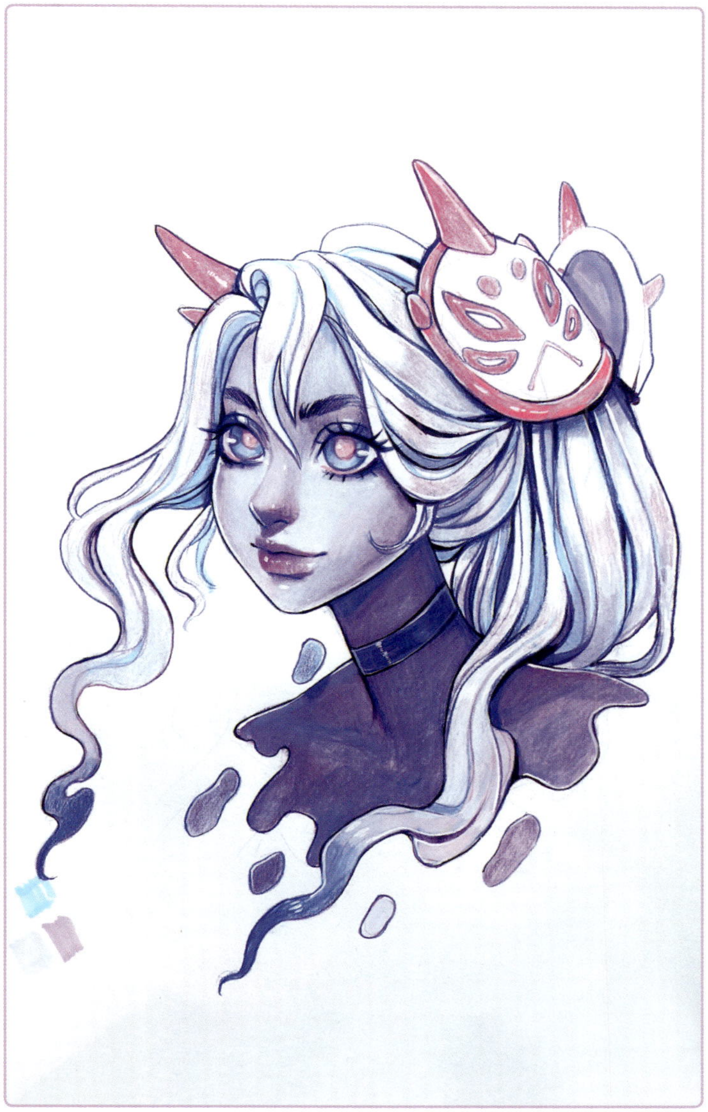

A colored pencil and Copic marker portrait on Arteza Mixed media paper.

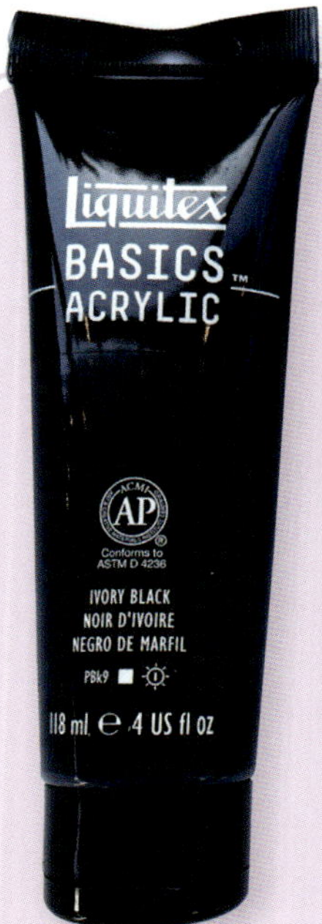


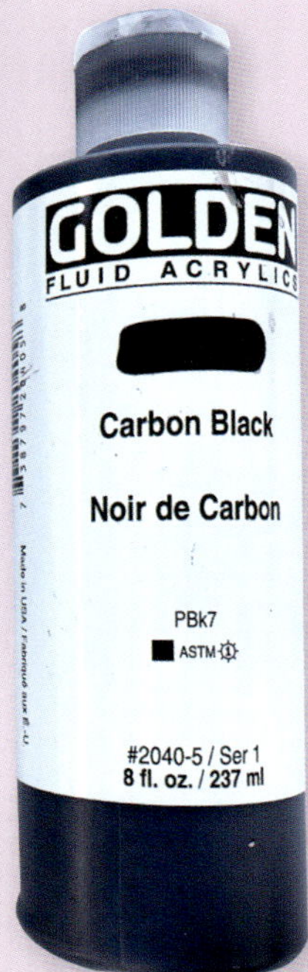


TRADITIONAL SET-UP:

# painting

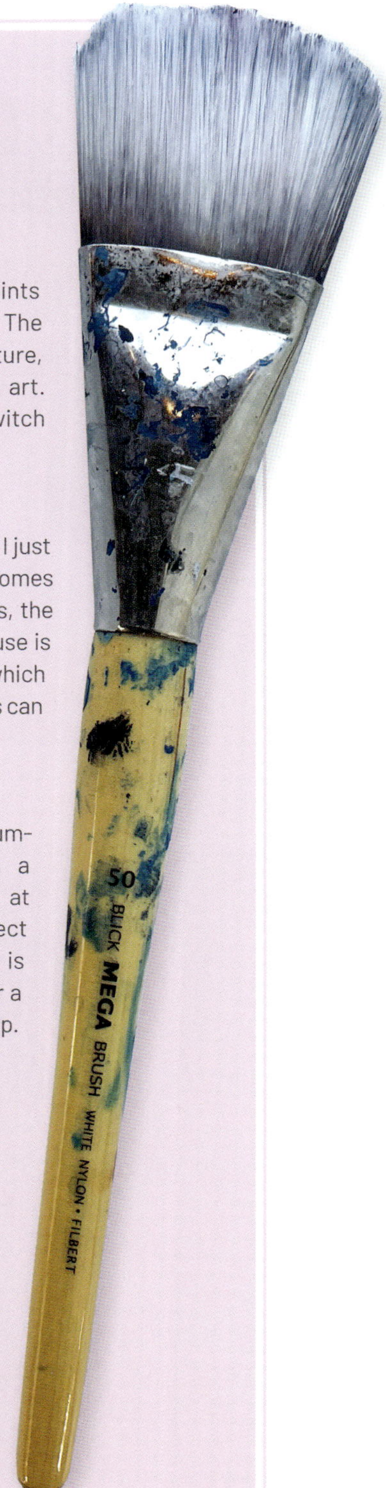


**Paint** When I create acrylic paintings, my favorite paints to use are Golden Fluid Acrylics and Liquitex Basics. The Fluid Acrylics are opaque but have a loose, fluid texture, which is just amazing for blending and creating line art. When I feel like I need my paint to be a little thicker, I switch over to using the Liquitex Basics paints.

**Brushes** I don't have a paintbrush brand that I favor — I just buy highly reviewed brushes online. However, when it comes to the large brush I use for creating background blends, the Blick Mega Brush is the only brush for me. The brush I use is soft with a round tip and I find the bristles don't fall out, which is the biggest issue with cheap brushes, as loose bristles can get stuck in the paint and cause unwanted bumps.

**Canvas** I work pretty much exclusively on medium-density fiberboard (or MDF board for short). It's a lightweight, inexpensive, smooth wood available at most hardware stores. The smooth surface is perfect for creating textureless paintings and the light weight is handy if shipping the finished product off to a client or a gallery, as shipping costs with paintings can really add up.

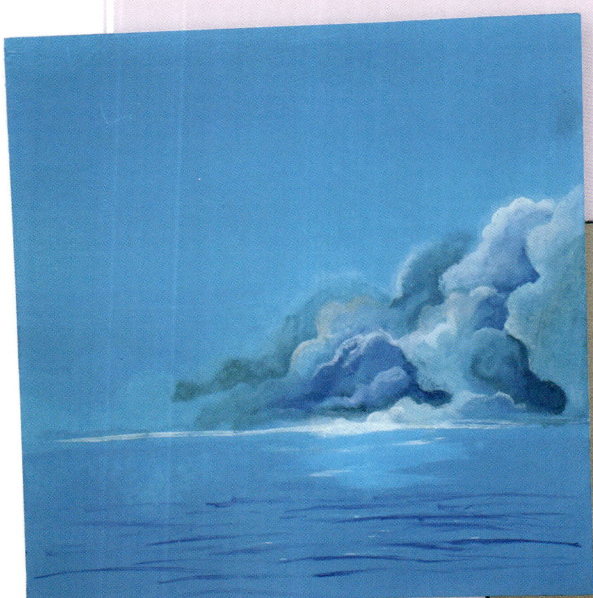

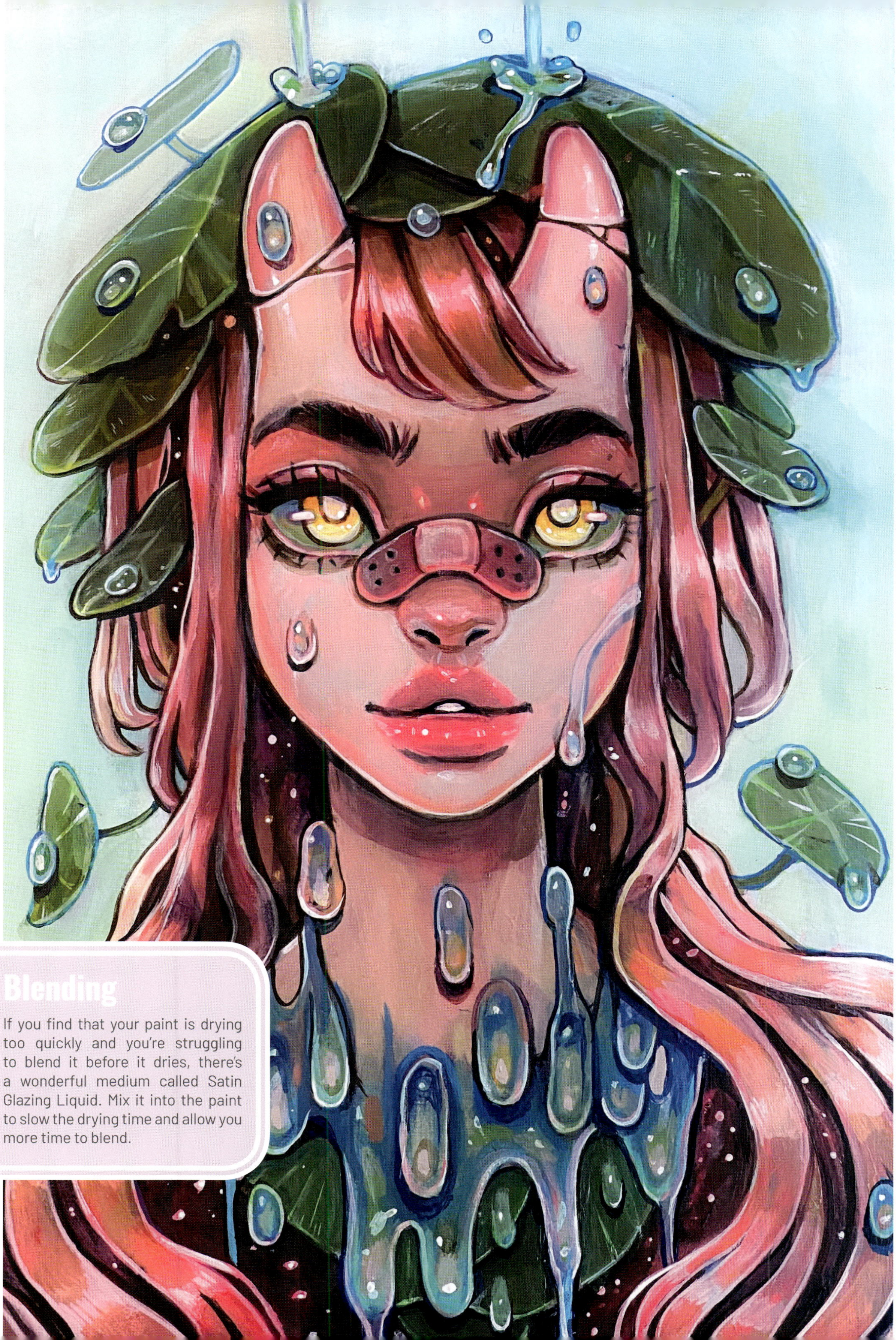

## Blending

If you find that your paint is drying too quickly and you're struggling to blend it before it dries, there's a wonderful medium called Satin Glazing Liquid. Mix it into the paint to slow the drying time and allow you more time to blend.

# traditional meets digital

"Tradigital" coloring, a combination of traditional and digital painting, is something I started in college when I first had access to digital tools. The technique was born of a frustration I felt, lacking proper art tools both traditionally as well as digitally. I loved the feeling of drawing traditionally, but didn't own effective tools for coloring my art; I did, however, have access to Photoshop on my home computer. At the time, I didn't own a drawing tablet and stylus to draw with so I had to use my mouse, which (as you might have guessed) wasn't very easy or comfortable to work with. Nevertheless, forced to use what tools I had access to and based on a technique I saw a few artists online use, I scanned my sketches and shaded drawings in to the computer and colored with Photoshop. I often added paper textures at the end of the painting process to reintroduce the beautiful textured finish that I loved, but couldn't achieve with the tools I had.

As time went on it became a technique that felt very comfortable for me and to this day, I almost never complete a piece using solely digital tools. Sketching on a screen feels foreign and awkward to me, so I almost always create my line art traditionally using pencil and paper.

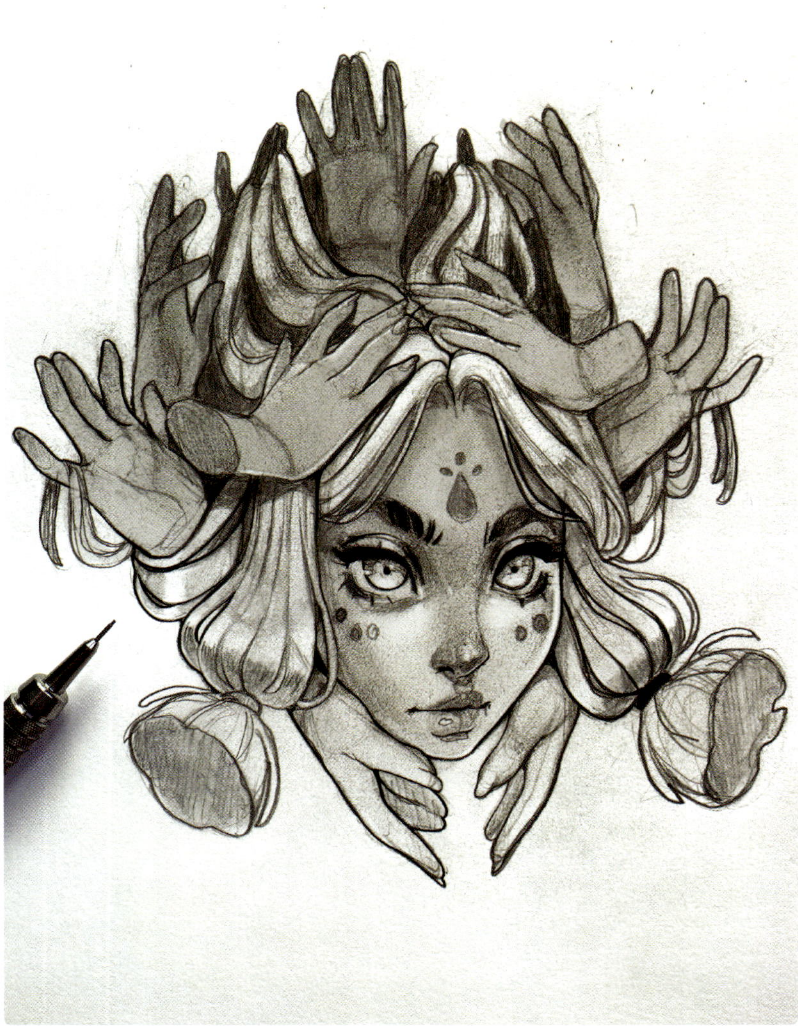

I often added paper textures at the end of the painting process to reintroduce the beautiful textured finish that I loved...

## 90s influence

As a person born in the 90s, who grew up in an analogue world that transitioned into a digital one, having an art style that bridges these two types of art in a way feels very fitting for my life experience.

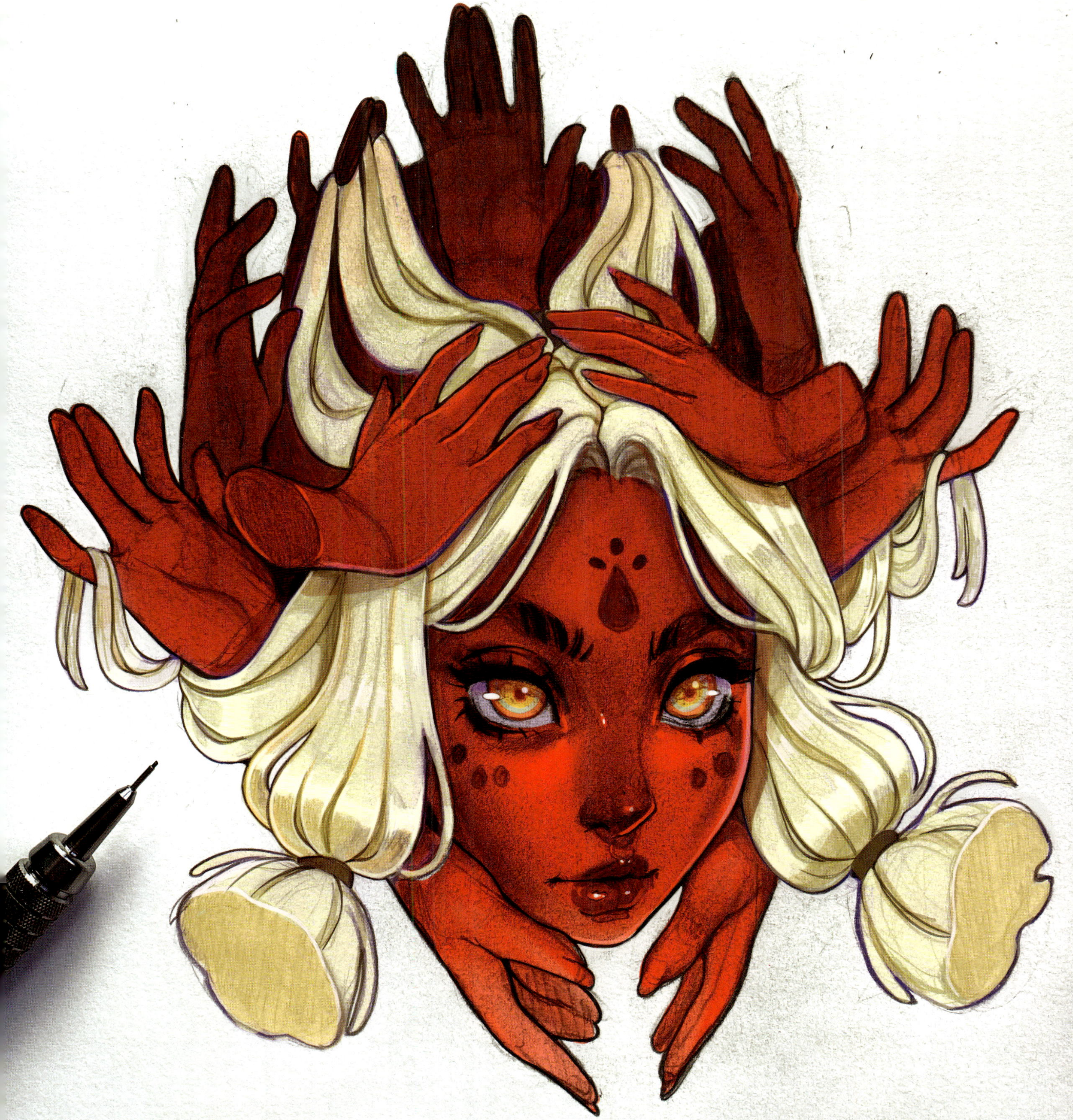

TUTORIAL:

# working tradigitally

**I've created this tutorial to demonstrate how digital coloring can be applied to a traditional sketch without compromising the beautiful original linework. I'm using the Procreate app on an iPad Pro, but the tools used are basic features of nearly every drawing app, so feel free to use whichever program you feel most comfortable with.**

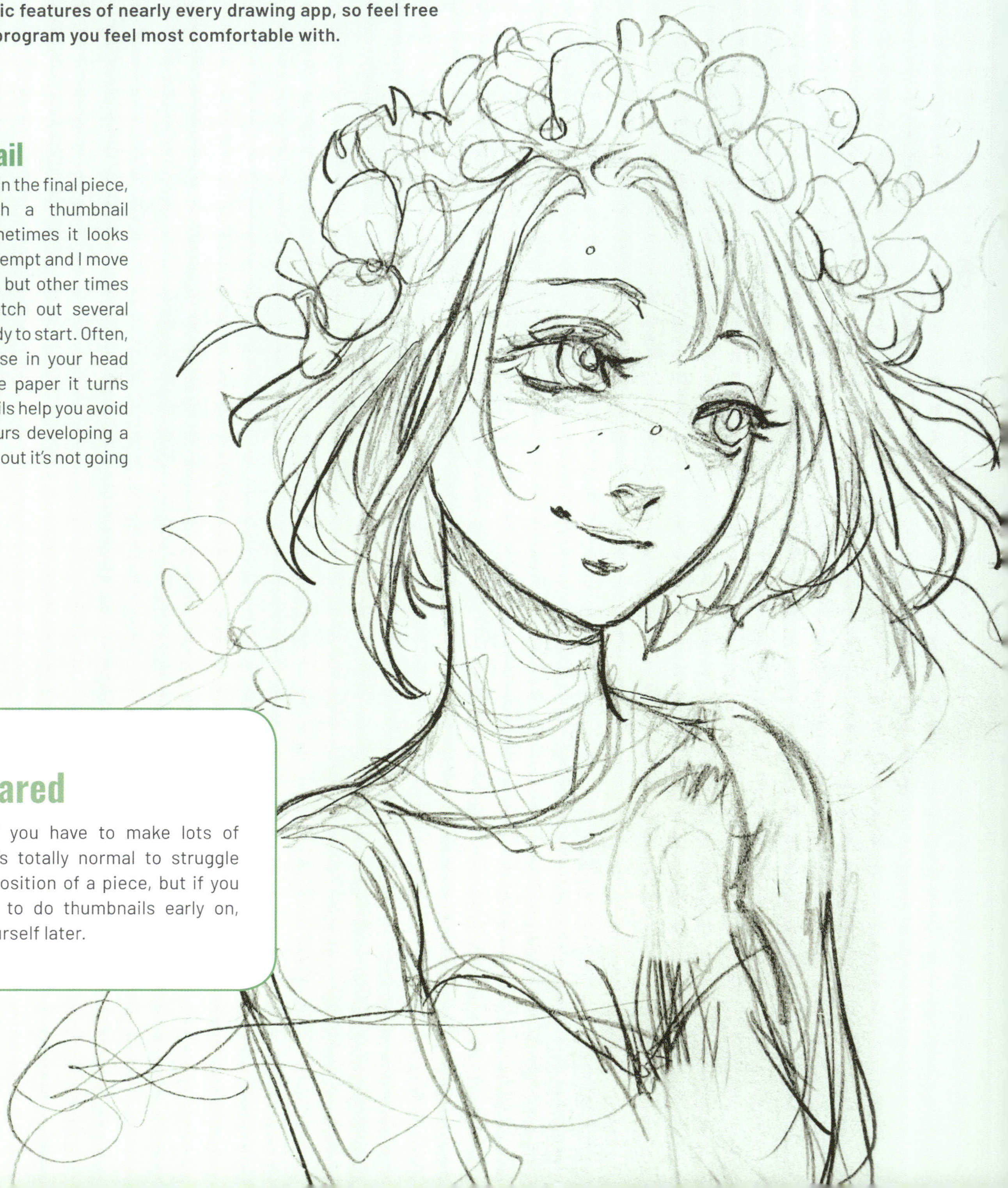

## 1 thumbnail

Before I begin the final piece, I start with a thumbnail sketch. Sometimes it looks good on the first attempt and I move on to the full piece, but other times I may have to sketch out several ideas before I'm ready to start. Often, an idea makes sense in your head but once it hits the paper it turns awkward. Thumbnails help you avoid wasting several hours developing a drawing only to find out it's not going to work.

### Be prepared

Don't worry if you have to make lots of thumbnails! It's totally normal to struggle with the composition of a piece, but if you take the time to do thumbnails early on, you'll thank yourself later.

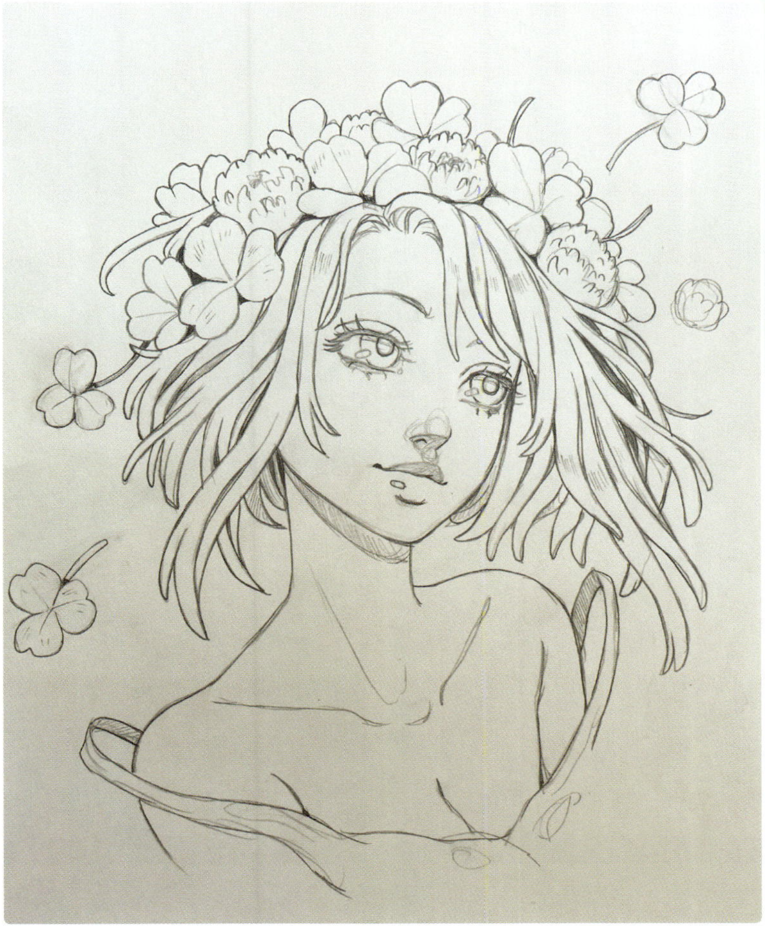

## 2 sketch line work

When it's time to make the final drawing, you will have to choose how you want to split the drawing into traditional and digital methods. You might decide to sketch out just the basic line work and do the rest of the shading in the color portion, or you can complete all the shading traditionally too – both work with this method! Depending on the mood of the piece, I will flip between the two. Doing the shading first gives you a much moodier piece with beautiful texture. With this particular drawing, I drew just the line art traditionally. I like to work with a Moleskine sketchbook because the paper is smooth and textureless, which helps in achieving even lines. I sketch the design with a soft pencil and then draw the final lines with a 0.5mm Pentel drafting pencil.

### Smooth lines

If you want beautiful traditional lines but are having trouble with a messy page, take a picture of your sketch and use your digital tablet as a makeshift lightbox to create a sleek drawing on a new piece of paper.

## 3 capturing the photo

There are two different ways to take a sketch into the digital world – with either a photograph or a scan. If you have a scanner and you're comfortable using it, then go for it! For ease and accessibility, I try to do as much as I can on my phone – I take the picture with my phone camera. To achieve even lighting, my favorite place to photograph art is near a window with diffused light. Avoid direct sunlight and overhead lights, as your hands will cast shadows over the paper.

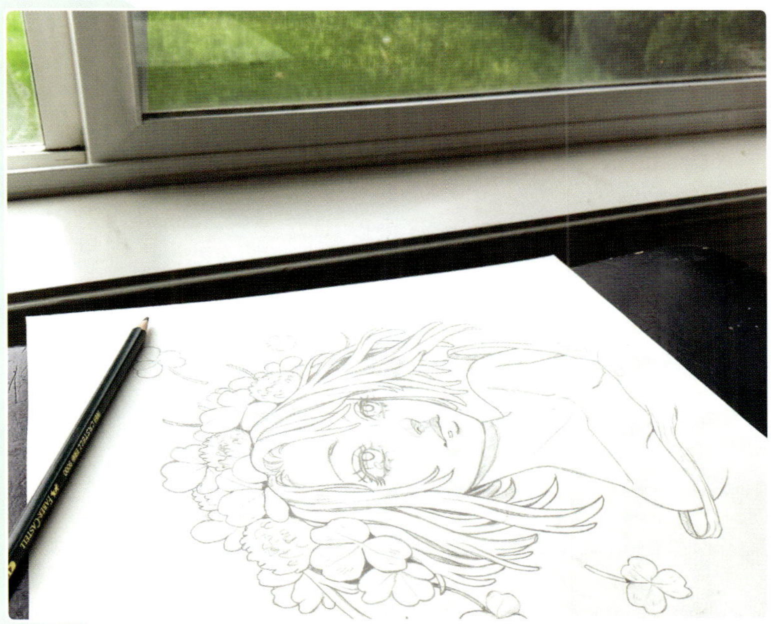

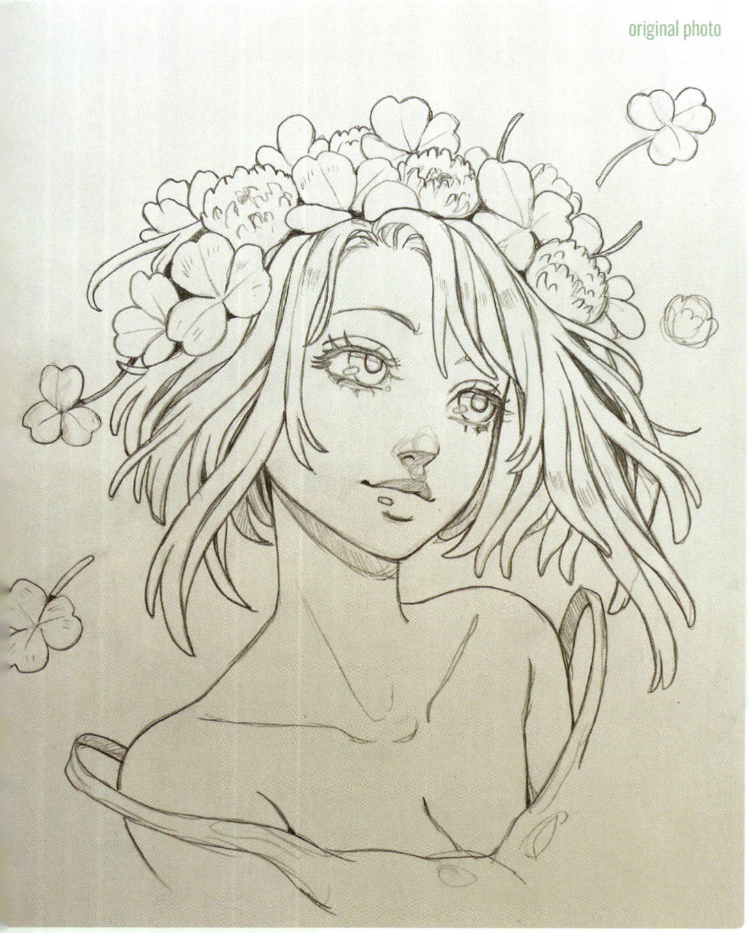

original photo

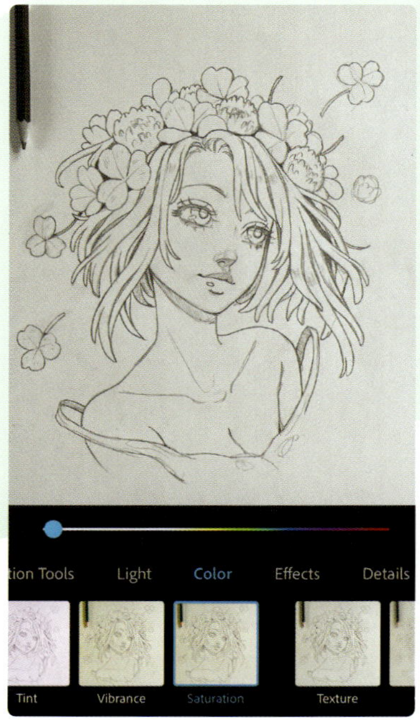


reduce saturation

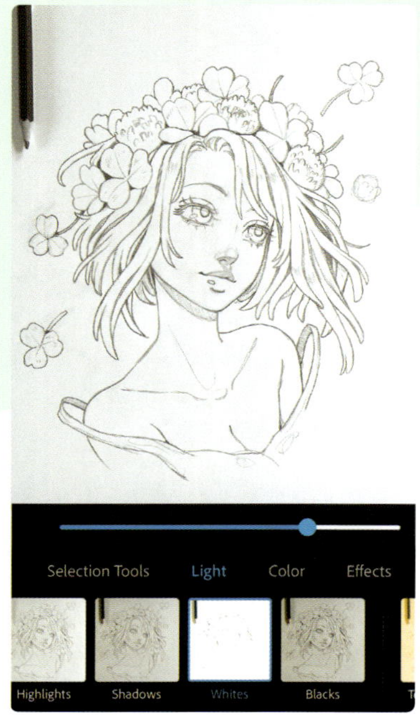


adjust white balance

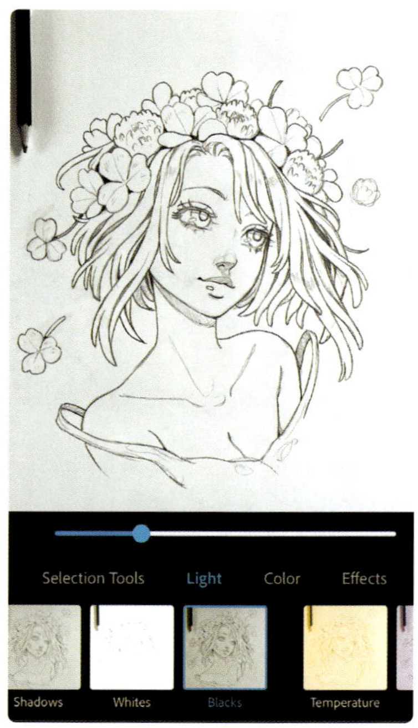


increase blacks

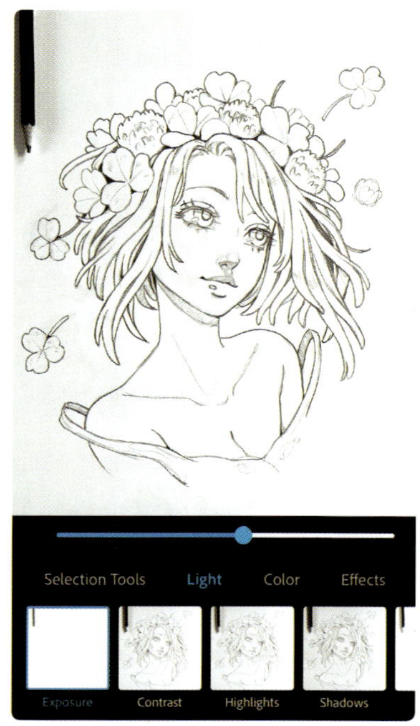


adjust exposure

## 4 editing the photo

No matter how amazing a photo you take, you will probably find that it is much too dark to work with. Also, it may be tinted blue or yellow depending on the light, and so needs to be edited before it can be used.

Open the photo in a photo editor (I use the Adobe Photoshop Elements app on my phone) and make adjustments. I use a few different adjustments to clean up and lighten the image. First, I reduce saturation levels to zero to eliminate color tints, then adjust white balance to show the true white of the page. You may lose some of the darks doing this, so I increase the scale on the "black" setting. If the piece is still too dark after that, I will carefully adjust the exposure (work cautiously as this step can cause line work to disappear). These are basic settings found in most photo-editing software.

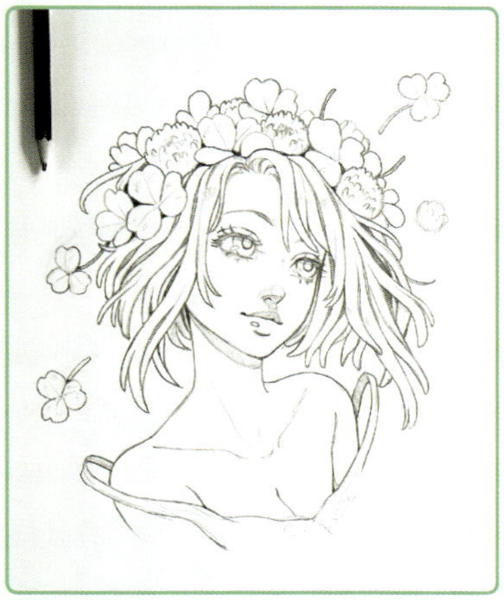

edited photo

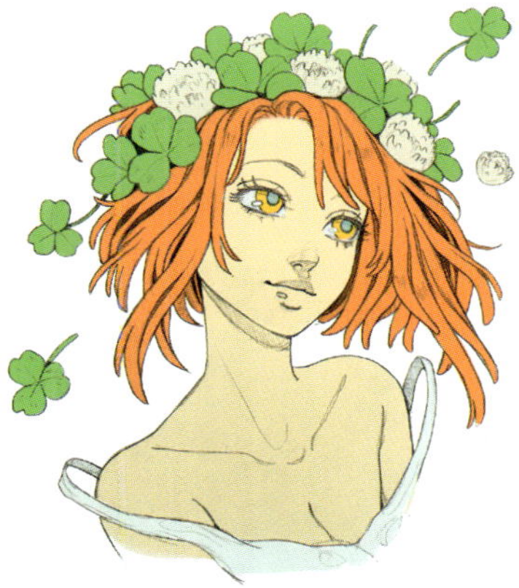

first base layer

## 5 adding base color

Adding color to your digital sketch is much simpler than most people expect — all it takes is changing the layer setting. I work in Procreate, but this layer, called Multiply, is a staple in pretty much any drawing software. Once you set your sketch layer to Multiply, it will project itself over any layers you place beneath it, so make sure any layers you're adding to color the image get placed *beneath* the sketch layer in the line-up. In fact, the only layers I will place *above* the sketch are Screen and Highlight layers (which I will talk about in later steps), unless I need to correct a mistake in the original line art. Begin to add the base colors.

add color beneath the Multiply layer

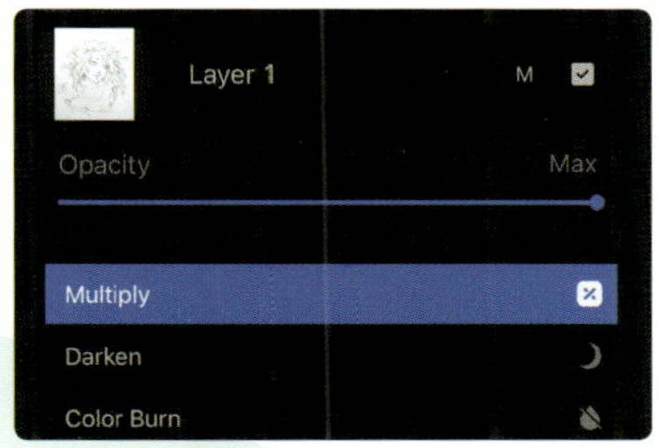


## 6 adding soft shadows

Once the base colors are in place, I add soft shadows. I always start with warm shadows to round out my shapes. I aim to use these shadows to help build dimensionality into the shape, focusing on areas such as the nose, the cheeks, and the arms.

**Brush settings:** My favorite pen to use is one of the basic brushes in Procreate called the Studio Pen — it's a fairly standard inking pen, but unless I am laying down base colors I never use the brush set to full opacity — this helps me get a textured look with my art.

**Smudge Tools:** To round out shapes or get an even blend, I use smudge tools with the opacity set very low, otherwise the blending can get "streaky" instead of smooth.

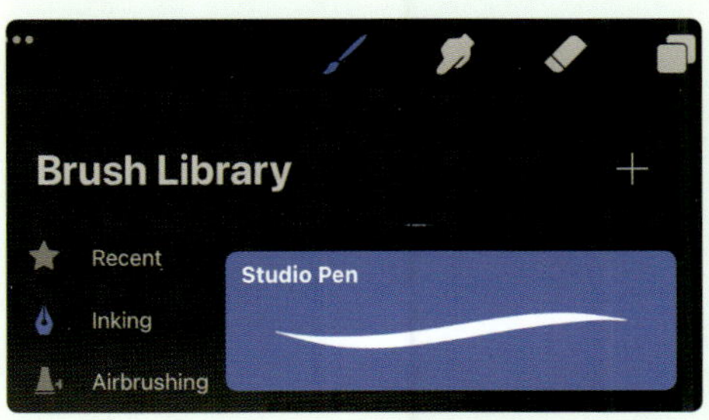


brush set to low opacity

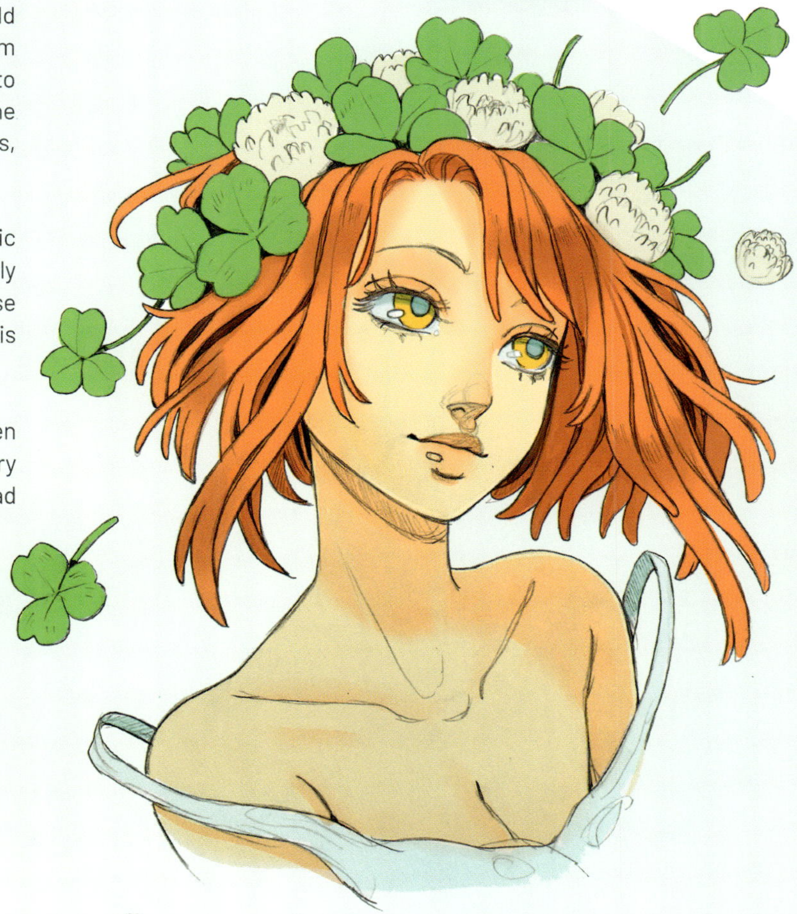

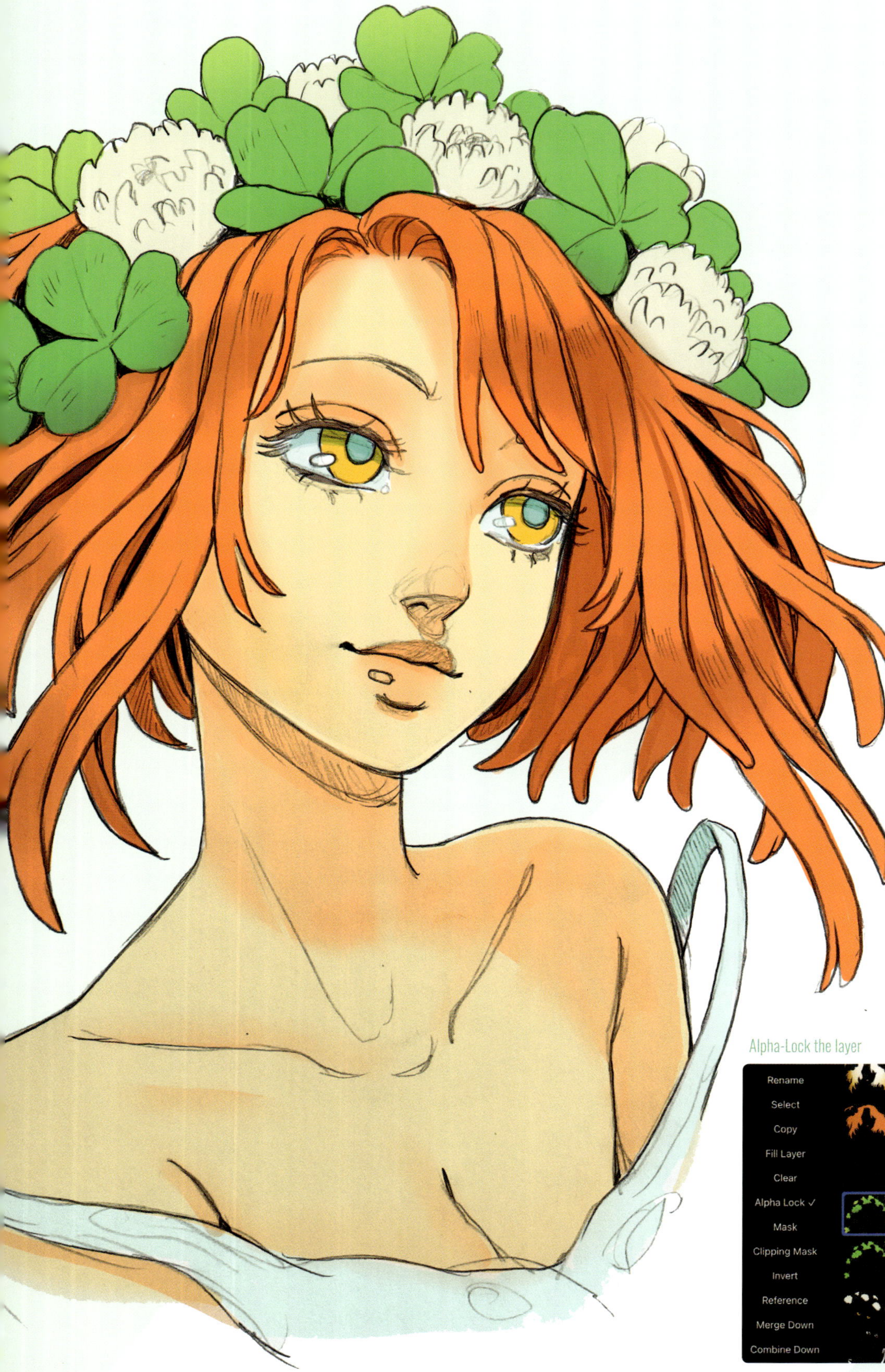

## 7 applying gradients

I always try to include gradients in my art in some capacity. For example, in some designs I apply them to the hair, but for this piece I create a gradient on the giant clovers. The clover leaves fade from a bold green to a yellowish hue, helping to break up what would otherwise be a monotonous color palette. The introduction of color gradation also guides the eye effectively around the image.

To achieve a gradient in specific areas, the key is a layer setting called Alpha Lock. I create a new layer, draw entirely over the areas I want the gradient to cover (the color you use for this part doesn't matter – I usually use black to make sure I got everything covered) then Alpha-Lock the layer. This will lock the layer so that you cannot draw anywhere except the areas that have already been drawn on. Once it's locked, draw the colors you want to blend together and use the Gaussian Blur tool to achieve a perfect gradient.

Alpha-Lock the layer

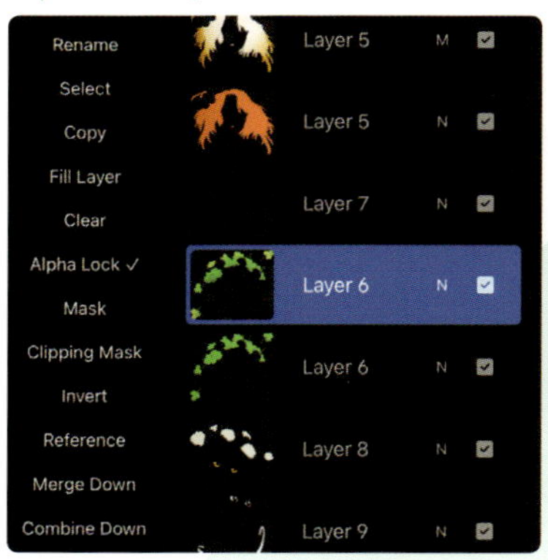


use Gaussian Blur

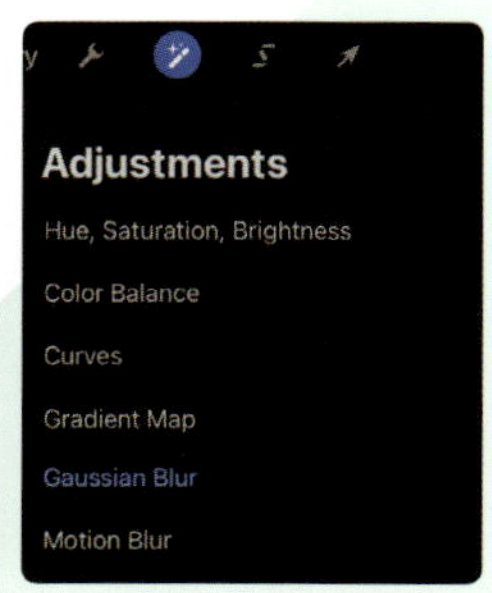

## 8 painting cool shadows

Next, I introduce cool shadows where direct shadows are cast — for example the nose, bangs, or chin may cast darker shadows. To give a more natural look, when adding the cool shadows, I leave a rim of warm shadows, or more specifically, I allow the warm shadows to extend further out from the cool shadows. To keep them from looking too sharp, I then blend them a little with the Smudge tool. Shadows that are closer to the object casting them will have a harder edge, and become more diffused the further away they get from the object.

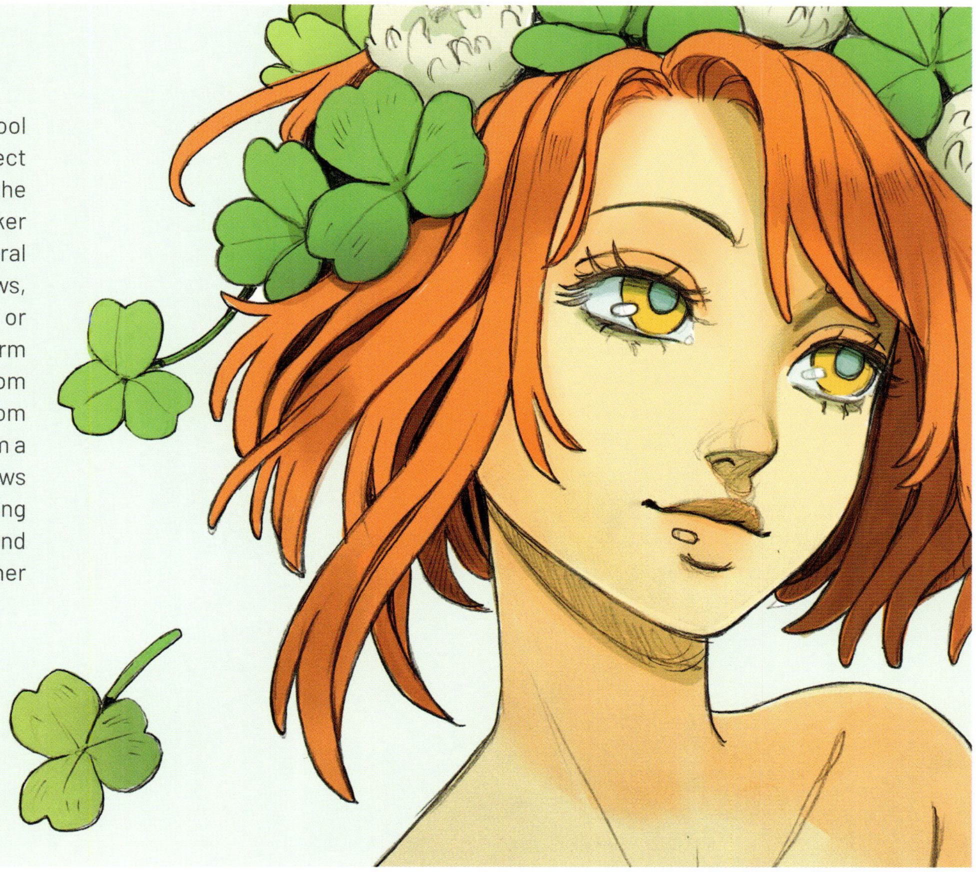

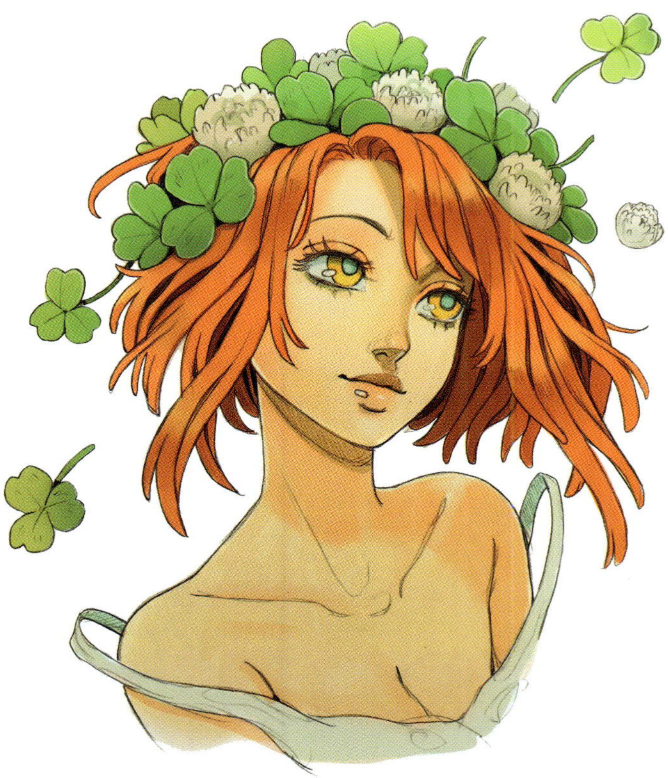

## 9 darkening

At this stage, the piece may feel too light, especially if you hope to achieve bold highlights, backlighting, or elegant atmospheric effects. To help make the piece pop more as I build layers of shadows and highlights over time, I use a Multiply layer to darken the entire piece (you can see here that so far, all layers have been created *beneath* the initial sketch layer). The color I choose depends on the type of mood I'm trying to set. I want this piece to feel warm and summery, so I select a warm shadow, but for a cooler, watery piece I might choose a cool blue shadow.

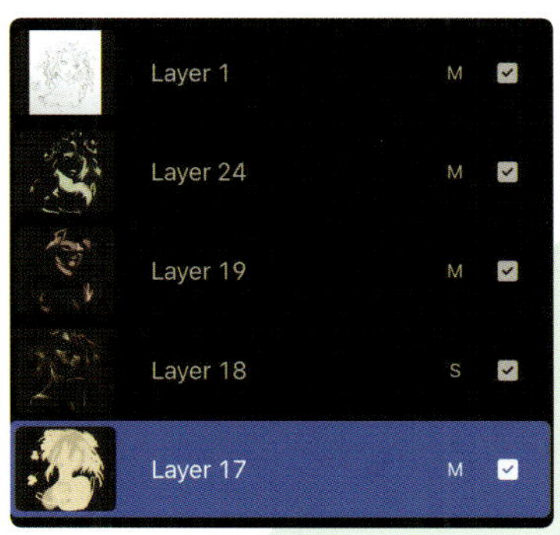


darken using a Multiply layer

## 10 adding highlights

It's time to start highlighting the piece. To add highlights, I use a Screen layer placed *above* all of the existing color layers. I use screen layers instead of plain layers for highlights because they add light to a layer while still interacting with the layers beneath. This way, you don't feel like you're covering up progress already made. I tend to add a lot of highlights around the contours of my characters to achieve a lustrous, rim-lighting effect. I mostly shy away from true white highlights, using colors instead. For the hair, I use a yellow tone to highlight the orange base, and for the face I use a soft beige. Rarely will I add stark, hard edged, unblended highlights, saving those for only the shiniest areas, such as the bridge of the nose, lips, or chin. Otherwise I will softly blend my highlights to create roundness. Here you can see I added blended highlights to the cheeks, forehead and neck.

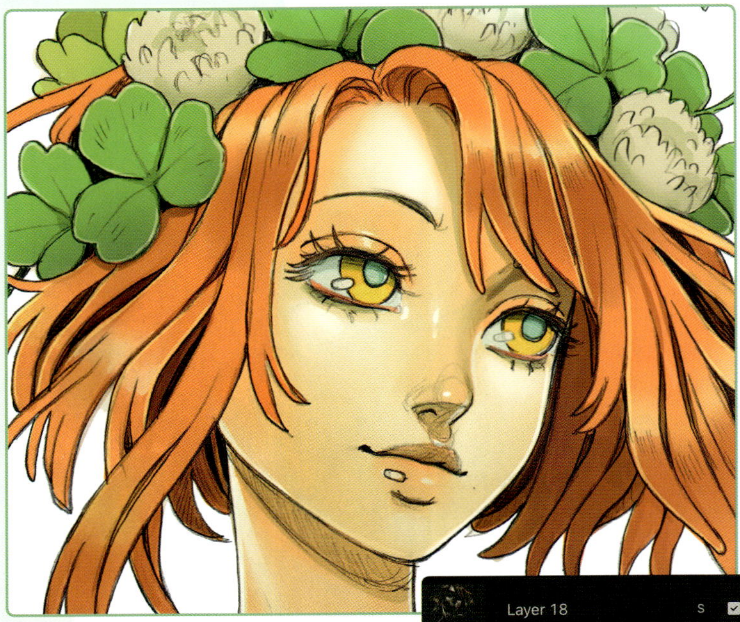

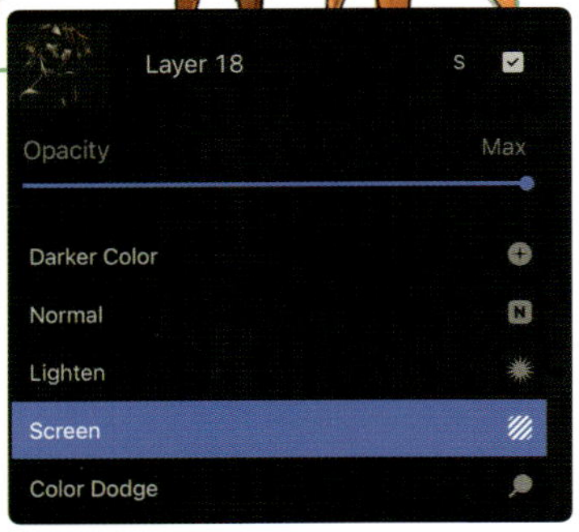


create more Screen layers

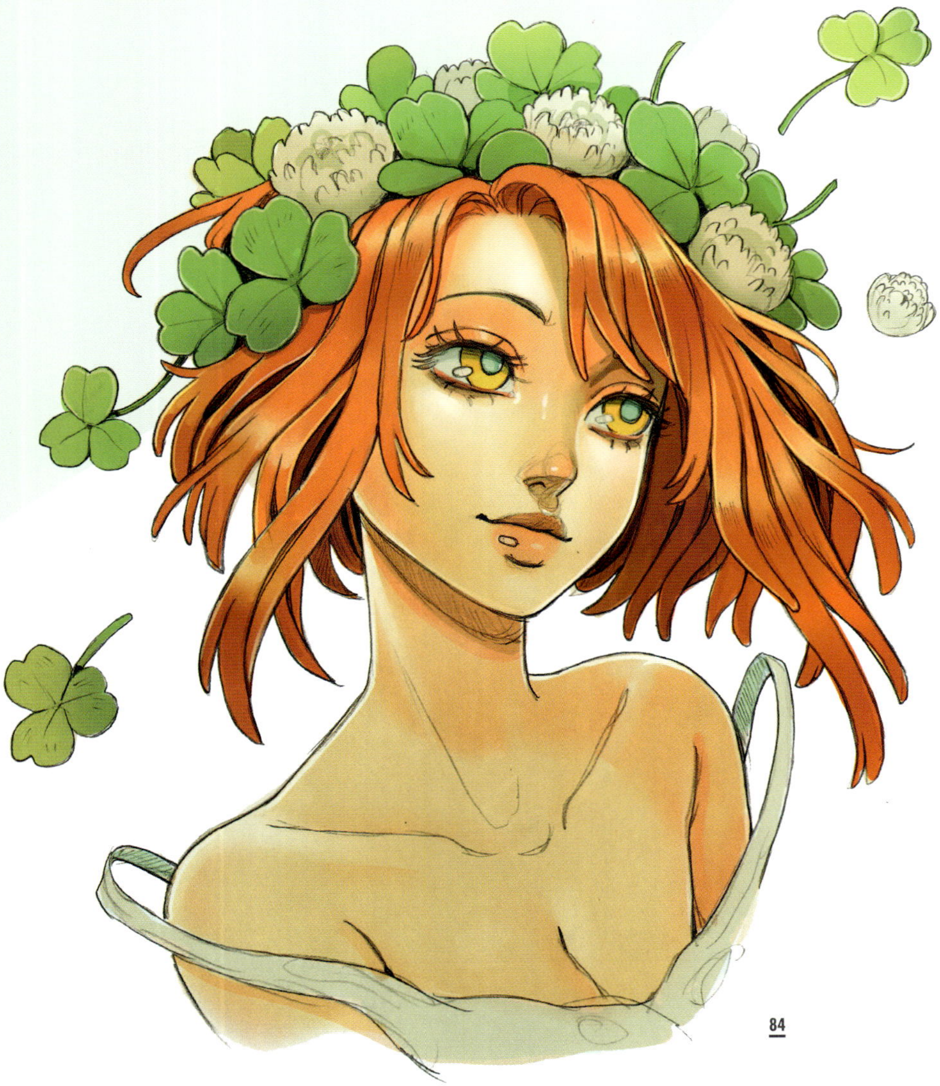

## 11 pushing depth

This is the stage where I go back and forth pushing dark and light to the limits. I create more Multiply and Screen layers to push darker areas further backward, such as areas of hair that may be in shadow or the neck area, and begin to bring bright areas further forward. This is based on your personal style preference, but I like to build up strong contrast over time. On this piece, I darken the areas around the eyes as well as parts of the arms, and cast stronger shadows from the leafy crown on her he ad. I also add stronger highlights to the hair, offering further definition to individual strands, and add an extra gradient to the hair to make it pop more (for more hair coloring tips, check out my hair-drawing tutorial, page 142).

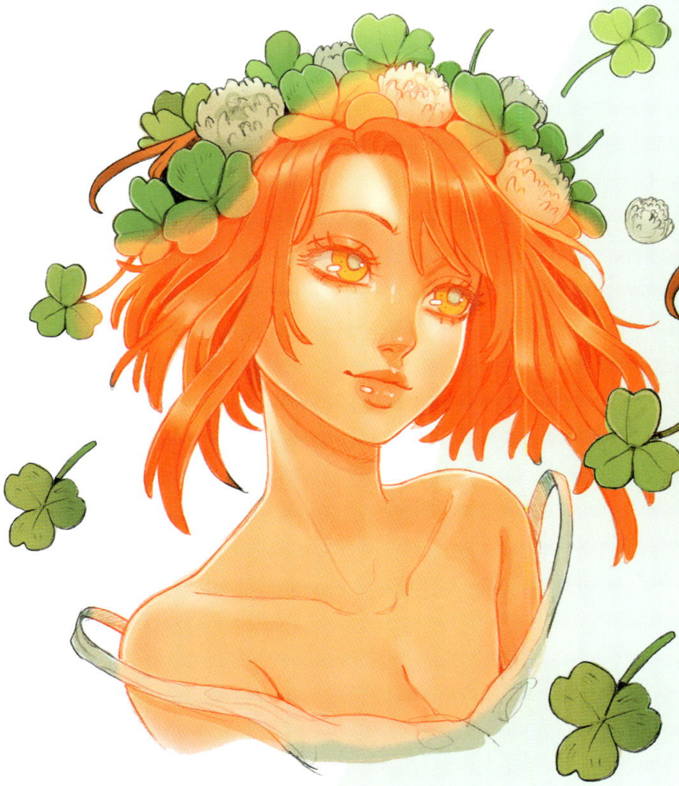

a

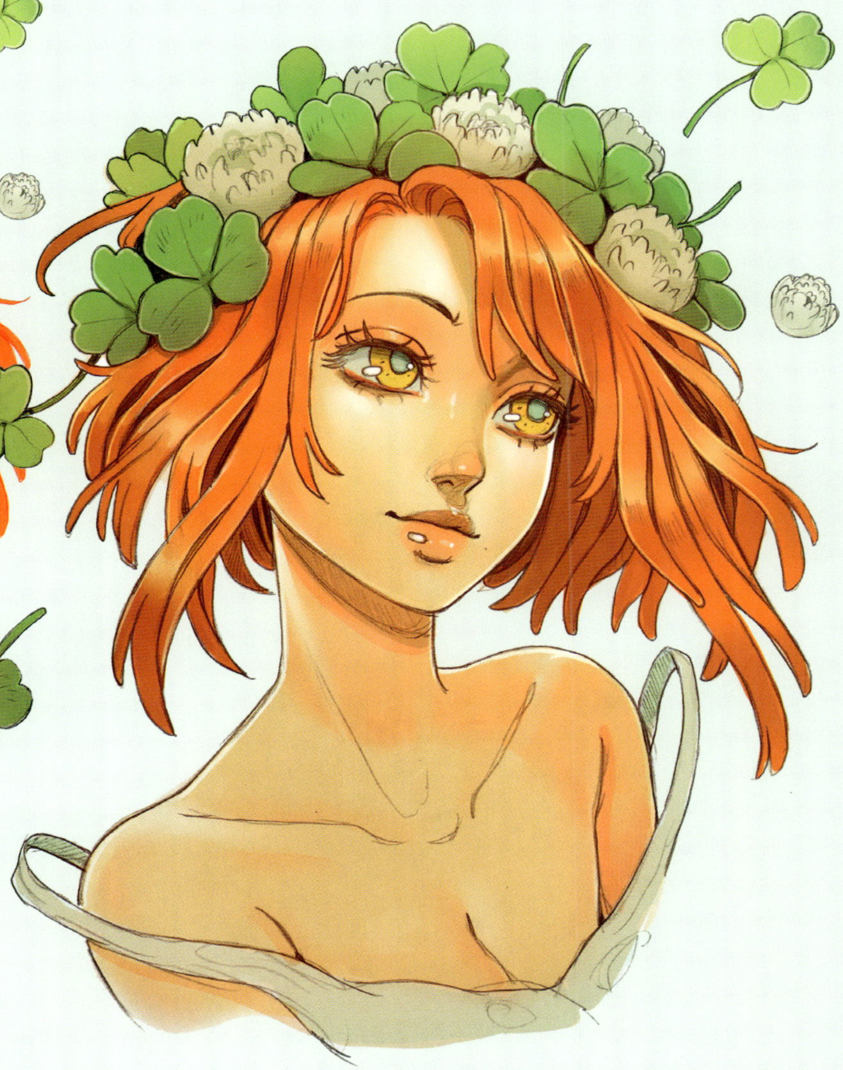

b

## 12 adding a tint

When it comes to tradigital art, this may be one of the most important steps! At this point, you will probably feel like your piece is very gray, especially if you drew all your shadows first with graphite. But you're in luck – the fun part is here! To introduce color into your lines and shadows, you can create a screen layer to tint the entire drawing. This will be the first layer that is placed *above* the initial sketch layer. Create a layer above the original sketch layer and set it to Screen – this layer can be used to add color to areas that feel a bit dim. Often I will use multiple Screen layers for different parts of the drawing to introduce a range of different colors. For this piece, I use a single Screen layer because I want to use the same color for the skin and hair. I use a bright reddish-orange and allow some of the color to bleed into the clover crown to allow for a warm radiance from the hair **(a)**. Next, I use the Gaussian Blur tool to blend the Screen layer and then lower its opacity **(b)**. Feel free to erase some areas if you feel it mutes the color – typically I might erase the eyes or dark outlines I want to keep untouched, such as the nostrils, eyebrows, or corners of the mouth.

use a Screen layer to add a tint

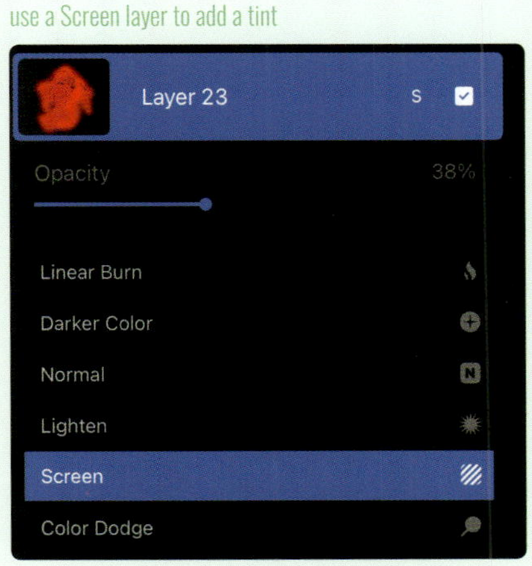

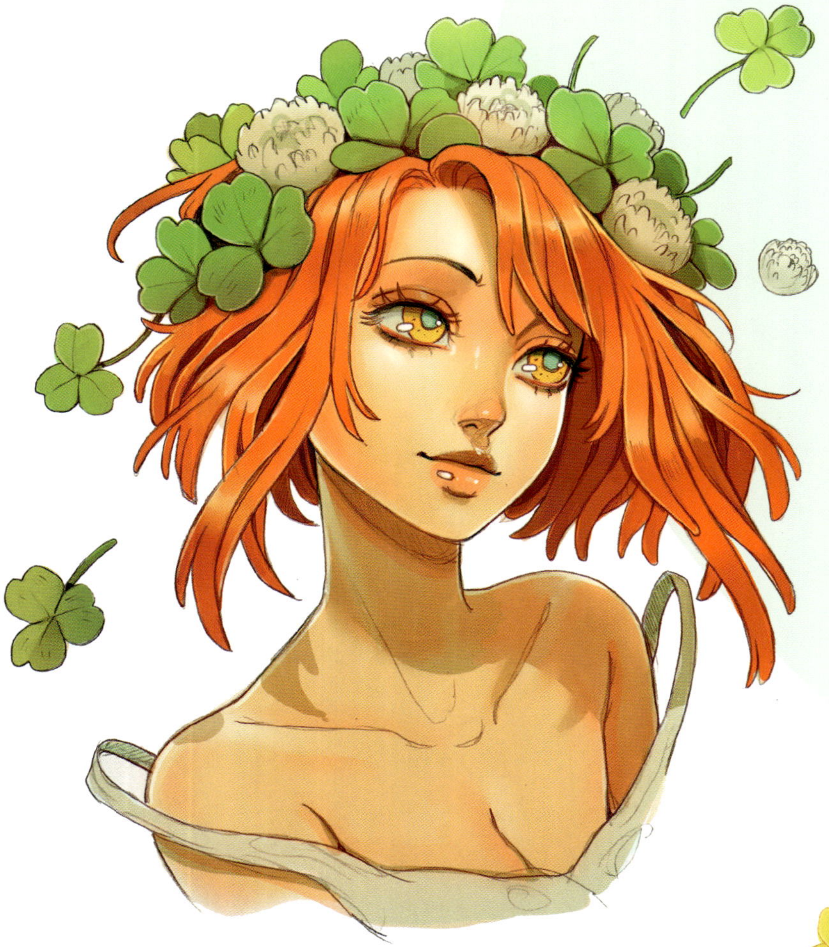

## 13 reintroducing shadows

Through the previous Screen layer application, some of the darkest areas of the image may be softened too much and therefore the contrast is lost. Now is the time to assess the image and decide where to add final shadows back in. I add deep shadows and redefine key areas such as the eyelashes, shadows on the body, and the centers of the clovers.

## 14 creating atmosphere

You'll see this step on most of my pieces. I love making my images look as if they're being engulfed by a bright light. To achieve this effect, you'll once again use a Screen layer positioned above your sketch layer so that it can brighten the outlines. I pinpoint areas around the drawing where light might break through from behind the character (areas such as around the shoulders or between strands of hair) and add a bright color. To give the look of a cool midday color, I use a bright blue; for a warm twilight feel, I select a bright yellow. In this piece I add a bright yellow to make the piece feel summery and warm. I use a Gaussian Blur to diffuse the light, then lower the opacity of the layer until it looks right.

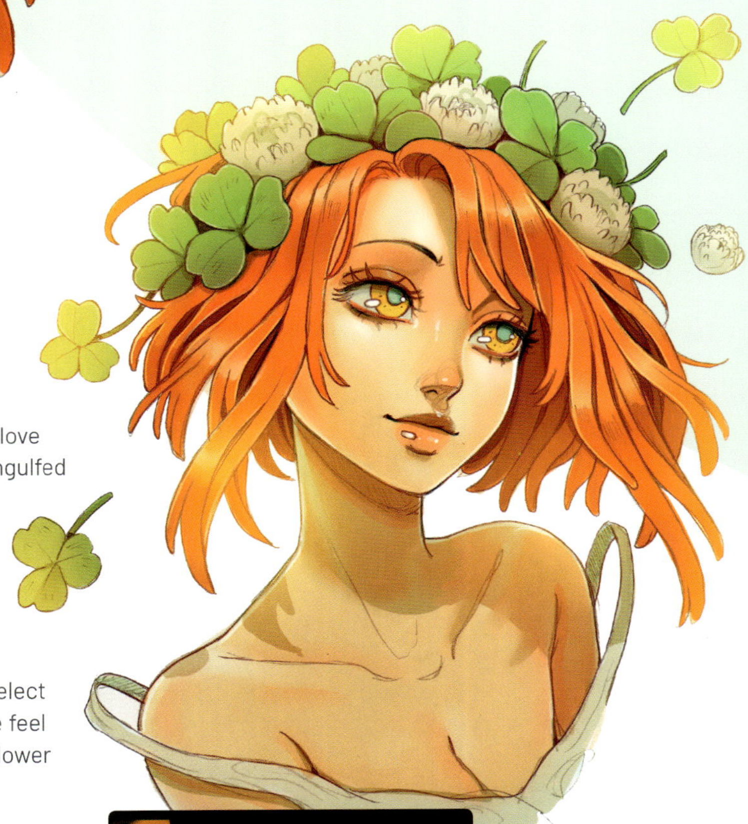

### introduce texture

If you want to add extra texture to your piece to give it a sense of being crafted from traditional media, upload a paper texture file and set it to Multiply. The texture will likely be too intense and busy for the artwork, so you may need to lower its opacity. You can either take paper texture photos yourself, as I did for the photo used here, or you may be able to find stock photos online.

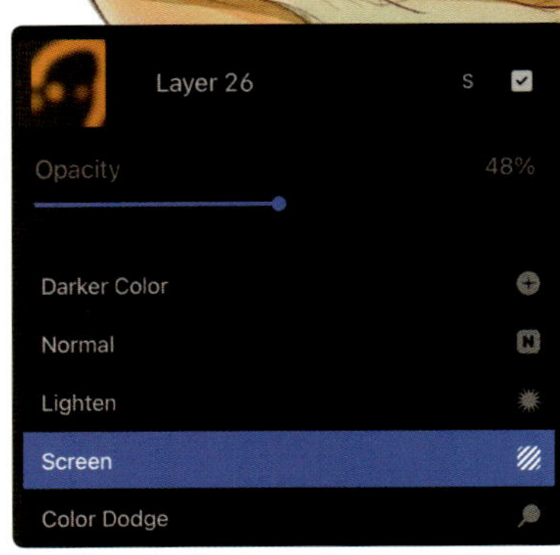


use a Screen layer to brighten the outlines

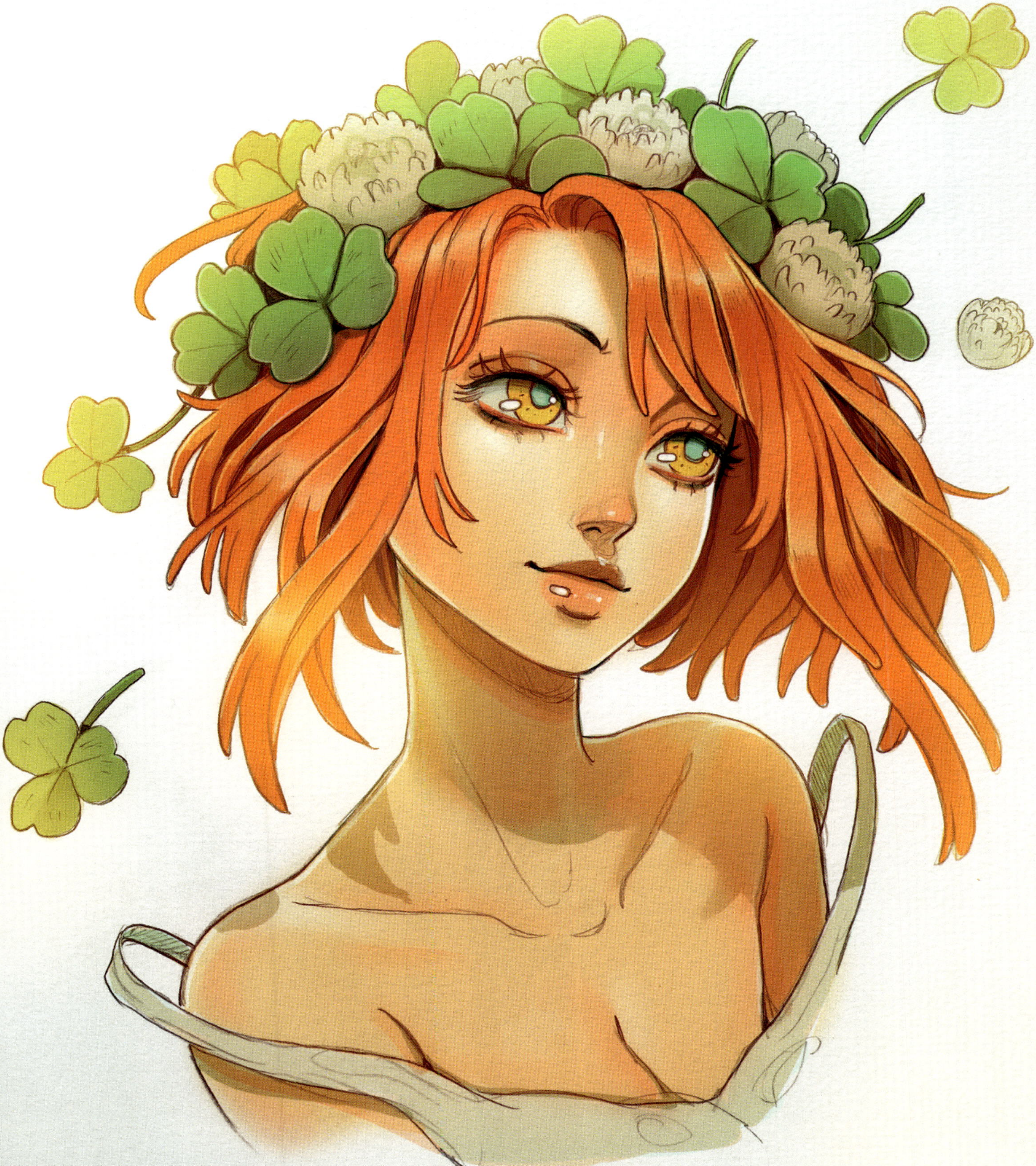

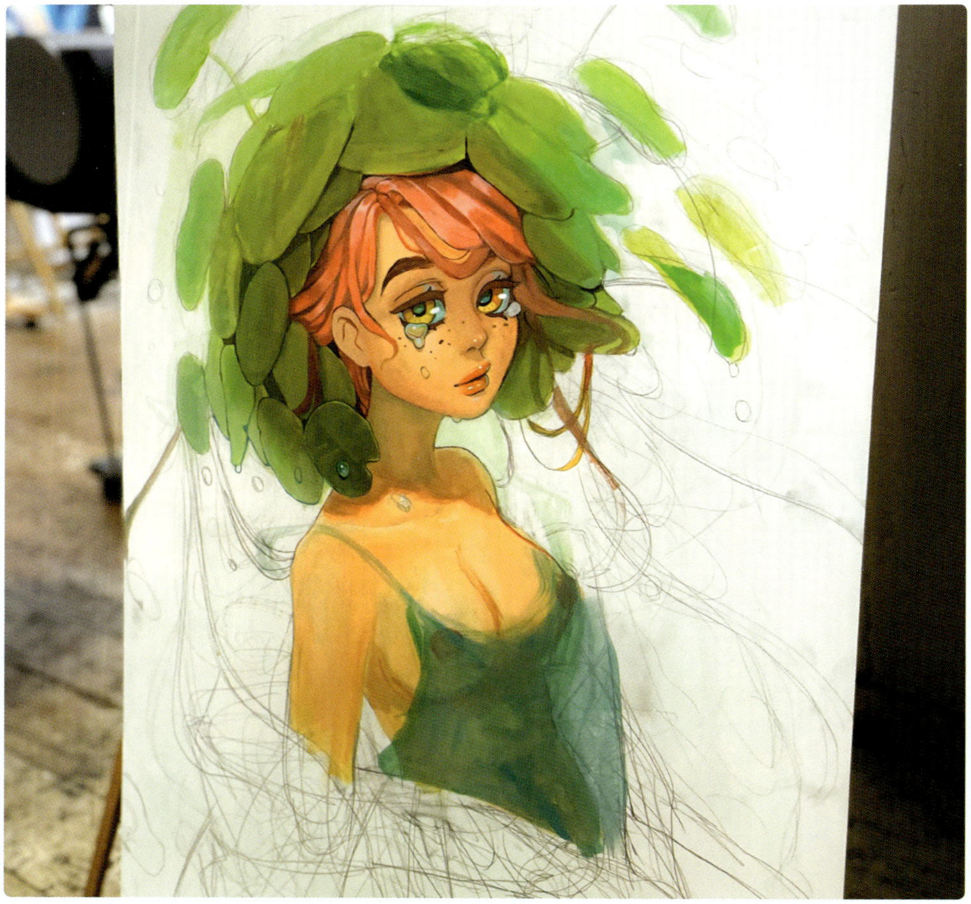

***The Pride of the Wise*** | 2018 (opposite page)
This is still my favorite painting I've ever made, and it's the painting that landed me my first gallery show as well. I was working on it during a local Drink & Draw event. The gallery owners posted a picture of it to social media, which led a gallery in New York to reach out and ask if I'd like to exhibit with them.

***Lily*** | 2020 (this page)
This is the biggest painting I've ever worked on (part of the reason it's not finished yet) and depicts my character Lily, who is also on the cover of this book. She's one of the few characters of mine that I liked enough to recreate multiple times. She represents the beautiful sunny summer days of nature, and has a counterpart named River who represents the cool, moody blue tones of nature instead.

# traditional painting

**I find acrylic paintings the most rewarding art to make. I enjoy working with all mediums but there's nothing quite like having a tangible, one-of-a-kind piece of work that you can hold in your hands. The time commitment for traditional paintings is higher than digital work, so I don't have enough time to create them as often as I would like, but my dream is to create them full time.**

The first time I encountered acrylic paint was during a high-school art class. Up until then I had only used colored pencils or crayons to color in my work, so being able to add a full range of color to my pieces was an exciting thought. However, at school, I wasn't given much instruction on how to work with acrylic paint, as the class ended up being mostly a free period to mess around. I struggled to achieve the desired outcome and felt frustrated with the medium so didn't use acrylic paint much after I graduated. I didn't pick up acrylics again until years later when I met Matt Linares, the painter with whom I share a studio. Initially, I was looking to hire him. In the years between quitting college and developing a career as an artist, I pursued myriad other avenues, one of which was game creation. At the time I met Matt, I was attempting to make a video game and needed an artist to create background assets. I happened upon Matt's artwork in an online game development group and thought his work was spectacular and so I asked if he wanted to help on my project. Although the project was unsuccessful, we stayed in touch and one day I asked if he would be willing to teach me a bit about his traditional painting techniques. Specifically, I was transfixed by his backgrounds – he made exceptional clouds, mountains, and celestial paintings – and much of his work seemed to glow!

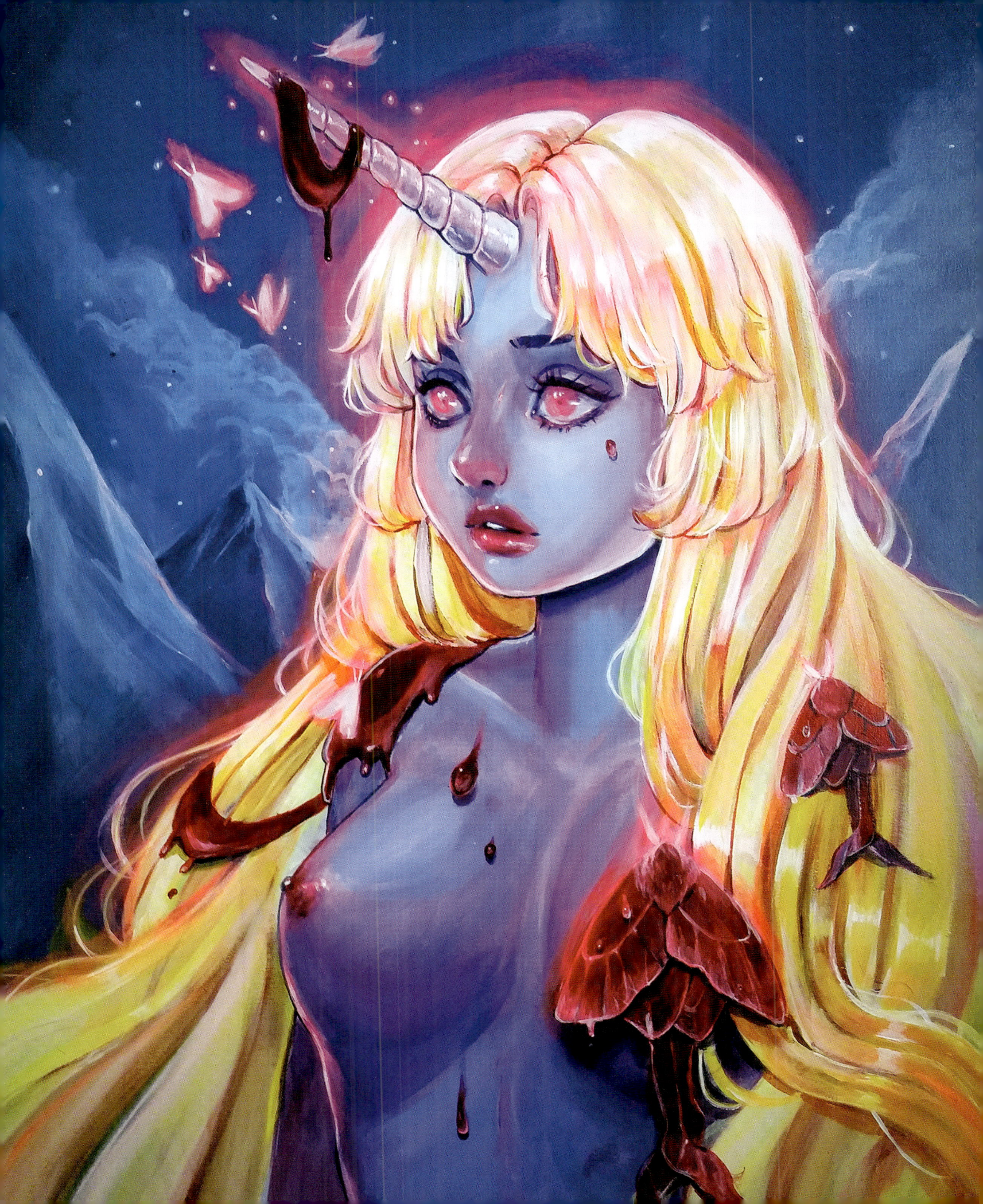

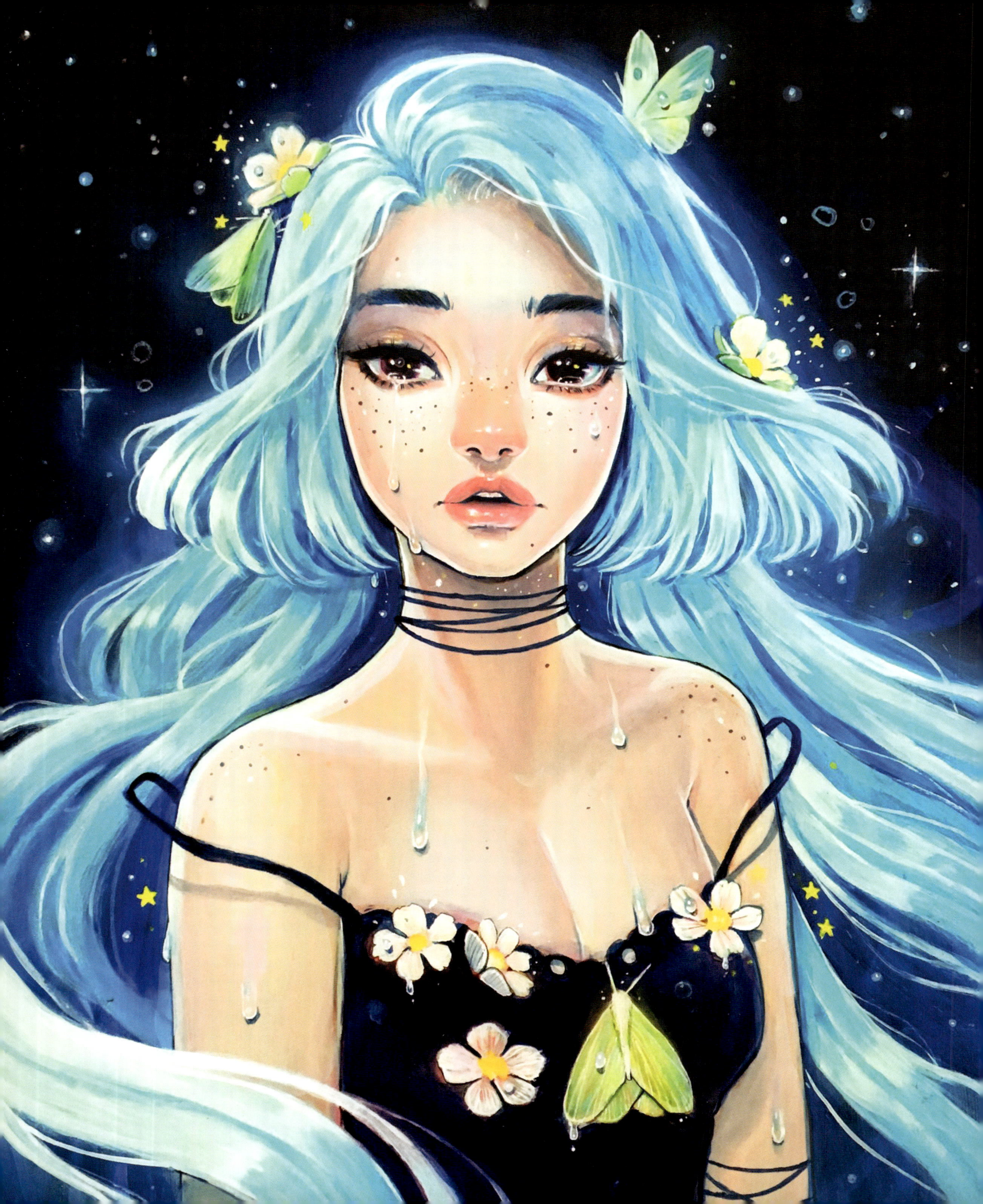

Matt very kindly allowed me to come to his art studio to paint. During those invaluable sessions, I learned from him everything I know about painting with acrylics. I have included many of the helpful tips he shared with me in my tutorial Working with Acrylic on page 94. From using MDF board for its smooth surface and Mega Brushes for seamless backgrounds, to those small bits of technical advice that kick-started my interest in painting again. The lessons were so important to me because I finally felt like I had the direction to create the paintings I wanted.

Even though I had instruction, I wasn't amazing at painting right away. The first painting I made after Matt's instructions was a girl with whipped cream on her head. I was still learning to control paint — I struggled to get the blends I wanted, and to create thin lines. I ended up using a Sharpie marker to create her eyes, nose, and lips. I still have that painting hanging on the wall of my studio space and I laugh whenever I look at those Sharpie marker eyelashes.

The day I sold my first acrylic painting was the day I felt like I'd truly "made it" as an artist. Someone purchased it through my online store and I was so panicked that they were going to change their mind and ask for a refund, or get it in person and feel disappointed, that I had a nightmare about it that night. The first thing I did the next day was ship it out before they could change their mind. It meant so much to me when later they sent me a nice message about how much they loved it, along with a picture of it hanging in their kitchen.

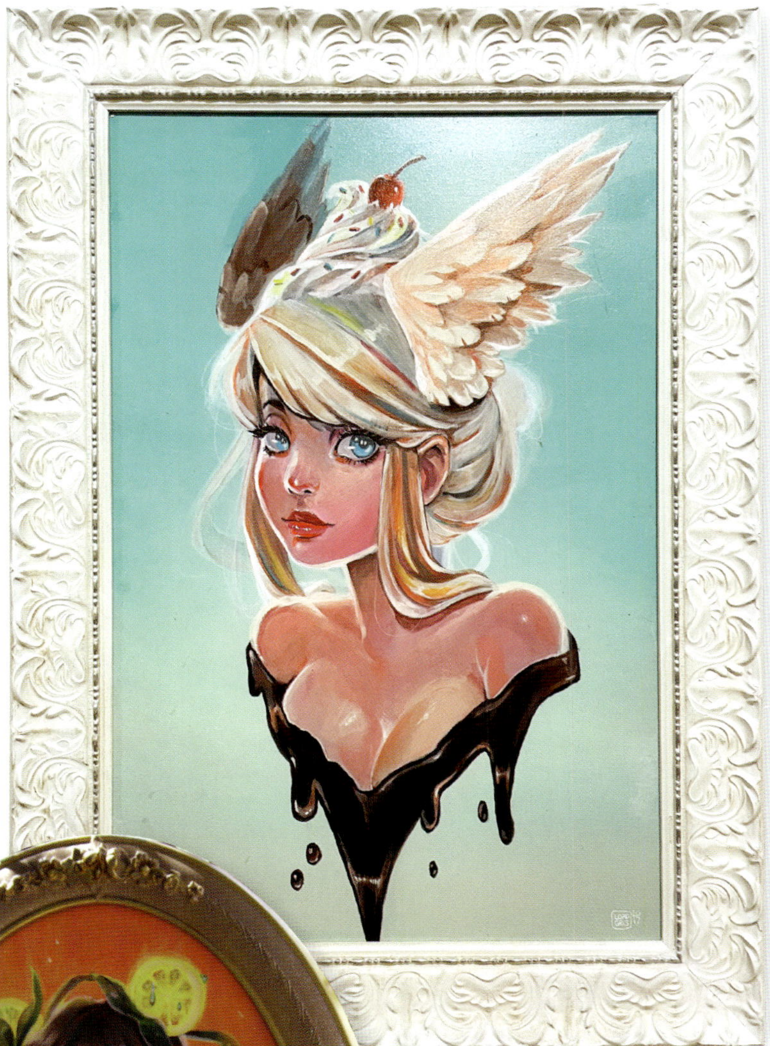

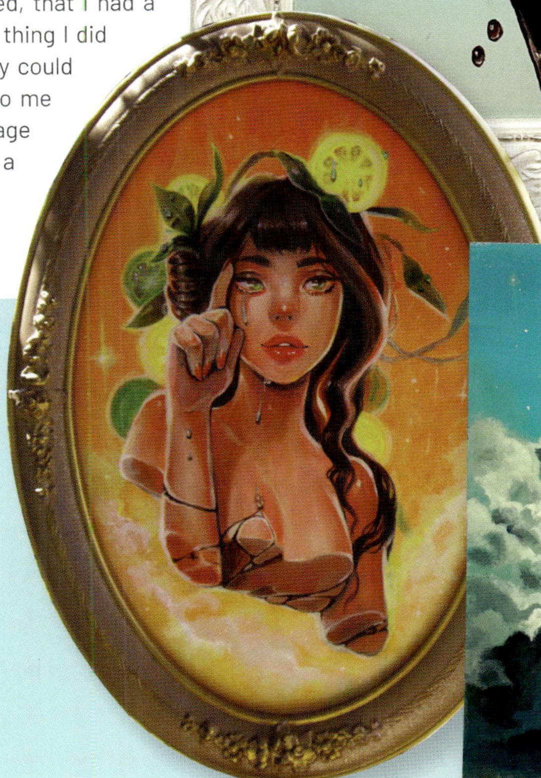

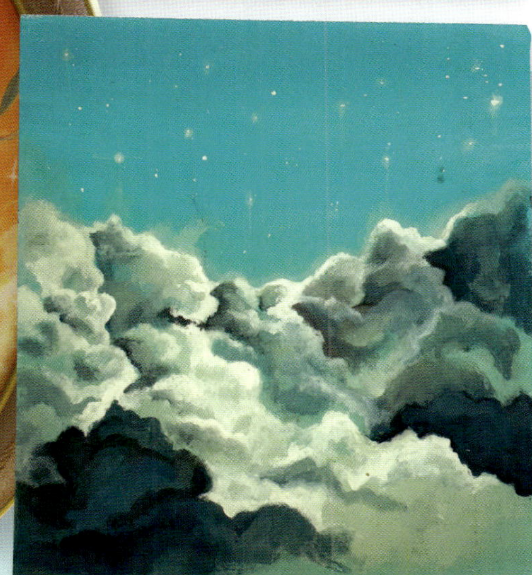

***Water From the Underworld* |** 2018 (opposite page)
I made this painting for my first ever gallery show at Haven Gallery in New York. I was so nervous that no one would want it, but the painting sold on the opening night. I love how the glow turned out.

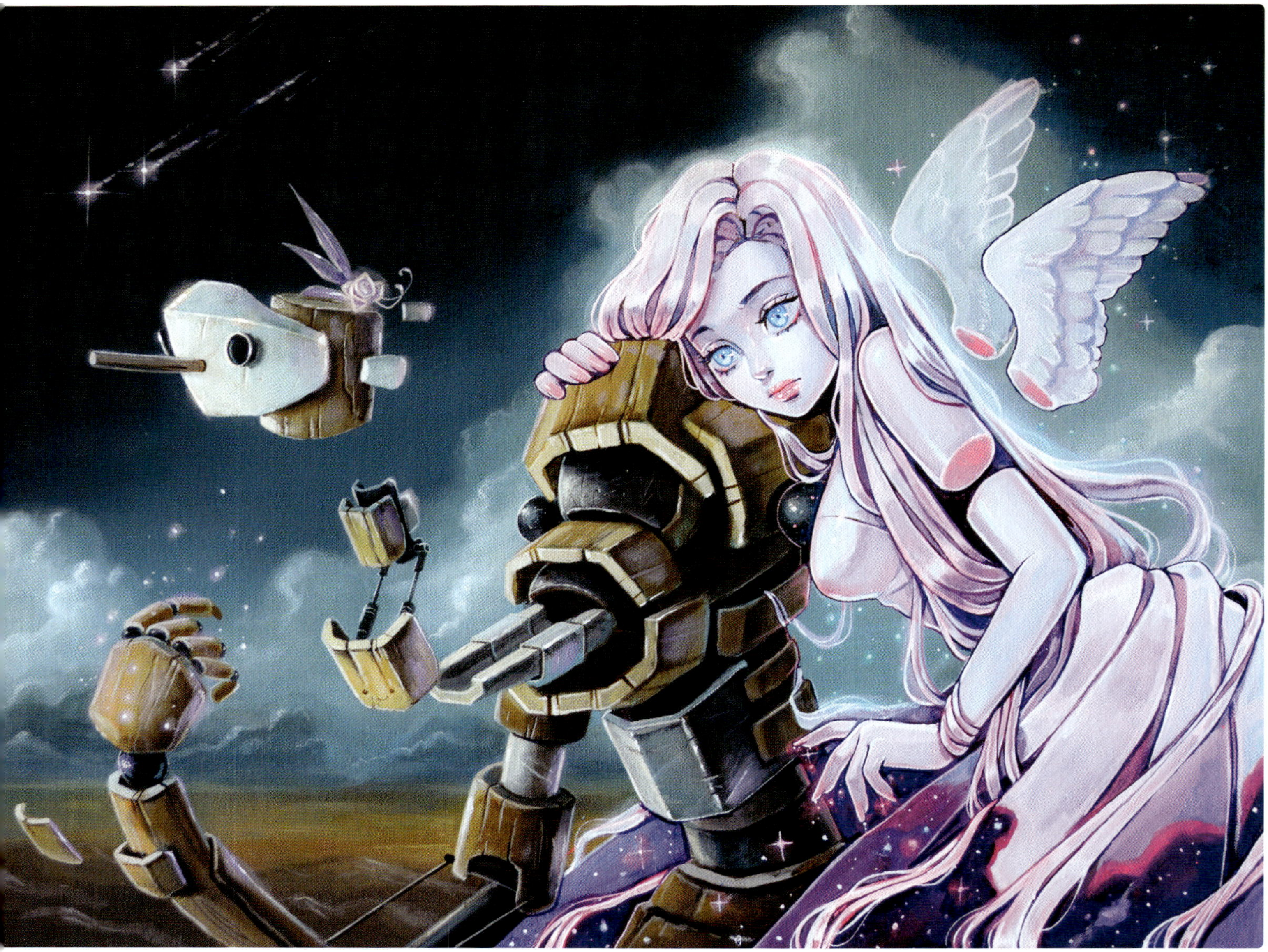

I have now been creating paintings for about six years and I've only just started to feel confident in my ability to create what I envision, but that doesn't mean the creation is without mistakes. There's an absolute graveyard underneath my studio desk of paintings I worked on and discarded because my artistic visions were outside of the realm of my technical skill. It's very frustrating to not be able to accurately depict a concept, but I just kept trying. I even had to restart the acrylic painting I created for the tutorial in this book; in fact, I restarted not once but three times because I messed up the background beyond repair. Creating is never seamless, nor easy, but if you are able to make it to the end, it feels truly amazing. I have big dreams for paintings I want to make going forward, including ones that are life-sized and include full-bodied figures. I'm excited for what the future brings!

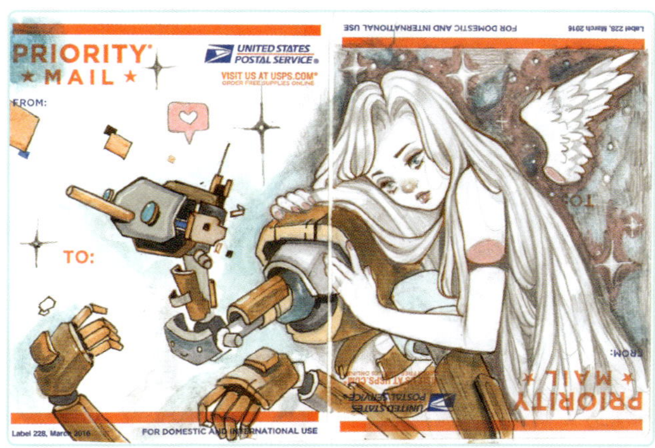

Creating is never seamless, nor easy, but if you are able to make it to the end, it feels truly amazing.

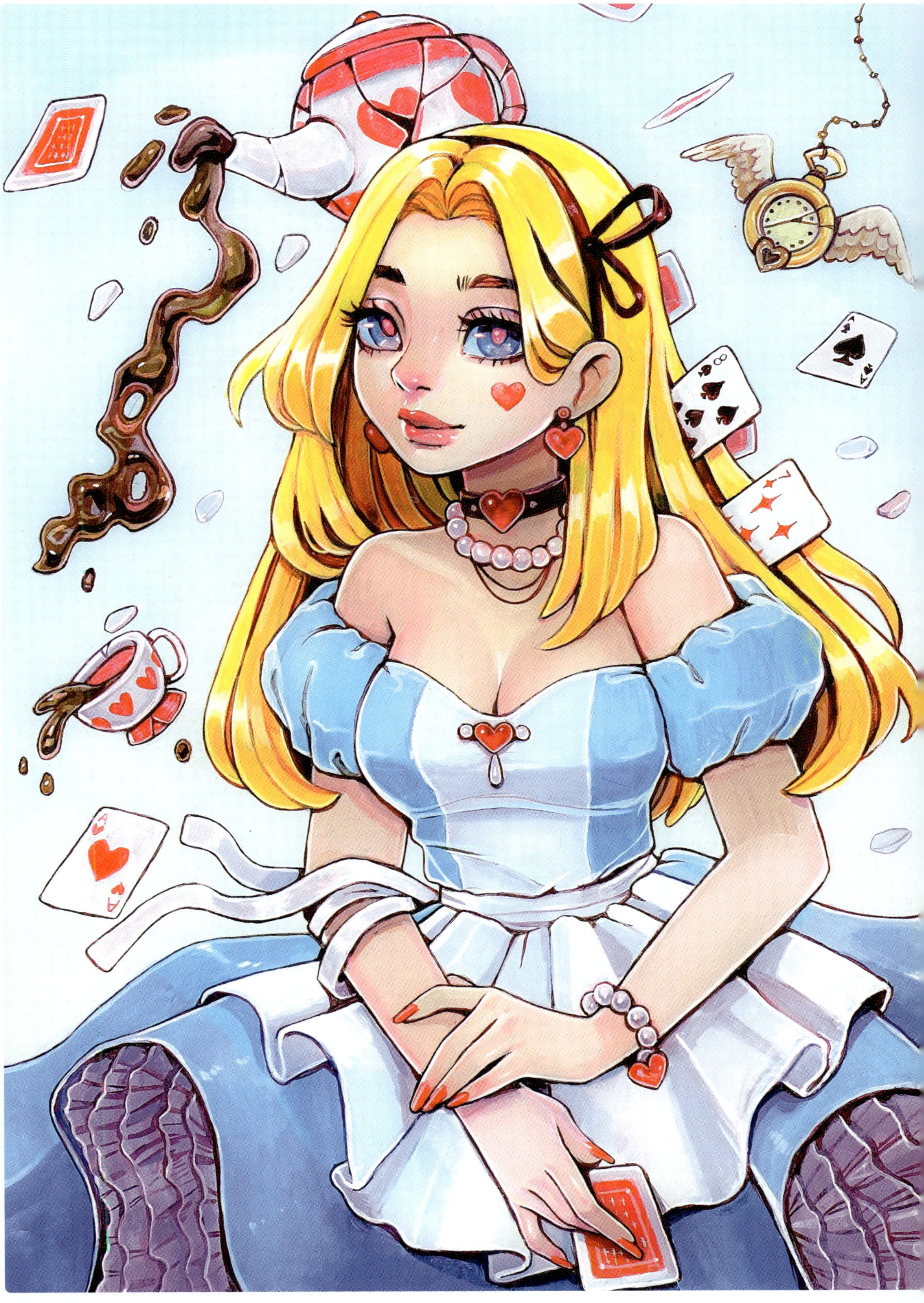

***Matt x Gris Painting*** (opposite page)
A collaborative painting between Matt and me, based on a doodle we made on an old shipping label many years ago.

***Alice* |** 2021 (this page)
*Alice* was made for another show at Haven Gallery. I had a lot of fun with the composition of this piece, allowing the objects to flow from the upper right to lower left.

TUTORIAL:

# working with acrylic

I used to find acrylic paint to be a very finicky and frustrating medium; it felt as if it dried too quickly, and I could never get the sort of blend I was looking for. Once I was given a few tips and introduced to a few mediums, the game changed for me and I got hooked on painting — I think it's one of the most fun ways to create art. Hopefully I can impart a few of the useful tricks I was given to you here.

## 1 make a sketch

Before I start my paintings, I always sketch out what I want to create. I used to not do this and try to wing my paintings, but would get stuck on anatomy mistakes or color choices, and end up ruining the piece.

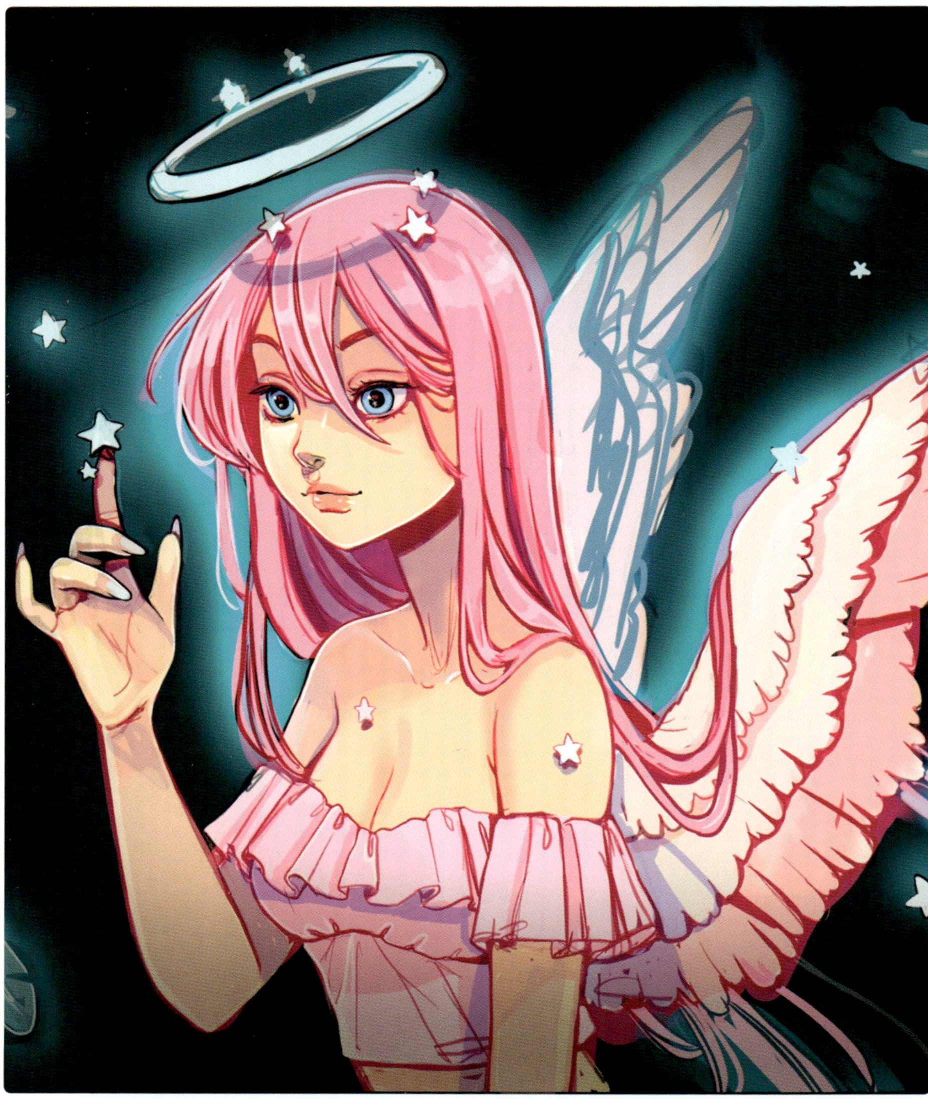

### mock-up medium

Sketches can be made with any medium you want, although I personally prefer to make a mock-up digitally. The benefit of making a digital sketch first is that it's much easier to fix a color or anatomy mistake digitally than in physical art, so any potential problems can be resolved early. Once I am happy with my sketch, it's time to start painting.

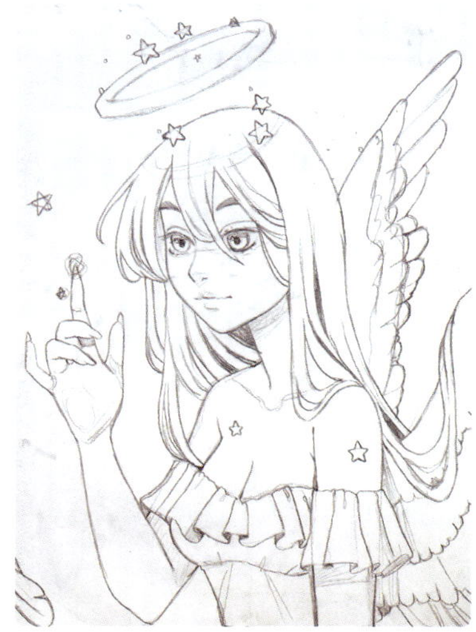

## 2 prepare an mdf board

As mentioned, I prefer to paint on smooth wooden boards instead of canvas – I create my paintings with lots of thin, sleek layers and find the texture of canvas gets in the way of how I prefer to work. I prepare the surface with a layer of gesso to create a sealed bright white surface. I use MDF and an extra-large, soft rounded brush for this. A cheap, low-quality brush is to be avoided as it might leave bristles in the gesso. If the gesso feels too thick when applying you can add a little water to it.

When covering the board, brush diagonally as well as back and forth to create an even, streak-free blend. Then, use fine sandpaper to smooth the surface until it is velvety to the touch. If you think your layer of gesso came out too thin, you can always add another layer and sand it again.

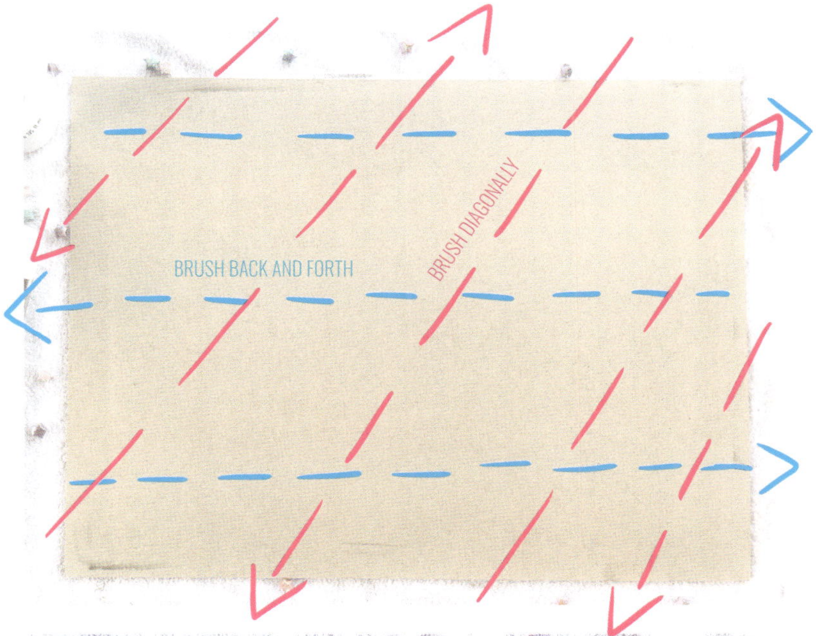


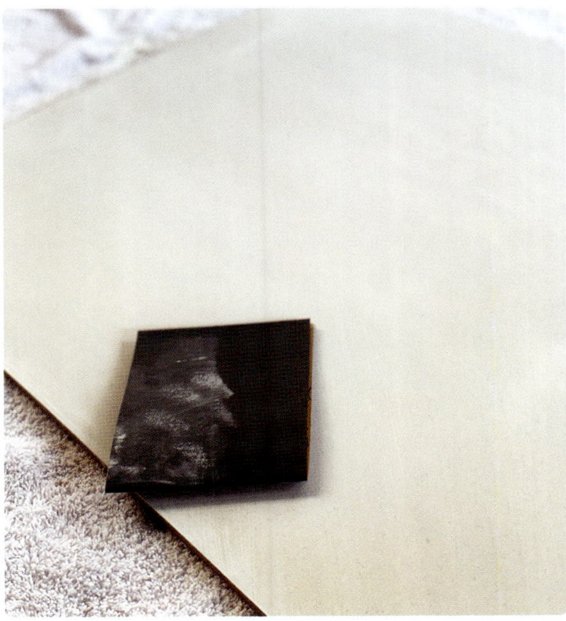

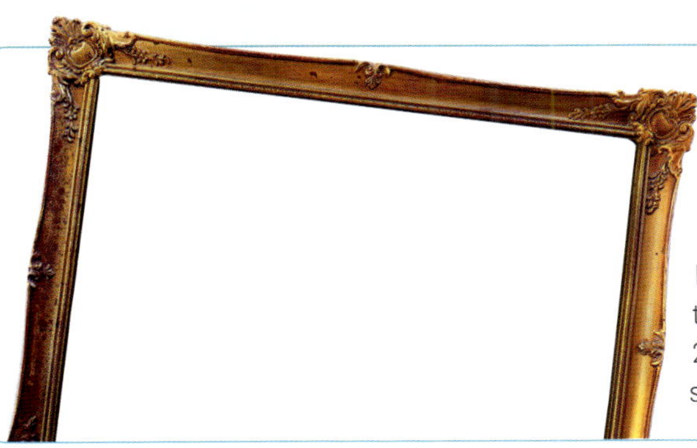

### consider frame sizes

MDF is available through most hardware stores in large sheets that you can then divide into multiple canvases. It's fairly inexpensive and can be cut in store for you. When cutting my boards, I try to pick traditional frame sizes in case I want to frame the painting afterward. For this painting, I cut my board to 20in x 24in (51cm x 61cm). I generally avoid making my paintings smaller than 12in x 16in (30.5cm x 40.5cm).

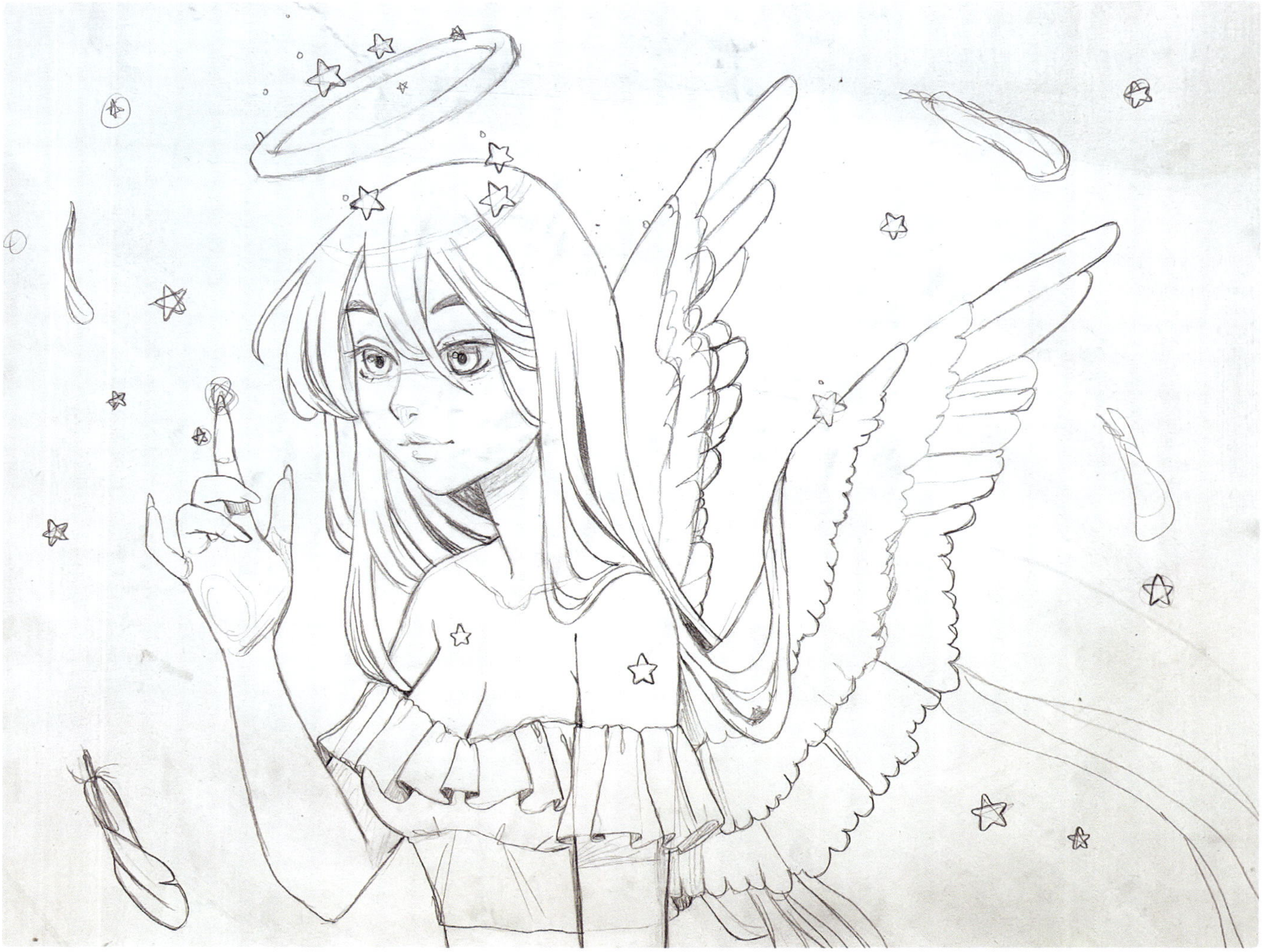

## 3 add the sketch

There are many ways to add your sketch to your canvas. If you are confident in your freehand abilities then you could sketch straight on to the canvas. My favorite method is using a digital projector to simply trace the original digital sketch. You do not need a high-quality projector for this since you are merely tracing an image.

Another way to transfer your image is to print it out on a regular piece of paper (or on multiple pieces and tape them together depending on the size of your piece). Cover the back of the paper with graphite and then trace over the top of the image while it's sitting on the canvas to imprint the line work on to the canvas (it's a messy option and not my favorite, but it does the trick). I usually use a light pencil to sketch at first and then a darker pencil for my final lines. Darker is better as you will want the lines to show up underneath your initial color layers, so don't worry about being too heavy-handed. If you go too light you might lose your lines during the base layer.

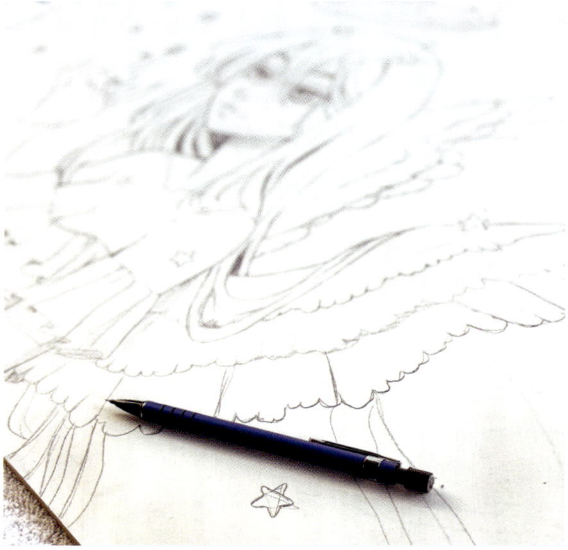

## 4 paint the background

As paintings are built back to front, it's easiest to paint the background first and the character second. Normally, if I'm painting a more light-colored background, I will actually paint the background color before even adding my sketch. However, since this background is so dark, I add the sketch first and paint the dark parts around it. When filling in large areas, it's best to use large flat brushes as often as you can because they apply color evenly. As I get closer to the sketch, I use a smaller flat brush – don't worry about overlapping the sketch a little bit, it doesn't need to be perfect!

I used a mix of black and teal to create this background color, adding more condensed amounts of black around the edge of the painting and making the area around the character more teal to achieve a slight glowing effect. If you're struggling to get an even blend because there are too many background elements in the way, paint over them and add them back in later (you will see I did this with some of my stars here).

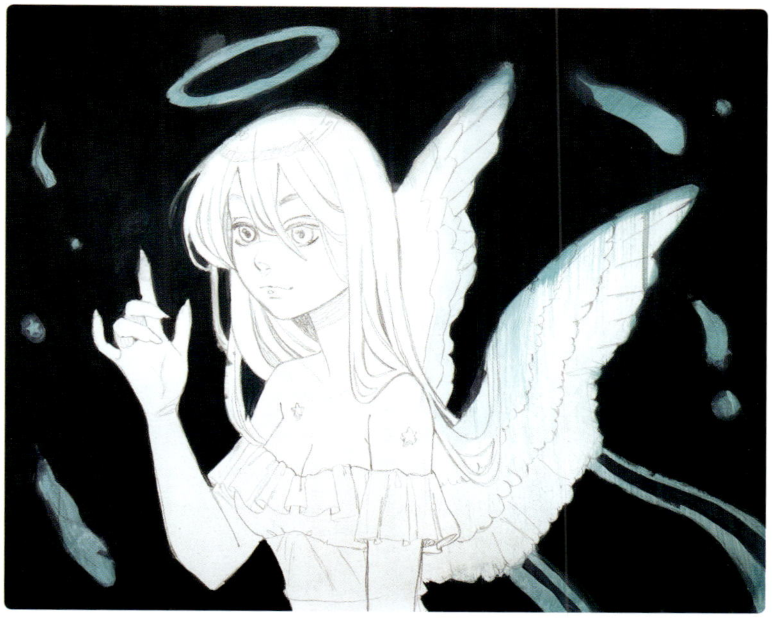

## 5 apply base colors

You can now begin to color in your painting. Lay down all the base colors – this is not going to look pretty, in fact for a long time your painting is going to look like a disaster. This doesn't mean you're failing or doing a bad job, it just takes a while for everything to come together, so it's important to be patient with yourself as well as the process. Just as with the background layer, this doesn't need to be perfect but it should be very thin! If you ever feel like you've laid down paint too thickly, you can always sand it down. Sanding is your eraser for this painting process. Sometimes an area may dry too quickly or just build up too thickly by accident and I have to sand it down and repaint – it's totally normal!

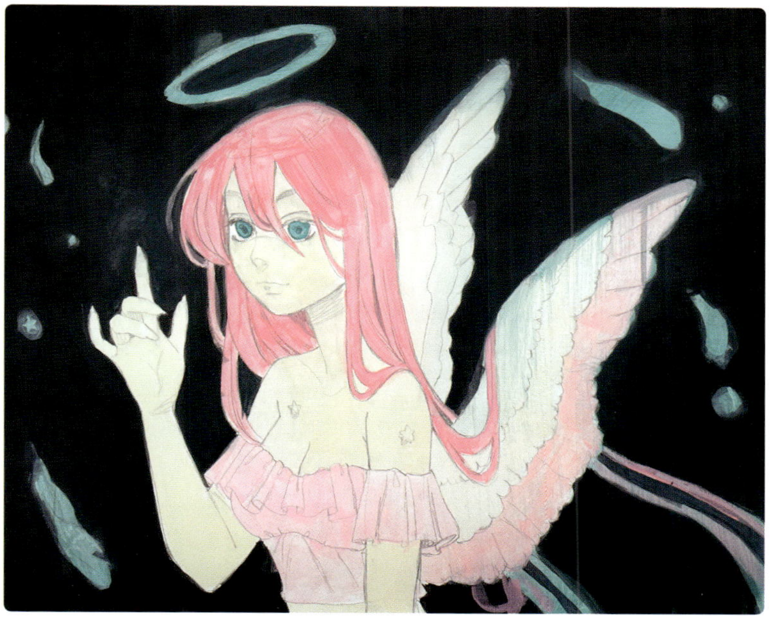

### even blending

My secret for getting very thin layers lies in the type of paint. I used to use very heavy-body acrylic paint and get frustrated when things weren't blending. Even worse, to thin it out I would add water, which would just result in a very uneven looking wash across my art. I now swear by Liquitex fluid acrylic paints, which are fully opaque in color but mix and move fluidly, resulting in a beautiful even blend across the canvas.

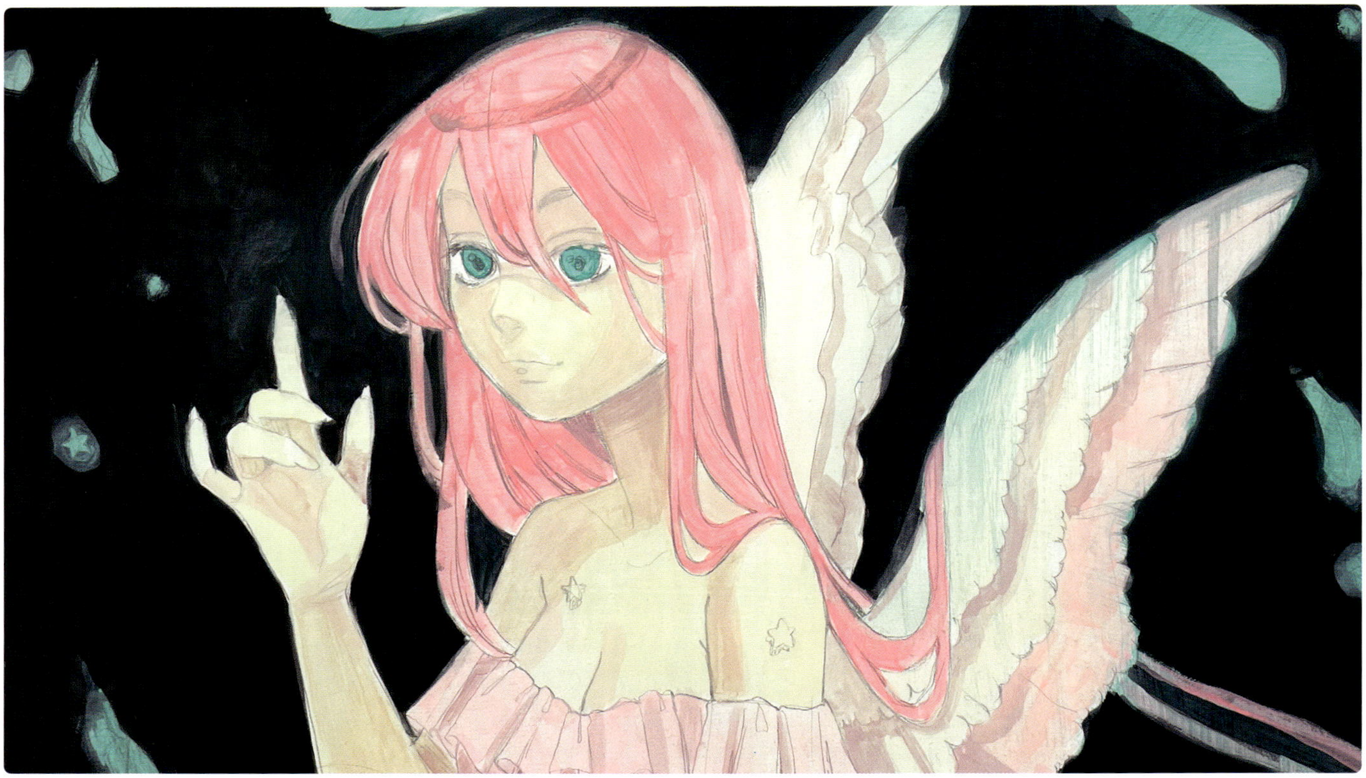

## 6 shadows

Once again, using a very thin layer, paint in all the shadows for your piece. I usually start very light with my shadow colors, beginning with warm tones. As I progress in the rendering process, I build up the depth and apply much darker hues. At this stage however, I am just painting in the loose starting points for the shadows.

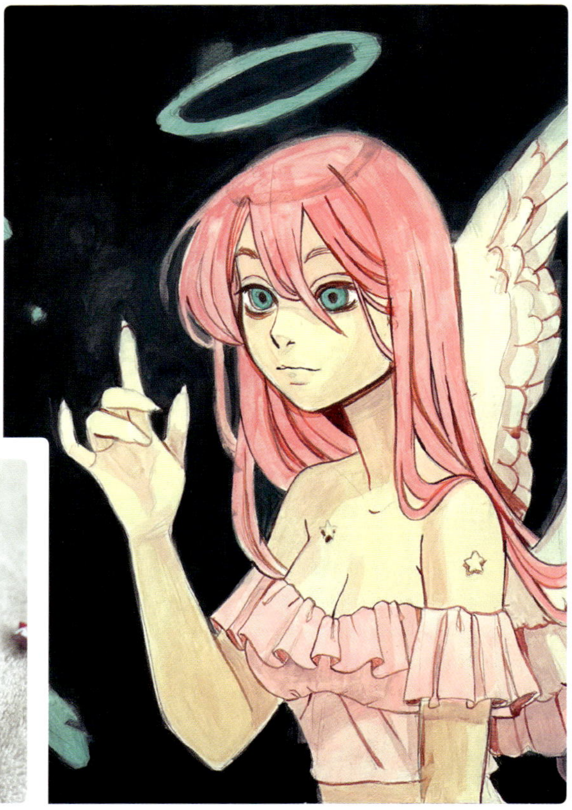

## 7 redefine line work

While many people wait until the very end to add line work, I like to add it in before the final render. I find that allowing the lines to build up under the rendered layers keeps the piece from feeling too flat and cartoonish. When I line the piece, I use a long, thin bristled brush and work with a burgundy or light-brown colored paint because I don't like my initial lines to be too dark. Using a fluid acrylic is especially helpful during this stage; avoid using full-bodied acrylics here as they do not have flow and can cause uneven and disjointed lines. If your character has eyelashes, strands of hair, or other small details, don't add them yet! Leave those until after you render the face, otherwise they'll get buried in the paint.

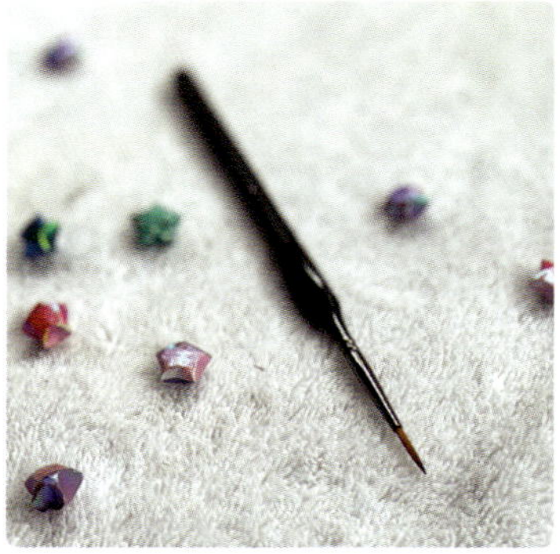

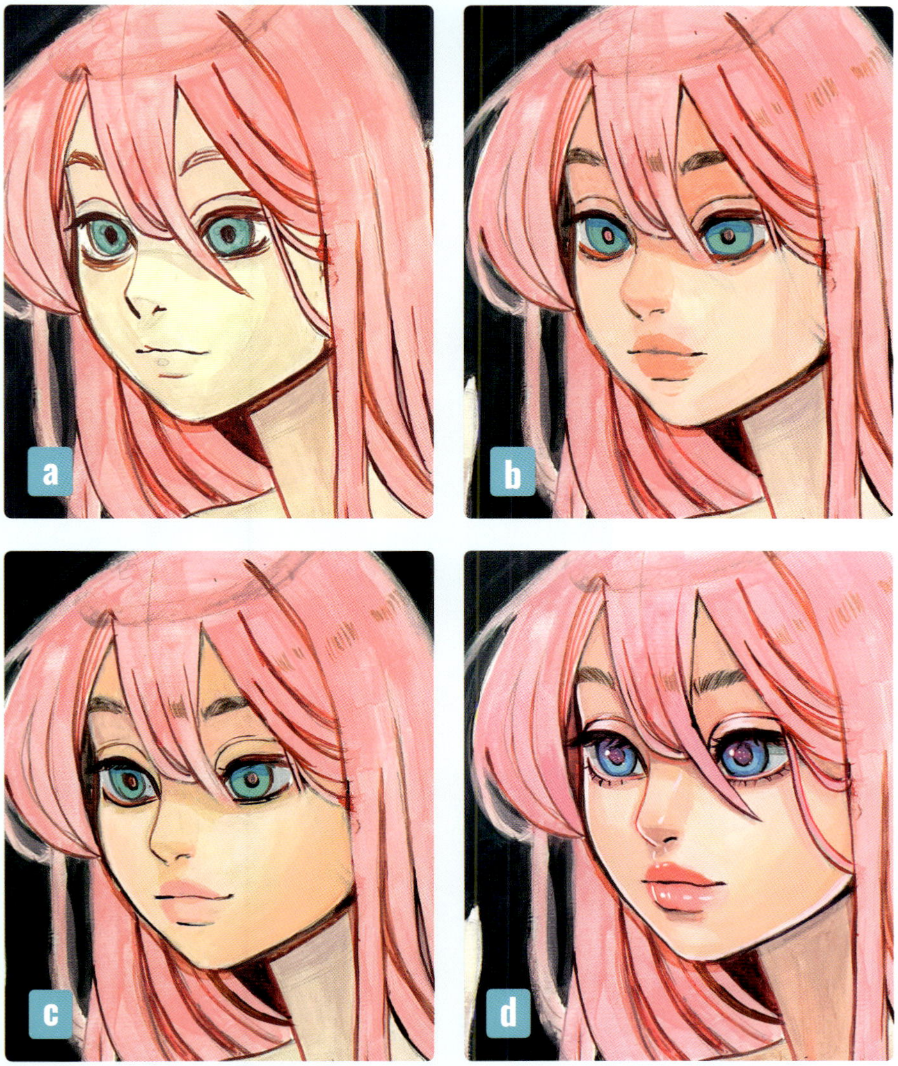


## 8 the face

When rendering, I start with the face, and match the rest of the painting to it. The face will take multiple layers of paint to completely render. It will look messy at first, but as the paint builds up over time, you will start to achieve a smooth, even blend. I try to blend all aspects of the face each time I apply a layer by adding the darks and lights, and brushing them together before they dry. I repeat this multiple times, layer after layer. You will never achieve a perfect blend in one layer, but the build-up of thin layers gives the illusion of perfectly blended color. Be patient — it may feel frustrating to paint the same thing over and over, but you'll be happy in the end!

I'm very sparse with highlights on the face, but when I do add them (such as on the eyelids, lips, or nose) I choose a bright color, usually a hot pink, and mix it in with whatever skin tone I'm using. Then I will use only the tiniest dot of white paint right in the center.

Images **a–e** show how any individual layer is probably going to look bad for a while; it took me 7–10 layers to blend everything. With each layer, the blend gets a little smoother until it's finally the even transition of colors I want.

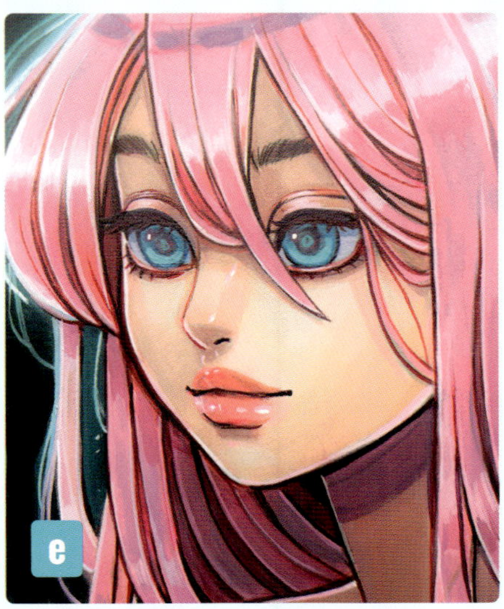


### digital corrections

I often struggle with painting eyes – you'll notice they change between each stage above. If you feel uncertain about a part of your painting, take a picture of it, upload it to your favorite digital painting program, and explore different ways to fix it. I did this for the eyes as they didn't feel quite right.

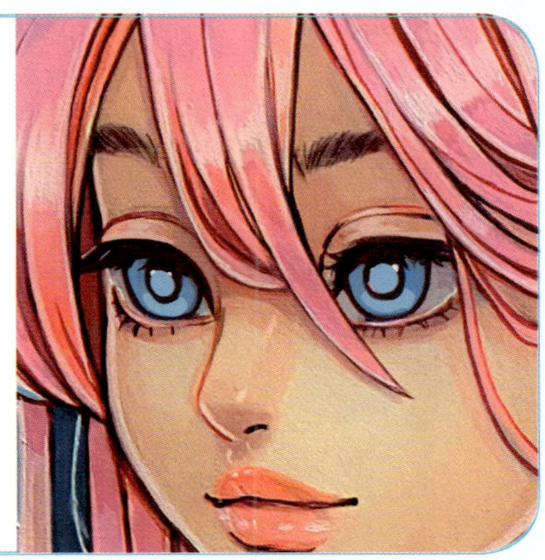

## 9 the hair

Because the hair is made up of many lines **(a)**, I use the same long, thin brush that was used for the line work, and a small flat brush for filling in the large blocks of color. First, I block the hair into general lights and darks, adding shadows, especially around the neck, and highlights to the bangs and the top of the head. Then I begin to line the sections of the hair with light and dark lines **(b)**. For a more detailed look into how I create hair, see page 142. While that tutorial is digital, the same general method is used here.

I begin to create the glow effect by lining the outside of the hair with a fully saturated teal color. Use your thin brush to create stray hairs that catch the light. For the strands closest to the viewer, I use pale pink. However, for the strands I want to push further back (such as the flyaway hairs near the bangs) I use the same bright teal that I used to create the glowing effects **(c)**.

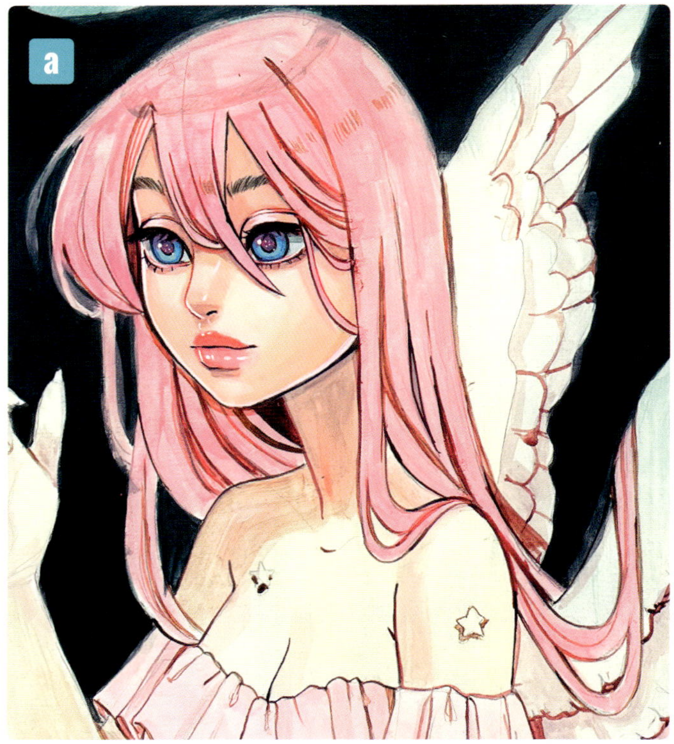


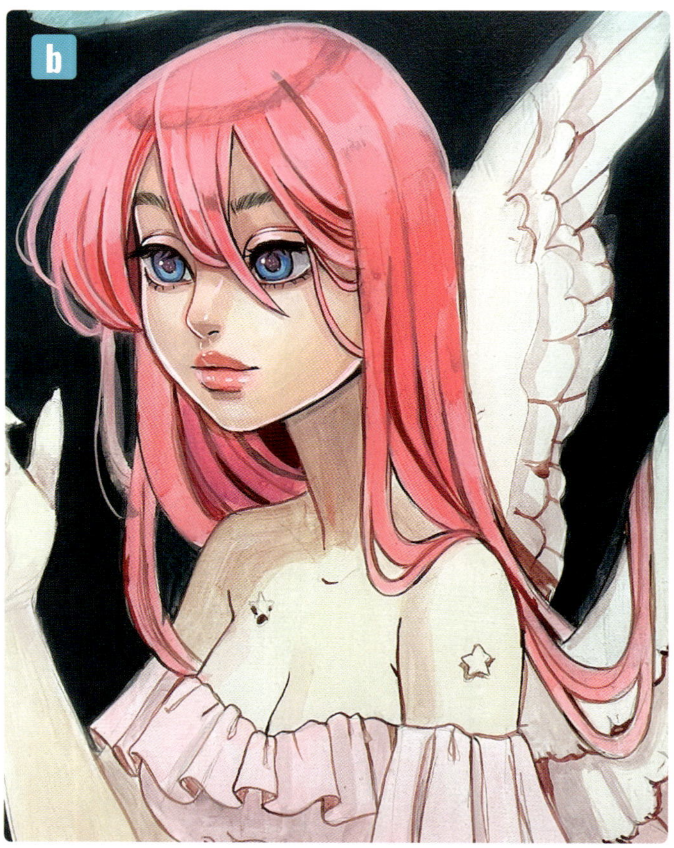


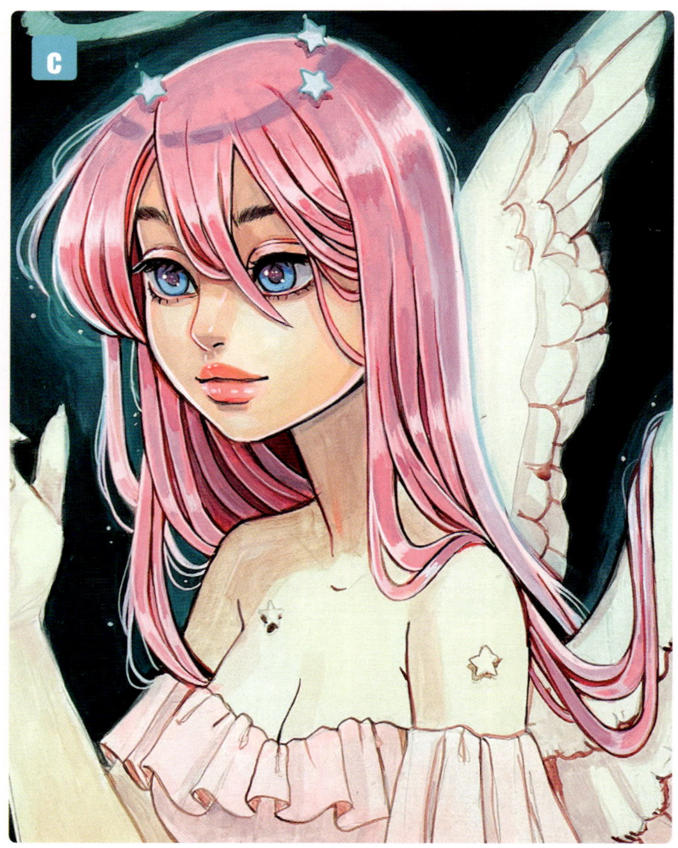

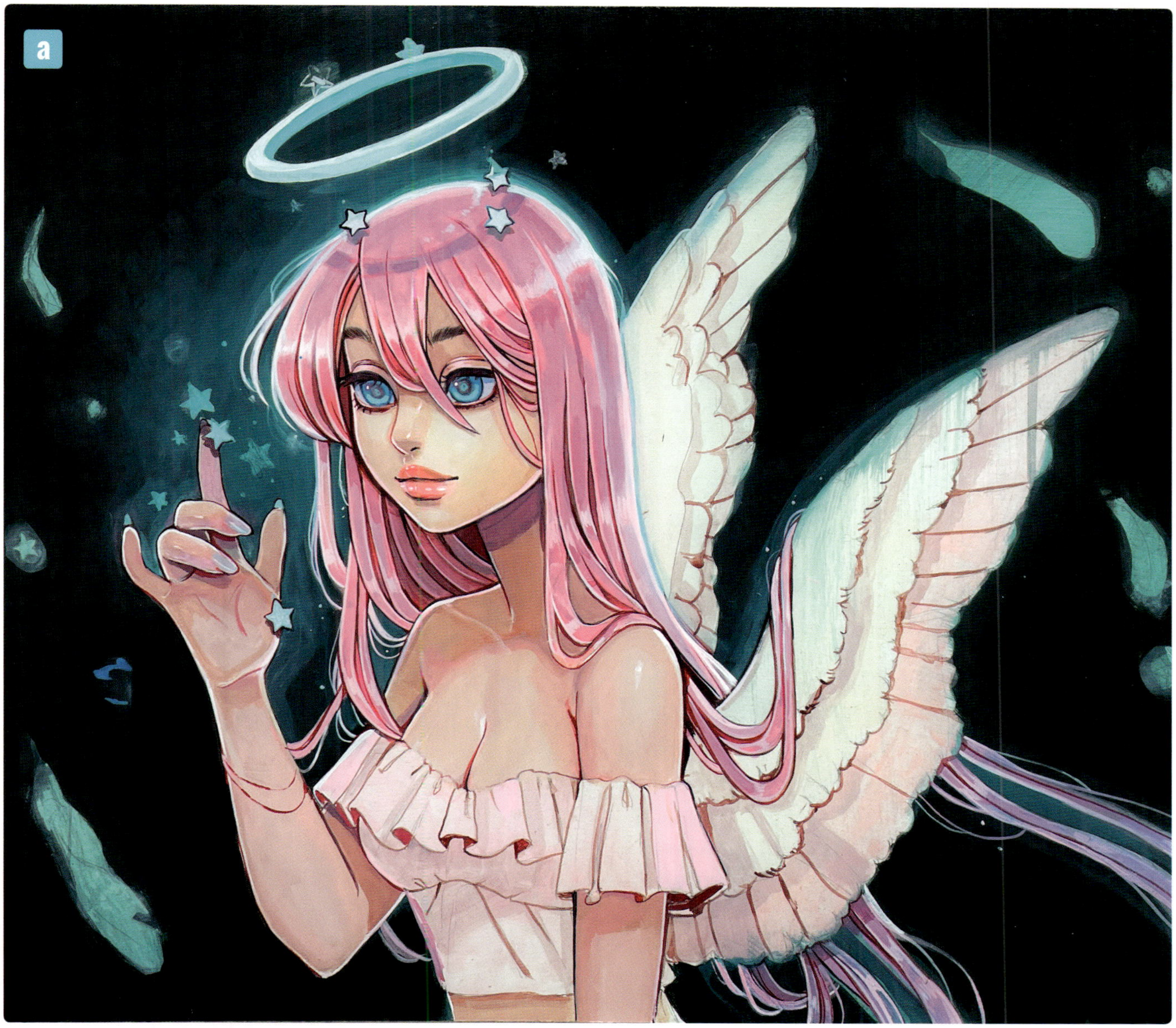

## 10 blending the body

This process should be fairly similar to how you blended the face — it takes patience and several layers to get a smooth blend. I want the face to be the focal point so I make sure that no parts of the body are as bright as the face **(a)**. To create the deep shadows that fall over the neck and shoulder, I mix a bit of dark blue in with the skin color. When laying down the shadows, I leave a bit of red shadow around the rim so you can feel the warmth of the light creeping into that shadow. Since this painting has a luminous blue light surrounding the character, I blend the skin tone with the same teal color I'm using for the backgrounds to add rim lighting to the shoulders **(b)**.

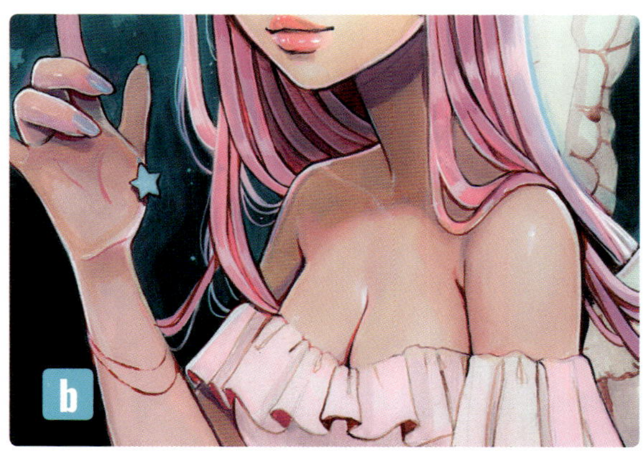

## 11 clothes

At this stage I paint the clothes, which feels like a mix of rendering skin and hair together. Clothes have a lot of line work but also a lot of open spaces that need to be blended **(a)**. I create strong contrast in the clothes, making the undersides of the folds one of the darkest parts of my figure **(b)**, and the parts that catch the light some of the brightest **(c)**. I also add lots of reflected blue light around the edges to give the clothes a contoured feel **(d)**.

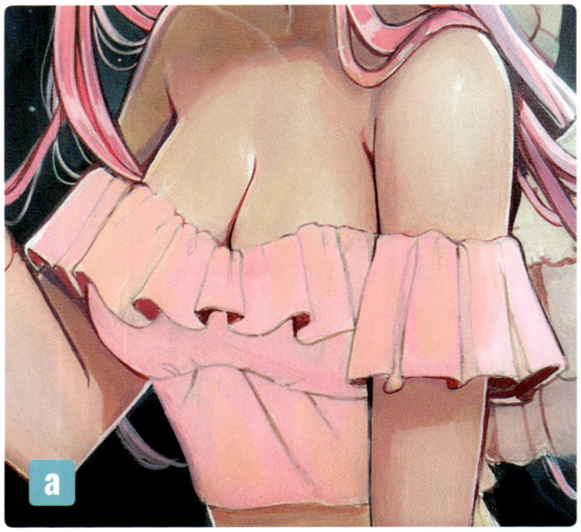


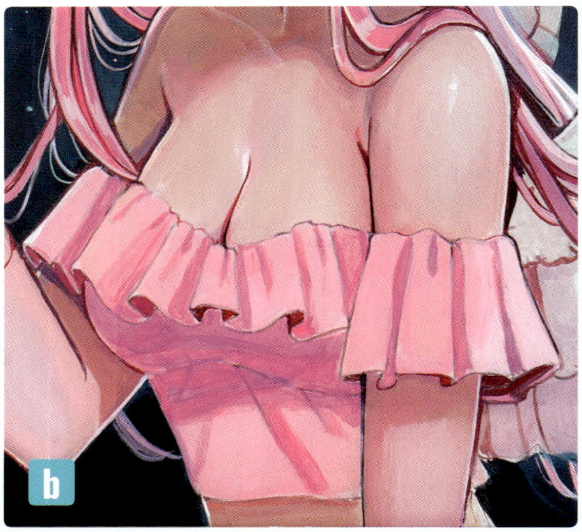


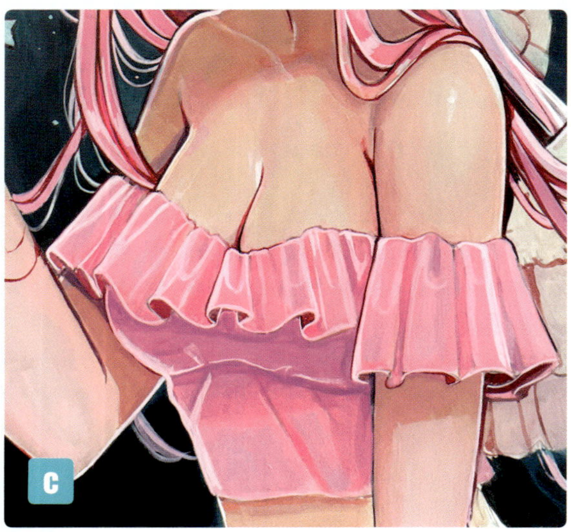


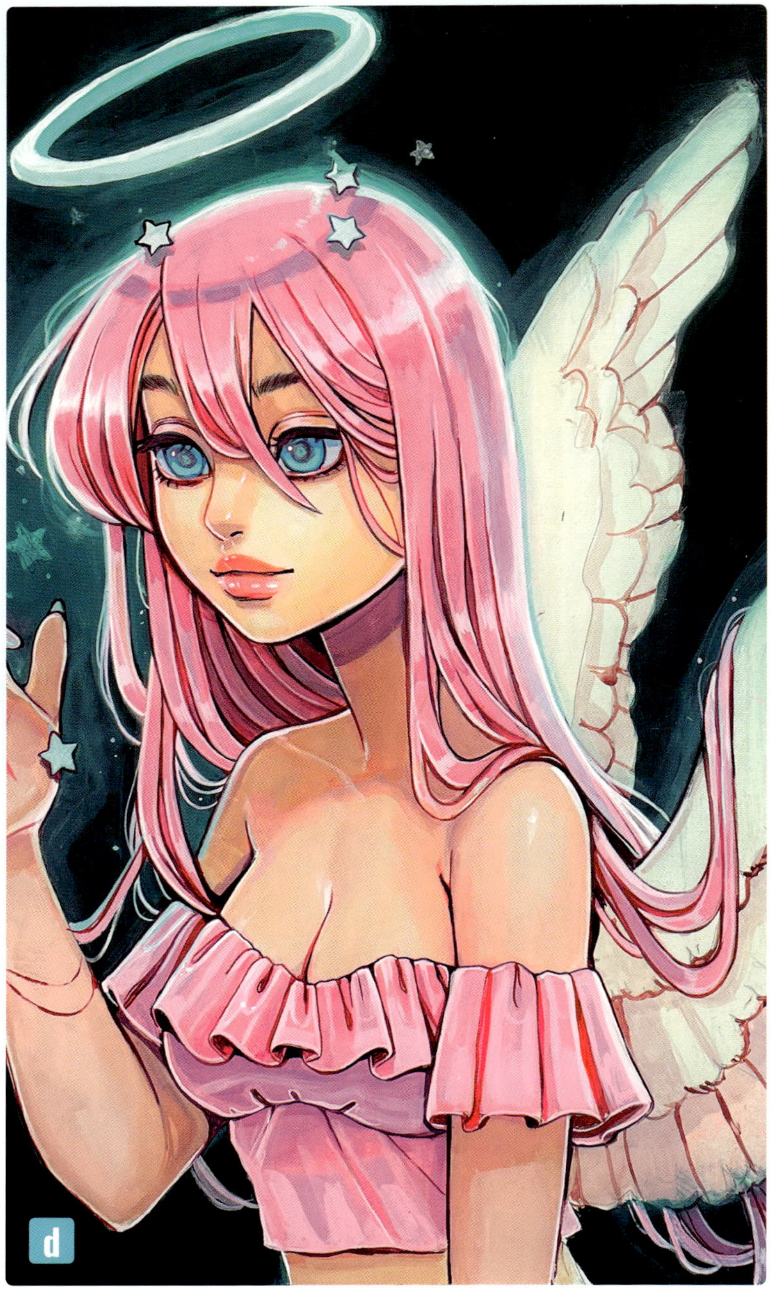

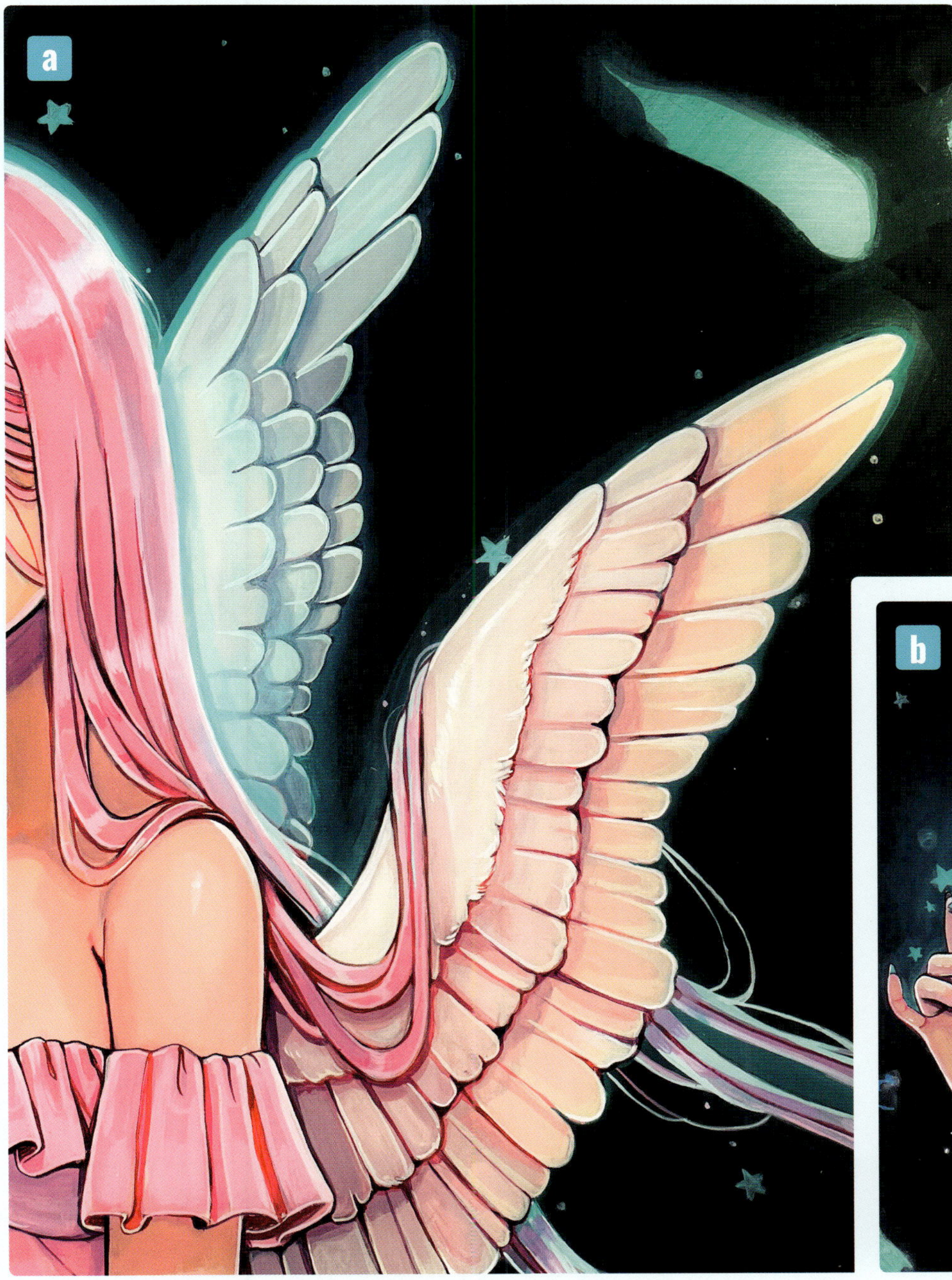


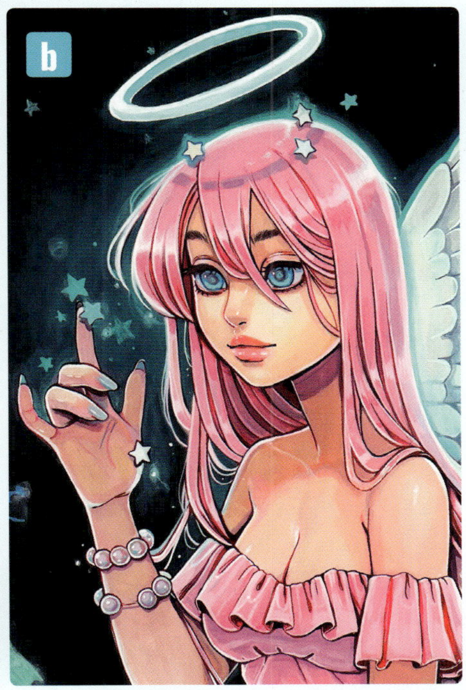


## 12 wings

On the wings, I work from bottom to top. I shade the lower layer first, then the middle, and finally the top layer. Feathers cast soft shadows that will not be as dark or aggressive as other shadows I've added to this piece, but adding these soft shadows creates distinct layers on the wings. Because I want the wing at the back to be pushed into the background and less of a focal point, I mix in a bit of teal from the background **(a)**. Notice that I added some pearls to the arm as well. It's normal to change aspects of your painting from the original sketch as you go along – you may find that things start to look off, or even think of better ideas than you did initially **(b)**. For a more detailed look into how I draw and paint wings, see page 148. There's no shame at all in deviating from your original design; art evolves over time and you should always give yourself permission to make the changes you think are best for the end result!

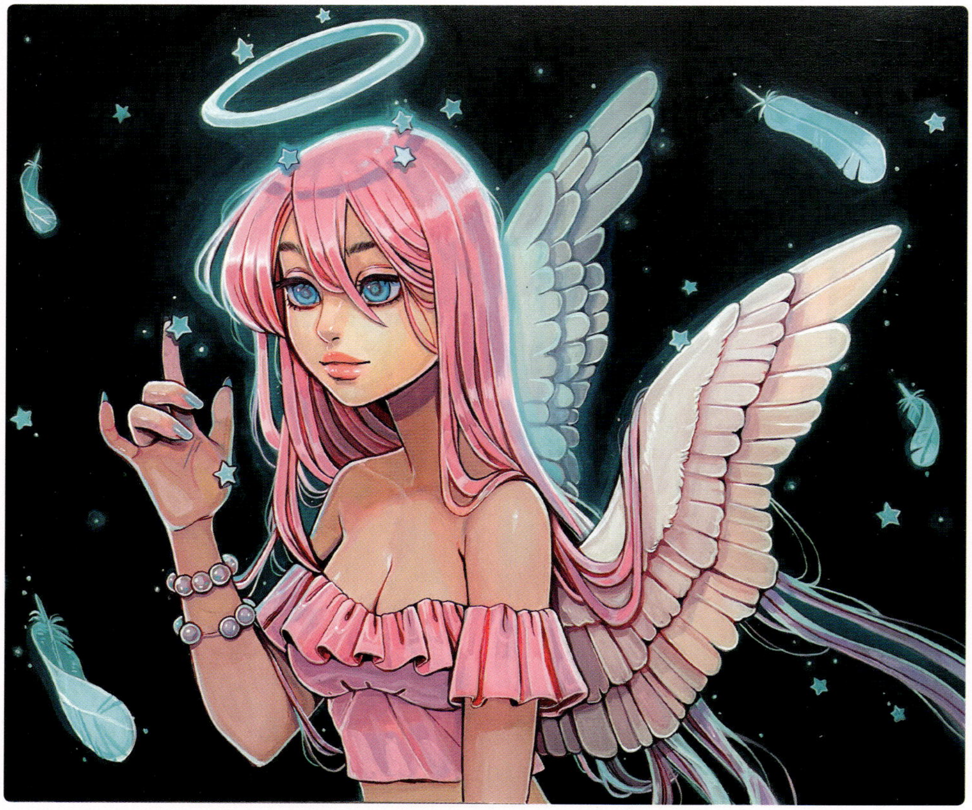

## 13 background

To create the glowing effect in the background I used pastel mint blue for the objects themselves, such as the stars and feathers, then to achieve the luminous glow around them I used a fully-saturated dark teal (see Creating glow, below). Objects that are glowing do not need much detail work, but any details you do add to them should be done with saturated instead of desaturated colors. I added white details around the rims of the objects to give them a bit of rim lighting to further boost the glowing effect.

For a more detailed look into achieving glow in your paintings, see the tutorial on page 150.

## creating glow

To create this light, glowing effect in the background, first take an old brush, cut the bristles down, and "mash" the remaining length up a bit (see right). Dip the dry bristles very lightly into a little white paint, then rub the brush on a paper towel a bit to leave a minimal amount of color on it. In circular motions, dry brush a soft circle on your canvas **(a)**, then place a small dot of white in the center **(b)**. Once dry, use satin glazing liquid and a bright color to create a thin wash over the top **(c)** — this should maintain the same values but change the color from white to whatever color you choose (in this case, teal).

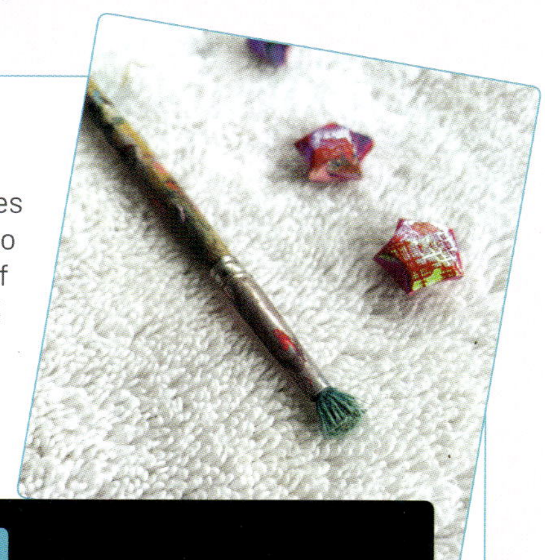

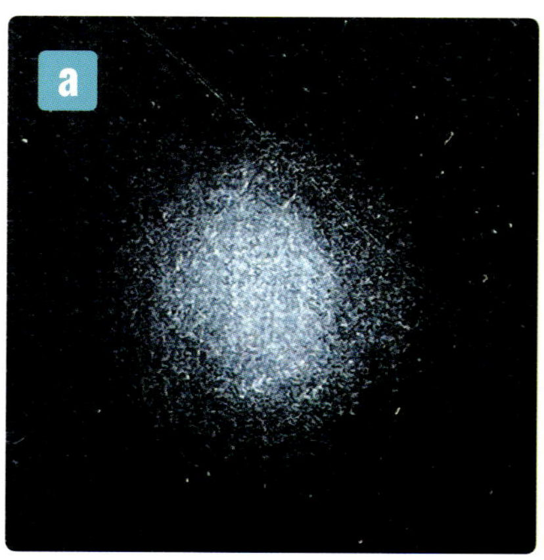

a

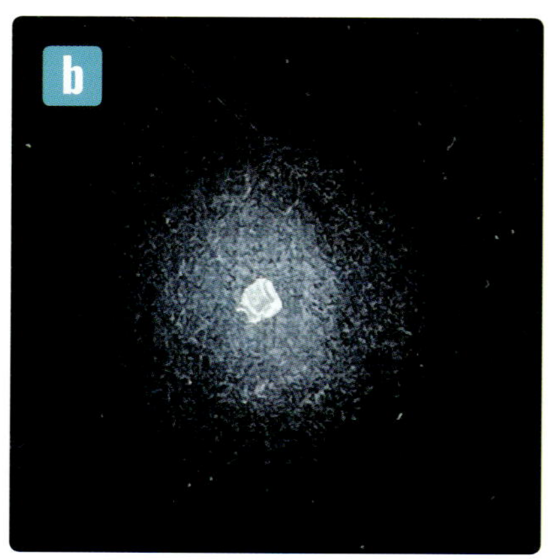

b

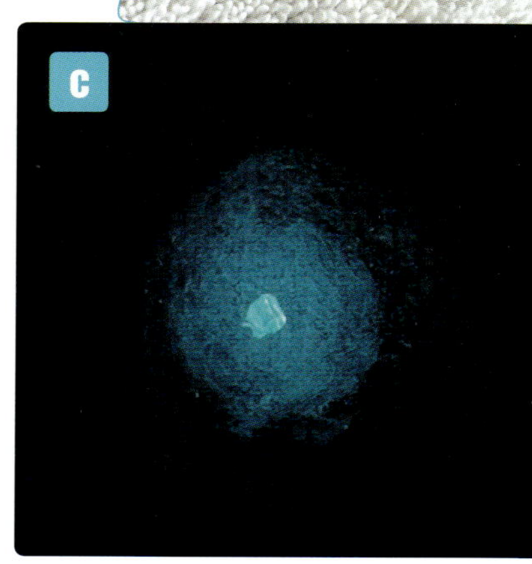

c

## 14 varnishing

Once your painting is complete it's time for my favorite part – applying varnish! Varnish will seal and protect your painting, as well as give it a lovely glossy sheen that makes the colors pop. There are many types of varnish to choose from, but I prefer a clear, glossy varnish that is specifically for acrylic paints.

To prepare, make sure you varnish outside or somewhere with good ventilation as the fumes can be toxic. I always lie my canvas down on a towel to protect my work surface from varnish spills. Pour a little varnish directly on to the canvas **(a)** and use your large flat brush to push the varnish over the surface of the painting. Use similar motions to the way you put down the gesso, going back and forth but also diagonally until the varnish has been smoothly distributed across the board **(b)**. I usually do a single layer, but there's nothing wrong with adding more than one if you feel like your layer was too thin.

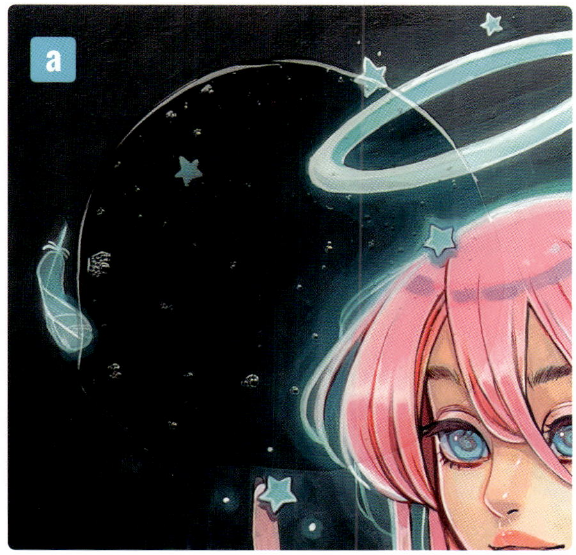


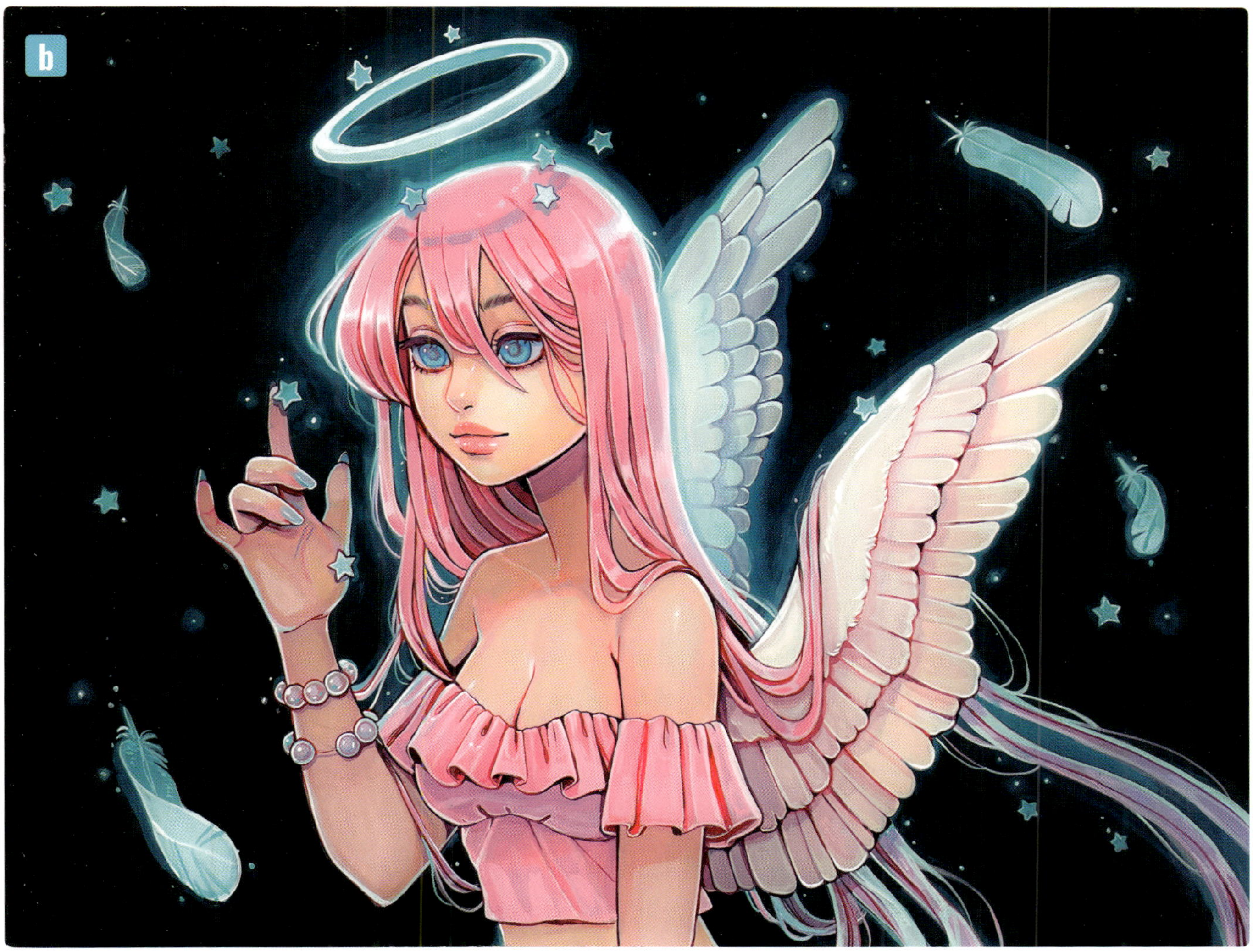

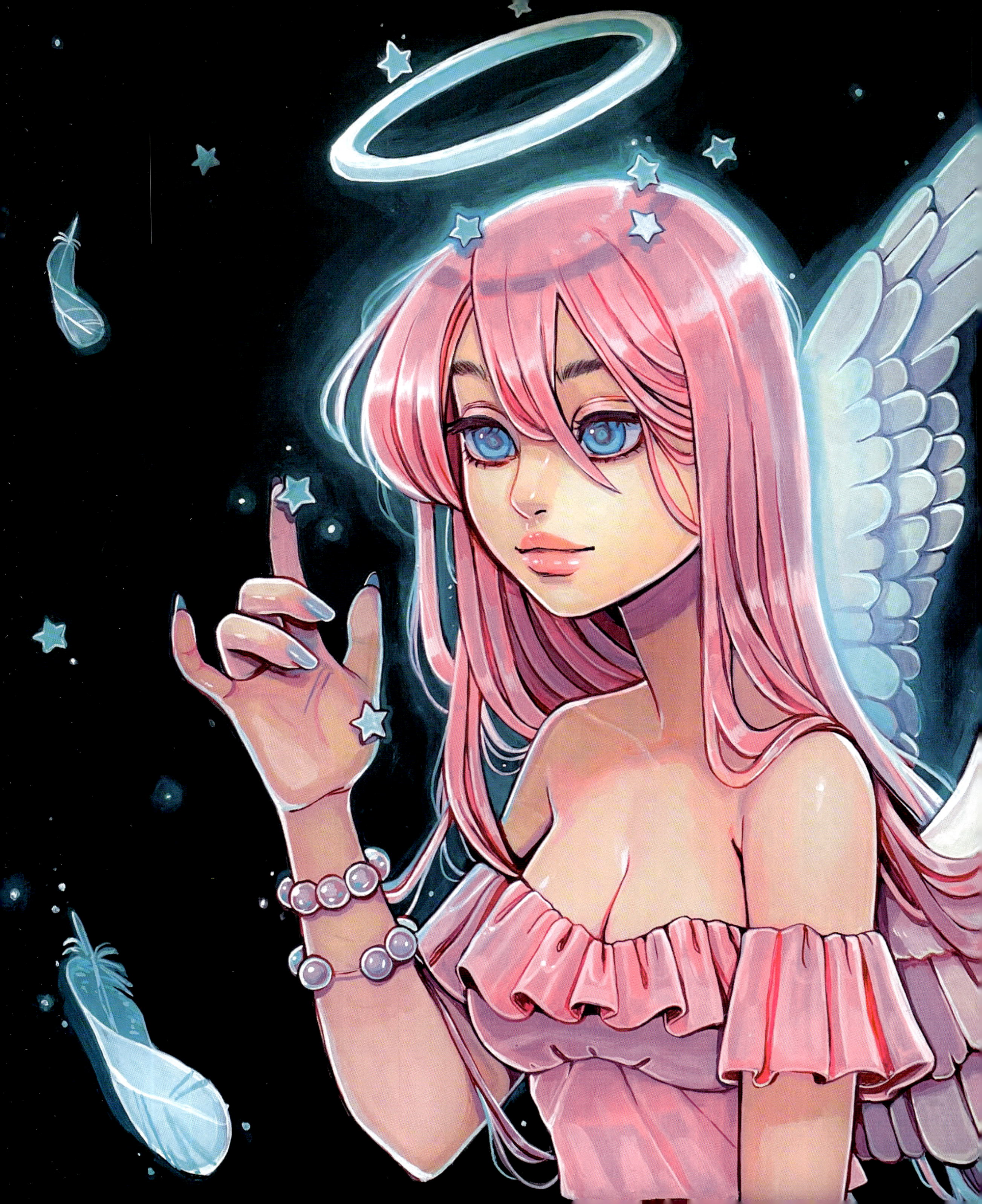

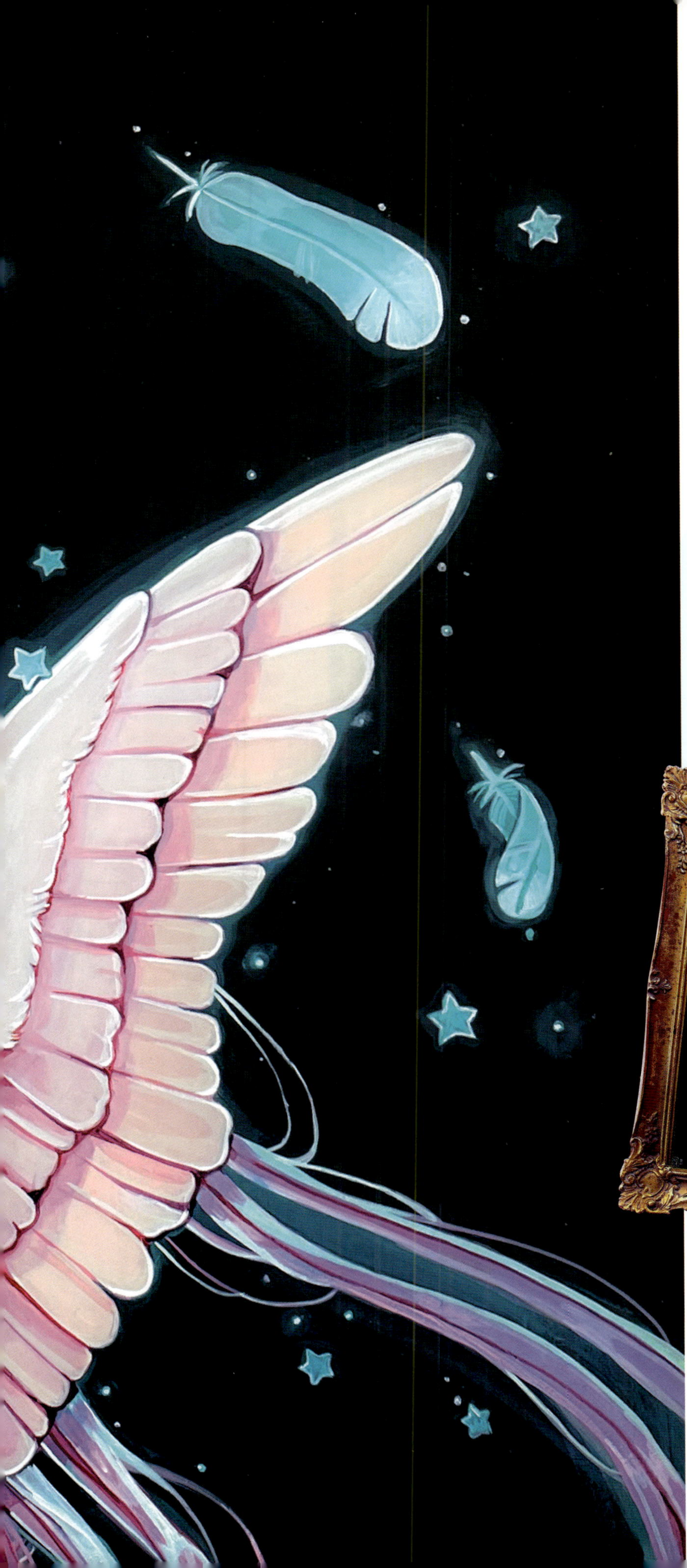

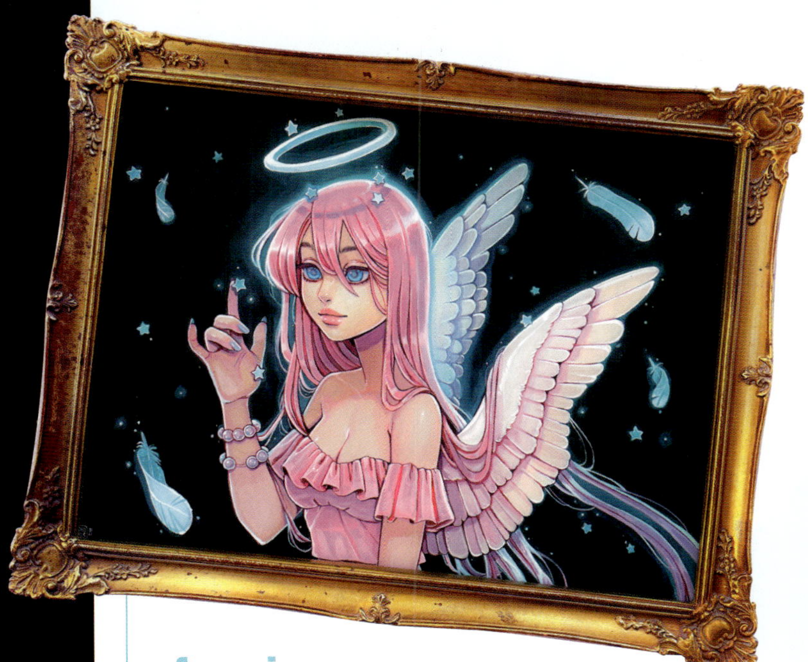

## framing

Adding a frame to your painting creates a professional-looking finish, especially if you plan to display it at home or exhibit in a gallery.

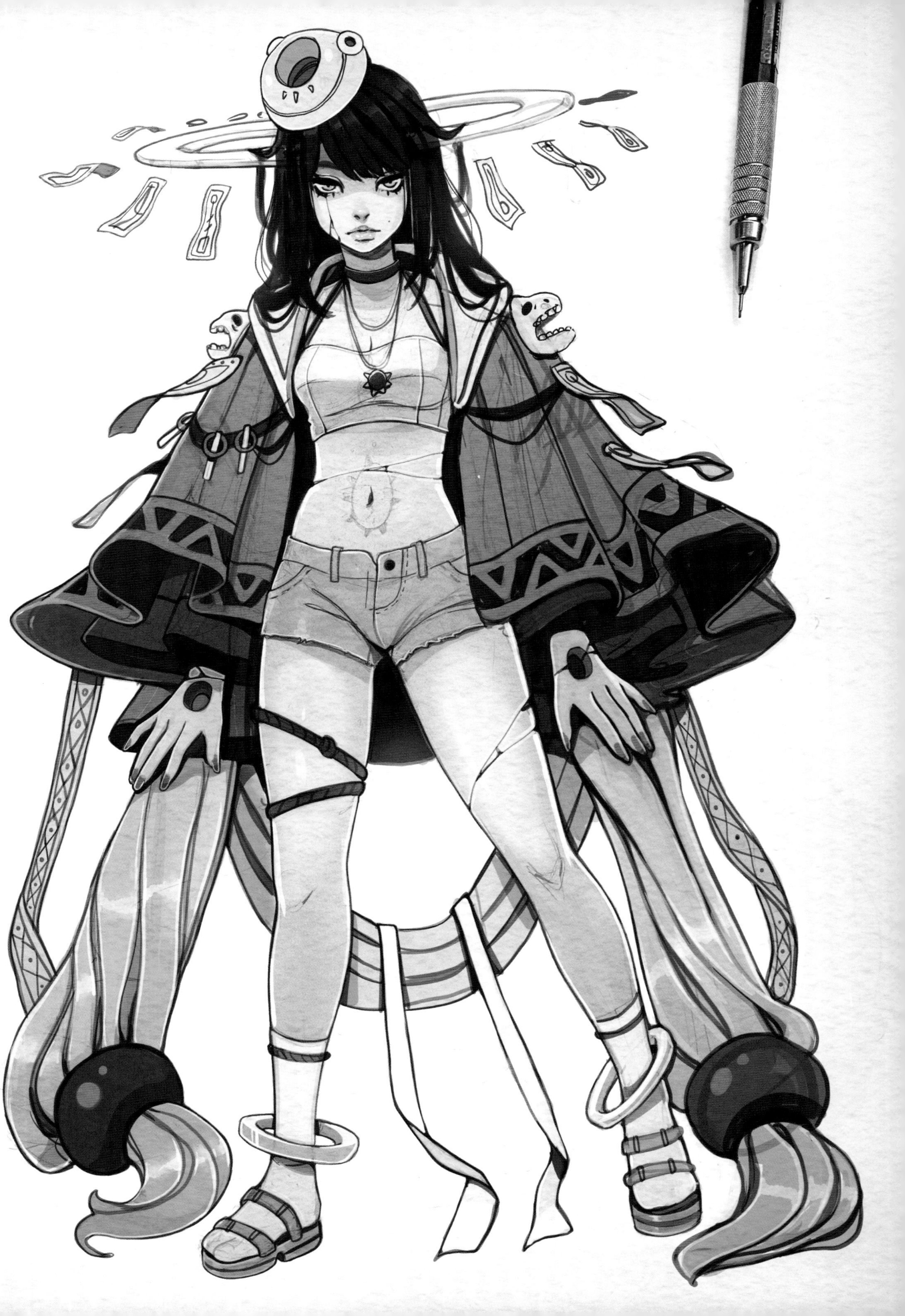

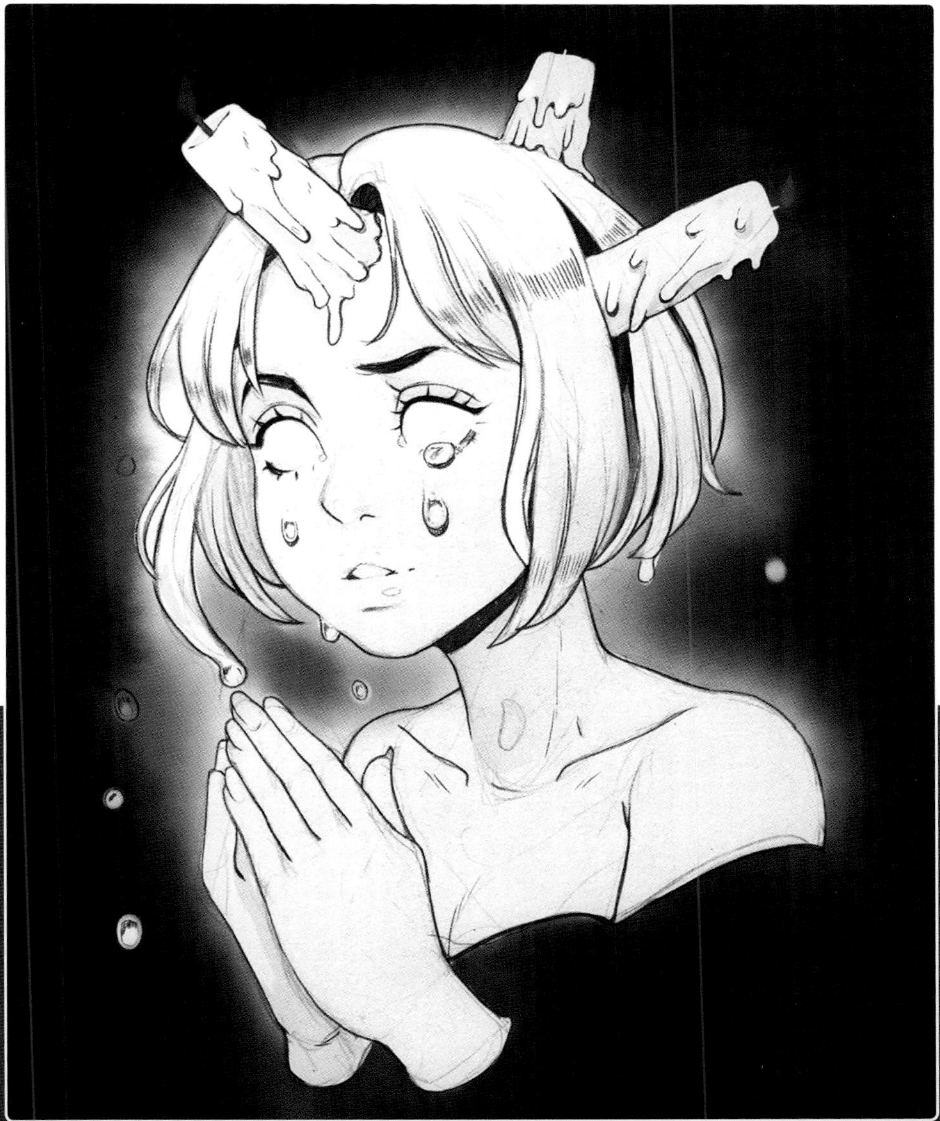

GALLERY:

# inktober

For those who don't know, Inktober is a social media challenge hosted every October. It calls out to artists to create a new ink drawing for each day of the month, led by a list of changing prompts. Although I've never participated in the true event (I don't use the official prompt list — I usually draw every other day and I sometimes use digital mediums) I do like to make my own spooky black-and-white drawings. I enjoy the challenge and limitation of creating in just black and white, as it pushes my art in a new direction. I look forward to making them each year and they often end up being some of my favorite designs!

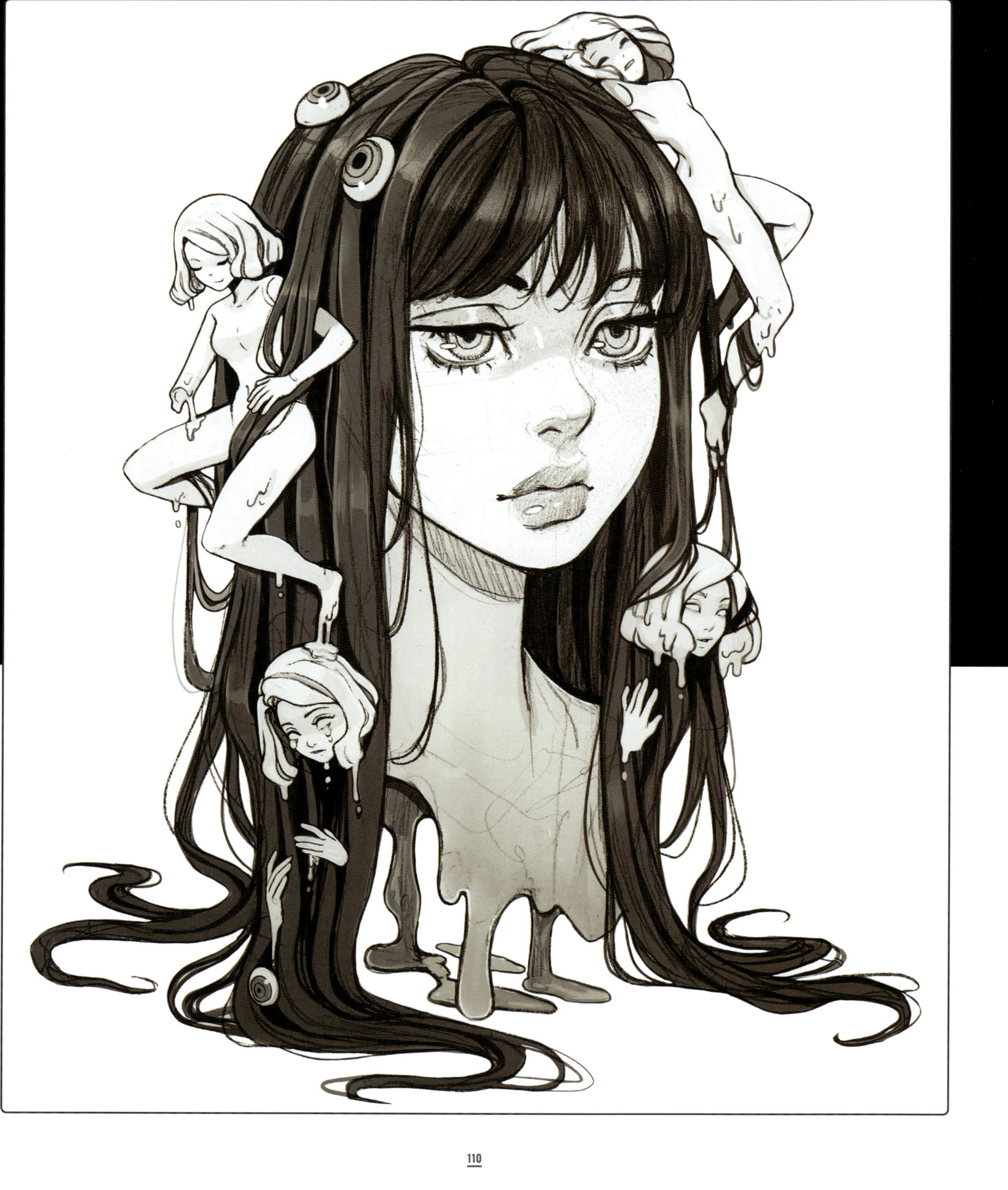

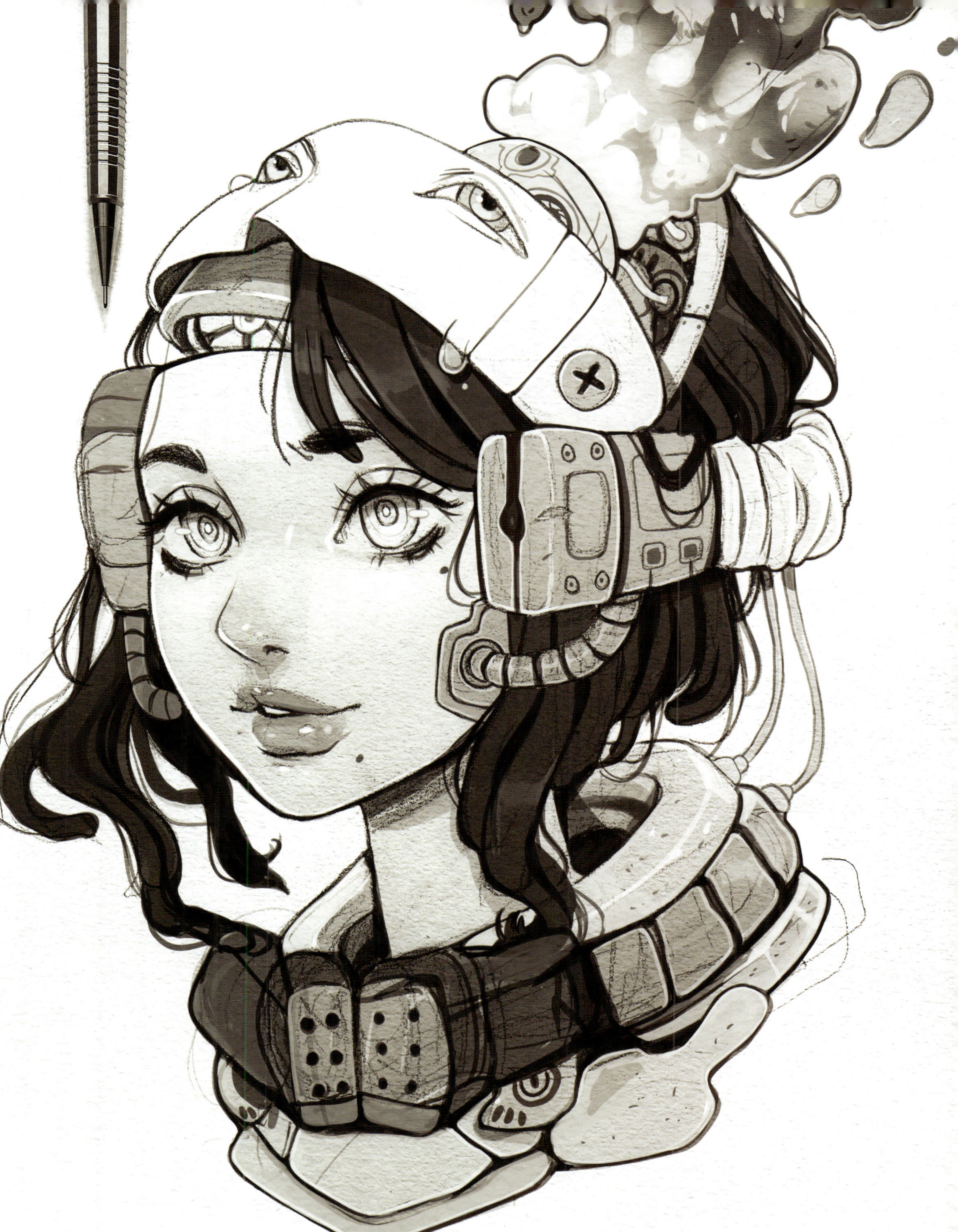

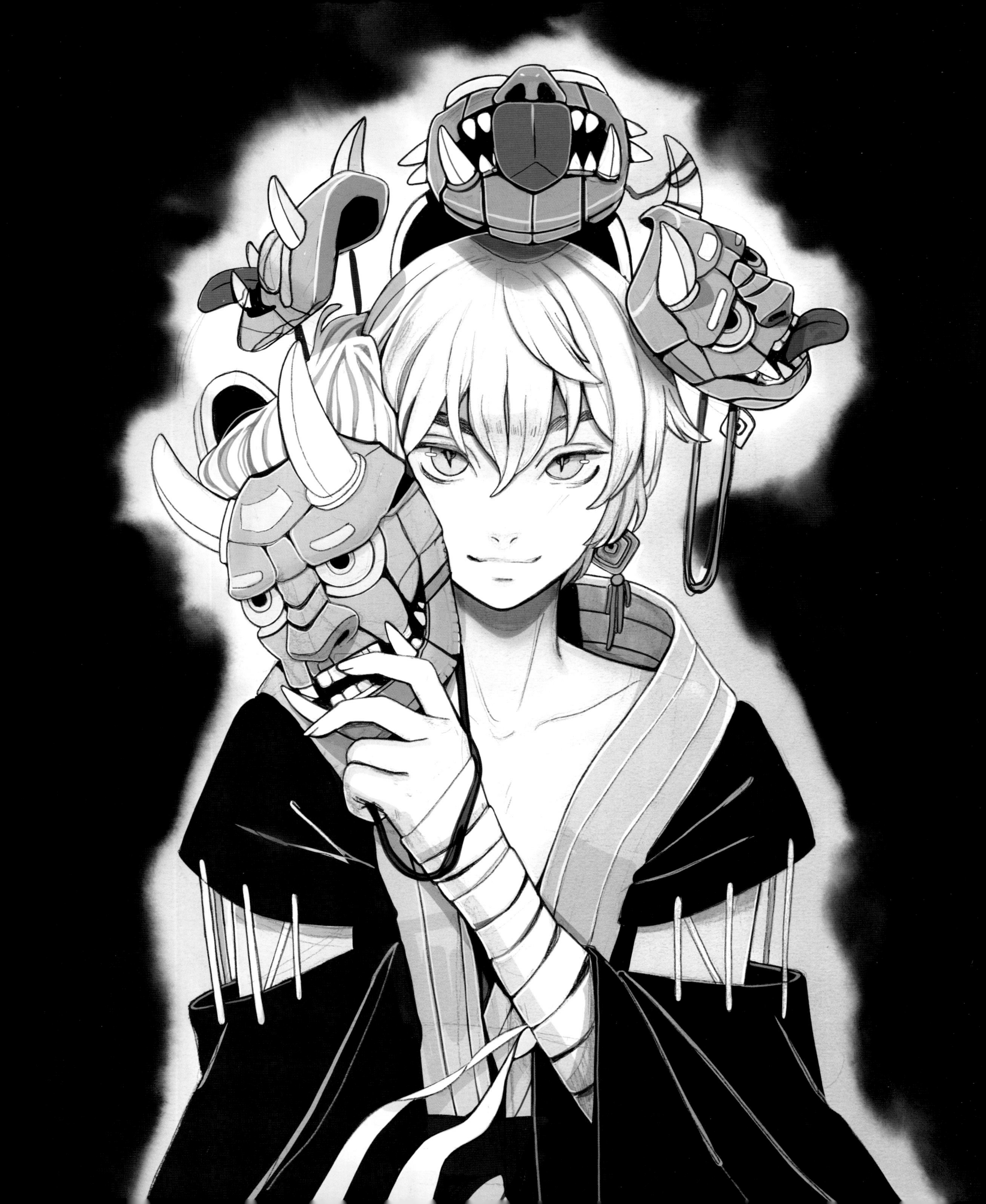

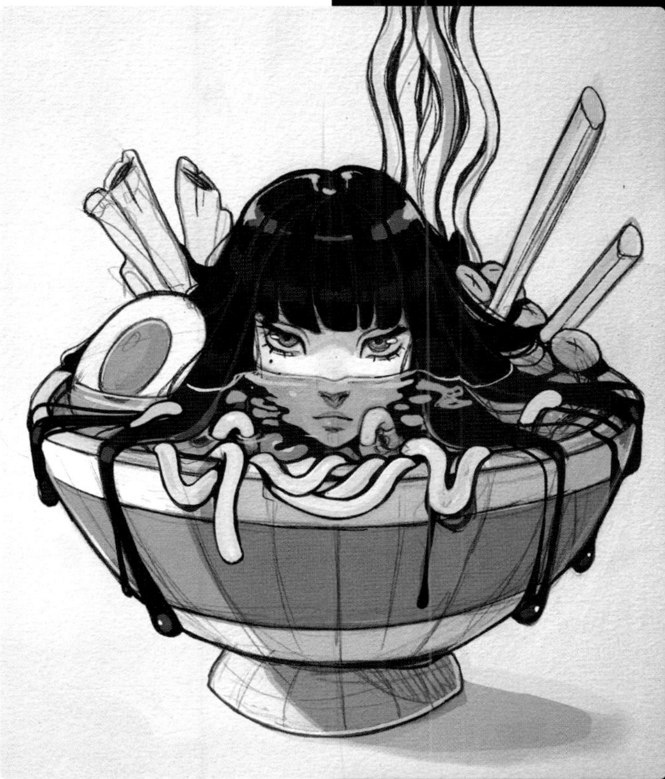

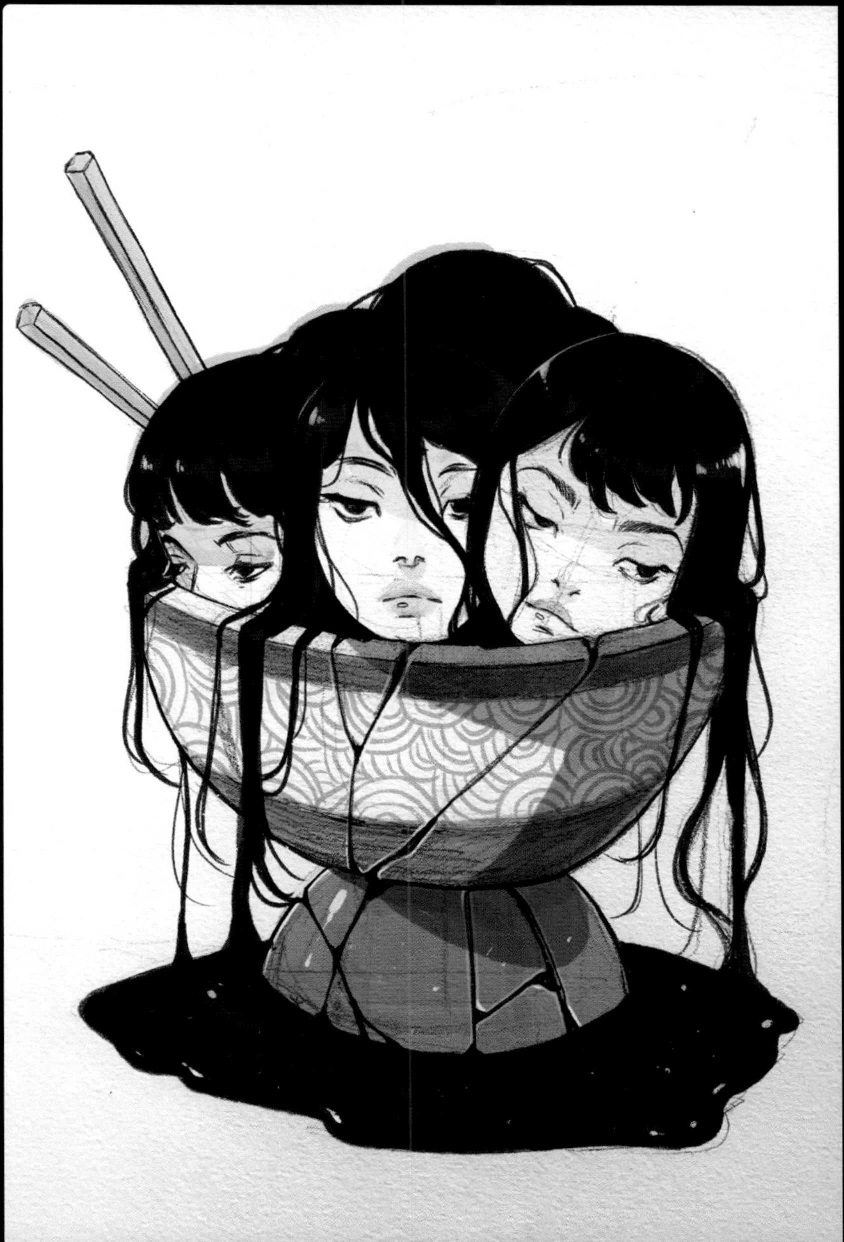

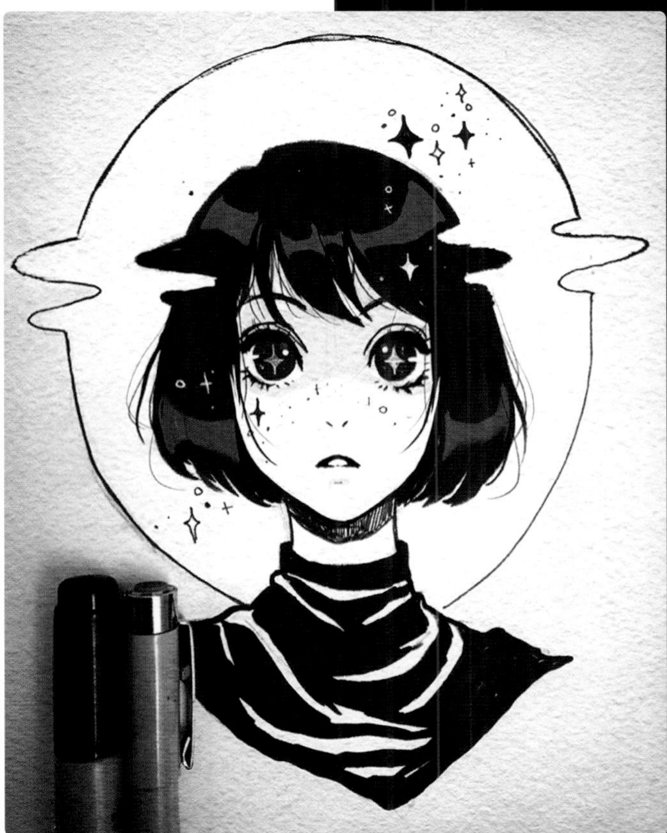

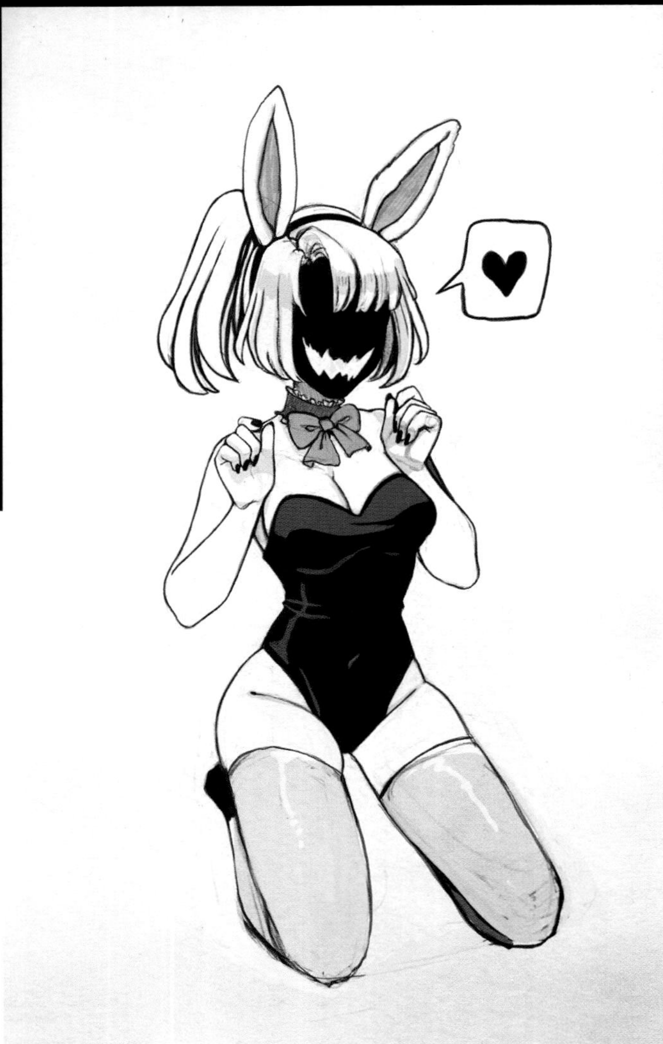

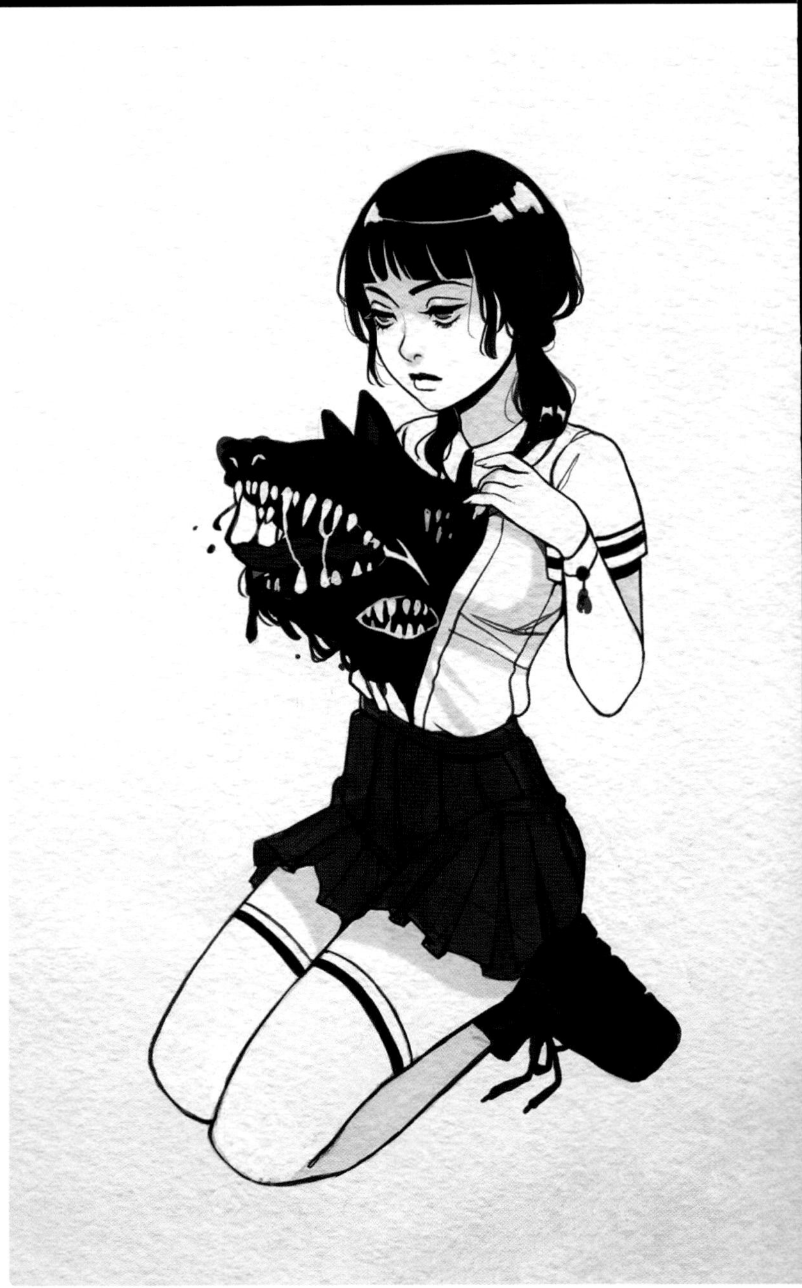

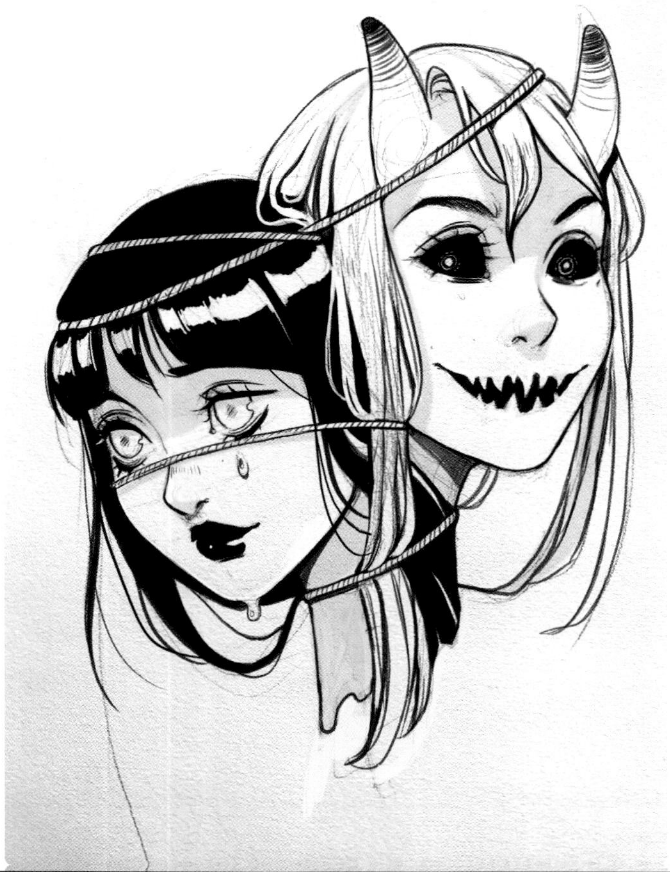

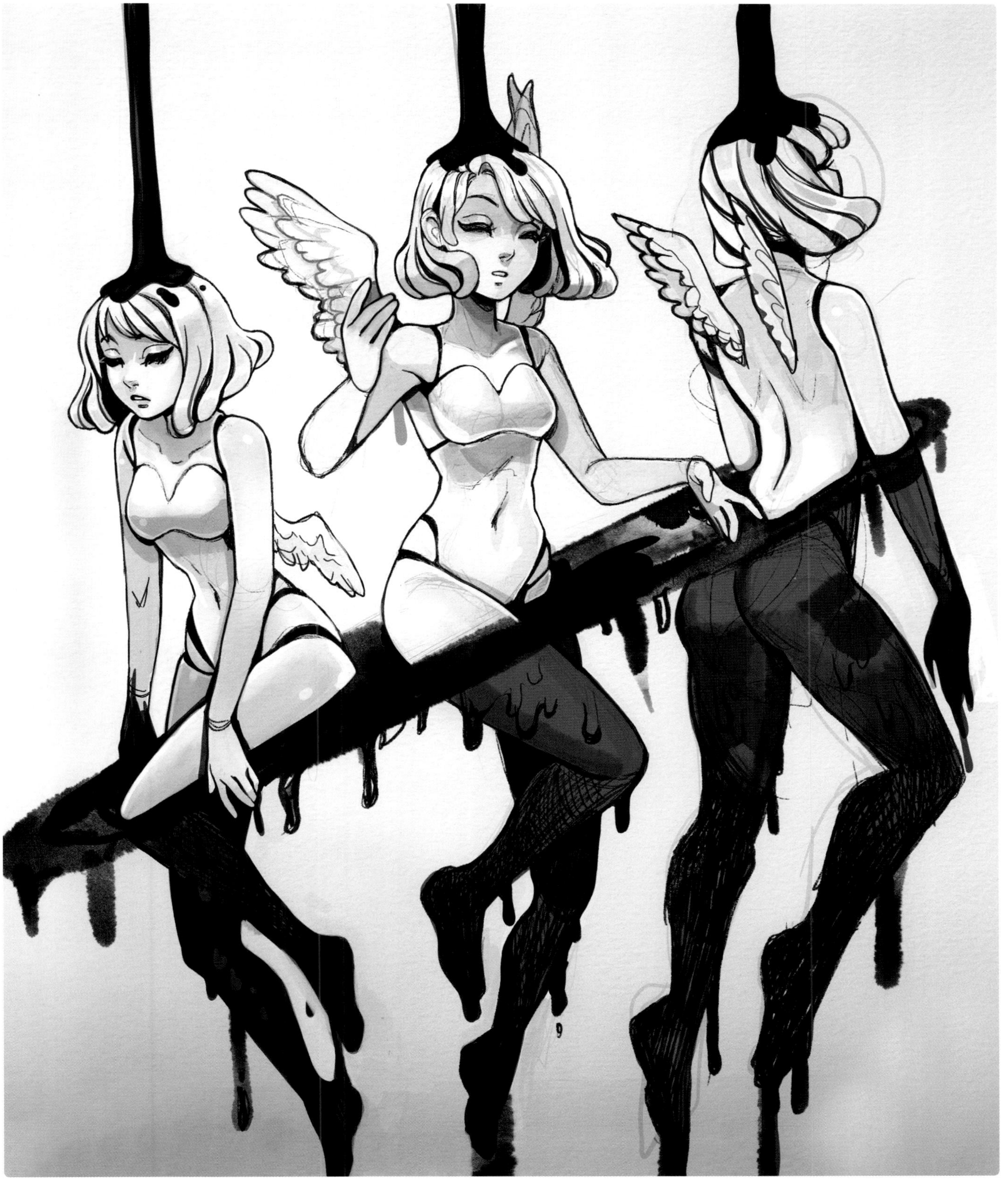

# GA

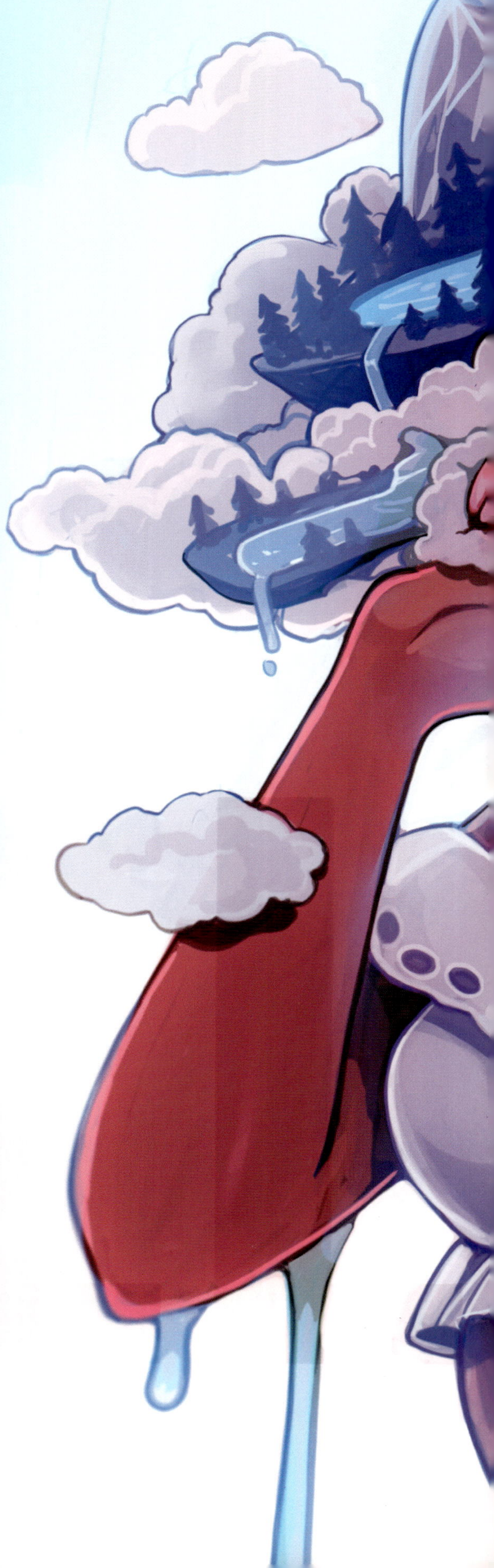

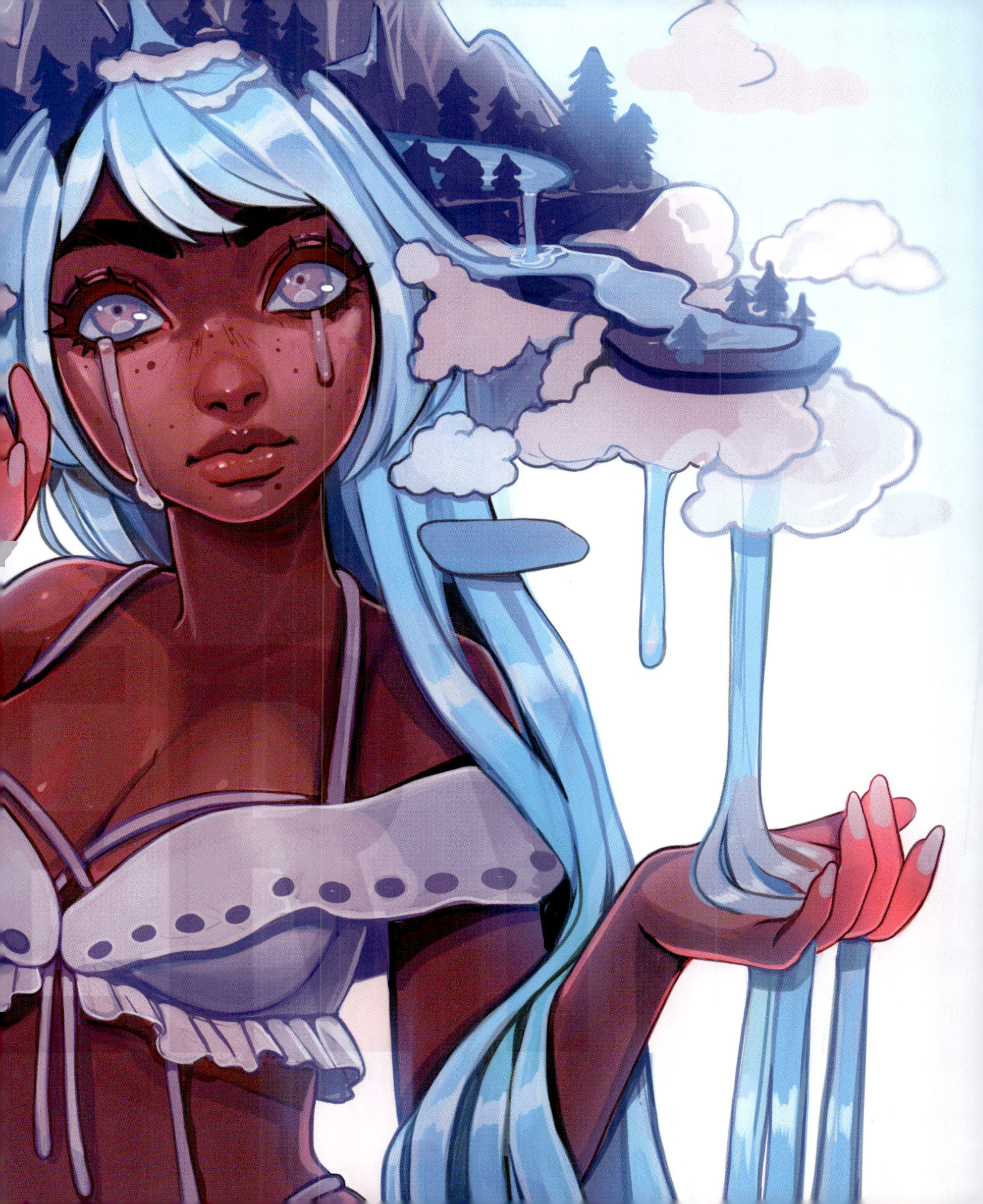

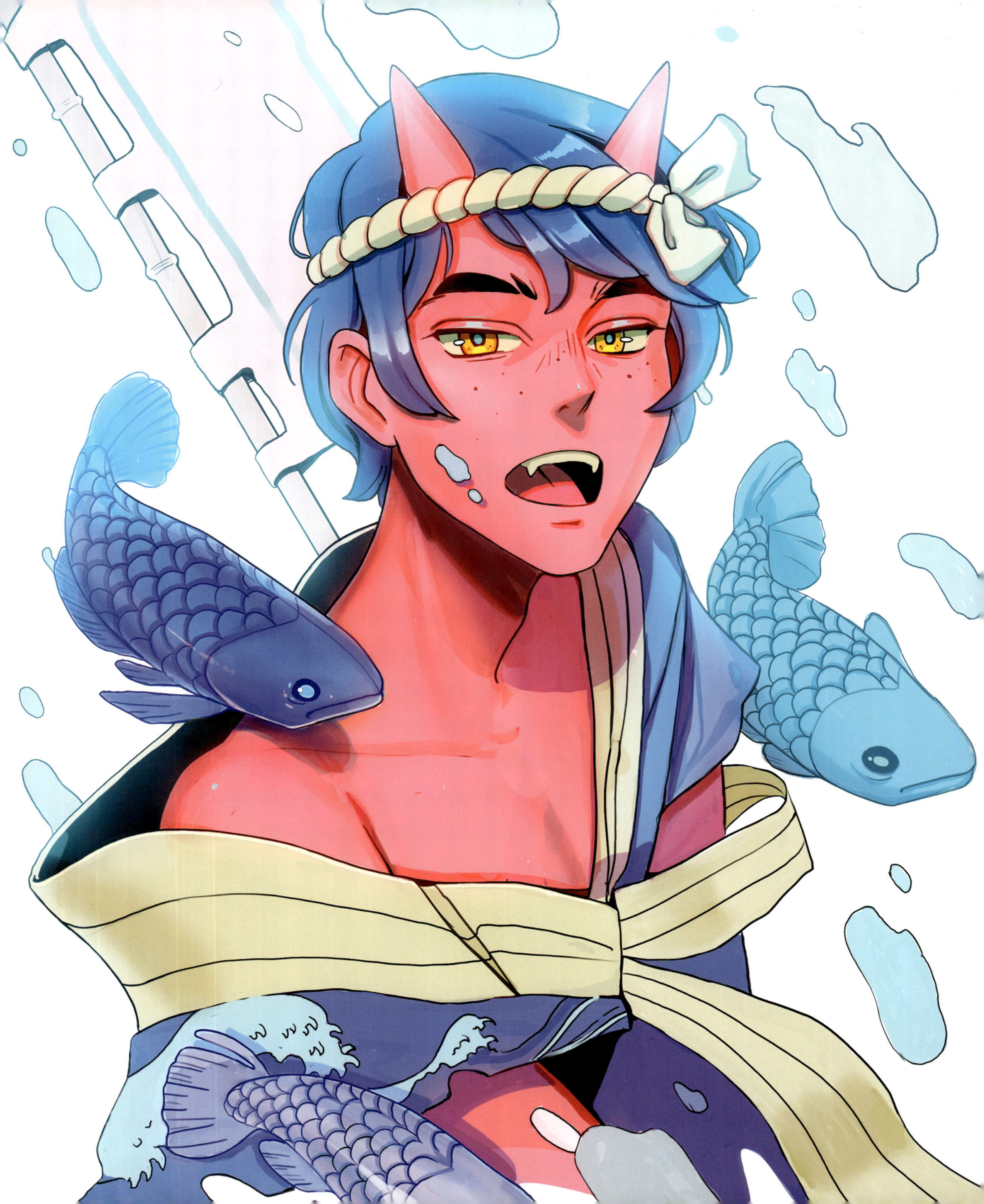

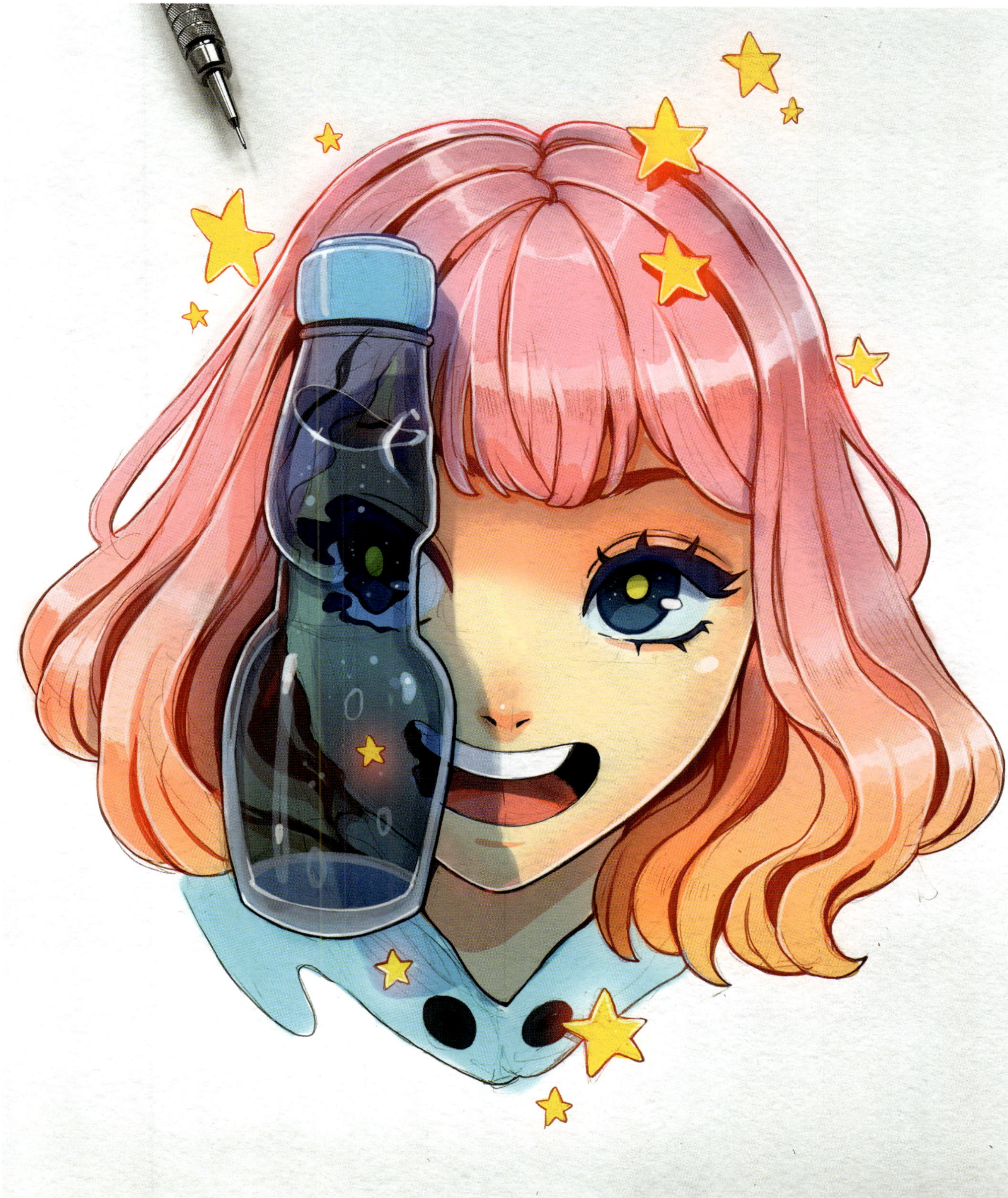

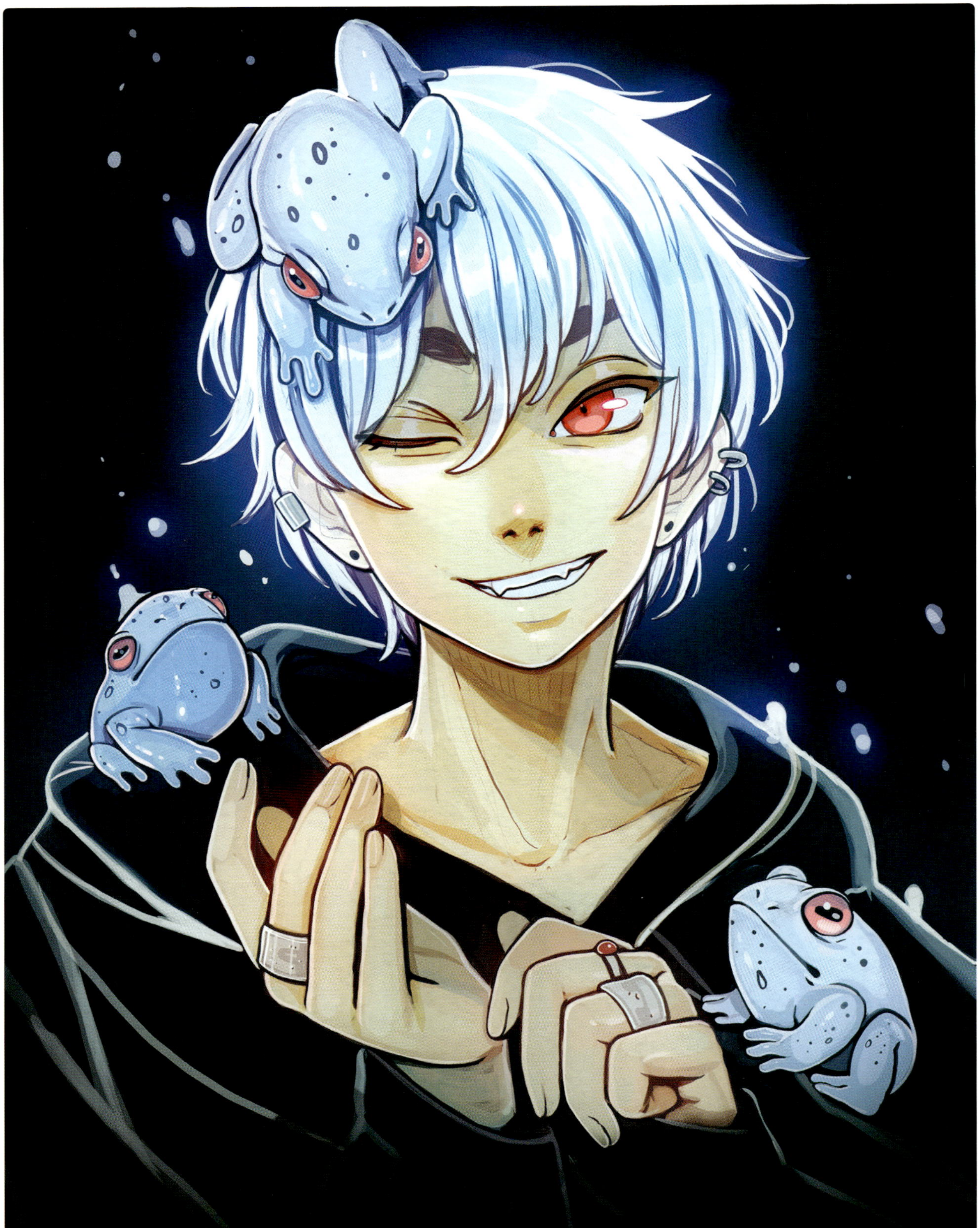

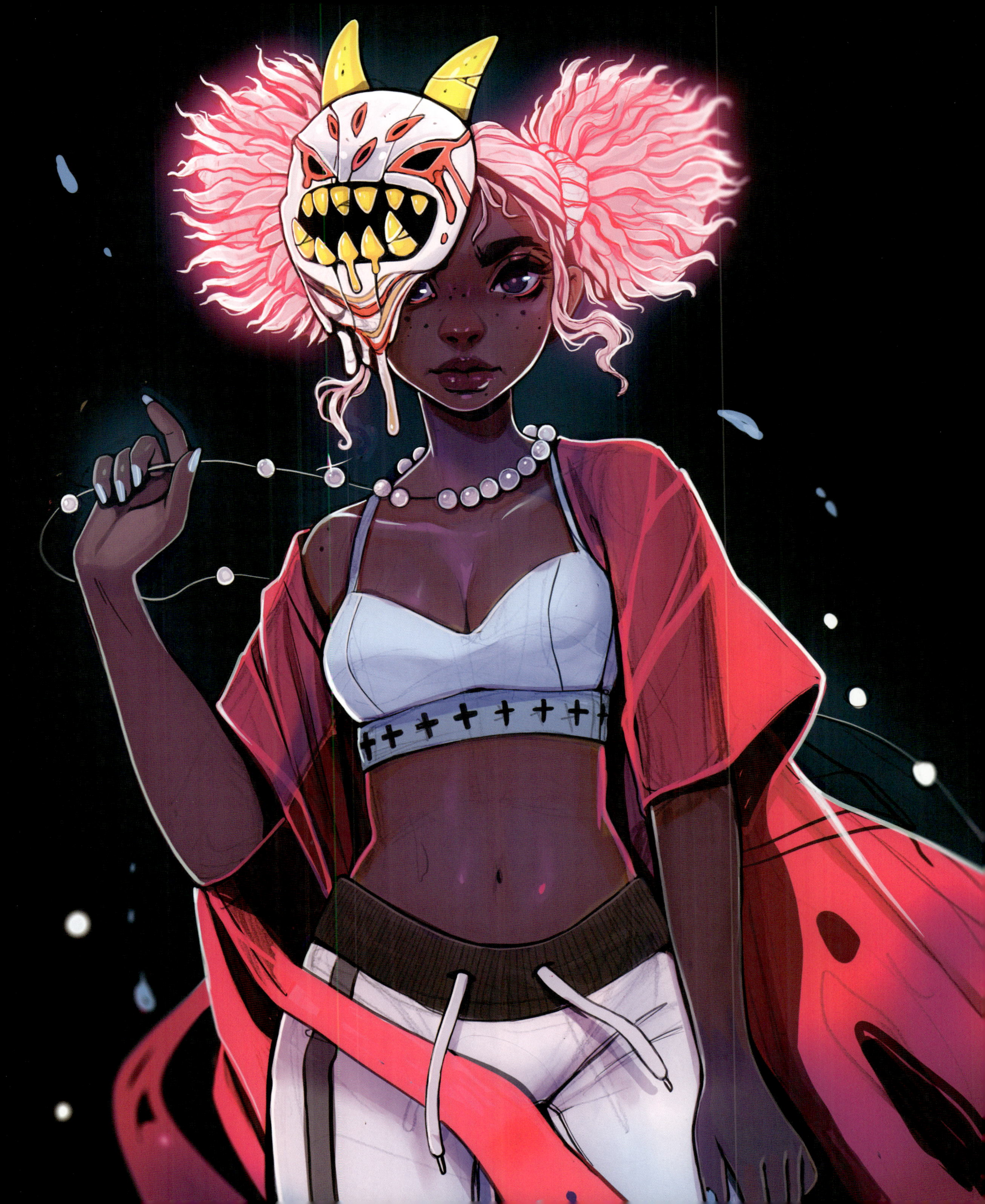

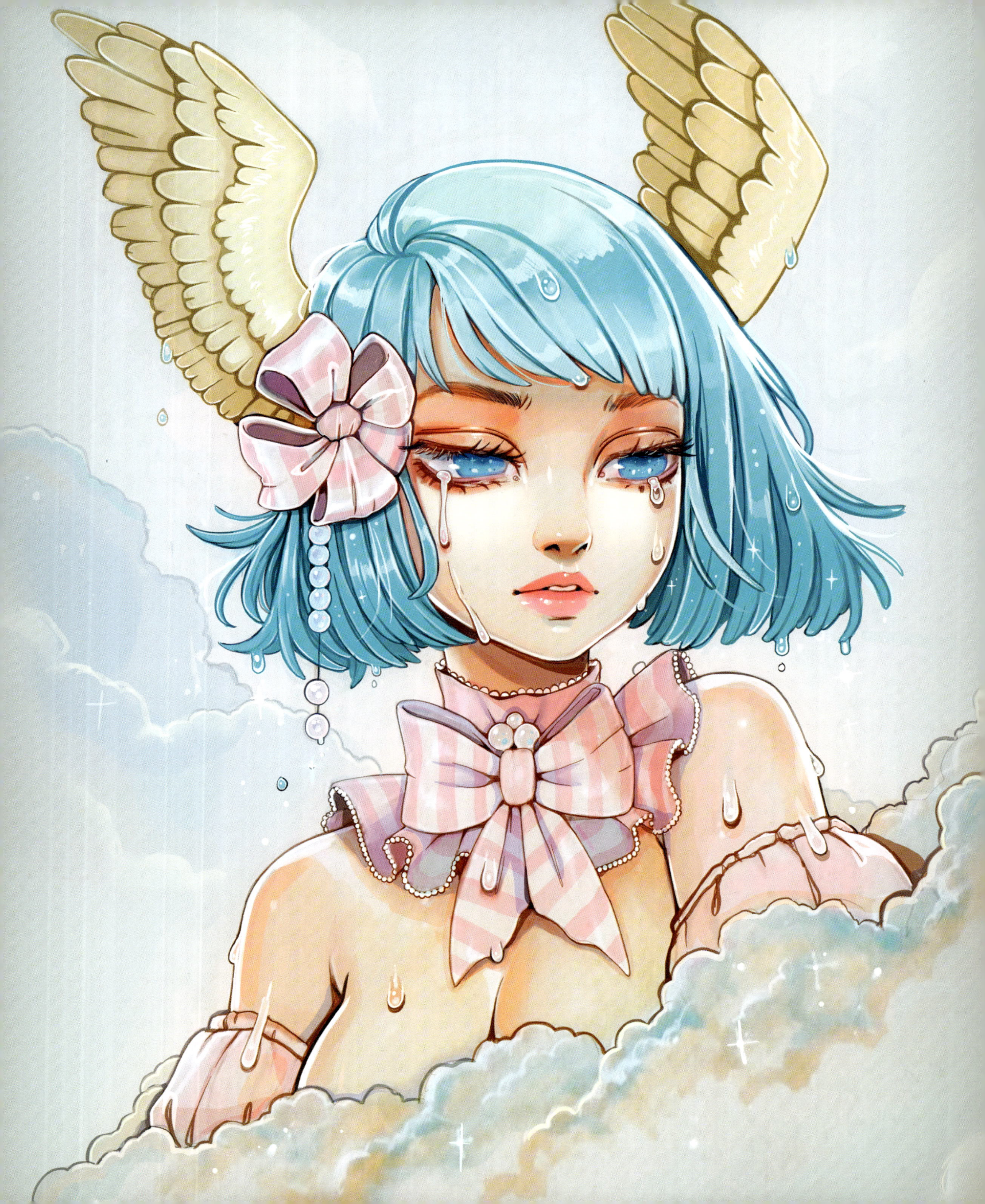

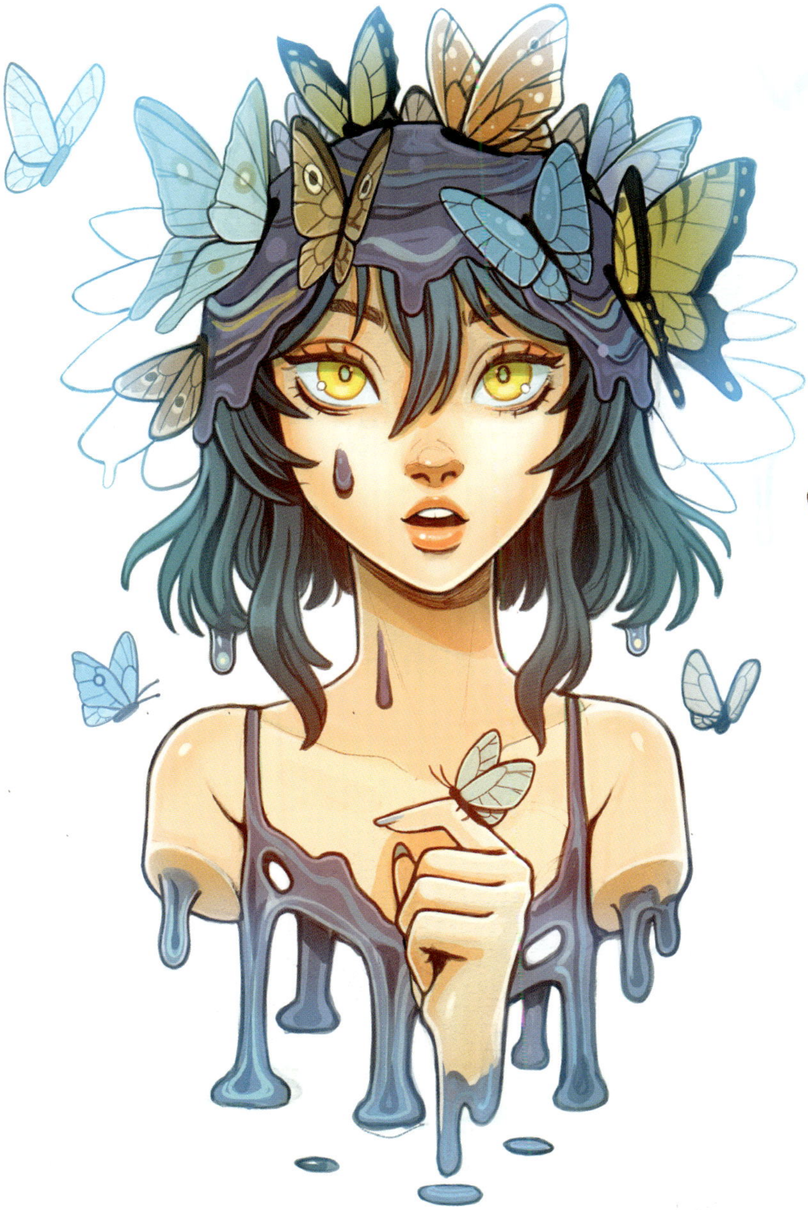

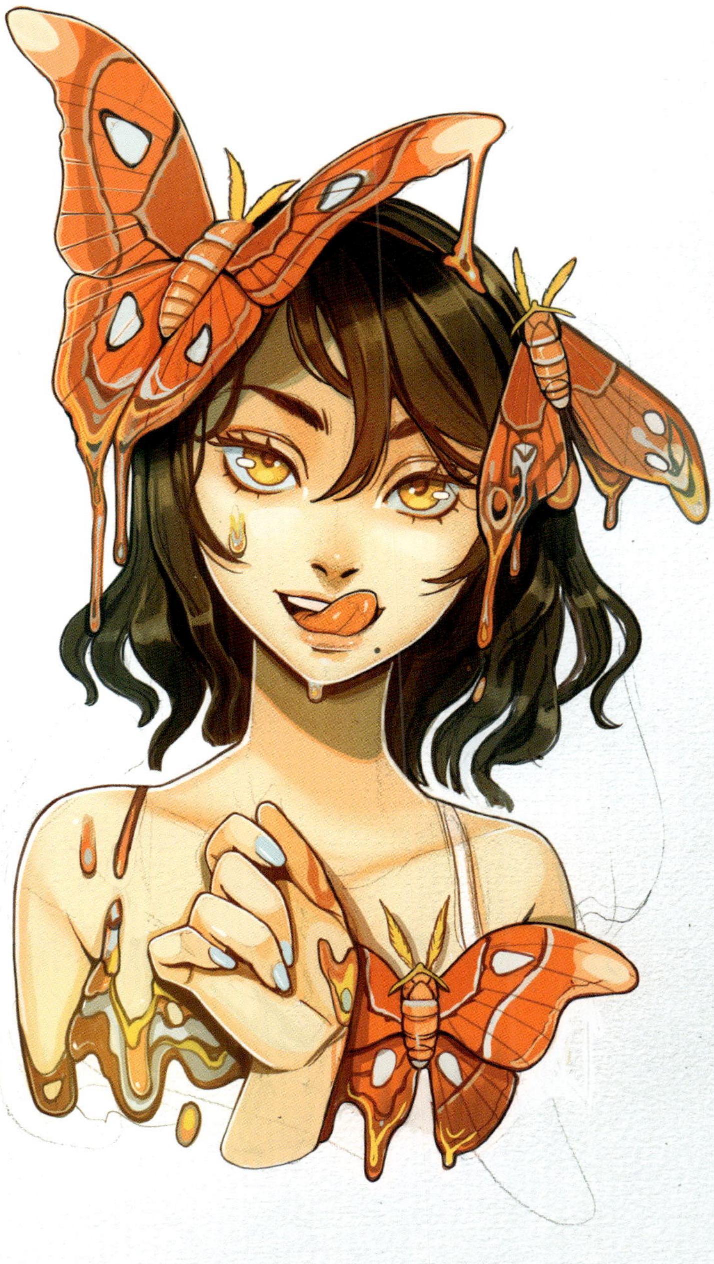

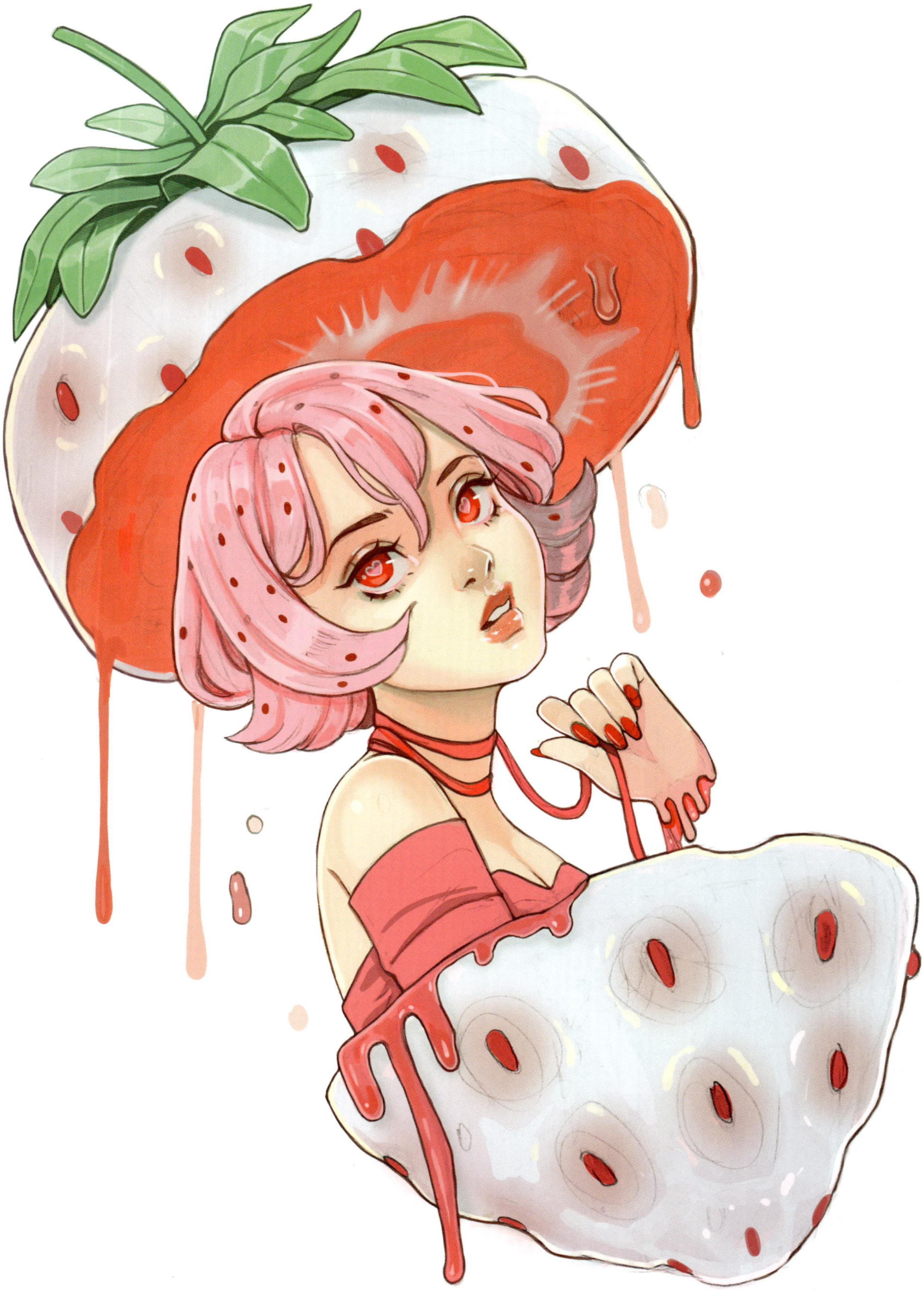

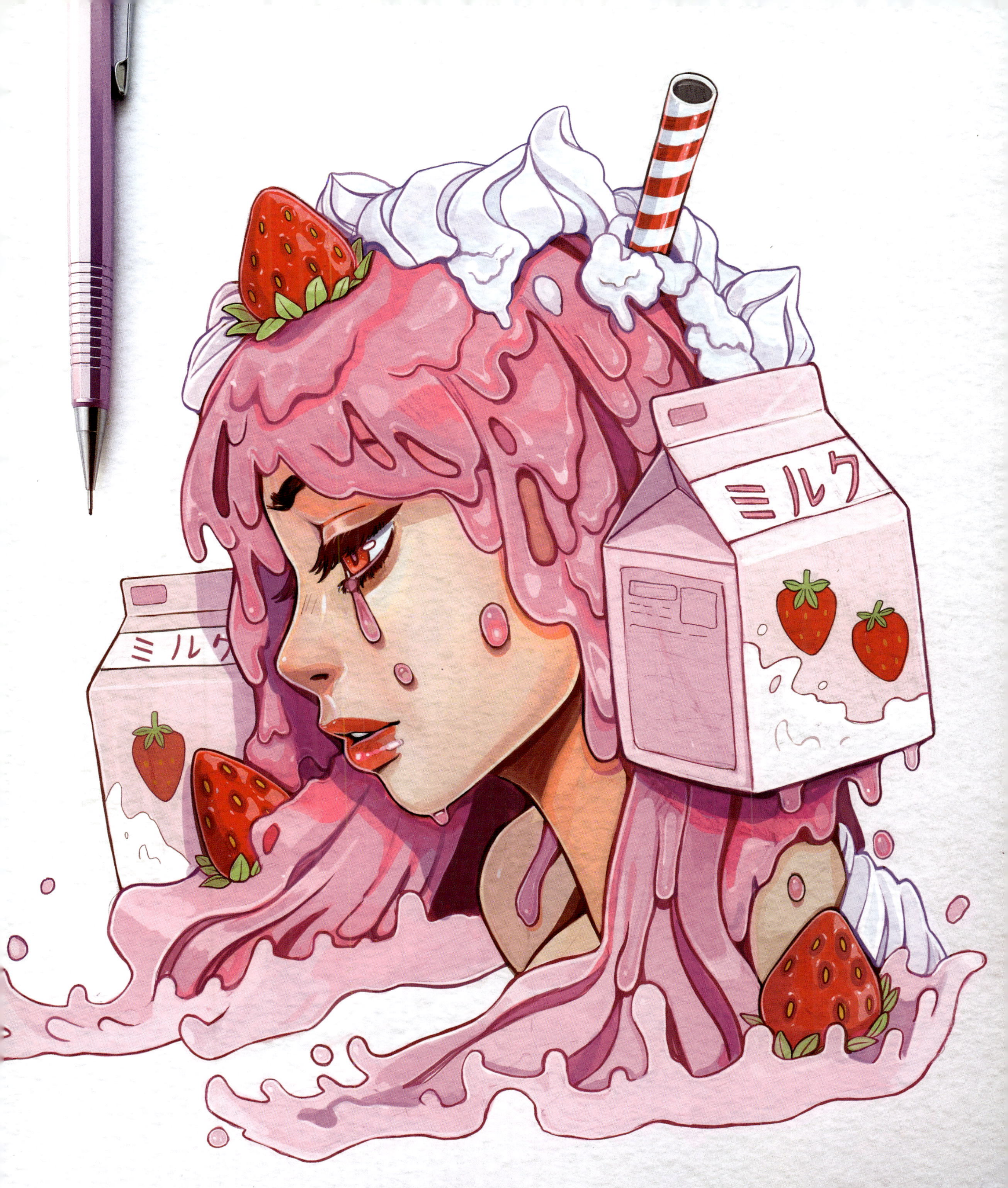
ミルク

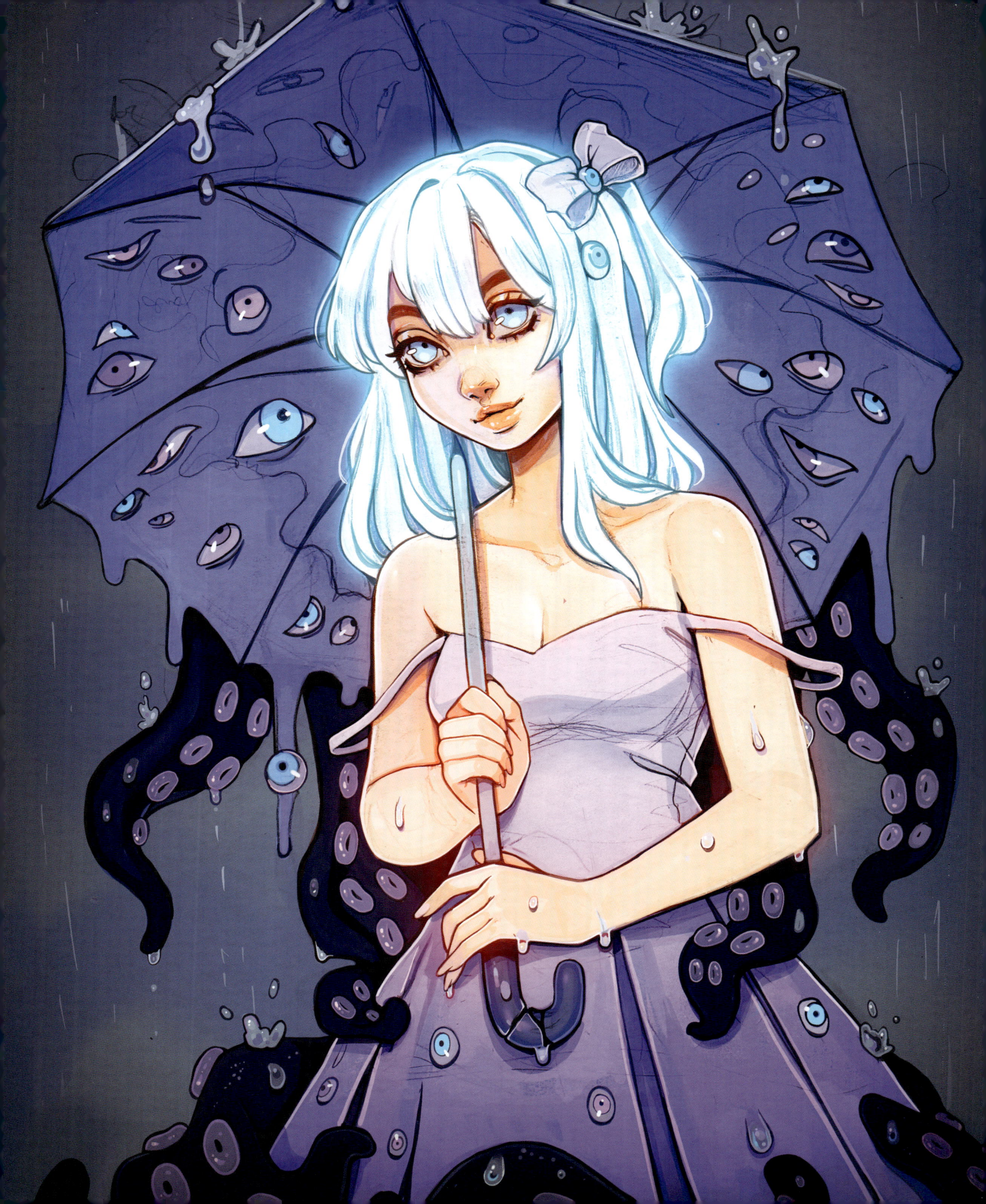

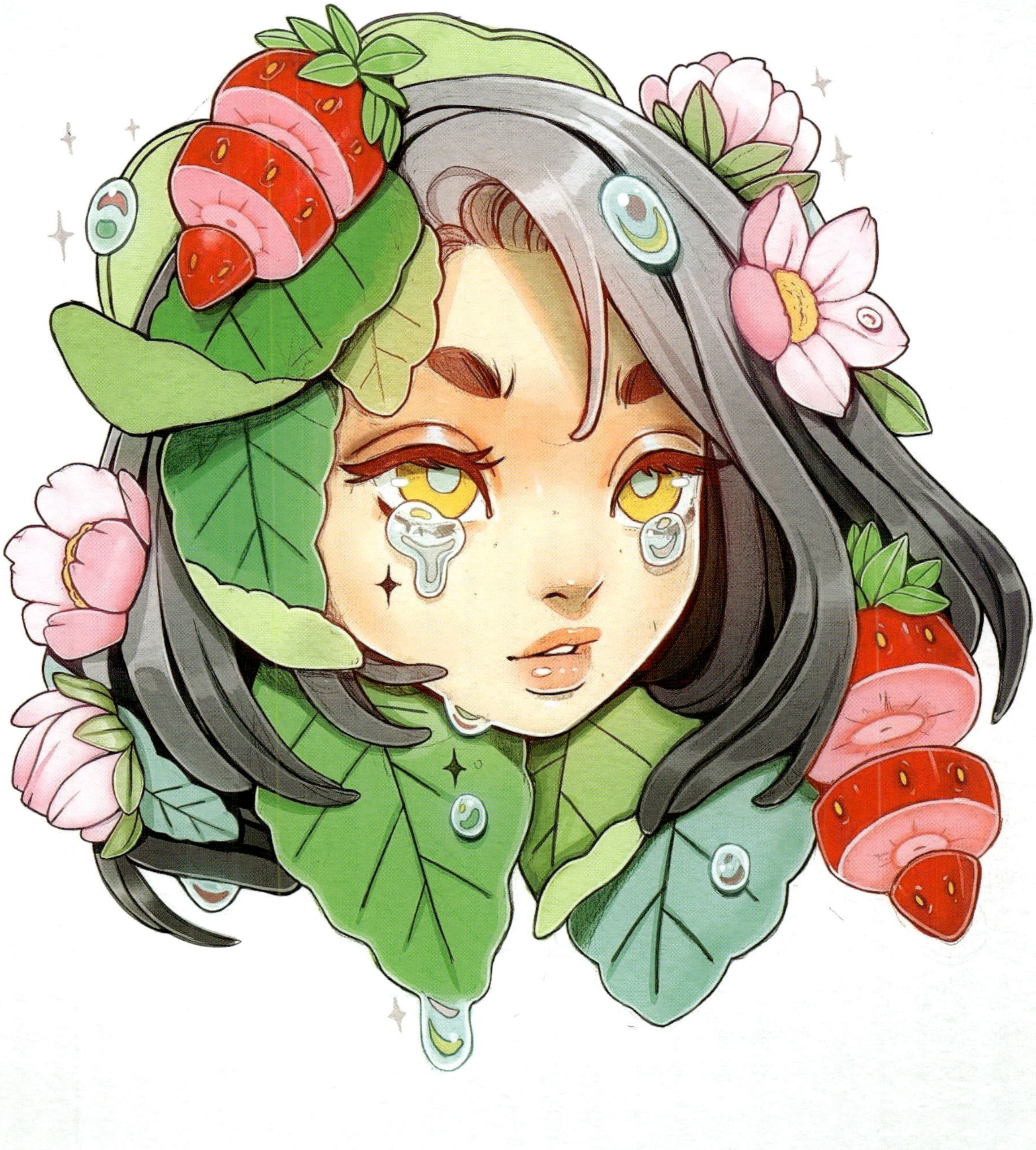

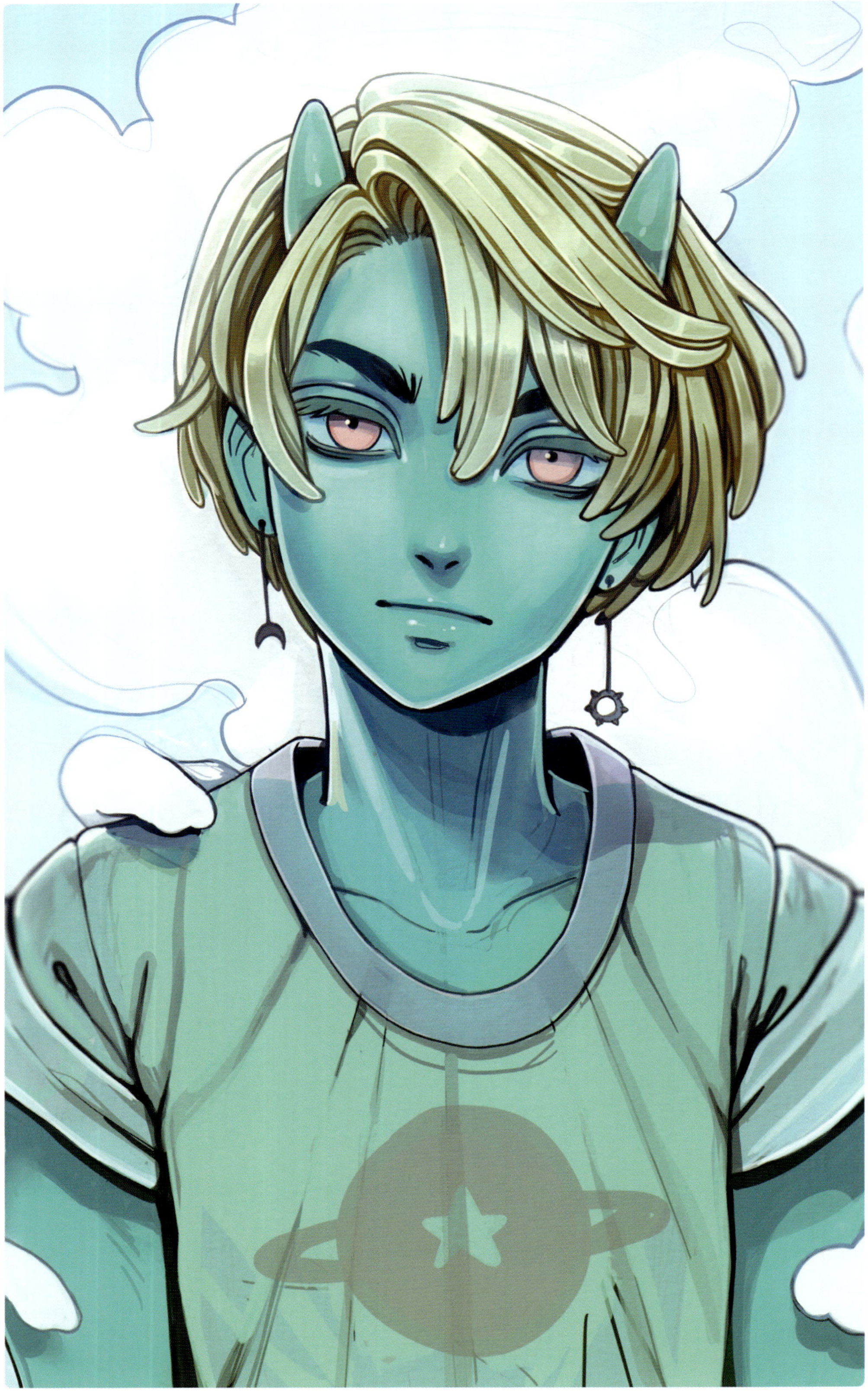

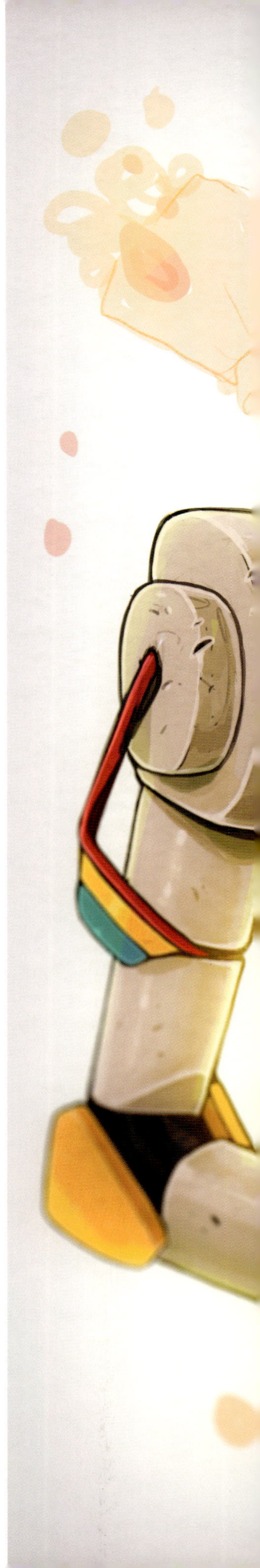

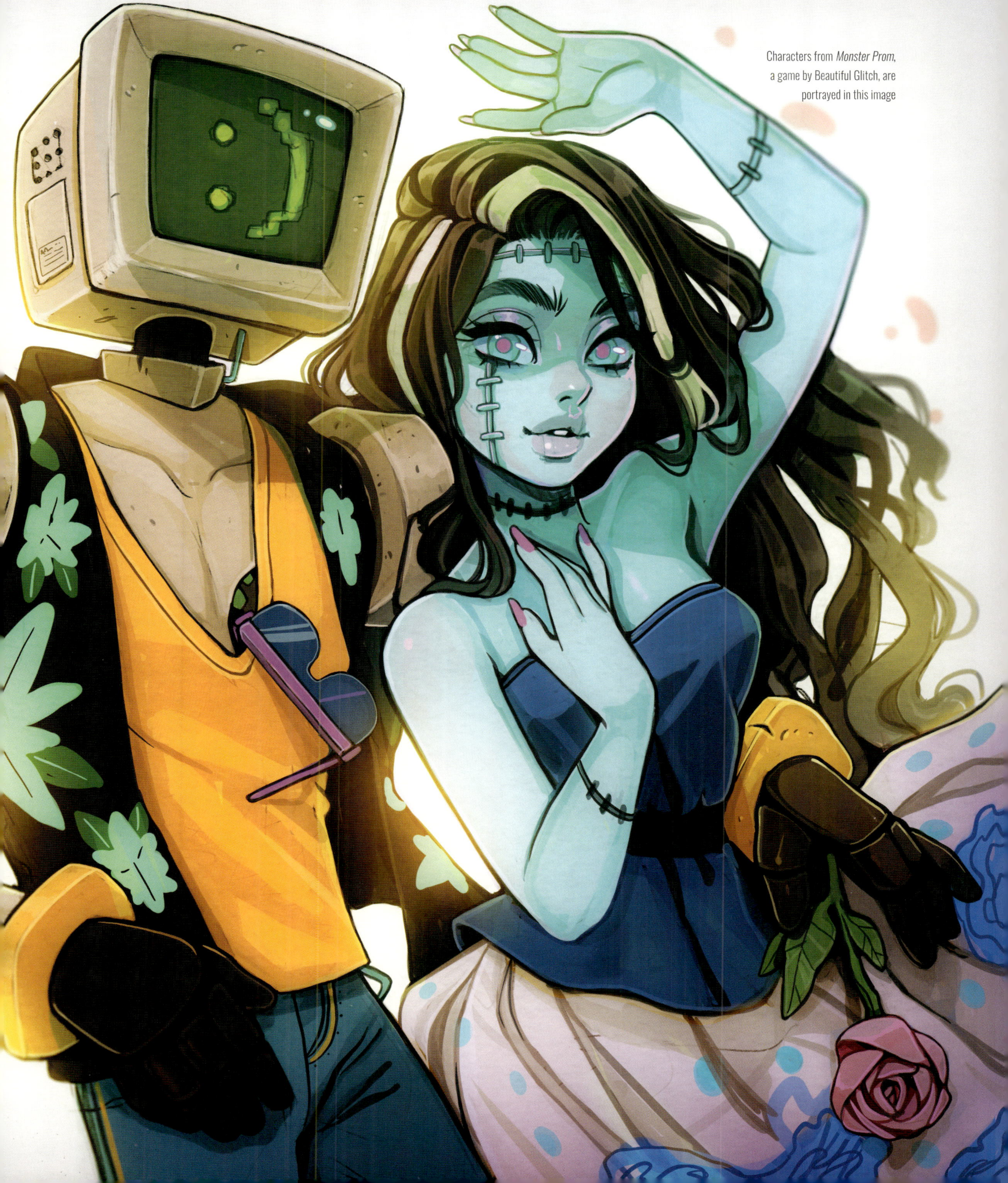

Characters from *Monster Prom*, a game by Beautiful Glitch, are portrayed in this image

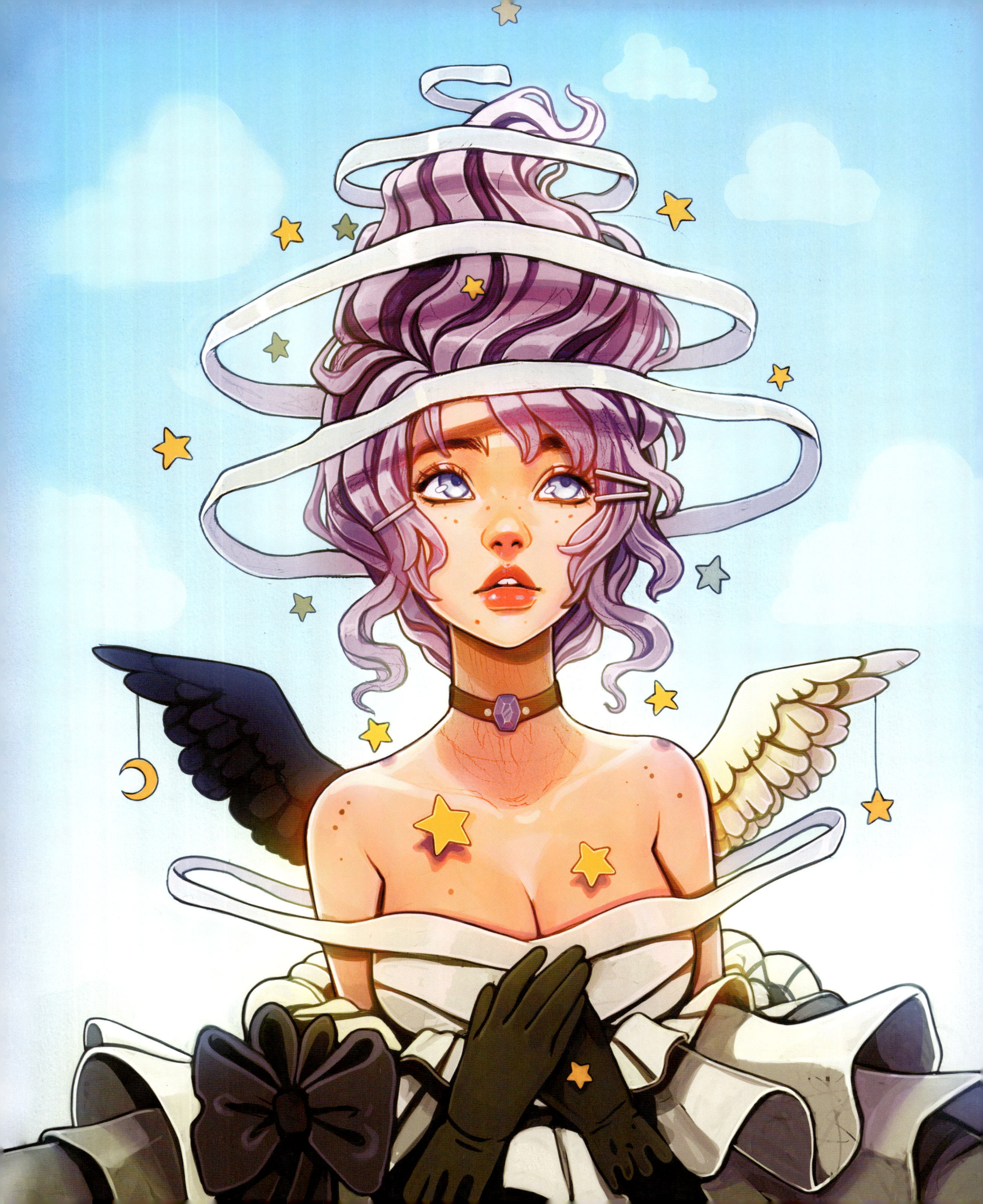

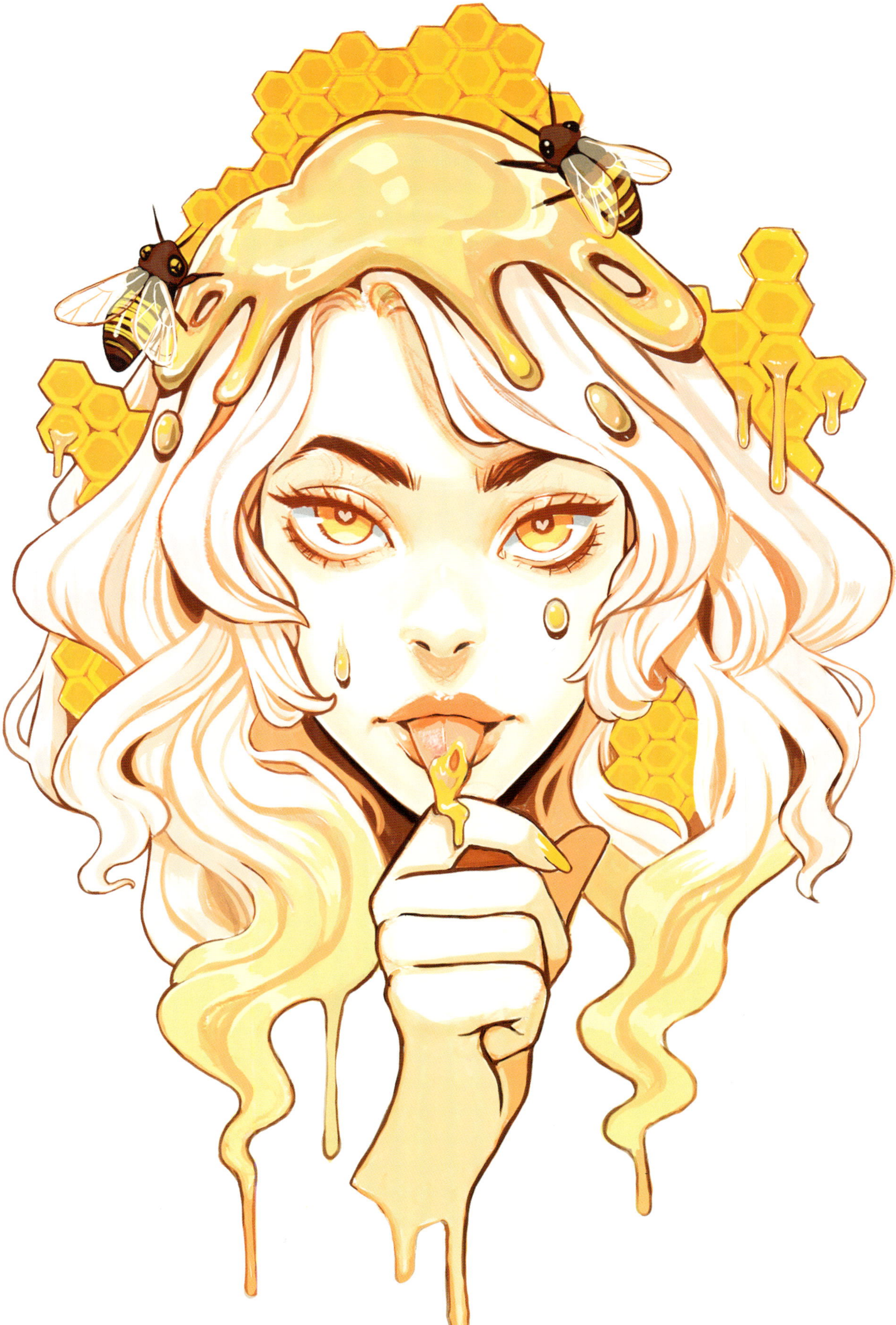

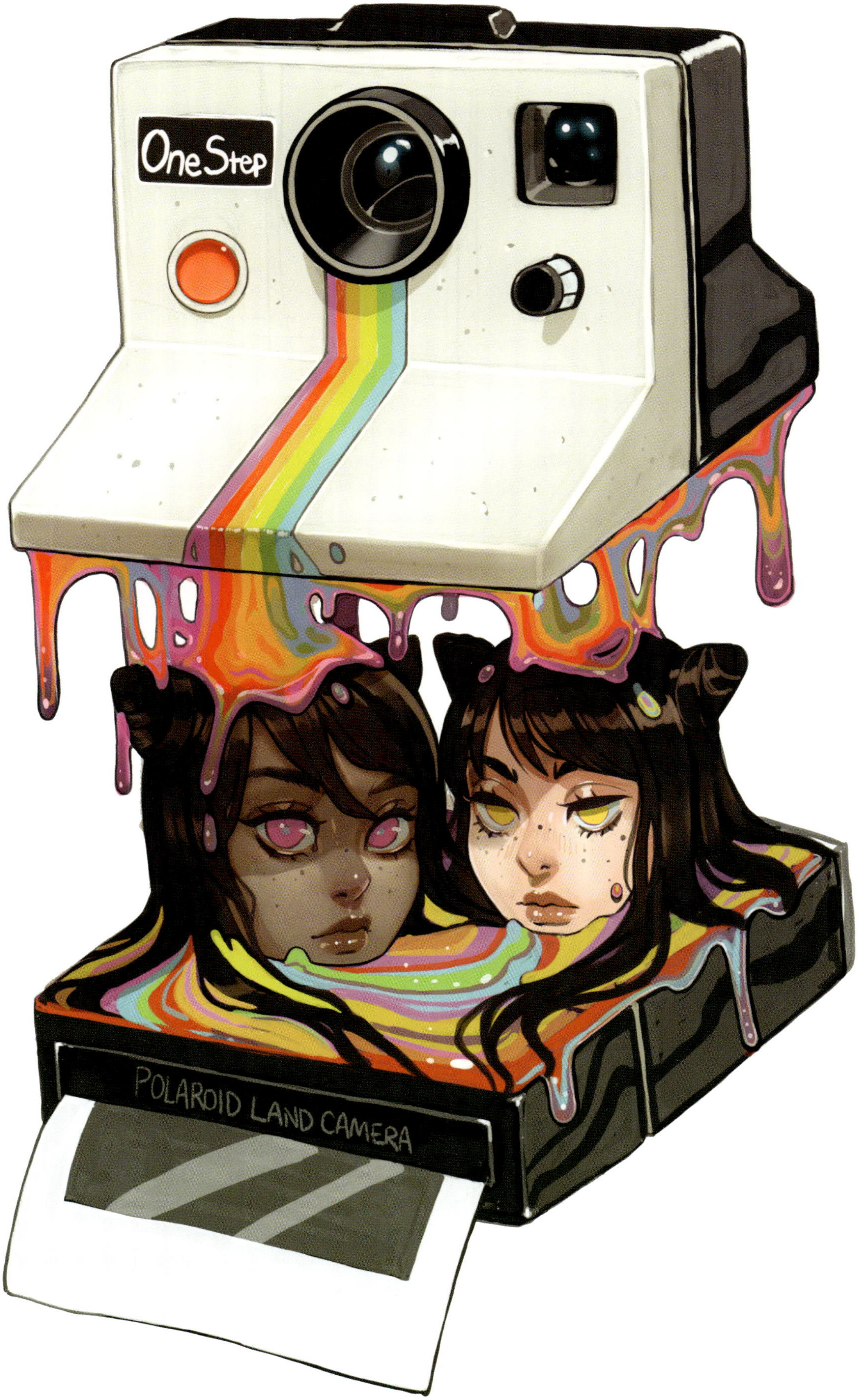
OneStep
POLAROID LAND CAMERA

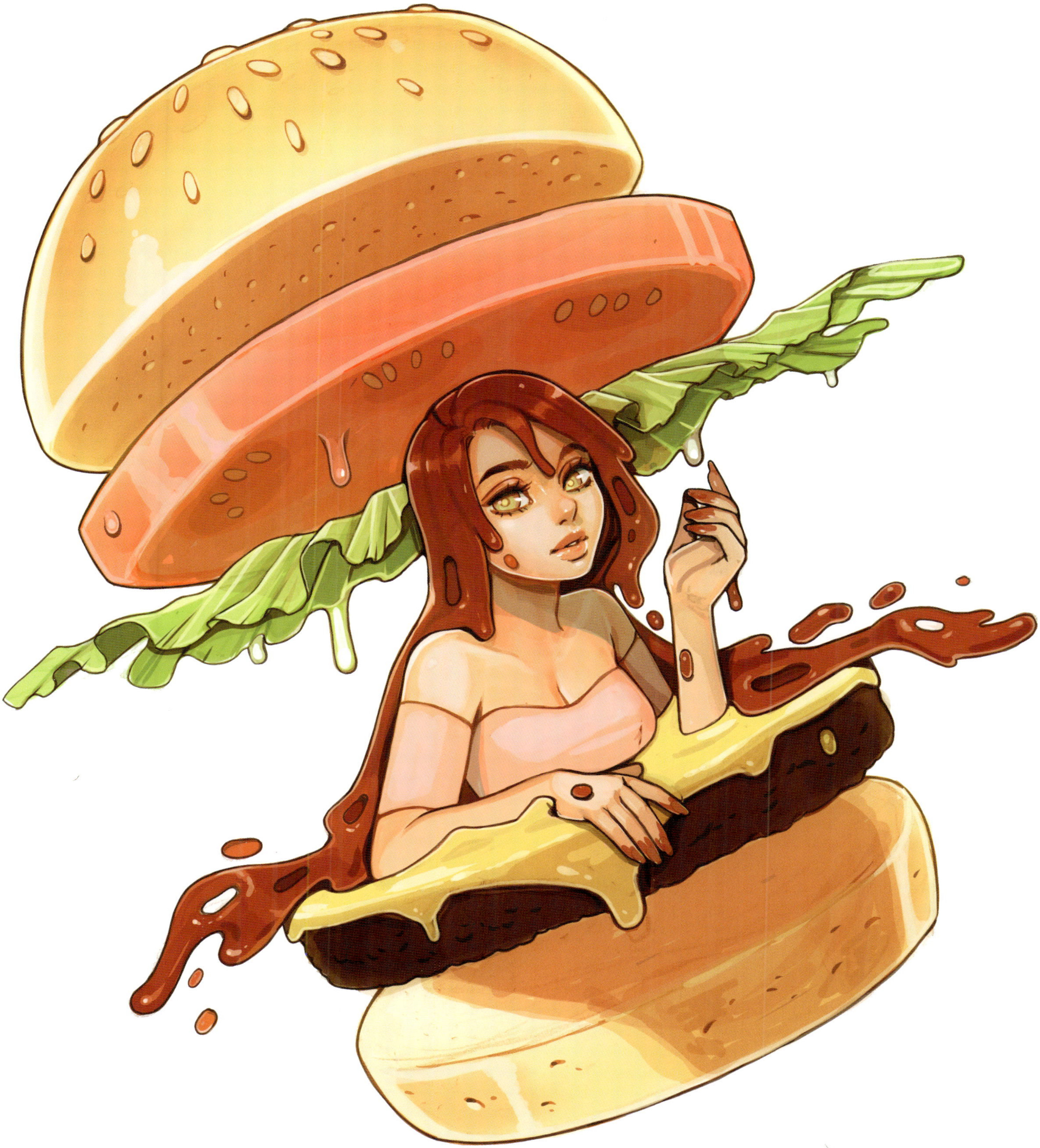

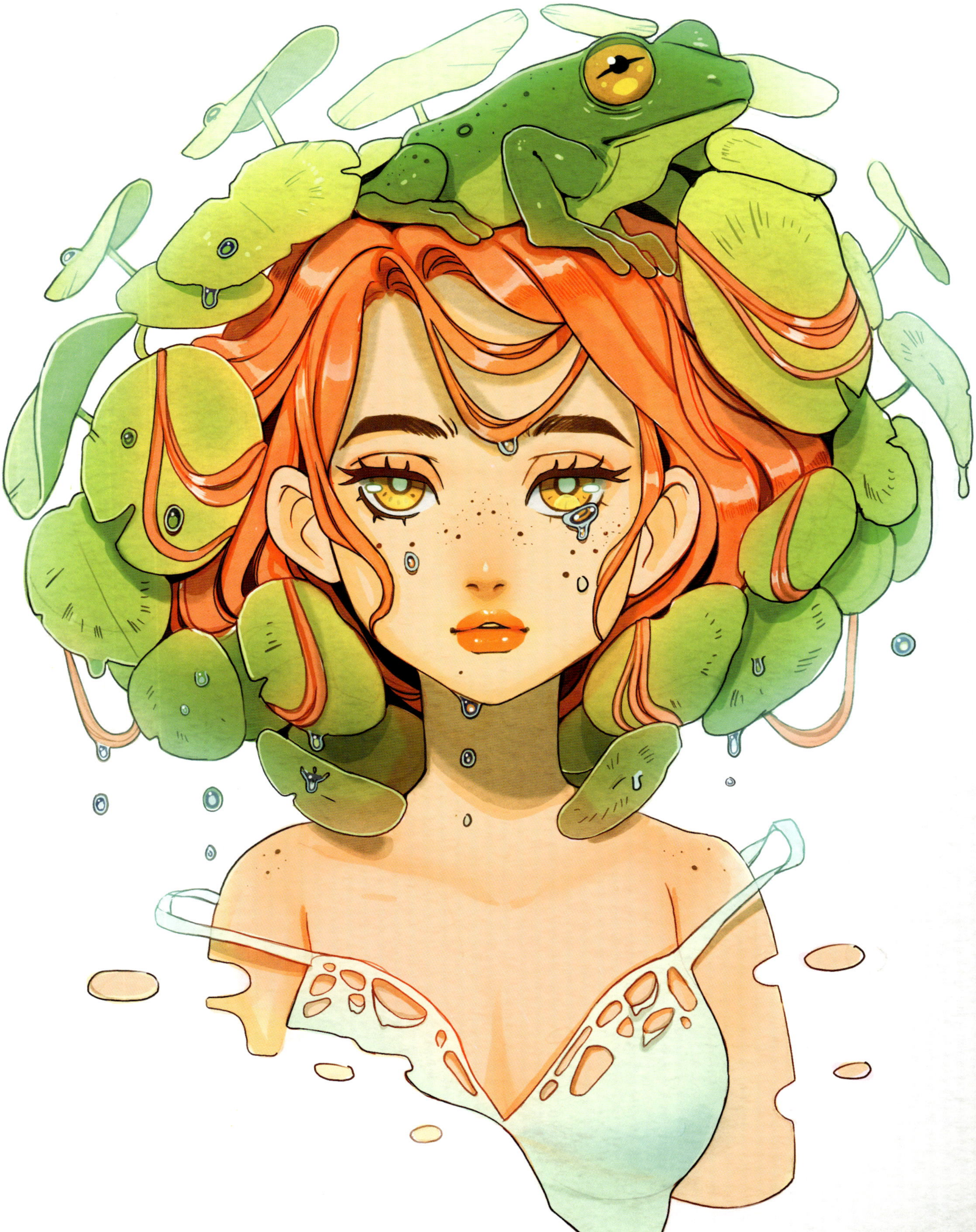

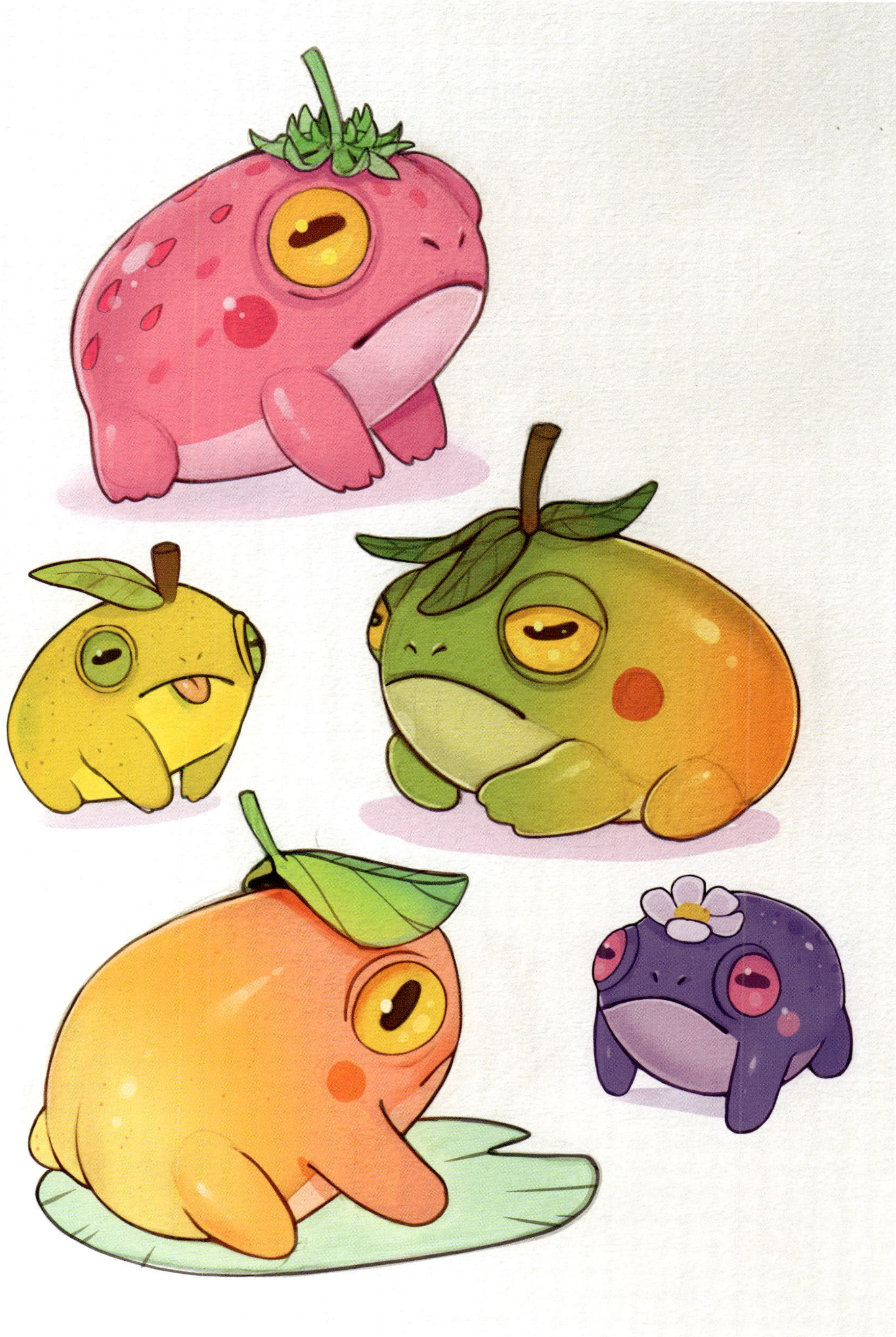

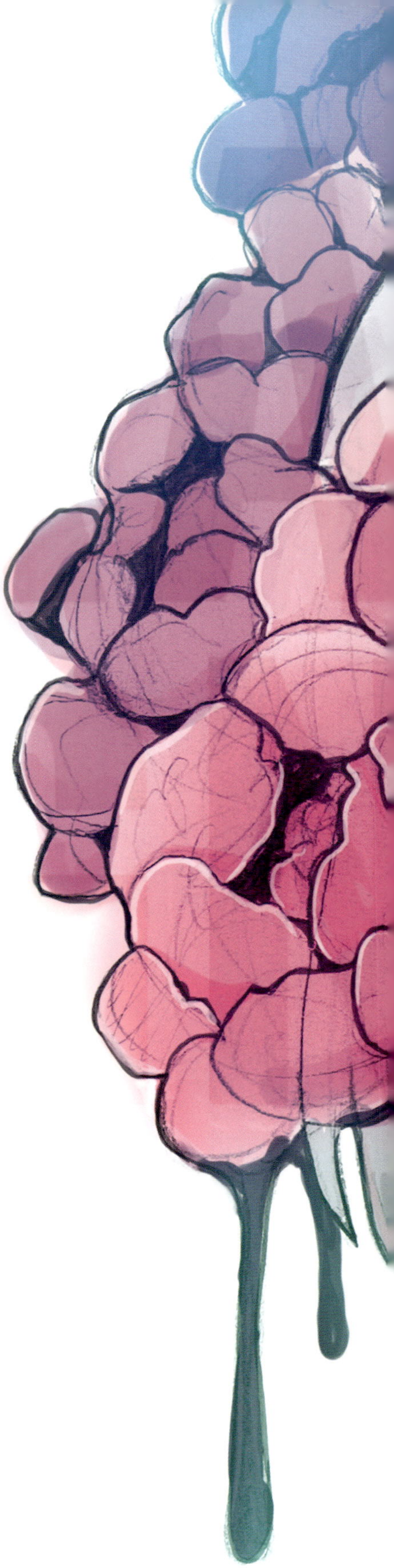

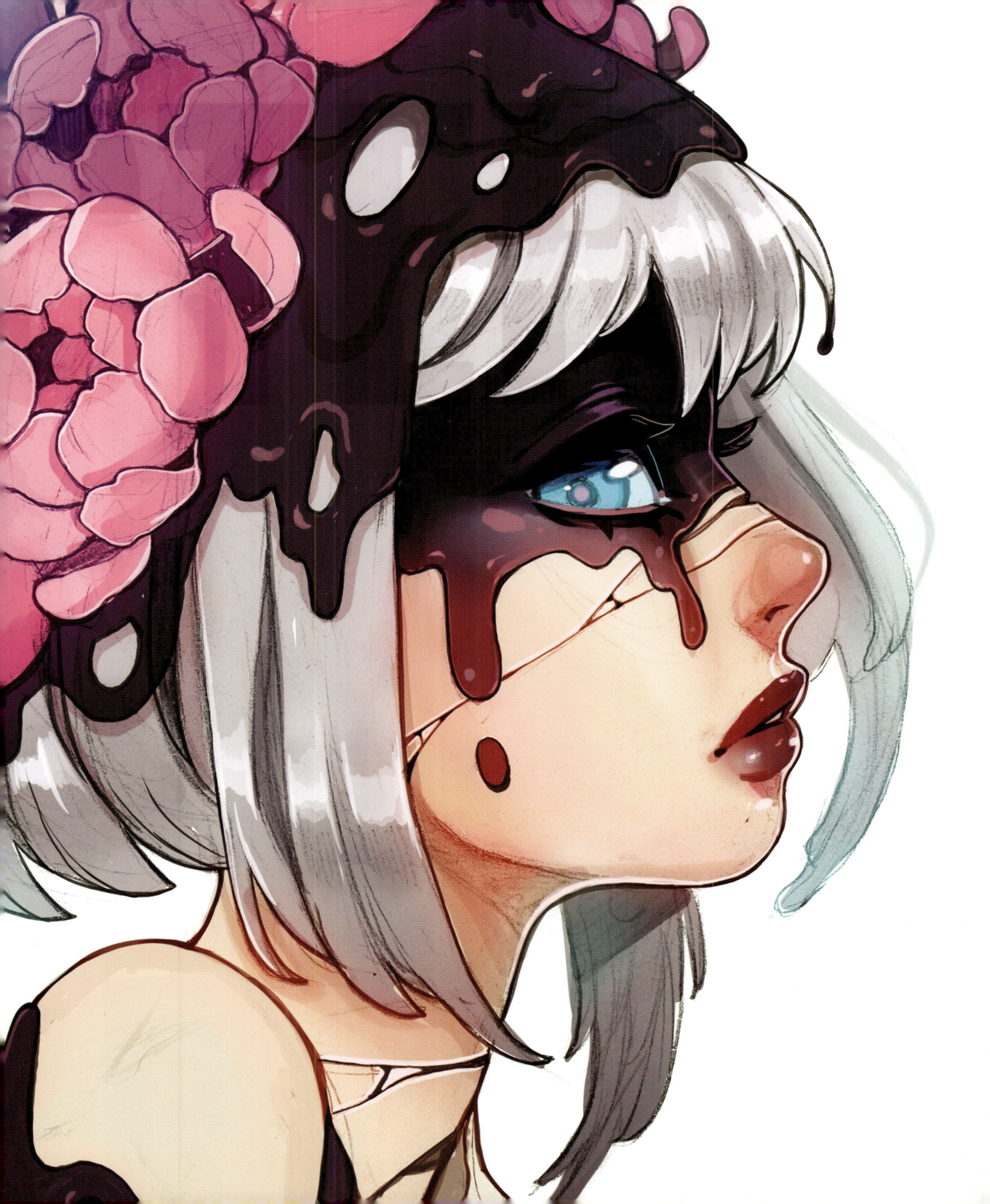

STYLE TECHNIQUE:

# fundamental facial proportions

It's important to state that "average proportions" are not the same as "how you should draw a face." There are many different types of faces in the world, including ones that do not have average proportions — they can all be fun to draw! However, knowing average proportions is a helpful starting point for when you want to create, whether average or not (if you want to draw wider-than-average eyes, it helps to know what average eyes are to begin with).

These are guidelines I read in a "how to draw" book I encountered when I was young and have gone on to use my whole life, so I wanted to pass them on to whoever encountered this book. When drawing, I always recommend using a reference photo to help create the face or pose you want, but any time something is starting to deviate from what you originally intended, I consult these guidelines to help you get back on track. Have fun experimenting with faces outside these boundaries as well!

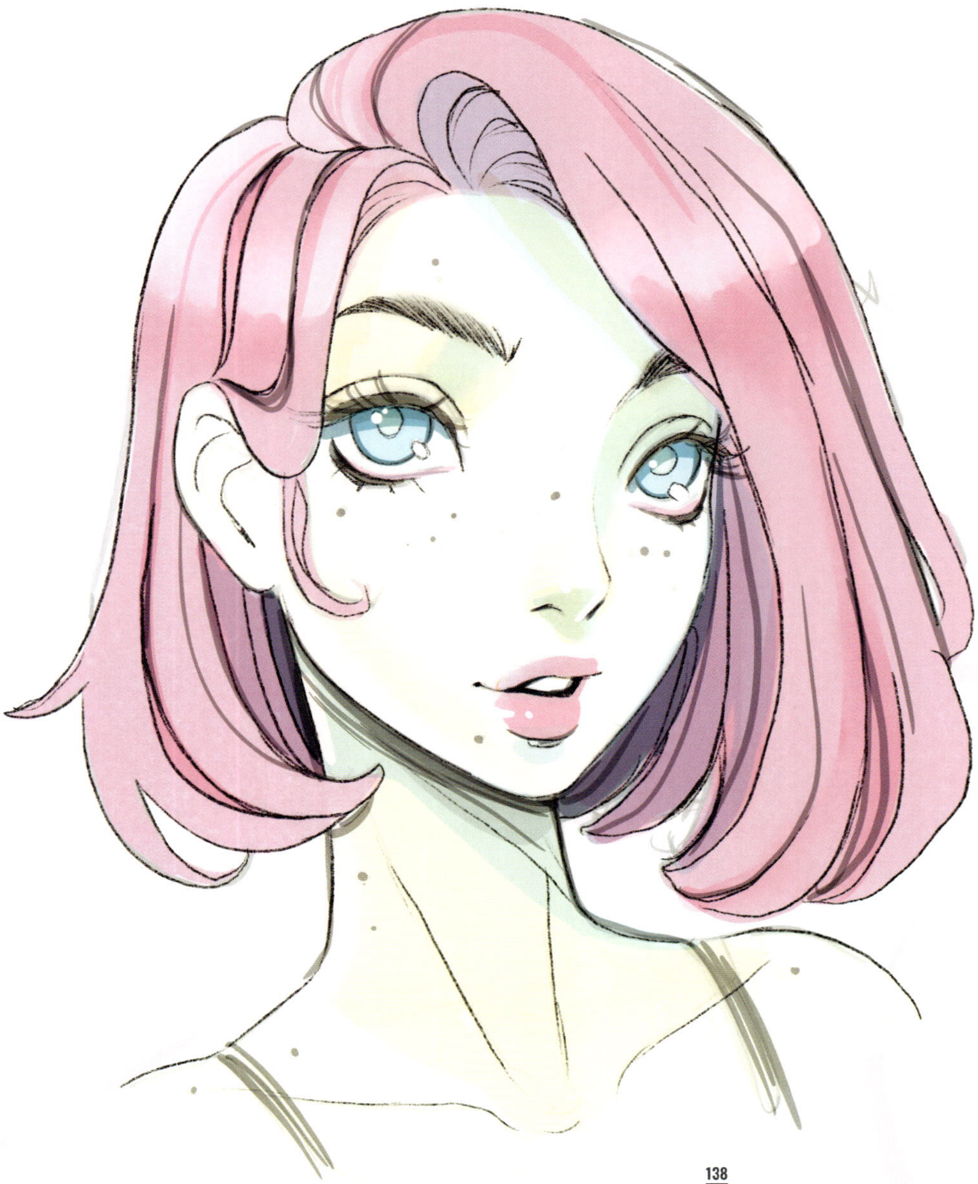

An example of a character with eyes that are wider apart than average

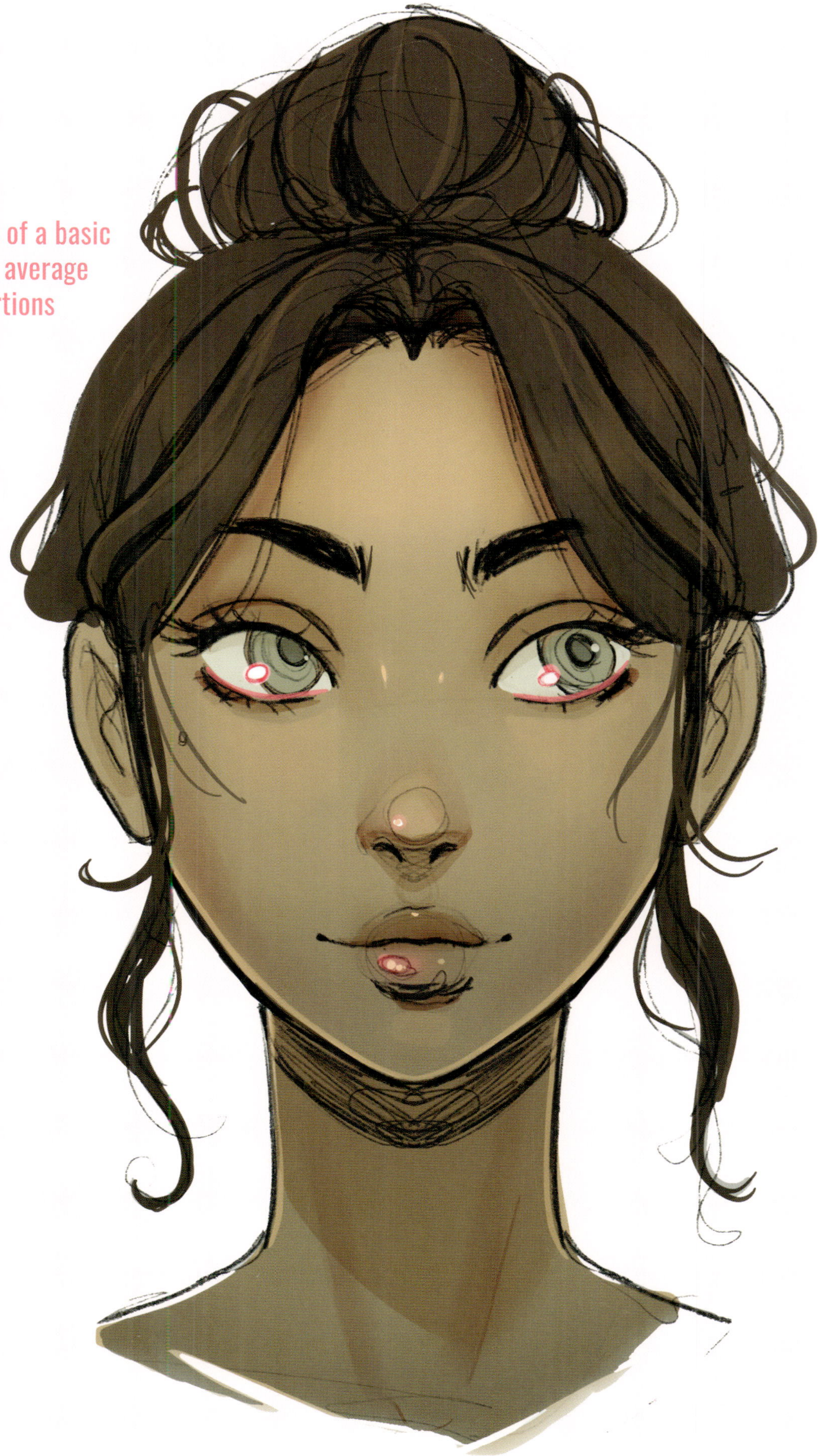

An example of a basic face with average proportions

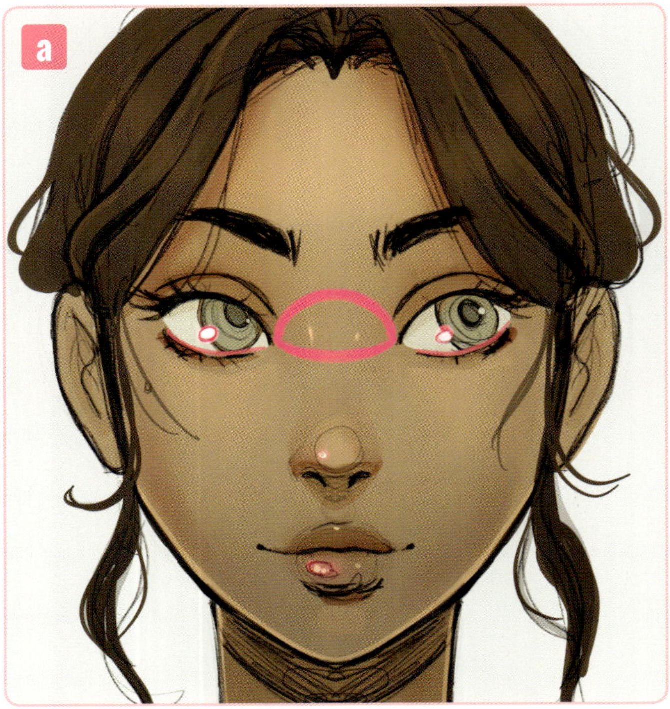


The eyes are one eye-width apart

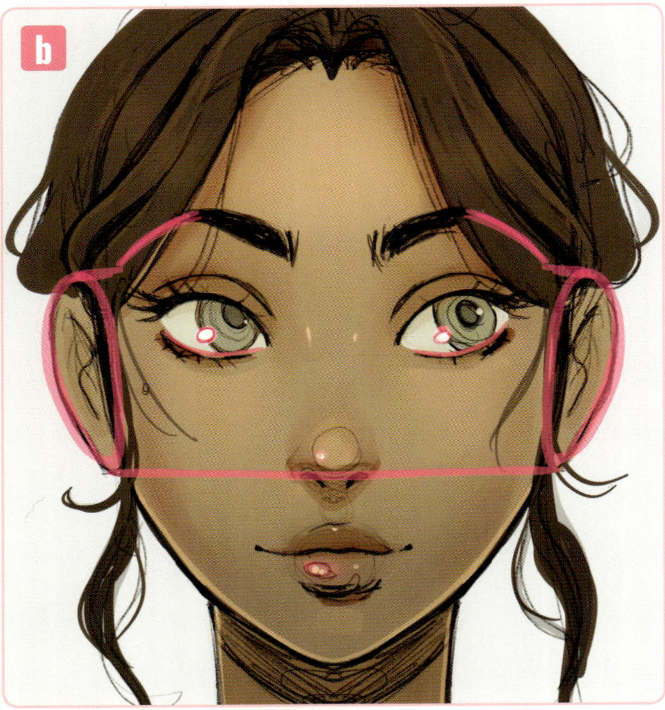


The ears line up with the tip of the nose and eyebrows

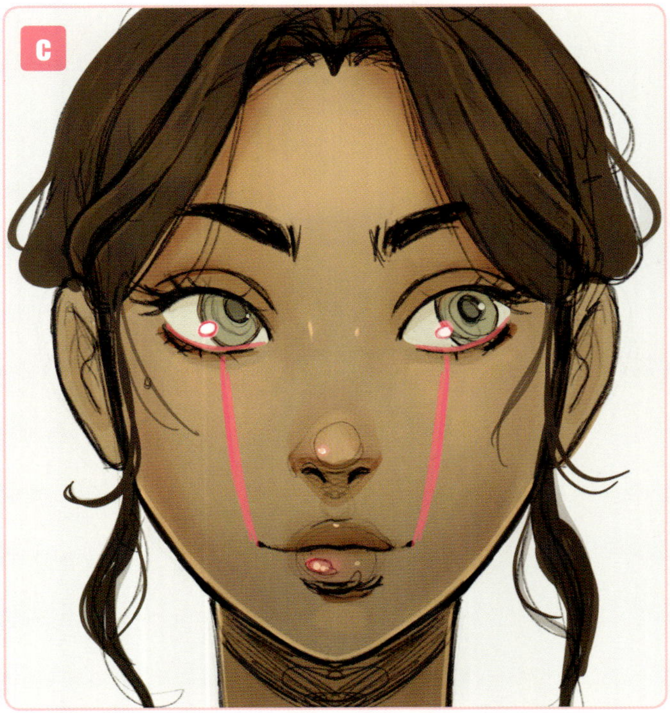


The corners of the mouth align with the centers of the eyes

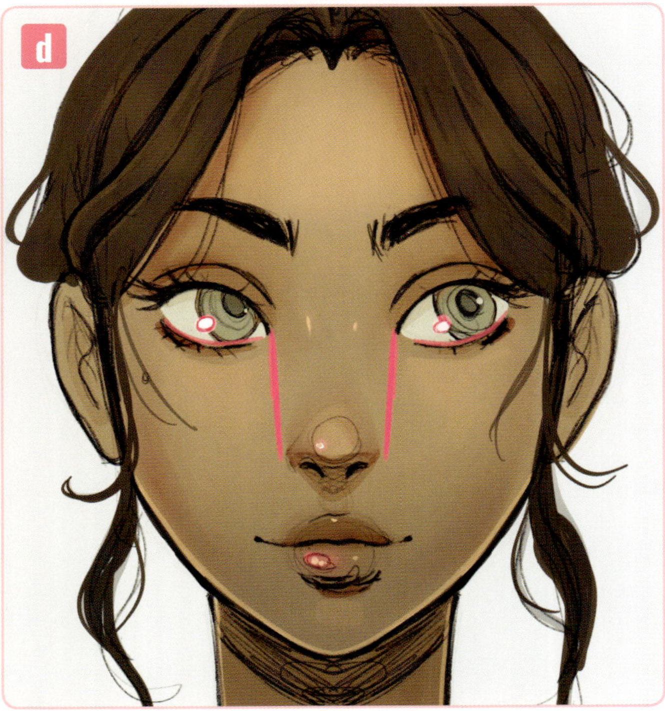


The outer edges of the nostrils align with the inner corners of the eyes

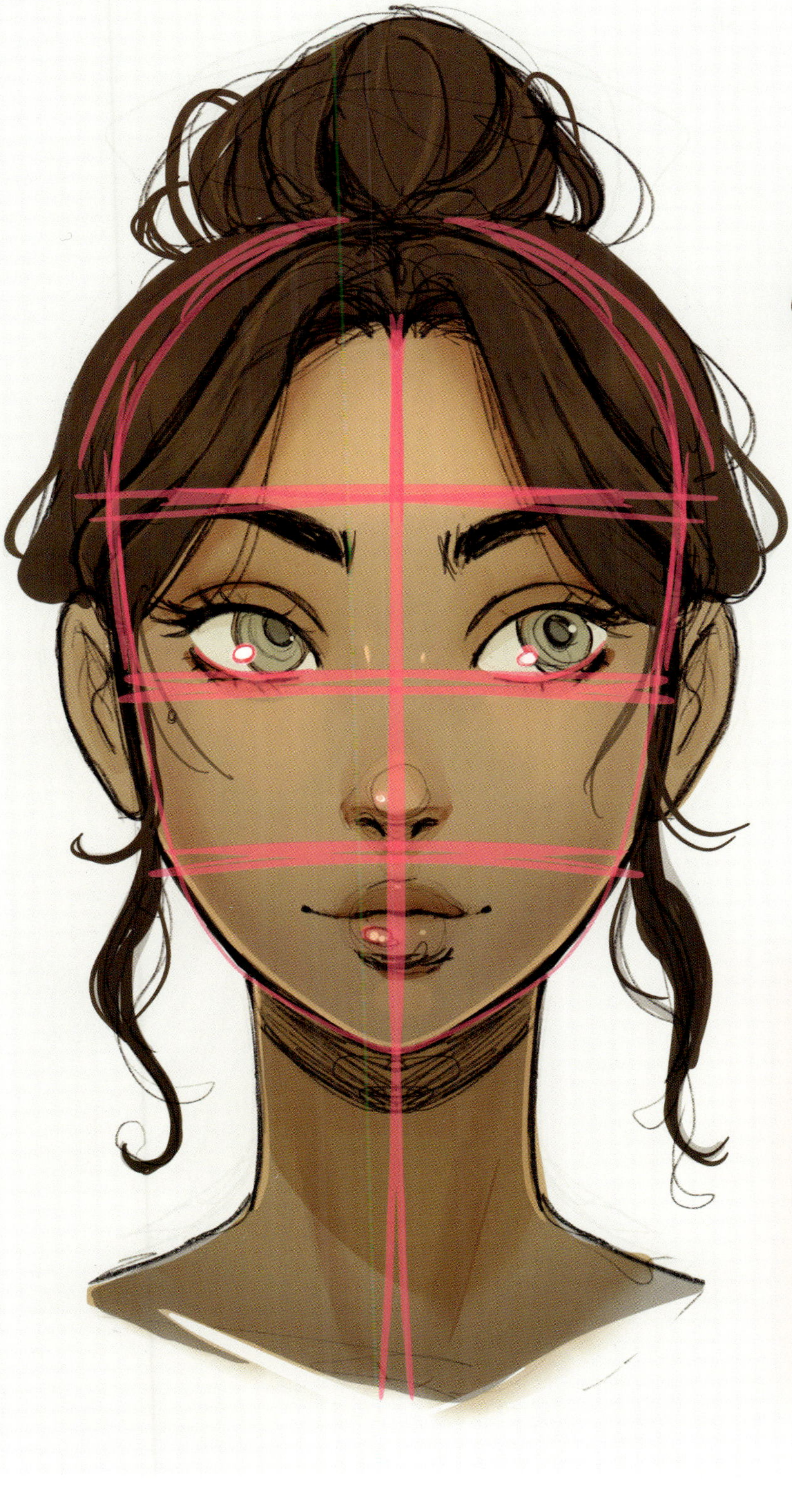

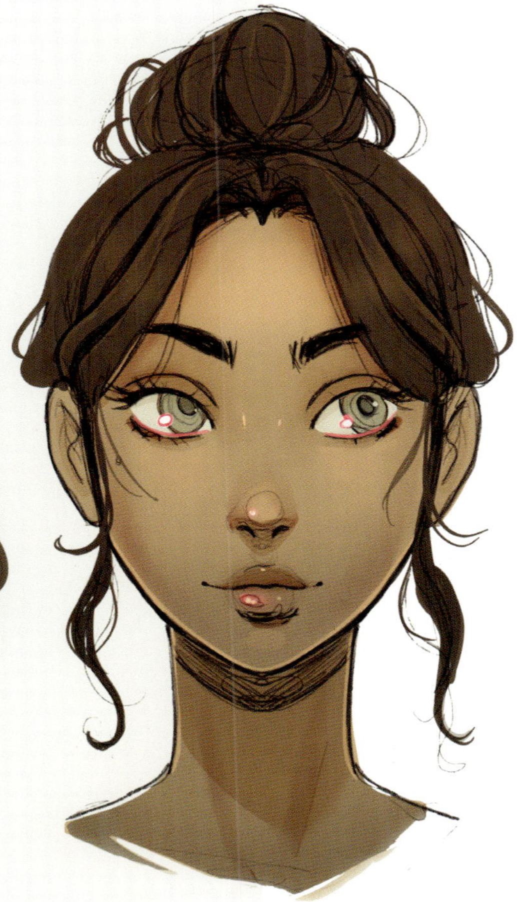

## facial proportions

If you break the head up into four even parts from top to bottom:

- The bottom of the eyes will sit in the middle of the face.
- The nose will sit at the bottom of the third quarter.
- The mouth will sit in the middle of the final quarter.

STYLE TECHNIQUE:

# hair with depth

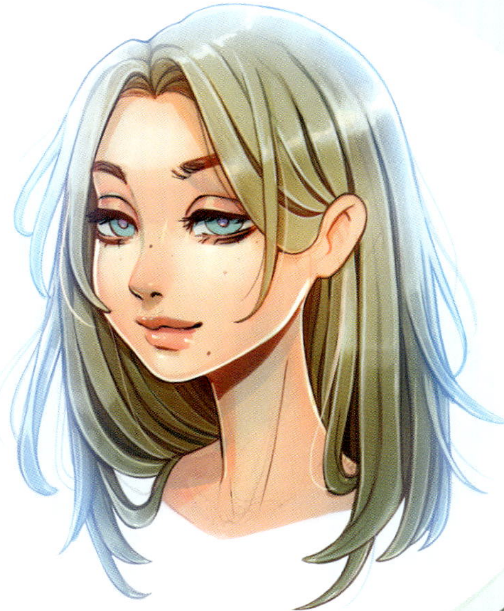

I am often asked how I draw hair, specifically about how I achieve such a great feeling of dimension. I love to draw hair in a way that feels substantial, focusing on creating areas of depth within. To achieve this effect, I build layers on top of layers — and it's honestly much more simple than it looks! No matter what type of hair or hairstyle I'm drawing, I use the same approach. So try using these tips as a general rule for straight, curly, long, short, up, down, or any other kind of hair you can think of. I demonstrate this technique using Procreate, but you can apply the methods to any digital or traditional medium.

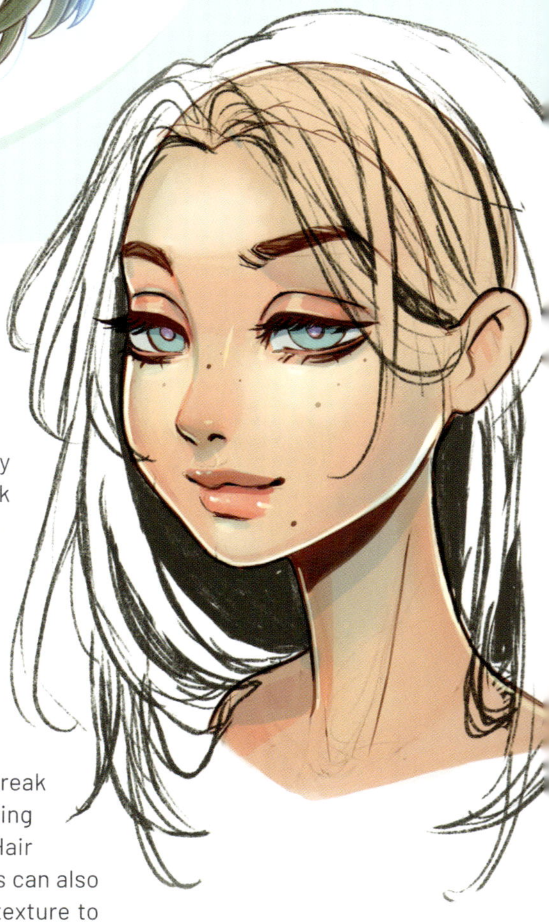

## mixing it up

### Vary the segments

Varying the segment sizes creates interesting compositions and guides the eye across the drawing.

### Change direction

Instead of having all the hair going in the same direction, try drawing strands that go against the natural flow or cross over each other.

### Create contrast

With long hair, I create dark spaces along the neck to ensure the face pops against the background. Short hair will float away from the neck.

## 1 sketching

Starting with the bald head, I do something I can only describe as "chunking." I break the hair up into different segments and separate them with thick, dark spaces. This gives the hair a feeling of depth, as if you're able to see into the different layers. Usually I look for areas where the hair might be breaking apart. For example, if a strand of hair is falling forward onto the shoulder, it will break away from the rest of the hair leaving a dark space I can fill in behind. Hair tucked behind ears or into ponytails can also create this effect. Hair with more texture to it may have more break-away parts, whereas straighter hair may be closer together.

## 2 inking

After I've sketched the hair, I will create the final outline. I fill in all the "chunks" with a fairly dark color here. You should already have a sense of depth to your hair at this stage. Whether I'm working traditionally or digitally, I like to leave a little of the initial sketch in the drawing. I never remove the sketch layer completely — I love the natural fluidity that sketches have. In the hair especially it can help add bits of texture that would otherwise be missing. If I'm working digitally, I will color in the dark areas of the hair totally black as they will be altered in color later. However with traditional art, it's important to be much more up front about what color those dark spaces will be from the start (see my tutorial, Working with Acrylic, on page 94).

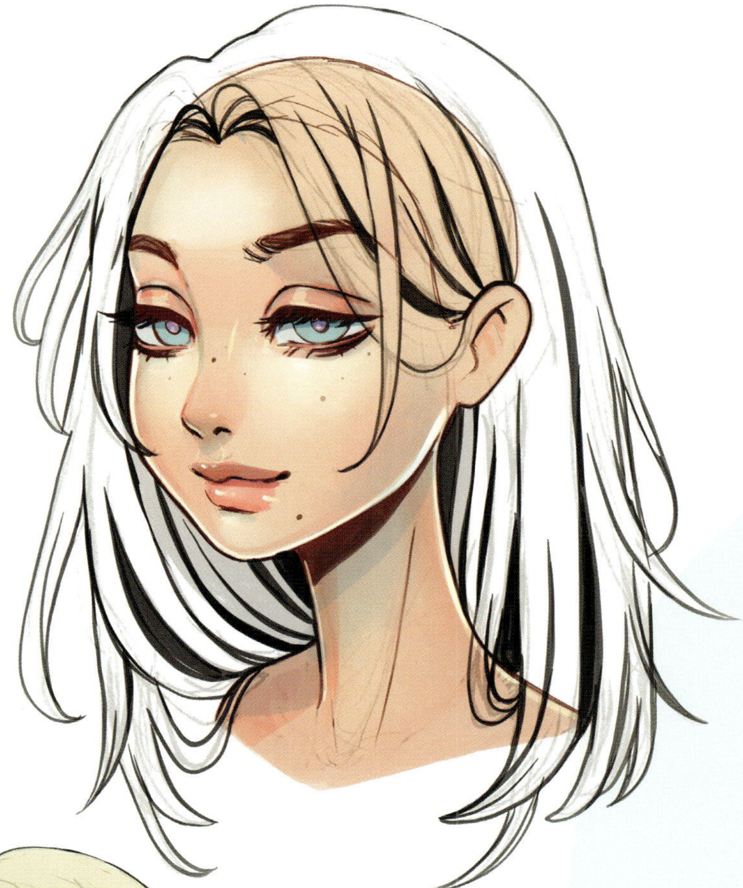

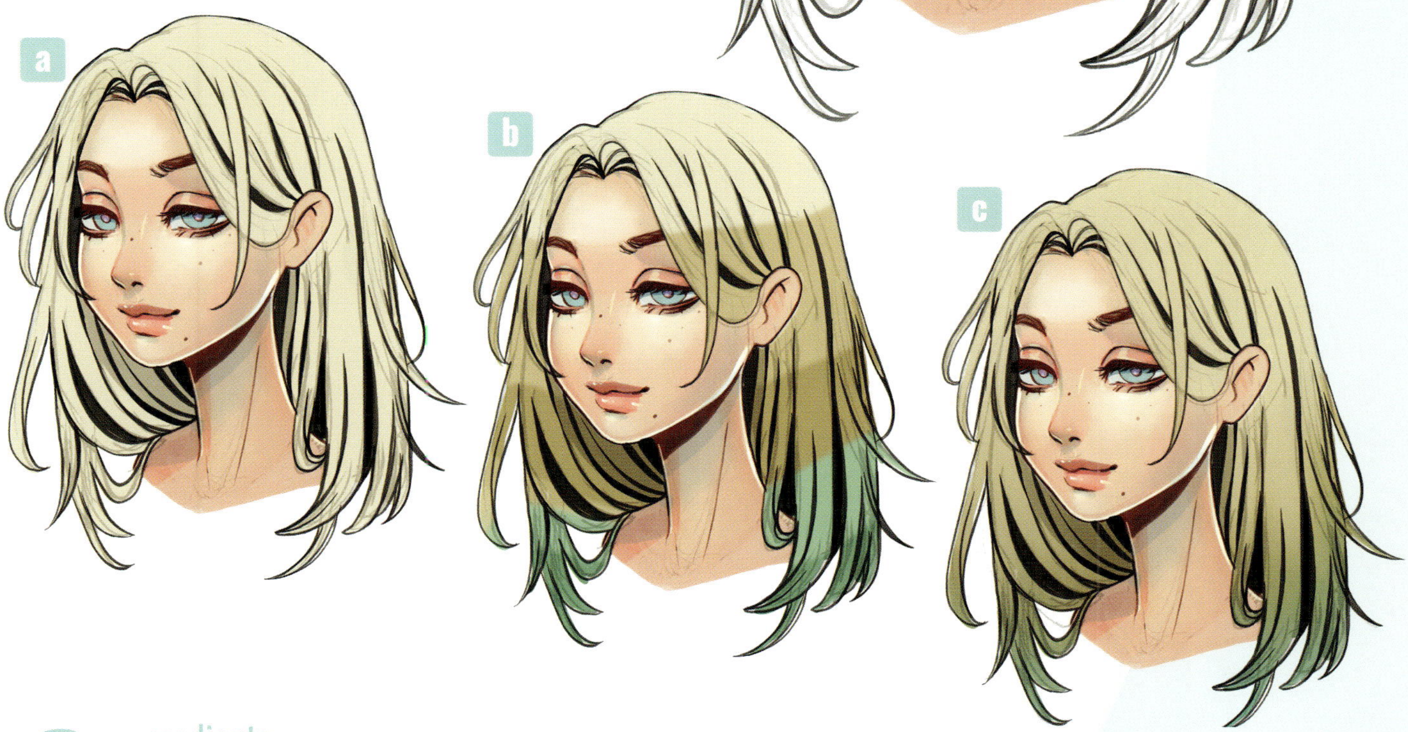


## 3 gradients

The first thing I'll do with hair once I've laid down some base colors **(a)** is add a gradient. You'll see this step in pretty much all my art — I love gradients. A large block of a single color can stagnate your drawing, and hair tends to be one large chunk of a single color, so I add gradients to help break the monotony. Here, the gradient transitions from one color to another **(b)**, but you could also create a gradient that simply transitions from light to dark. If I'm working with traditional methods like paint, I will create the gradient first before "lining" the hair, so that I can blend the colors together in one smooth motion **(c)**.

## 4 shadows

Shadows are really key for creating the kind of hair I produce, because you want to give the impression that some parts of the hair are further back than others. I add two types of shadows – one is to round out the shapes, and one is to create depth.

To round it out, it helps to think of the hair as one large object instead of several disconnected parts. Think of it at its core as a round shape, where the underside of that shape will be shaded. I add shadows to the hair and blend them softly to round it out.

To add depth, look for areas that you want to push further back from the foreground. Here for example, the hair around the neck is further back from the hair around the shoulder, so a heavy shadow is painted over it. Strands of hair that criss-cross over each other will also cast small shadows.

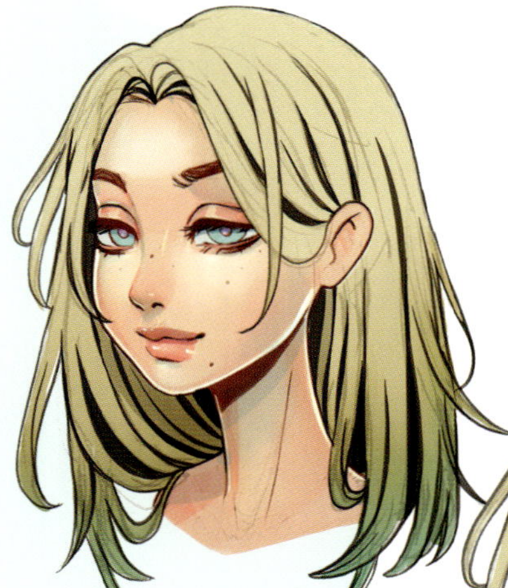

before

after

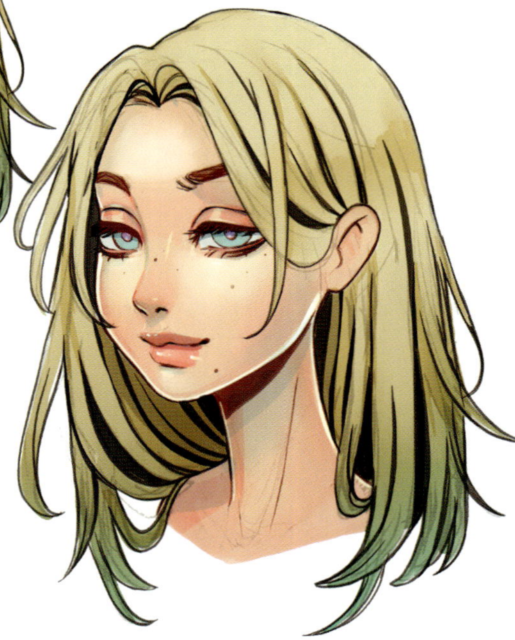

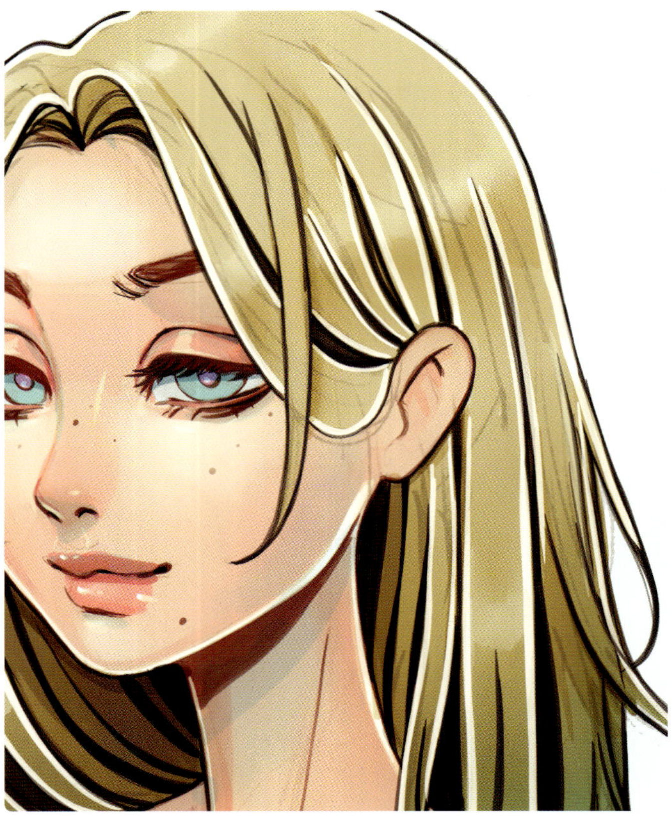

## 5 highlights

Highlights are fun to add because hair can be really shiny, but be careful – it is easy to overcrowd your piece with highlights. The highlights will help to create contrast that pushes the "dimensional" feel of the hair. There are several places where I add them. The first is directly above the "rounding" shadows that were added in the previous step. I add a bright but soft highlight to help further emphasise the roundness. I also add thin outlines along the hair strands. This helps to distinguish the hair segments from each other. These highlights are fairly light and will be at their brightest when they are closest to the rounding highlights. The third place I look for are areas where light might be catching the hair and causing shine – often close to the crown of the head or around the bangs.

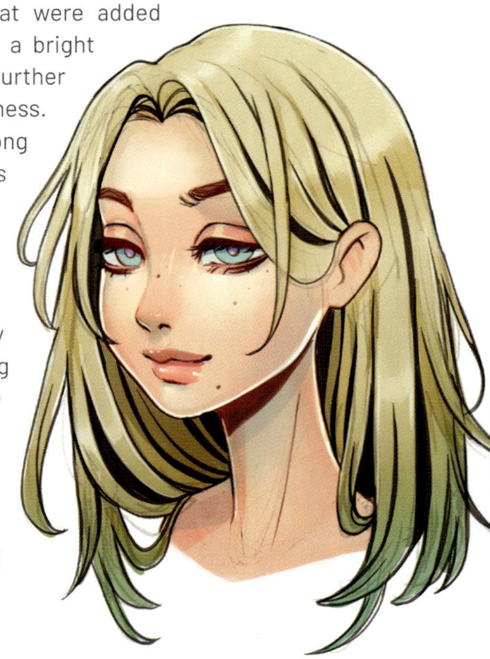

6

## screens

This is a digital-specific step, as your hair would be the true color from the start if you're working traditionally. However, as a shortcut for digital art, once I have all my highlights and shadows in place, I will use a Screen layer to show the hair's "true" color. This will turn all the darkest parts of the piece that color. For example if you're drawing pink hair, use a Screen layer to tint the hair hot pink. On this piece, I tinted the hair a yellow-blonde color.

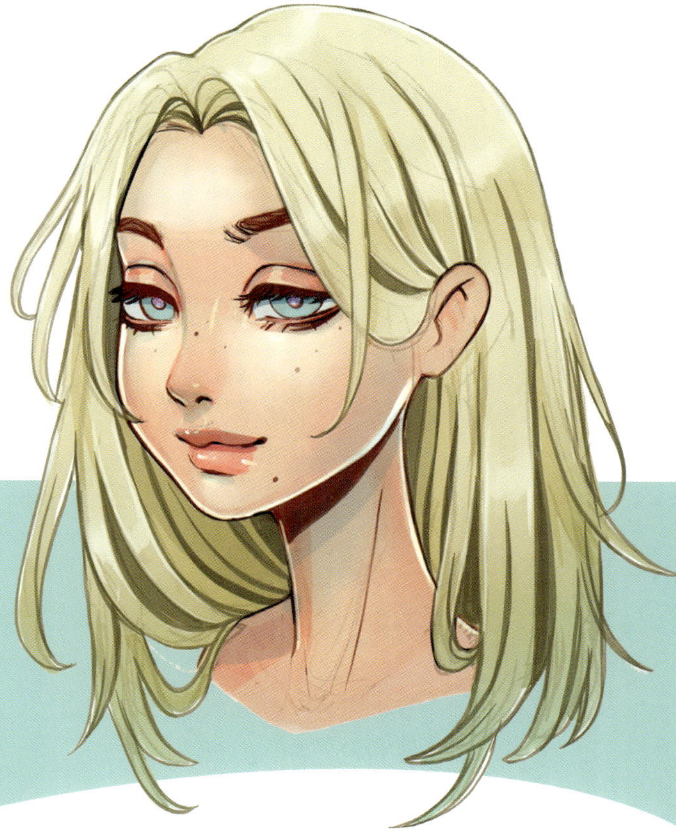

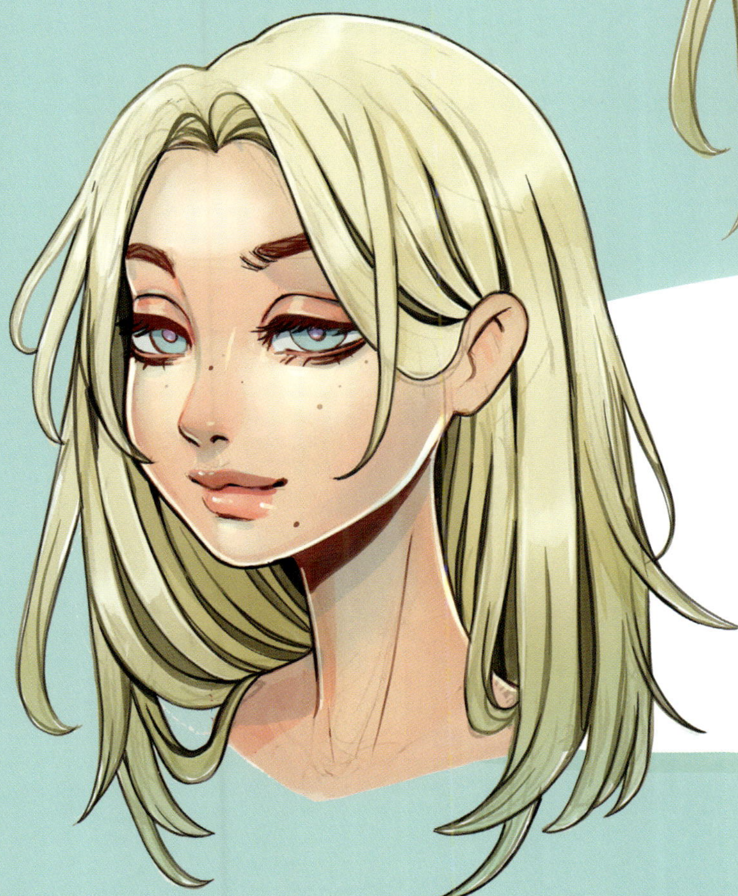

7

## redraw lines

Because you've lost your darkest "darks" with the Screen layer, it's time to add some (but not all!) back in. I'll add a few dark brown or blue lines (not black) around the dark "chunk" areas, but won't fill them in with the dark color. I may also outline the overall silhouette of the hair — you now have lines in the hair that transition from the hair color to a darker outline color.

8

## add more shadow and light

This is where I go back in and start pushing more parts of the picture backward or forward. I use cooler colors for shadows in areas that I want to feel particularly deep, such as the area around the neck. To bring forward areas of the picture I want to feel brighter, I add more aggressive highlights. In areas that are particularly bright along strands of hair, I will draw an almost "H" shape to accentuate the highlight that goes along the outline of the hair strand.

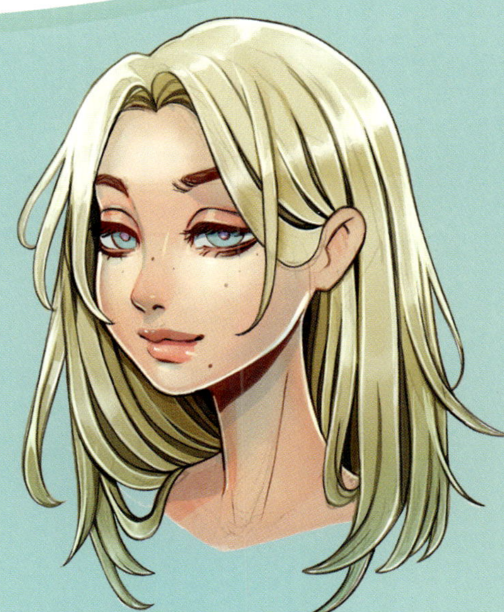

## 9 add warmth from the face

A fun trick is to extend a little warmth from the face into the hair around the edges of the face, giving your piece a radiant quality. This works for any skin tone — for warm skin tones, I mix in a bit of red **(a)**; for cool skin tones, I mix in some purple. Even for fantasy skin tones such as blue or green, I might mix in a teal color. Digitally, I will use the Screen layer to do this. With traditional tools such as paint, I will take a little of the skin color, blend it with the hair color, then paint that combination around the edges of the face **(b)**.

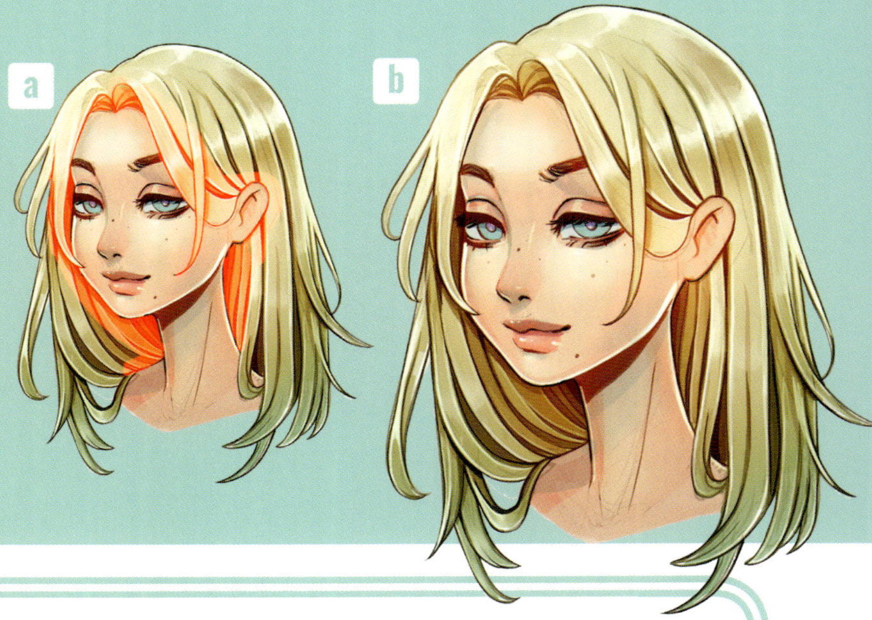


## finishing touches

There are lots of little things you can do to add finishing touches to your hair.

### Push lights and darks further

You can do this by adding another layer of shadow over your hair. I let the highlights shine through the brightest around the rim of the hair where the light is hitting it, but allow this shadow layer to push some of the highlights back.

### Add atmosphere

In the tutorial Working Tradigitally (page 78), we saw atmosphere added with a warm yellow light — here it is done with a cool blue light. With digital tools, you can use the Screen layer; with traditional tools, you can blend your hair color with a bit of light blue and blend it in around the outside of your character's hair.

### Add flyaway hairs

Add small, delicate hairs that break away from the larger chunks. I add most around the edges of the hair where the light catches them, but I also add a few crossing over the inside of the hair. When flyaway hairs cross over dark parts of the hair, I make them a very pale color for the sake of contrast.

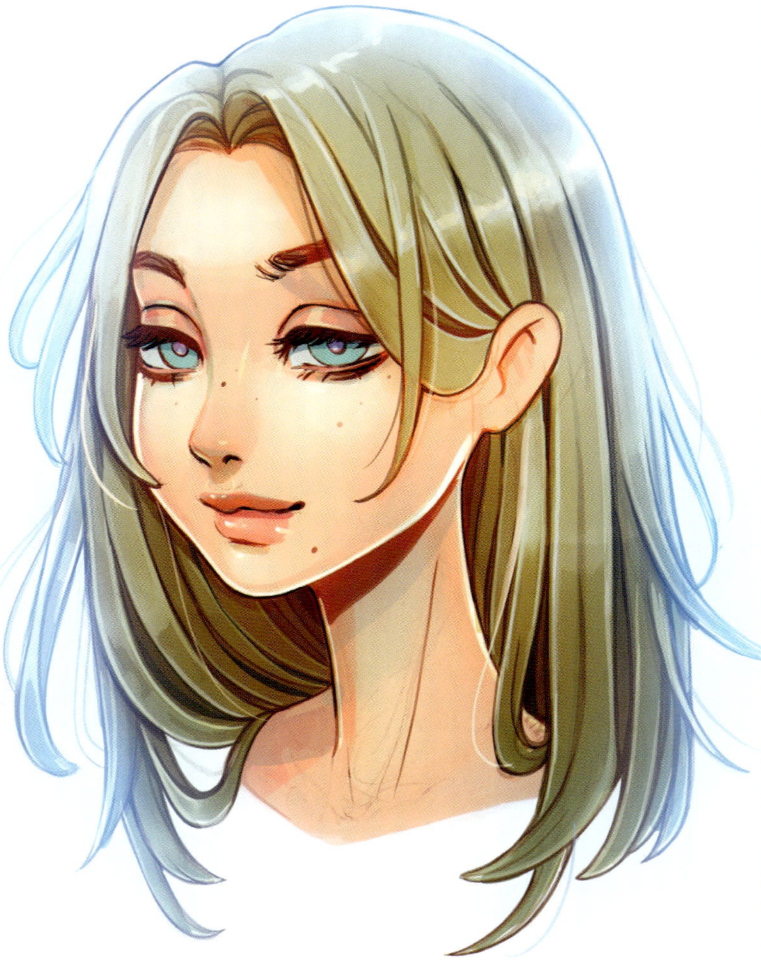

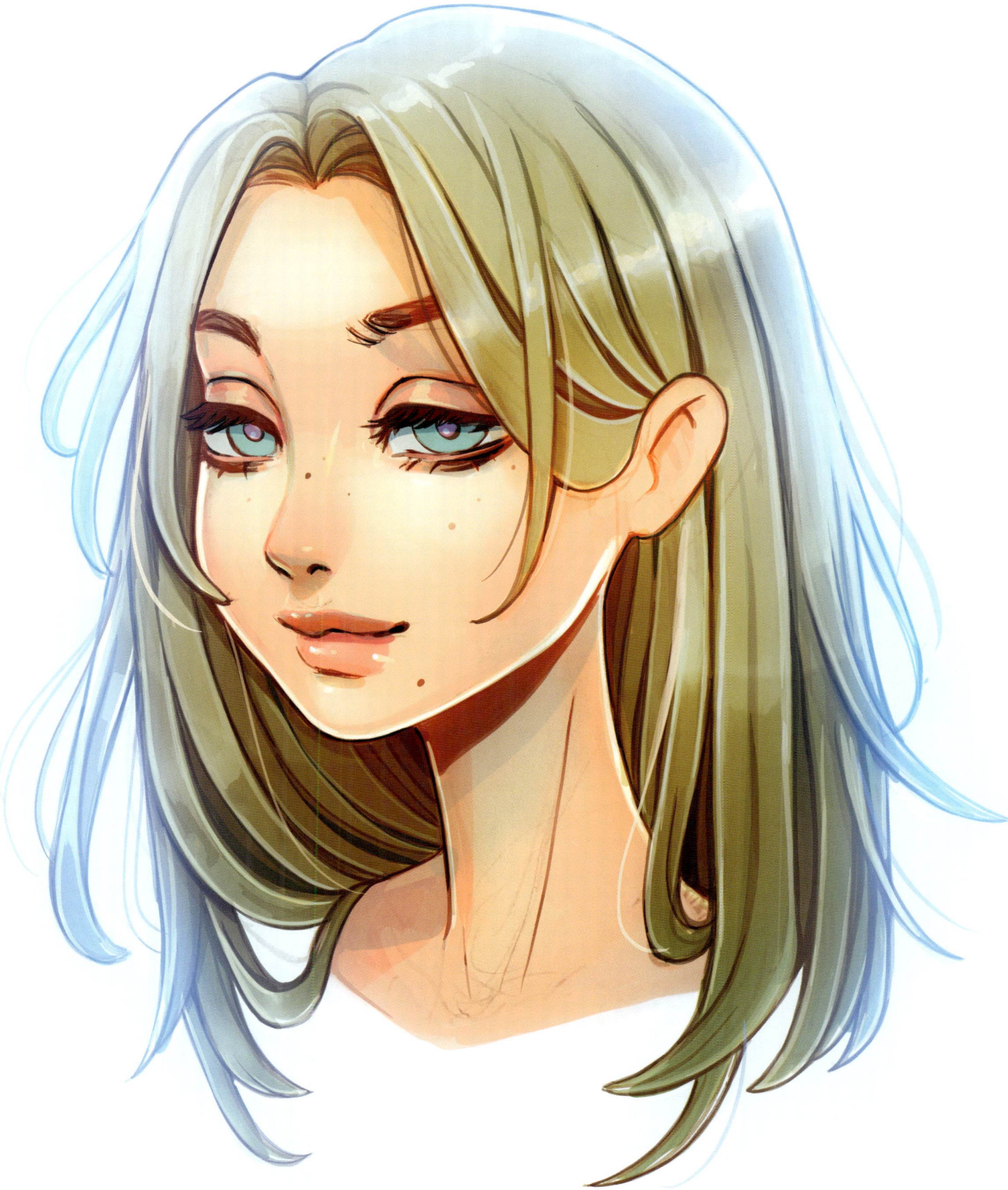

STYLE TECHNIQUE:

# drawing wings

I love adding wings to my art — feathers are beautiful, delicate, and elegant. Drawing wings may seem a bit intimidating at first, but it helps to break them down into basic shapes. There are many different kinds of bird wings, so always look up a reference photo for the one you want to create. My wings are imagined fantasy wings. They don't follow one specific bird's anatomy (a swan's is probably the closest) but are an amalgamation of the many different photos I've looked at.

## feathered tiers

Wings will typically have three or four "tiers" of feathers, with the top tier being the fuzziest. The feathers on each subsequent tier become a little longer, with the longest feathers at the bottom.

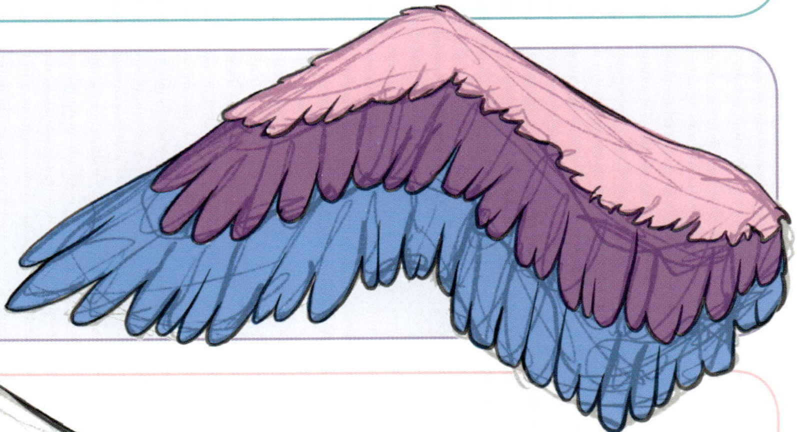

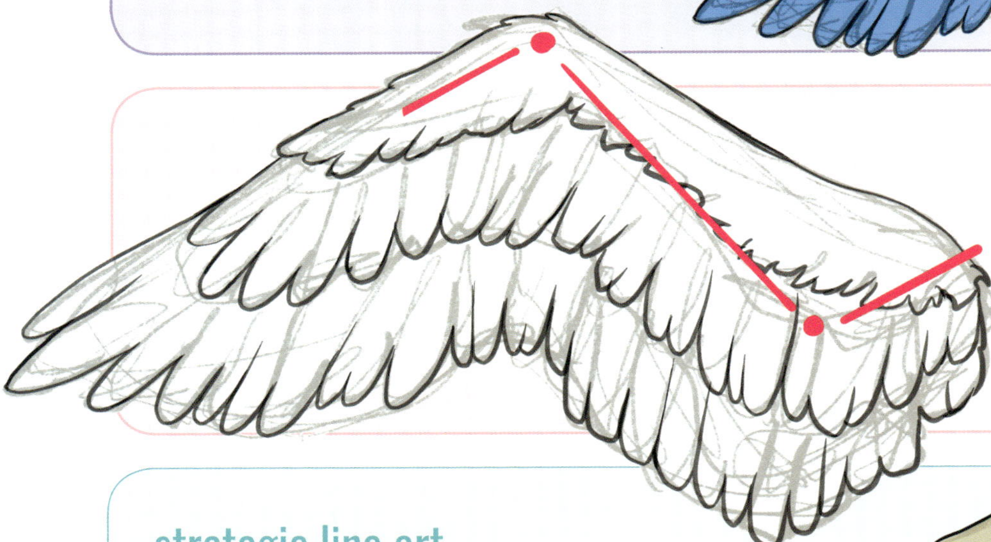

## bone structure

Understanding the underlying bone structure can also help to construct a believable wing structure and shape. The pink line work depicts the basic bone structure of an average wing.

## strategic line art

When drawing wings, remember that they are made up of lots of soft shapes and shading, and feature very few hard lines. When I do create line art for my wings, I will line the outside shape of the wing as well as the underside of each tier. However, I won't draw the individual feathers themselves — this helps keep the feathers feeling like they softly blend together.

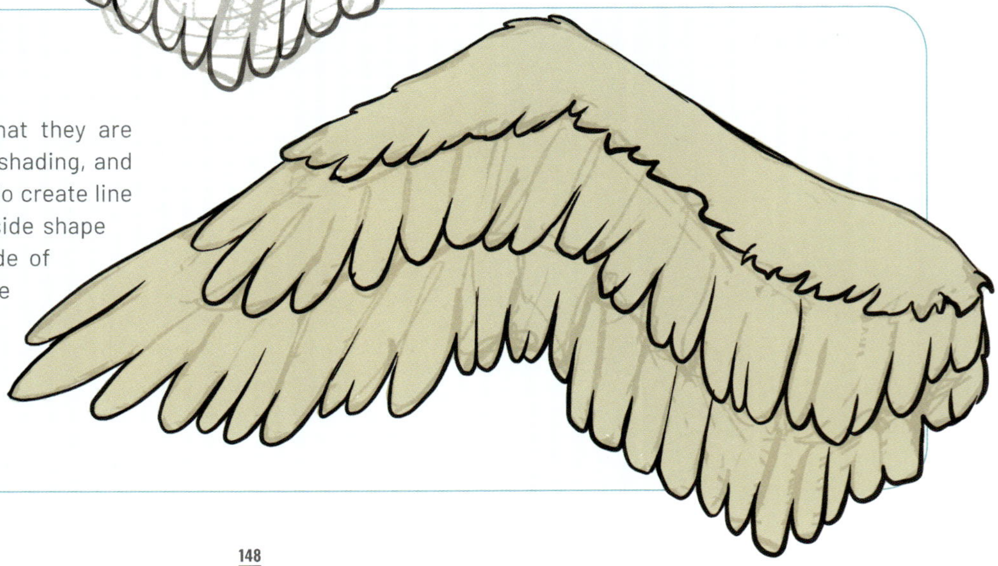

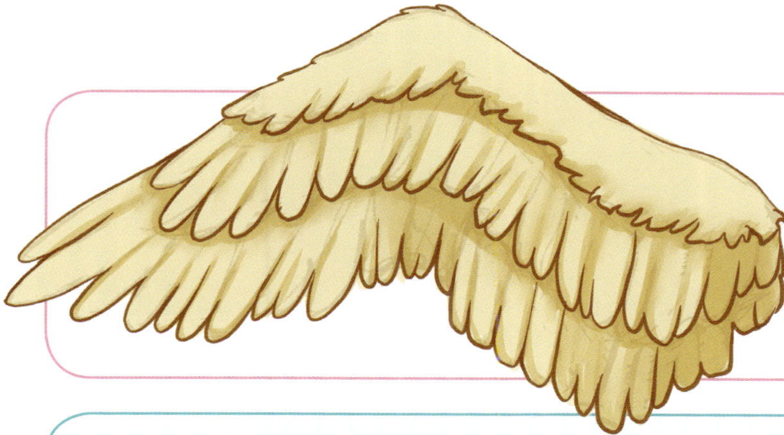

## creating shadows

To distinguish the feathers from each other, I will use soft, gentle, warm shadows instead of linework. Here, I used a warm red and blended it to softly distinguish the individual feathers.

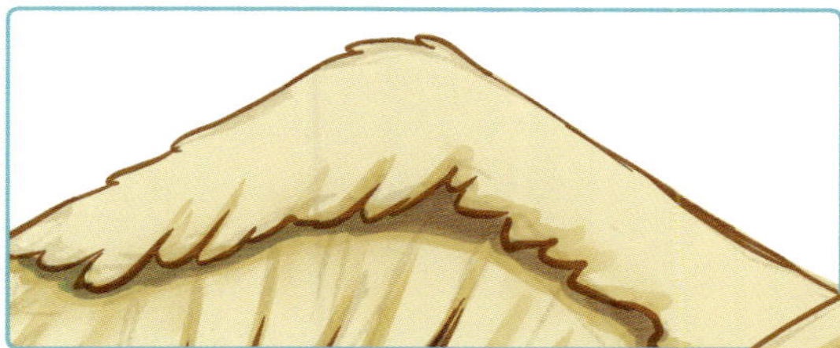

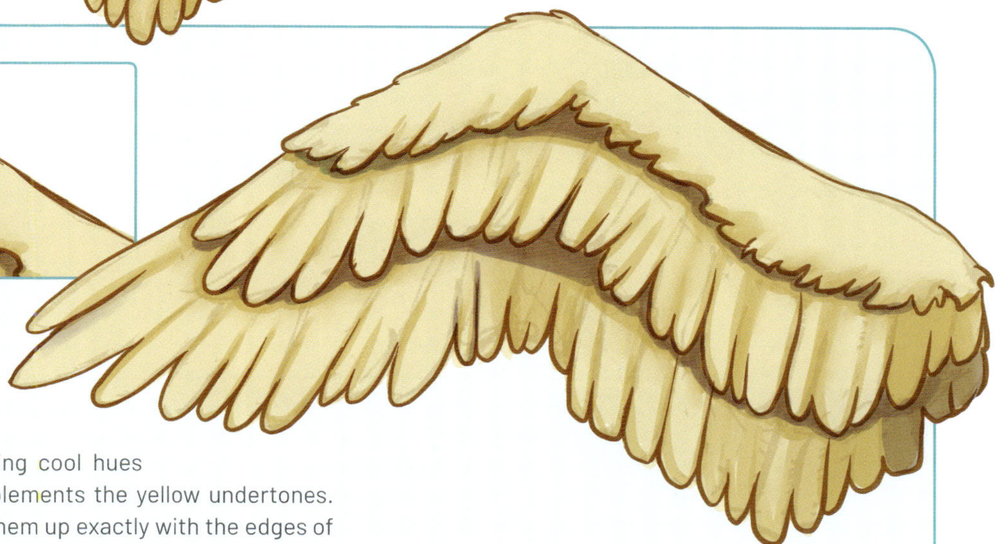

## shadow rims

Typically, deeper shadows feature where thick layers of feathers cast shadows on lower layers. I enjoy using cool hues for the shadows – here, purple complements the yellow undertones. When adding the shadows, don't line them up exactly with the edges of the soft shadows you drew previously. Instead, leave a rim of the soft shadow around these new, harsh shadows.

## highlighting

I find adding highlights really brings the entire image together and properly distinguishes the different tiers of feathers. Often, the edges of feathers will capture light, so I like to highlight them where one tier meets another as well as on the edges of the wing where the feathers may catch the light.

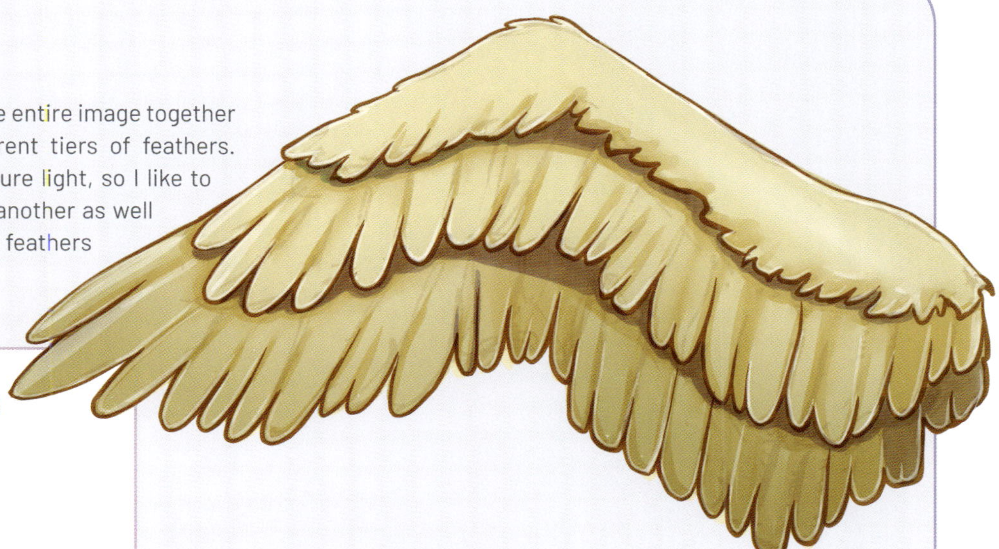

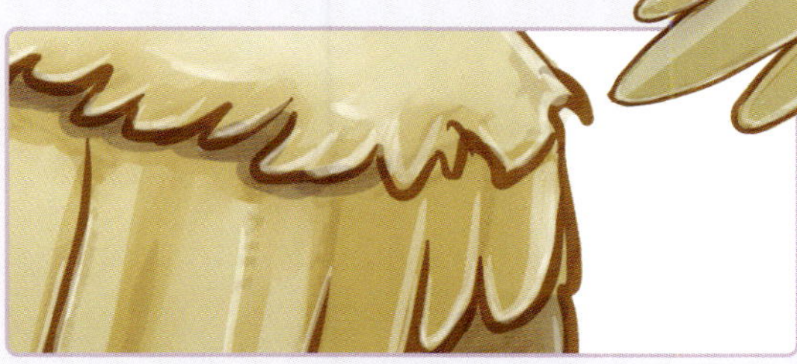

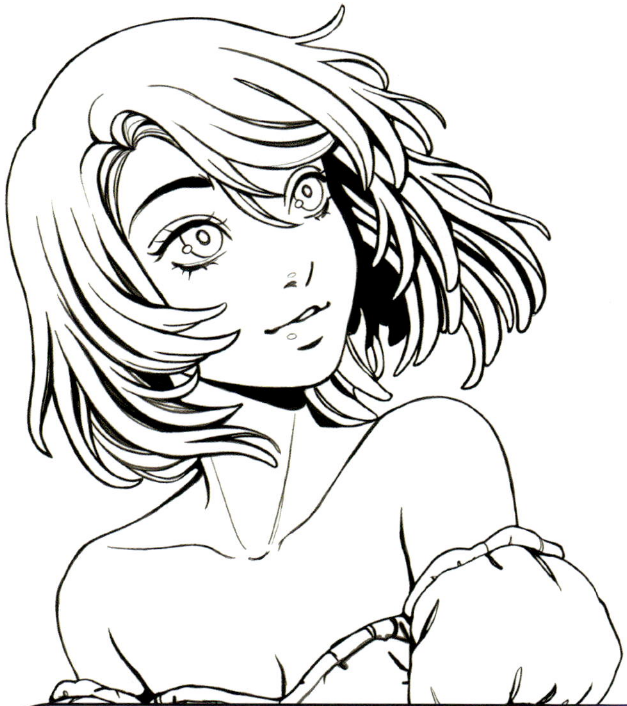

STYLE TECHNIQUE:

# glowing elements

Creating glow is a funny thing — once you learn the fundamentals, it's so simple. But for the longest time I really didn't get it, and my thought process was: light is white, right? So to add light you add more... white? I created a painting in high school that makes me laugh when I look at it now. It's of an anglerfish (one of those deep-sea fish with the luminescent headlamps), and my best attempt at getting him to glow was by adding lots of white paint. This was clearly unsuccessful, and I remember feeling frustrated — no matter how much paint I threw down, it still didn't glow!

This tutorial is about the concepts behind glow. Even though my examples are all digital, they can be done with any kind of media, traditionally, or otherwise. Some of the acrylic paintings I produce also have a glow to them.

## value and saturation

Not only is glow is about color and light theory, but it is also about understanding how value scales work together, and pairing saturation with desaturation to trick the eye into "seeing" light. It's important to understand what I mean when I talk about value and saturation.

- Value is how light or dark something is, white being the lightest on the value scale, and black being the darkest.
- Saturation is about color intensity. Picture a very vivid blue — the more you de-saturate that blue, the closer it gets to gray. A fully desaturated image would be entirely in grayscale. Light will reveal objects in the most vivid, saturated form of their true colors.

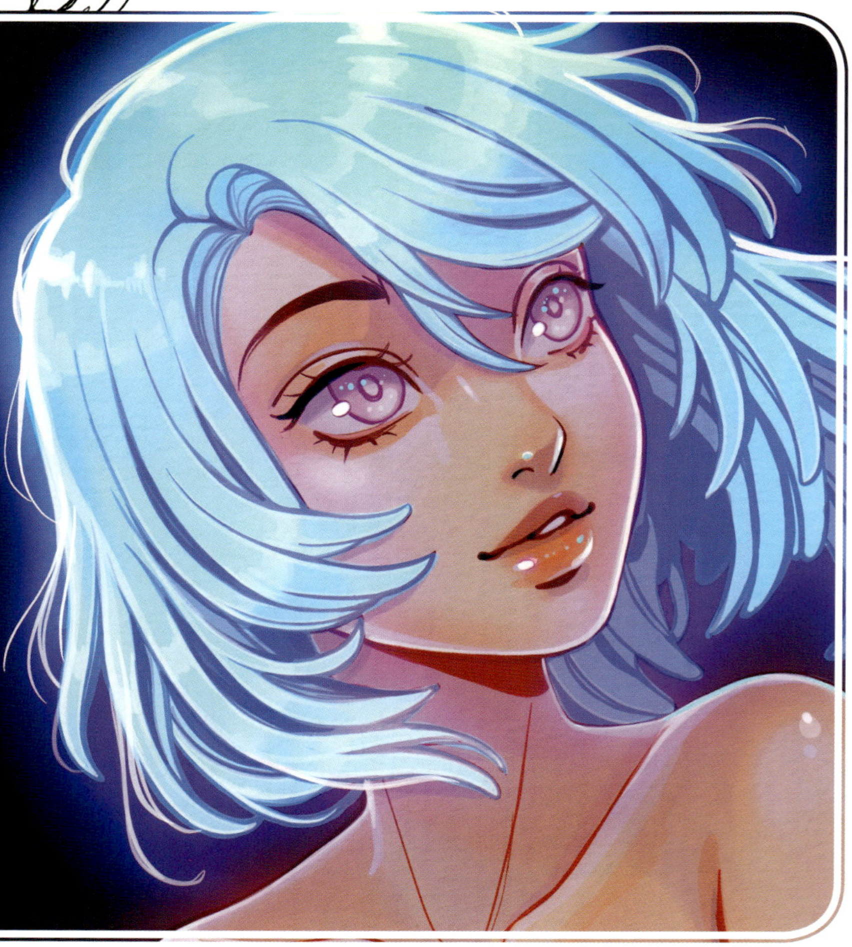

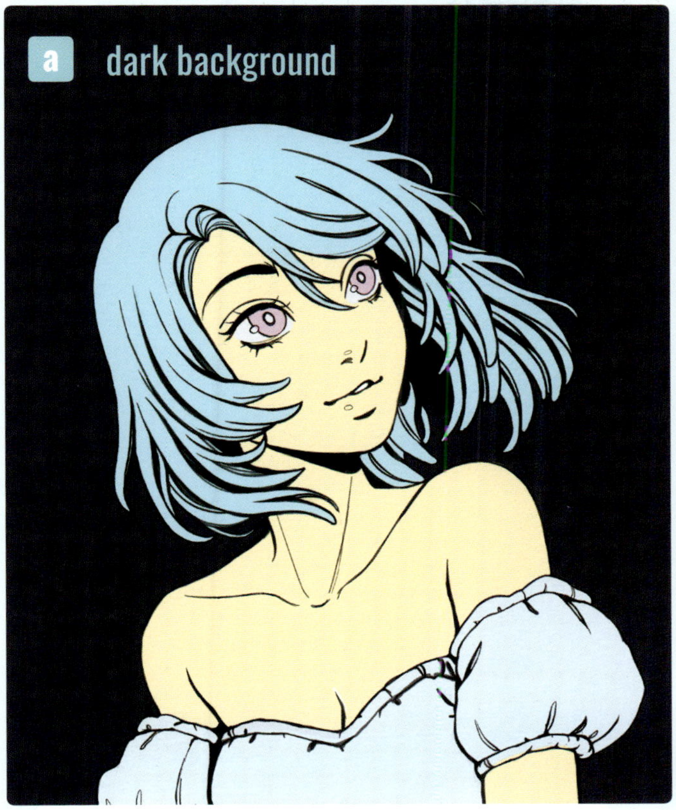


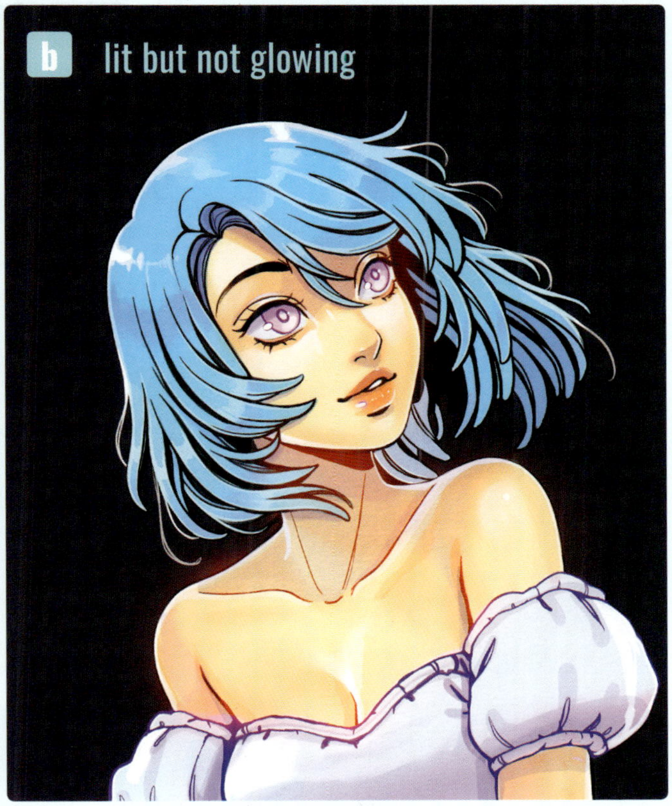


## 1 the background

If you want to create a glowing effect, you need to pair dark against light, and saturation against desaturation. You also need the diffusion of light. The quickest and easiest (but not the only) way to achieve a glow effect is by using a dark background.

A dark background will trick your brain into believing it is night-time, or that the character is in a dark room, and will expect the lighting on the character to match. Here, I've created a dark background, but have not colored the character to match the lighting my brain expects her to have **(a)**. The character appears to be in bright light despite being in a dark environment. There could be a bright flash or spotlight lighting her up, but it's not the glow effect we're looking for **(b)**. If we add a layer of shadow over the character, this is the lighting our brain expects to see in this dark environment **(c)**. But what would happen if part of the character is not pushed into shadow in this way?

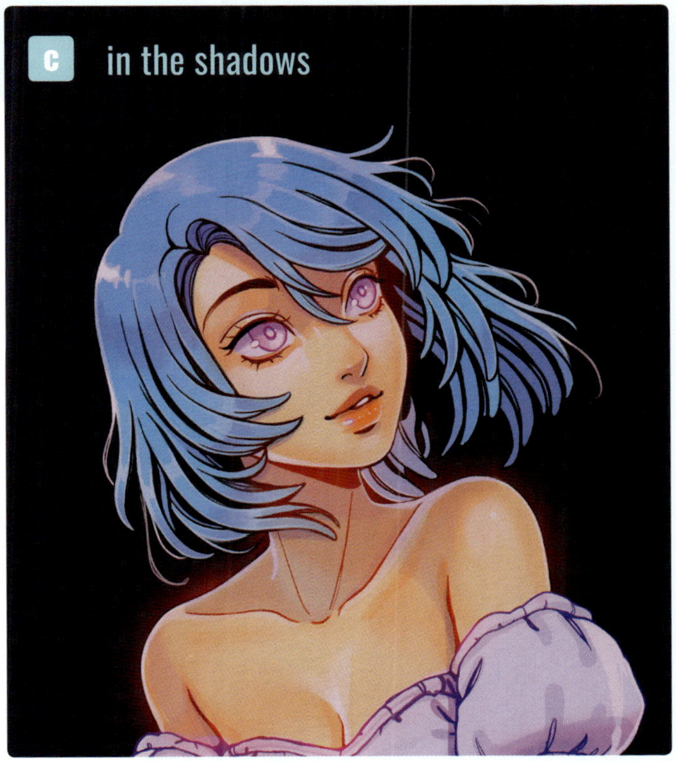

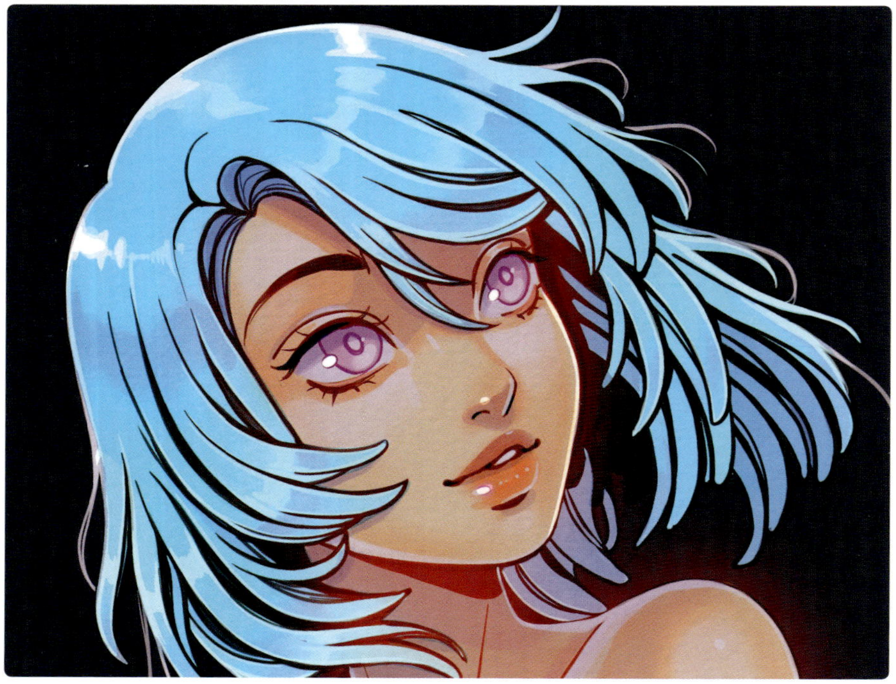

## 2 brightening the hair

Here, I have kept the character in darkness but have removed the shadow layer only from her hair, allowing it to remain its truest color, fully bright and saturated. This starts to appear strange to the brain, but it's not quite there yet.

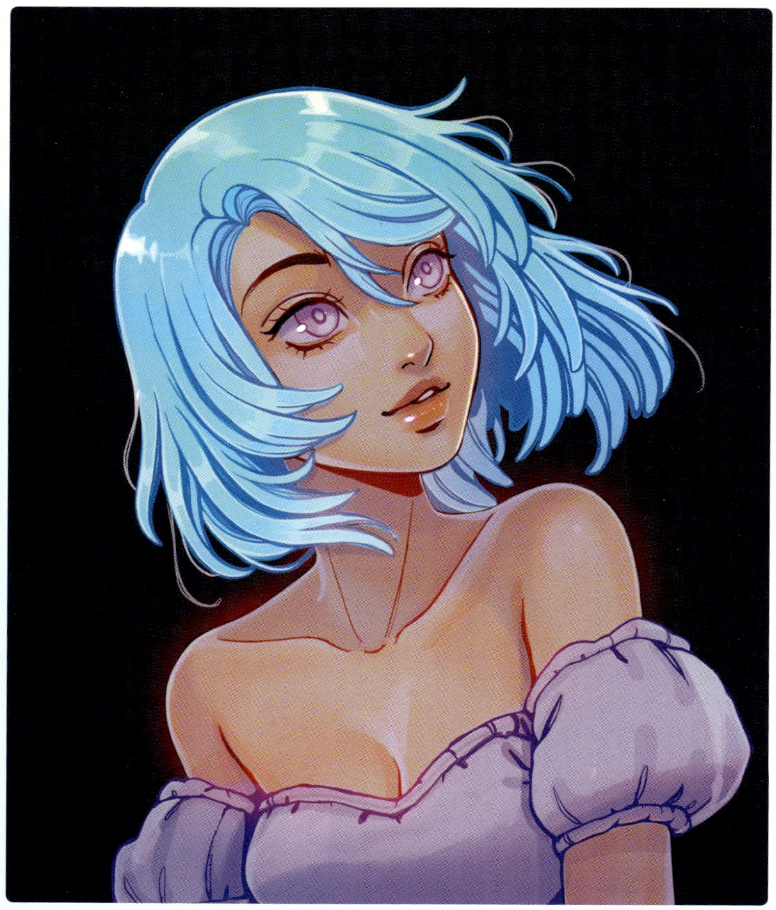

## 3 removing desaturated colors

To create an effect where it truly feels as if the object is radiating light, you must eliminate desaturated colors from the glowing object. Here, all the black lines have been replaced with a bright blue, so even at its very darkest point my object is still very colorful. We now feel that we are seeing the truest color of this object – at its core it is blue, and that blue is unaffected by the dark shadows we are otherwise seeing.

I started with the black lines to show how drastic the simple change from black to blue can be. When painting traditionally, I pick colors more intentionally from the start, and will try to pair a very intense, fully saturated color with a more pastel color. Here, it is bright blue against baby blue, but it could be dark, hot pink against pastel pink, a bright orange against a soft yellow, and so on. The key is that it's always colorful.

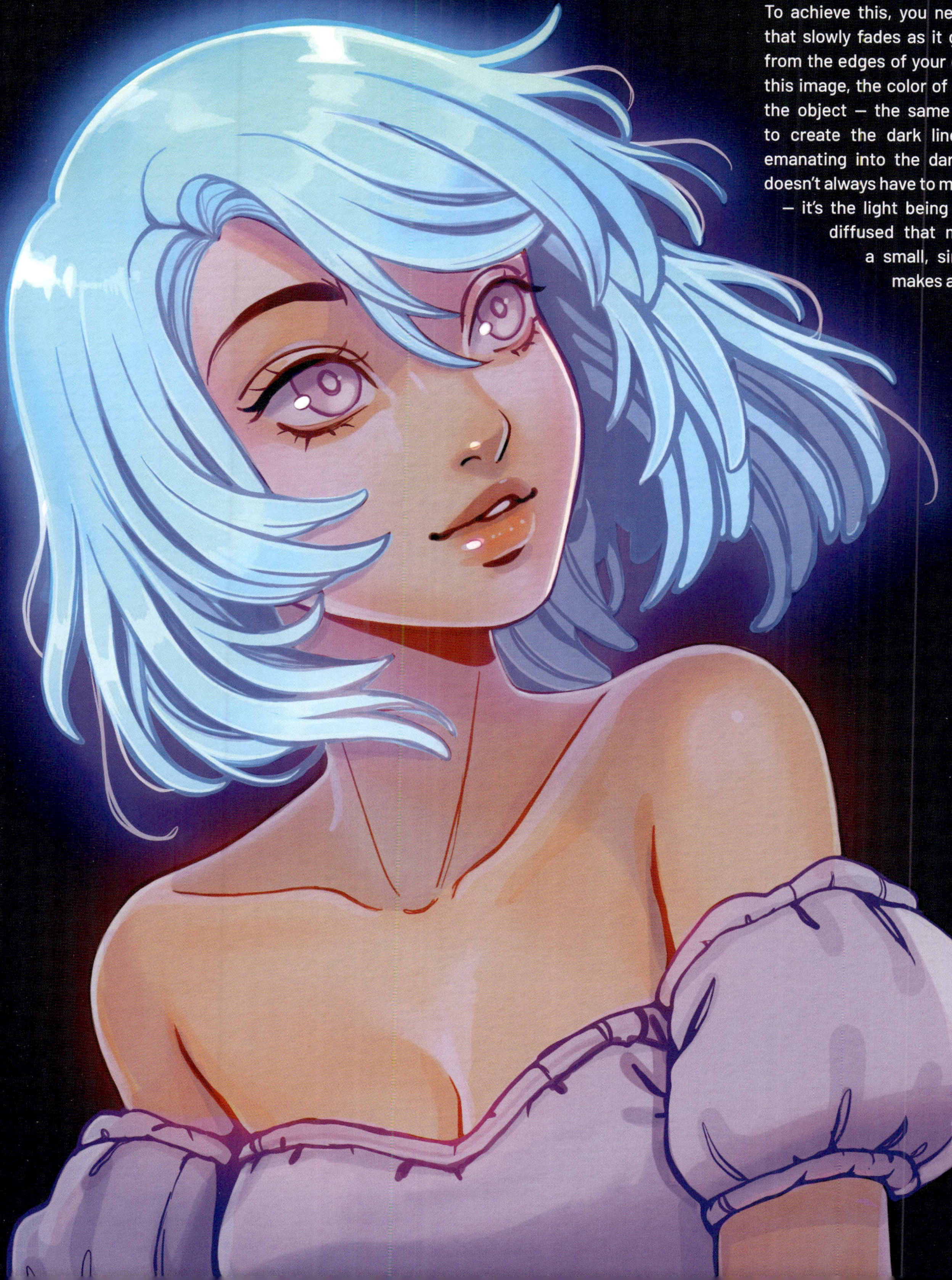

## 4 creating the glow

This is the step that takes your image from looking "bright" to "glowing." Light radiates outward in a lovely soft diffusion. To achieve this, you need a bright color that slowly fades as it gets further away from the edges of your glowing object. In this image, the color of the light matches the object — the same bright blue used to create the dark lines in the hair is emanating into the darkness. The color doesn't always have to match, it's up to you — it's the light being bright and softly diffused that matters. It's such a small, simple thing yet it makes all the difference.

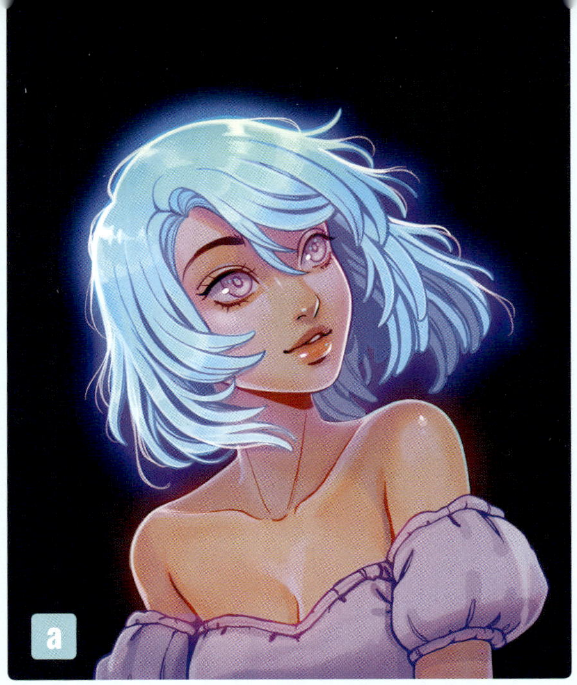


## 5 valuing white

When creating the anglerfish painting, I was missing what light truly did, which was to show the true, brilliant color of something. By adding all that white, I was missing the stunning colors in the deep ocean, but that doesn't mean that white has no value when creating glowing objects. Items that are backlit or drowning in the brilliance of your light may appear white, and it can be a nice way to add elegant little details to draw the eye toward the focal point of your painting. As shown here, I love adding strands of hair illuminated by the light **(a)**, or background objects hit by the brilliance of my glowing object **(b)**.

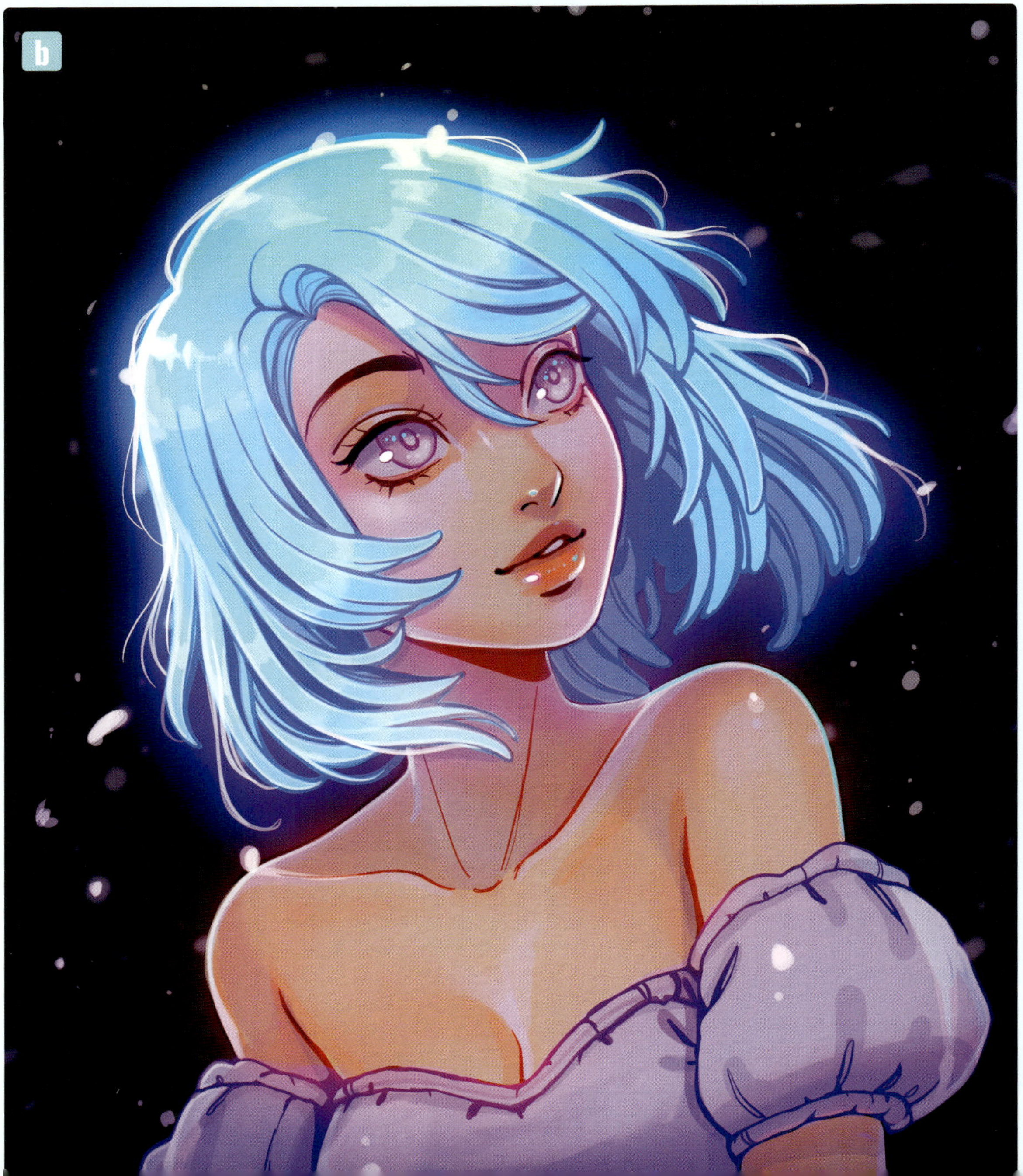

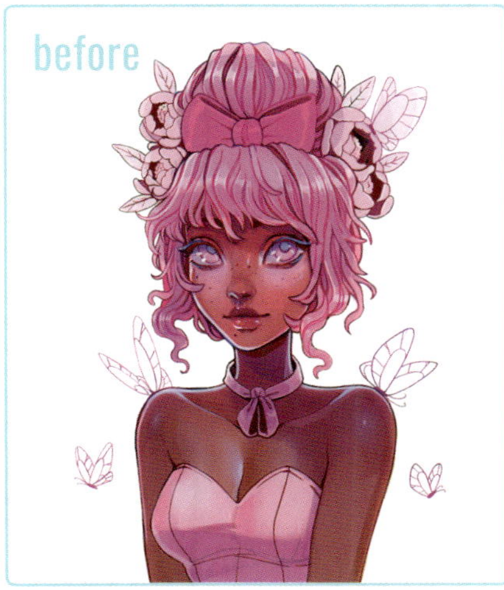

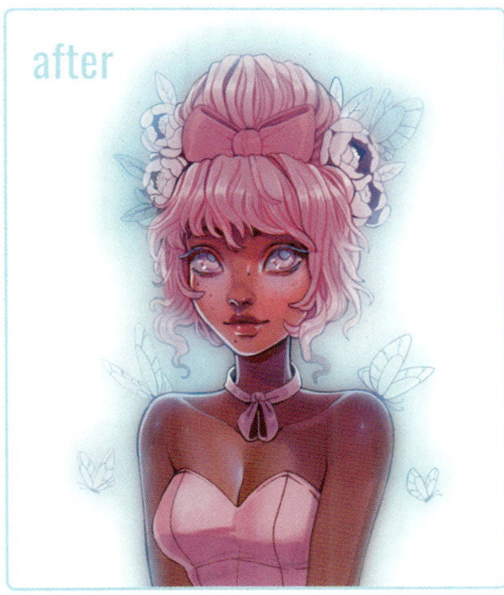

## using a light background

A dark background can be a powerful tool for creating glow, but it isn't an absolute requirement. You can still make a character appear as if they are radiating light with the one main, big trick shown in the previous example: a diffusion of color surrounding your character. Even on a completely white background, if your character radiates color they will appear to be glowing.

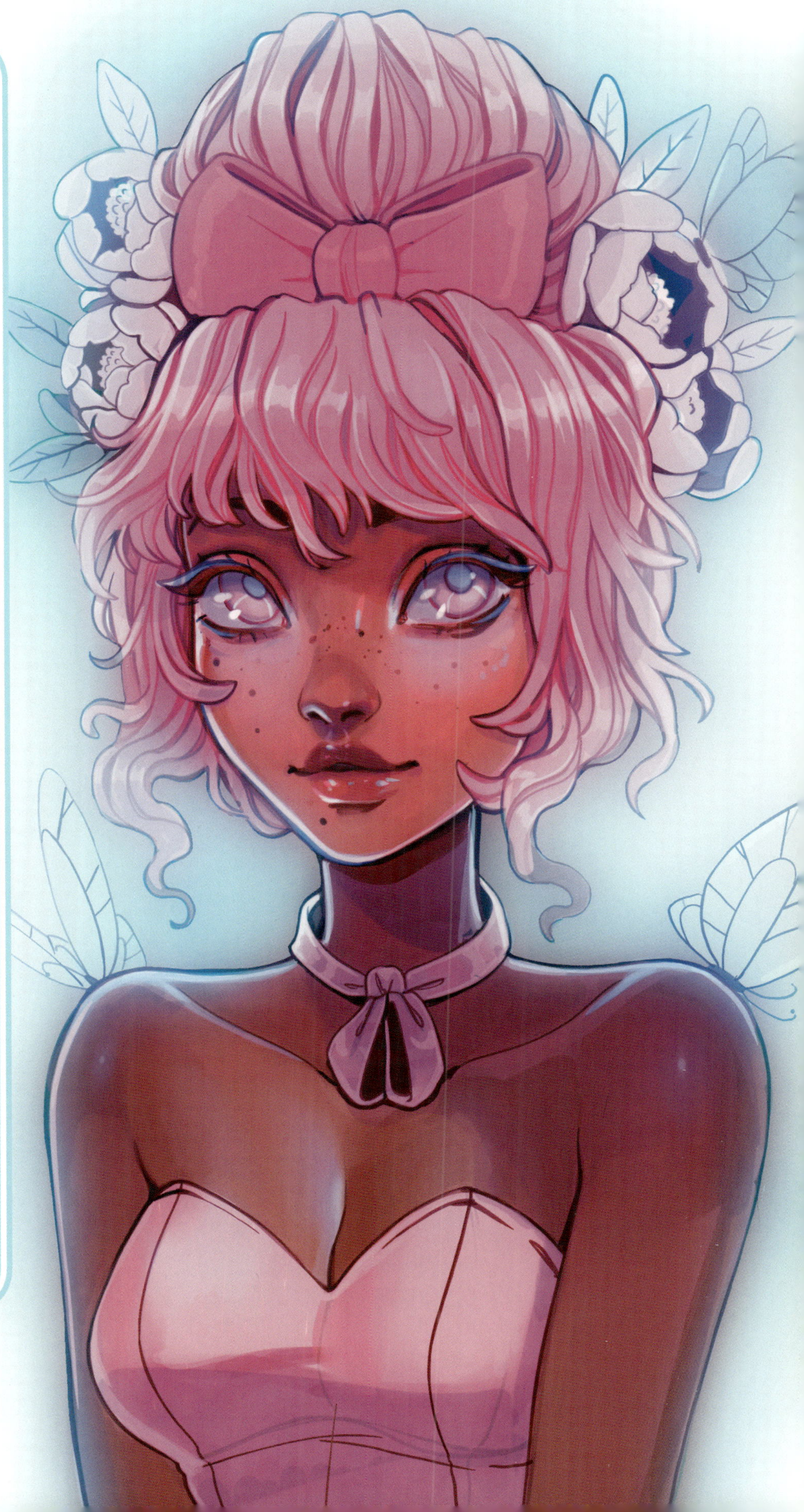

STYLE TECHNIQUE:

# get a fresh perspective

The way you choose to display an object can make all the difference to your art piece. It's easy to fall into the habit of automatically drawing an item viewed from straight on. But often, applying an interesting perspective gives a lovely sense of depth and substance to the object and overall piece.

These are a few of the steps I take when creating art to give it a unique and dimensional finish.

## turn it around

When drawing an individual object, I consider ways in which I can display multiple sides of it. For example, instead of drawing a milk carton facing to the front (where only one side can be seen), I turn it so that both the front and side are visible. This can be simple with objects that have very distinct sides (such as triangular or rectangular objects), but may be harder to apply to more organic shapes with less-defined planes.

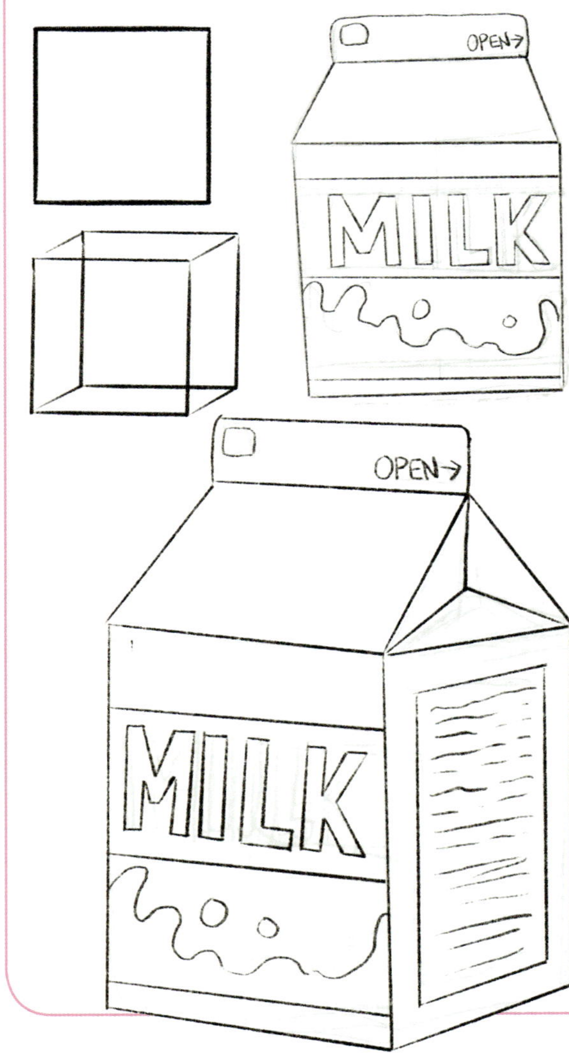


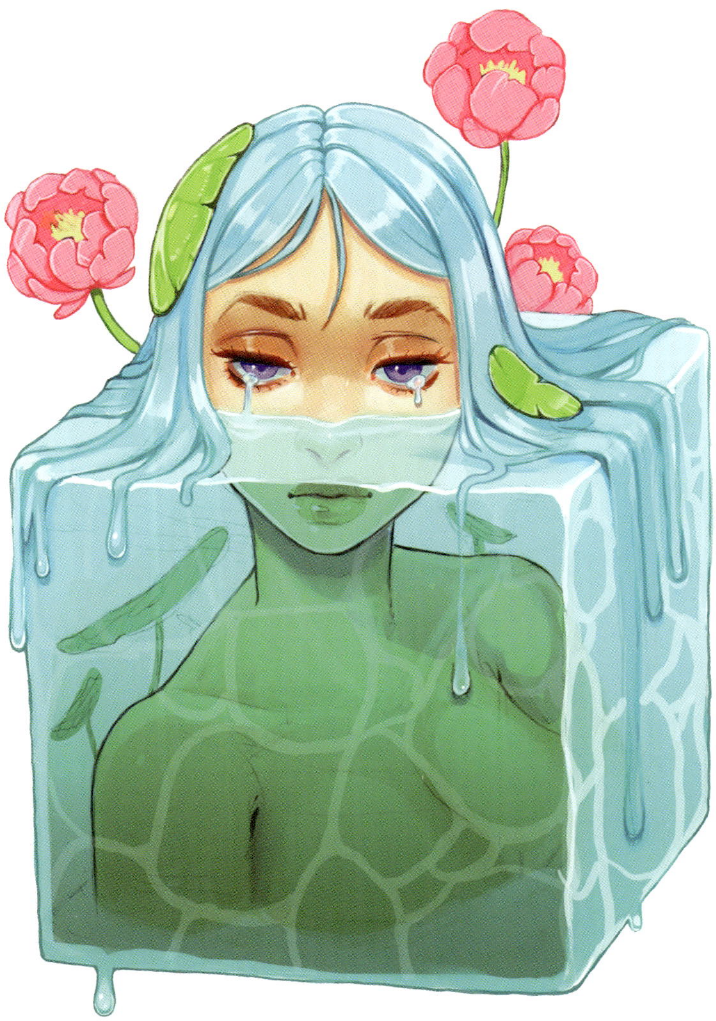

## try tilting it

Trickier organic items, such as flowers, can be tilted to offer a different viewing angle. Drawing them from a side angle displays their beautiful curled petals. You should be able to see both the front of the petals *and* the underside!

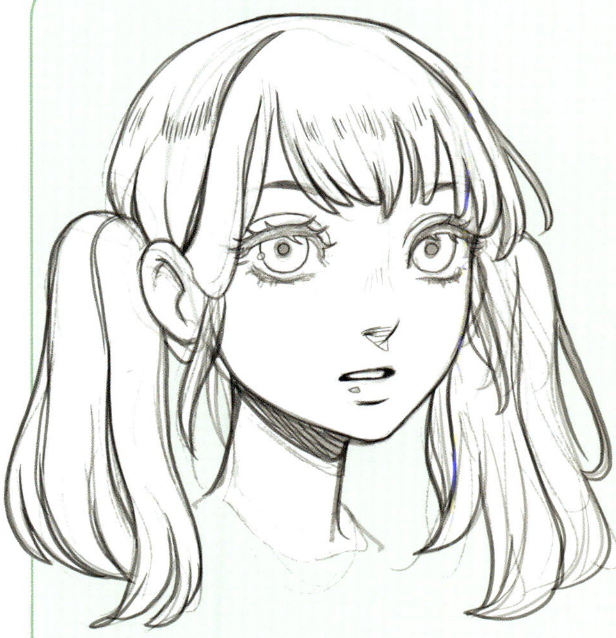

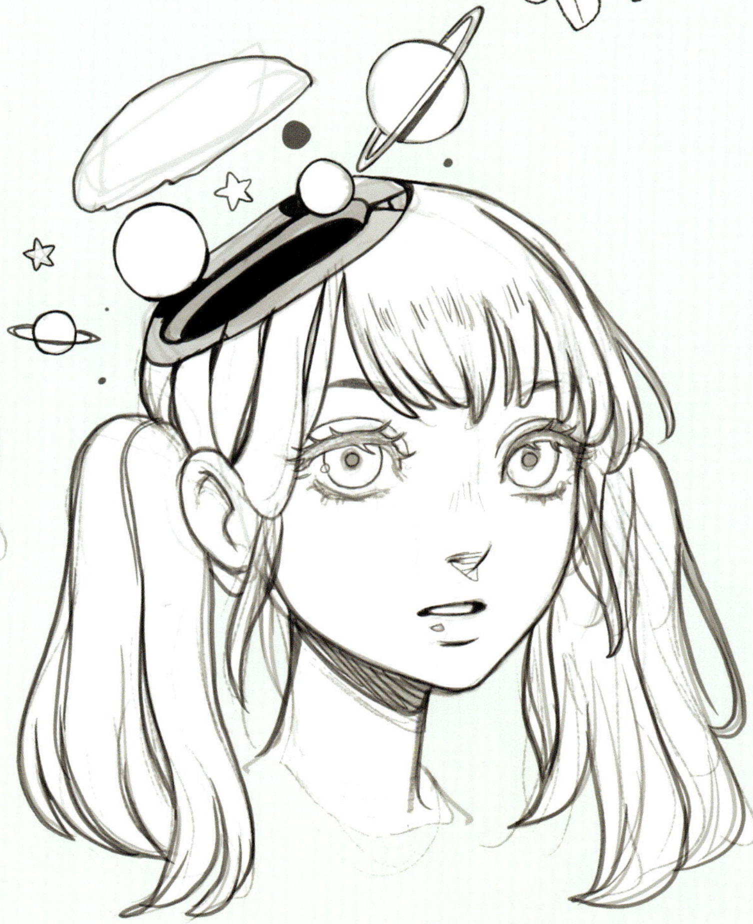

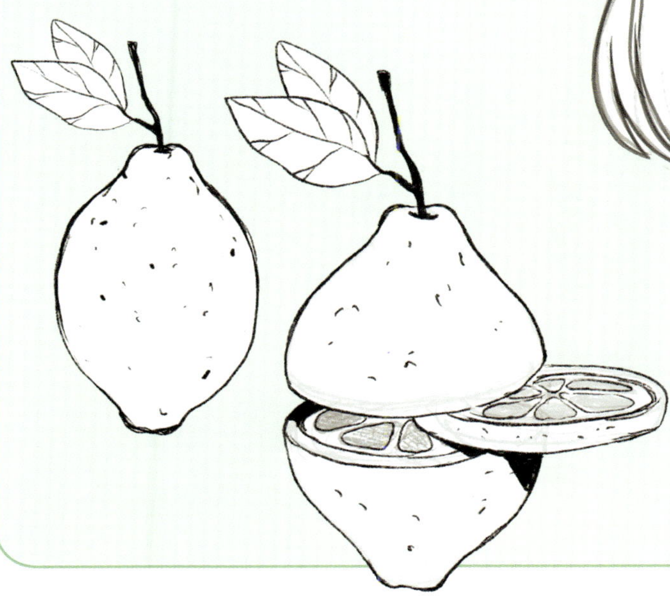

## take a look inside

Truly spherical shapes can be a little more of a challenge, because no matter how the object is tilted, it will appear round. In my own artwork, I often enjoy "dissecting" objects so that the viewer is able to see the outside and inside of them. This gives a very unique look, and it can be a lot of fun to experiment with dissecting different objects. Why not try it out with your own work?

STYLE TECHNIQUE:

# depicting cracked stone

Something that shows up in my work often is a cracked stone effect. It's surprisingly easy to create and can add lovely dimension and texture to your drawing. Here's a quick tutorial on how to add cracked details to your art. The steps I follow to create cracks are exactly the same whether I am using traditional or digital media, so feel free to try these out no matter which medium you prefer.

## 1 adding initial fault lines

When drawing digitally, I like to choose a textured brush, typically one of the sketching pencils, to create the cracked lines across the drawing. The textured brush helps to give the jagged look of cracked stone. Using a dark color (typically a shade of brown, blue, or purple, depending on the color of the surface you're coloring), draw lines where you want cracks to appear in your drawing.

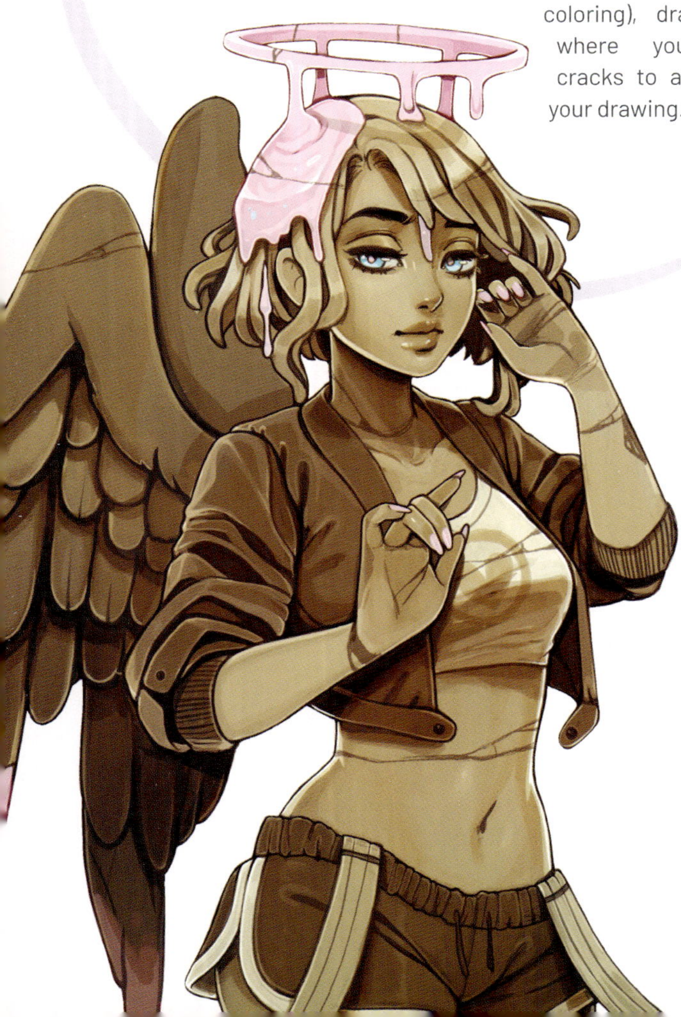

## line placement

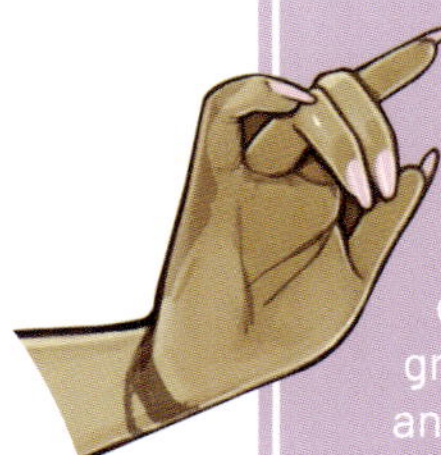

### Use natural joins

I usually add cracks in areas where two shapes meet, for example where the neck meets the body or the hand meets the wrist. In many ways these cracks are reminiscent of lines that are created when sketching that are removed later. I always love the life a drawing has when it maintains its original sketch lines, so cracks are a great way to keep those defining lines and make them feel like an important part of the piece.

### Keep it organic

Remember when drawing your lines not to draw them straight across the object, but instead make sure they follow the contours of your shape, as shown below. When drawing cracks, I often create large triangular shapes across the body/object. I will then break the triangular shapes up into multiple smaller triangles to give the effect of cracked stone.

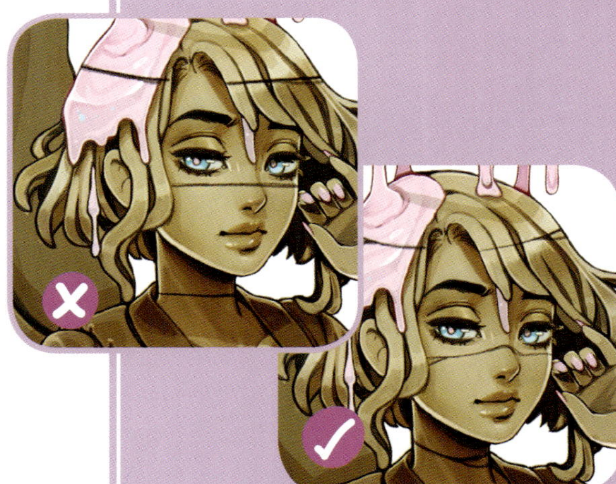

## 2 adding depth

Now that the sketch for the cracks is in place, I go back in and darken certain areas to create contrast. Typically, areas I look for are either the corners of my triangle shapes, or deep gashes that I want to appear deeper than the regular surface level cracks — diversity and an organic feel is key here! Keep the composition of your piece in mind, making the darker areas focal points.

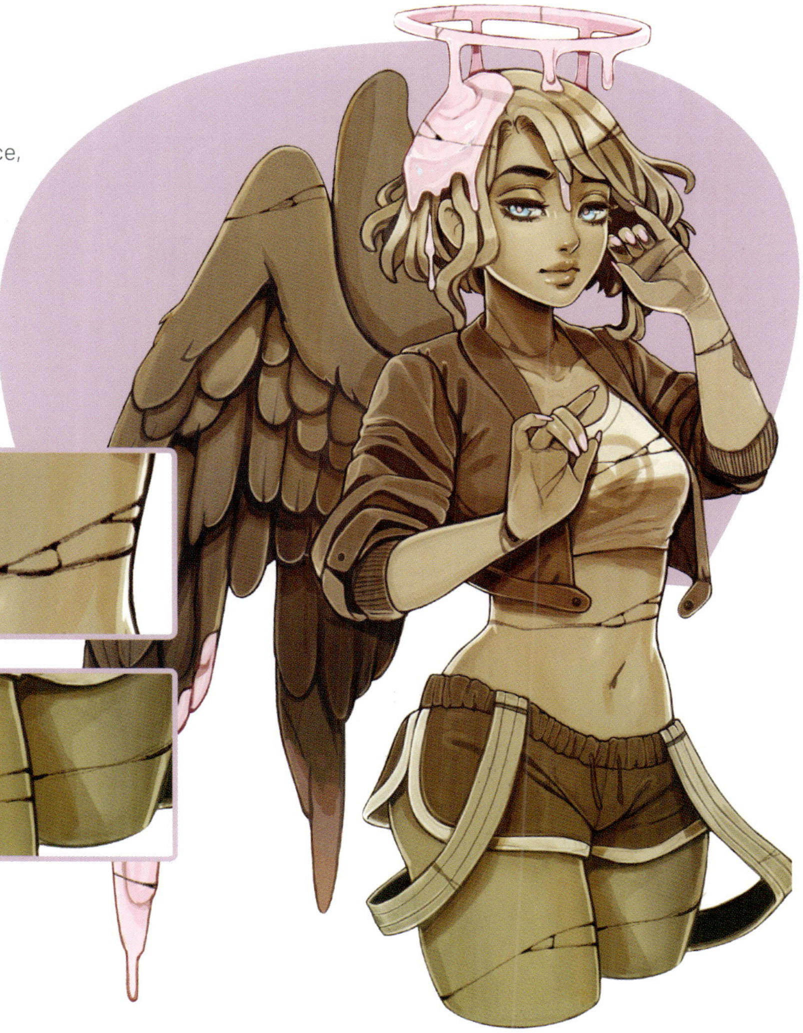

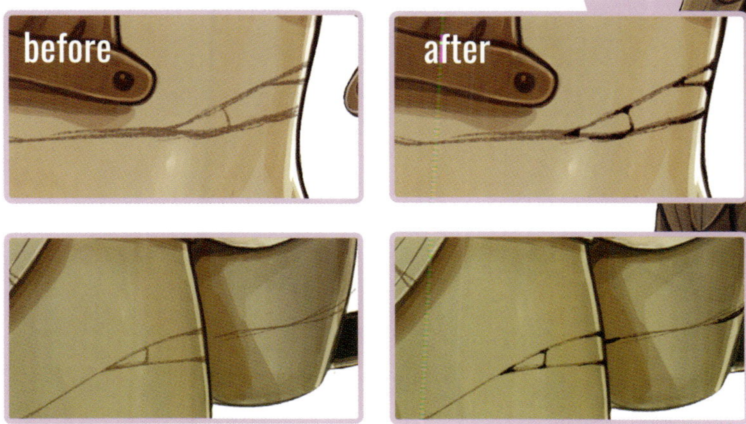


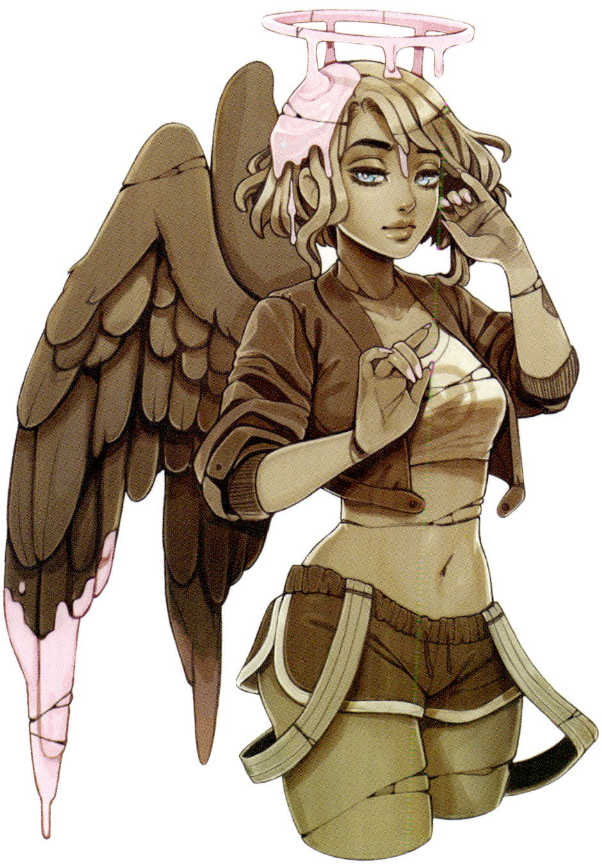

## 3 adjusting the outlines

You've now added cracks to the object or character, but the outlines will be too smooth and complete! Alter them slightly, tucking in areas that have cracked away, or bringing forward jagged pieces that may be sticking out.

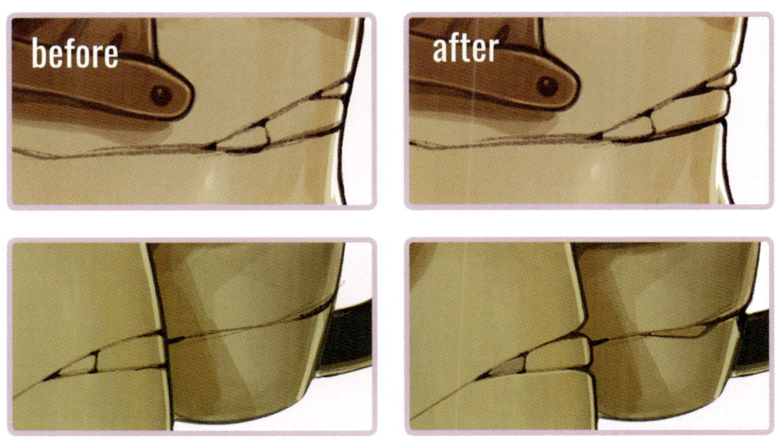

## 4 adding highlights

To enhance the rough jagged edges of the stone, add highlights around the newly created cracks. Follow along the crack outlines with a light outline, but try not to work too uniformly — as stated before, variation is important! Don't just outline with the same color and line size all the way across; make the brightest areas your focal points and let less-important areas be very subtle!

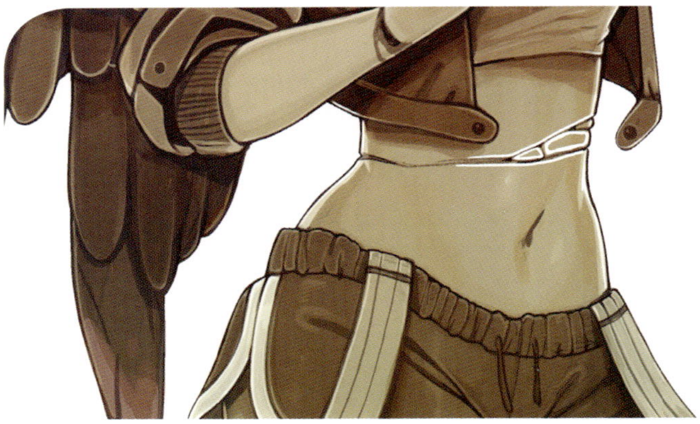

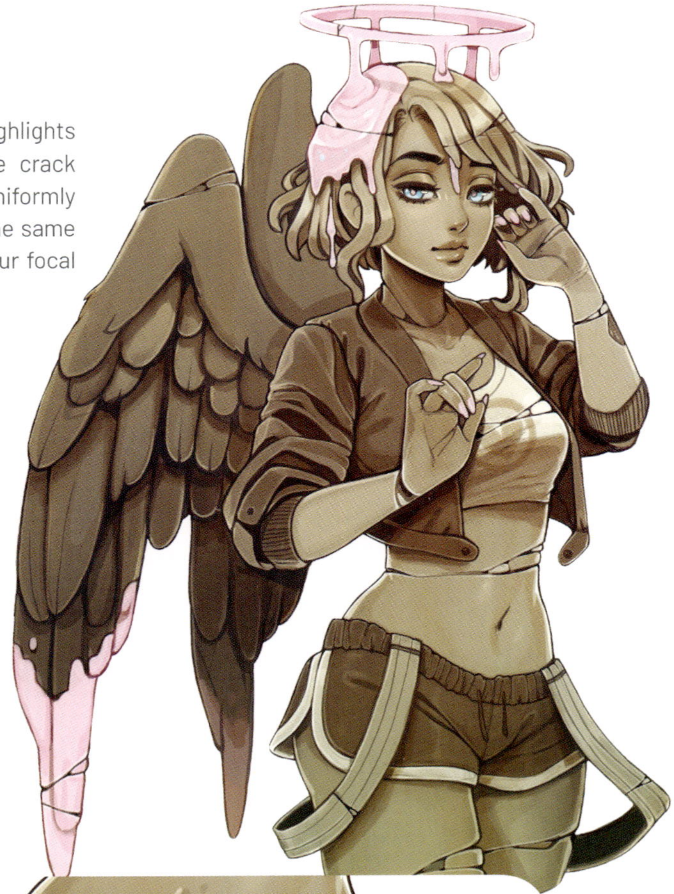

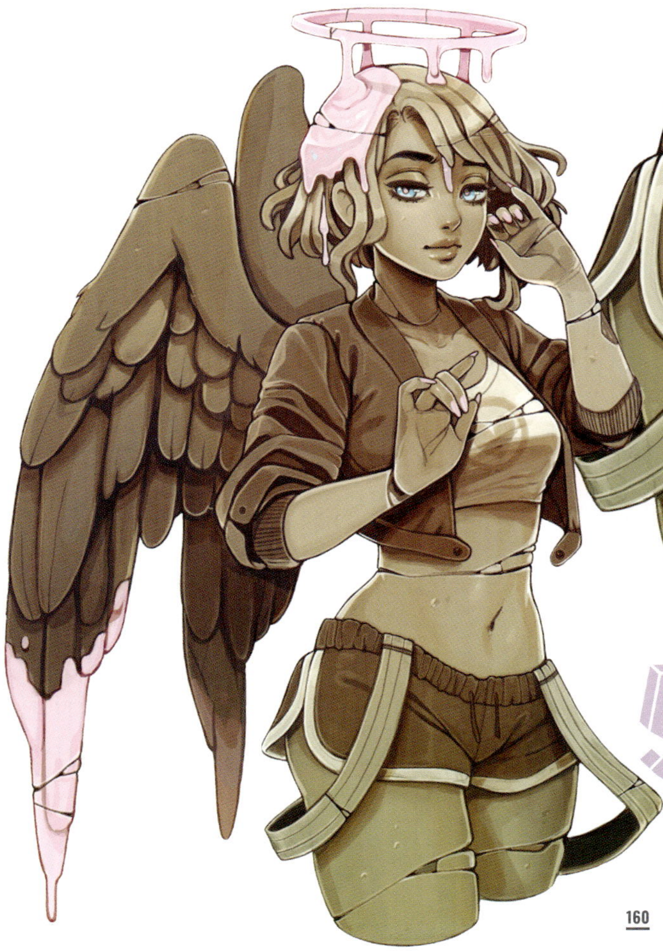

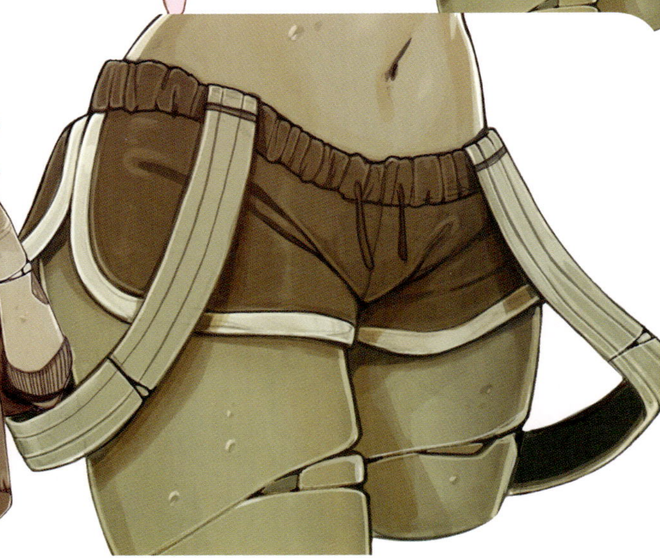

## 5 pock marks

Stone has a lot of texture to it, including rough marks. These can be created very simply by adding random-sized dark spots to your drawing and adding a light highlight to the top or bottom of them. These do not need to be dramatic additions but can be a nice extra texture to add to your piece.

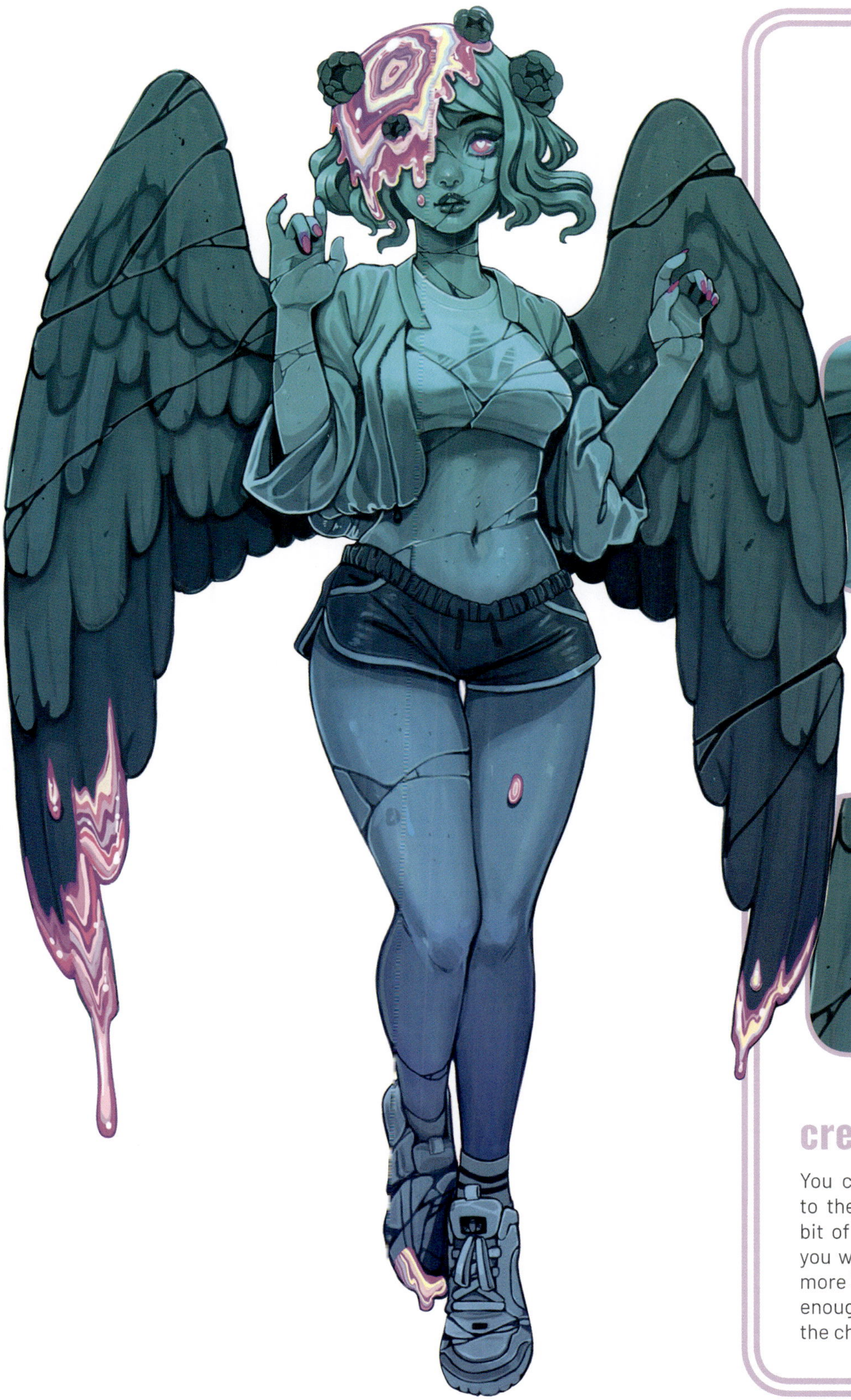

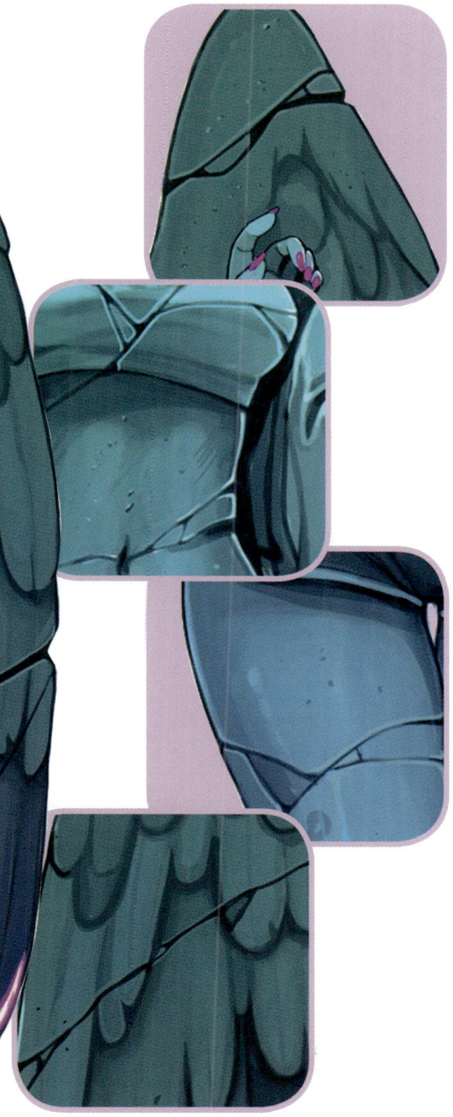

## creating chips

You can also add chipped-away details to the stone on your piece with a little bit of extra shading to the segments. If you want your character to appear even more 3D, make your stone effect cracked enough to show some of the interior of the character!

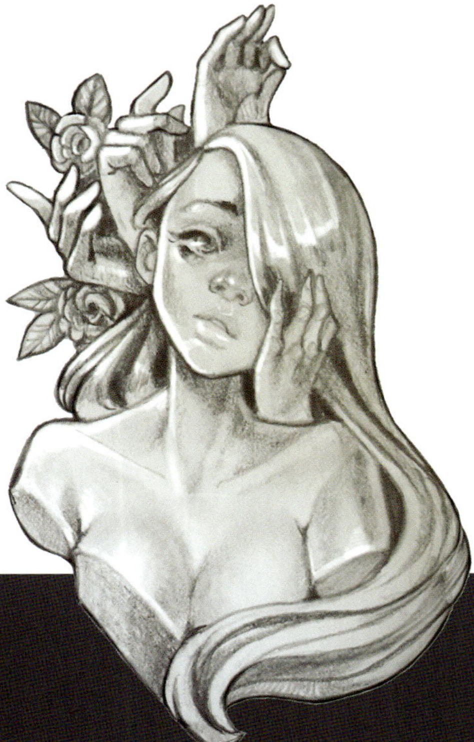
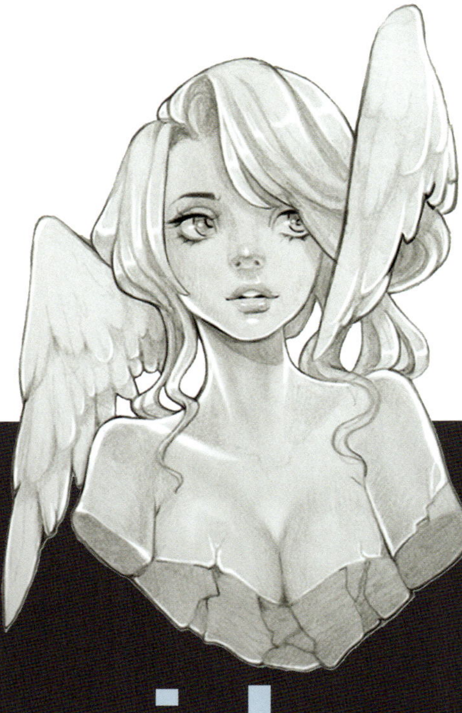
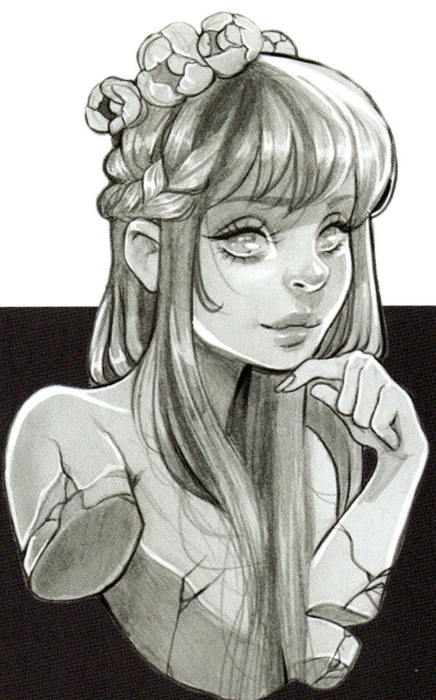

GALLERY:

# concrete girls

The inception of the concrete girl came with the first drawing I made after deciding to draw every day and just see what happened. I've been asked a lot about the meaning behind these crumbling statues, if they represent sadness, or decay, or disassociation, and subconsciously they might. But in truth, they came about because I struggle to draw arms. I'm not sure what it is, but arms always feel like this clunky part of the art piece that I'm always awkwardly trying to fit into the composition. When making that first drawing I wanted to draw a lot of hands, but didn't want to deal with a lot of arms, so I just... cut them off.

The drawing reminded me of a statue, so the next time I drew a character like this I added some cracks and the characters evolved from there. People seemed to resonate with these little broken girls, so over time I ended up making all kinds of concrete girls with all kinds of themes (they were named after a song by the band Switchfoot that I used to listen to when I was young). Even though I don't draw concrete girls as much anymore, I do think that crumbling elements are a huge ongoing theme in my work and still one of my favorite things to draw. (Turn to the Style Technique on page 158 to find out how to draw organic-looking cracks and splits in stone.)

In the end, if I could take one lesson from my experience making concrete girls, it's that much of art is about finding ways that you're broken and working with it instead of against it. I do think it's important to always be growing your skills and pushing yourself as an artist, but you might find that no matter how much you try there are certain things that just do not click for you. But when you do your best to embrace these parts of yourself and incorporate them into your work, you'll often create something that's truly unique.

I sometimes think about a story told by a teacher during my time at college. It was about a student who was fully colorblind – he could not see color, only value. He didn't ask people which paints he should work with. Instead, he would use totally random colors, choosing those with the right value scale for what he wanted to achieve. In the end he created paintings that were all over the place colorwise, yet still spot-on in value – they were unlike anything anyone had ever seen. I don't know if the story is true or embellished, but I don't think it matters. The moral behind that story has always sat with me: often, your weakness can be your superpower, and you may not even know it yet.

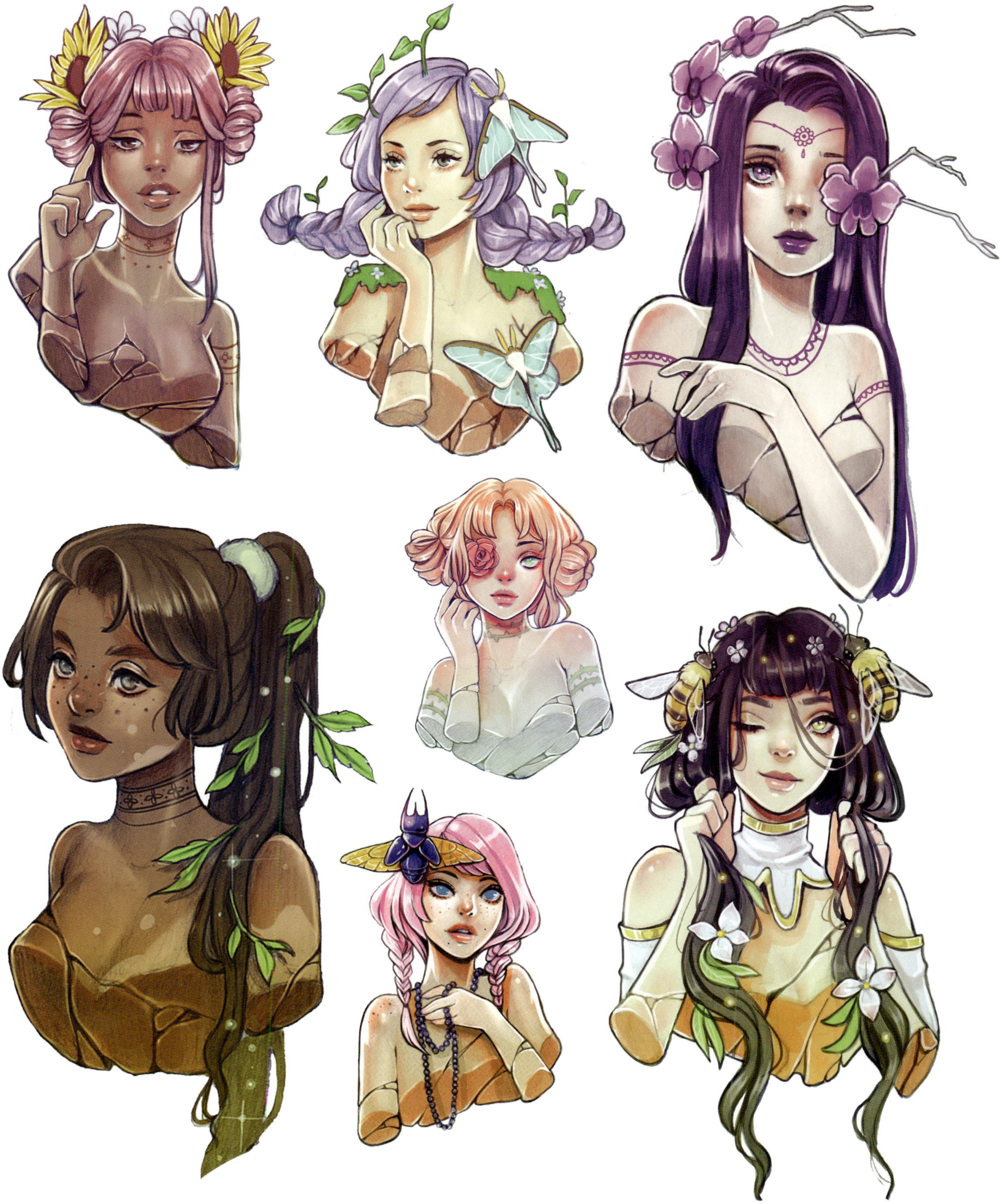

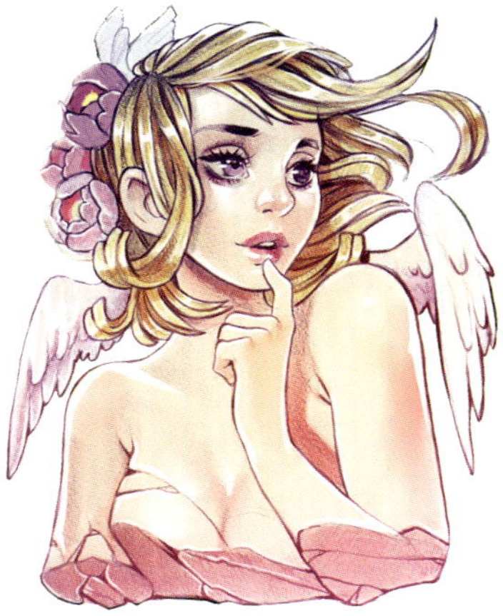

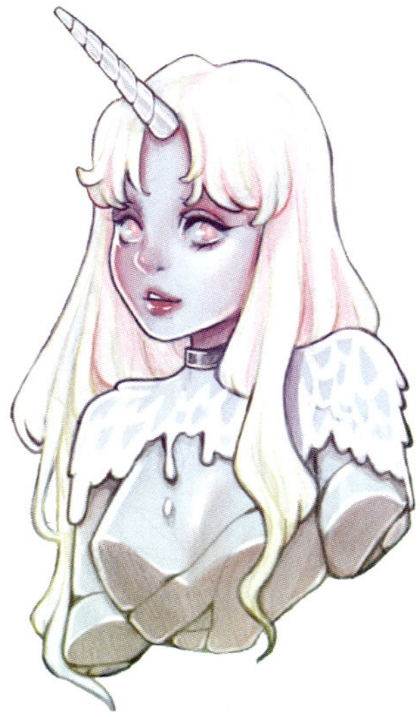

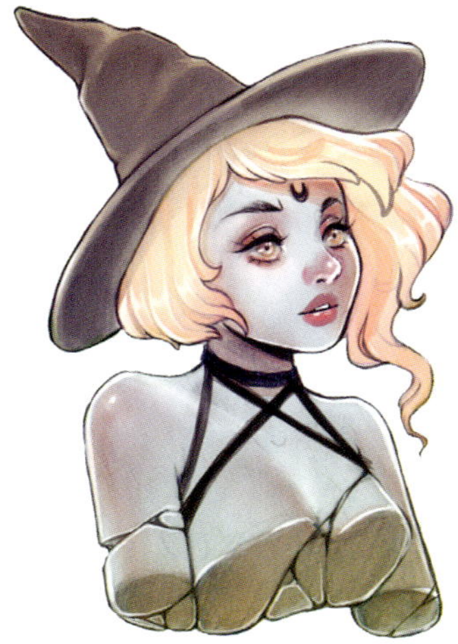

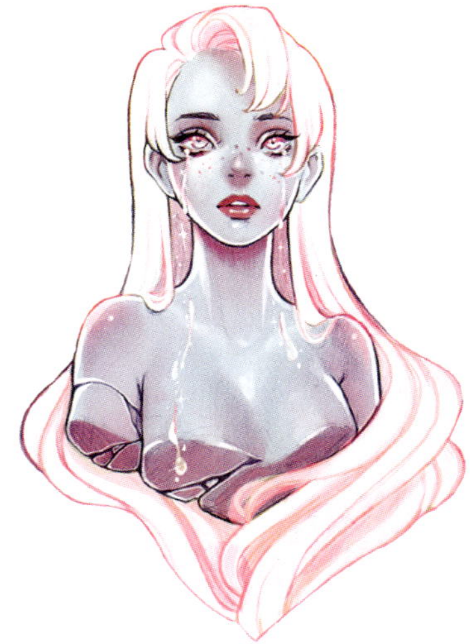

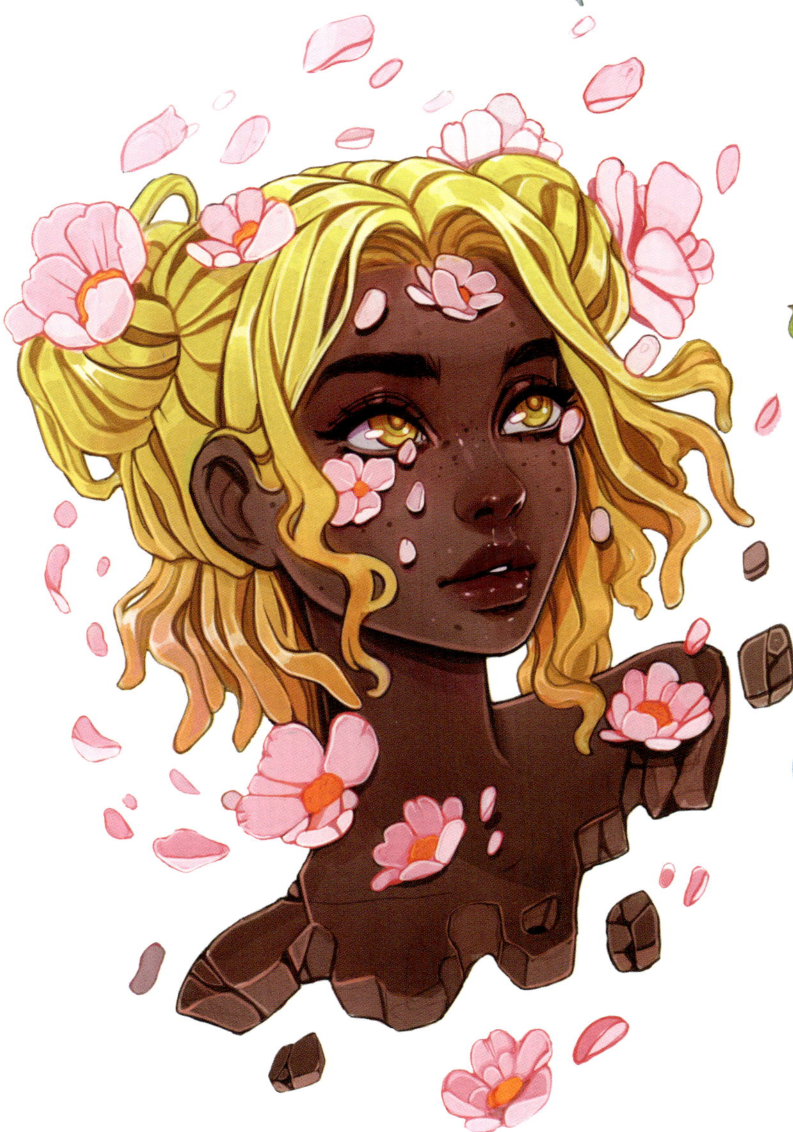

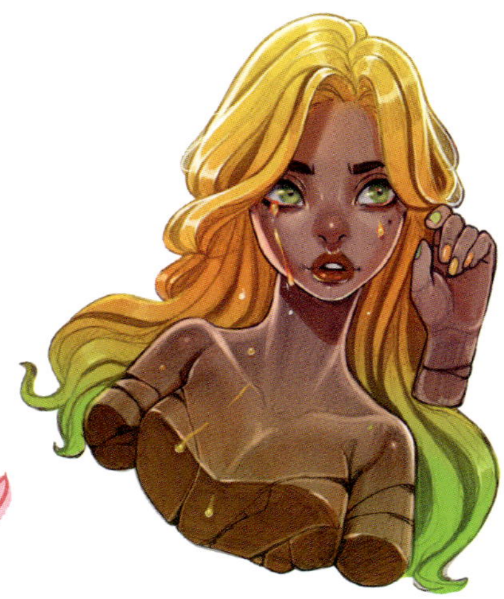

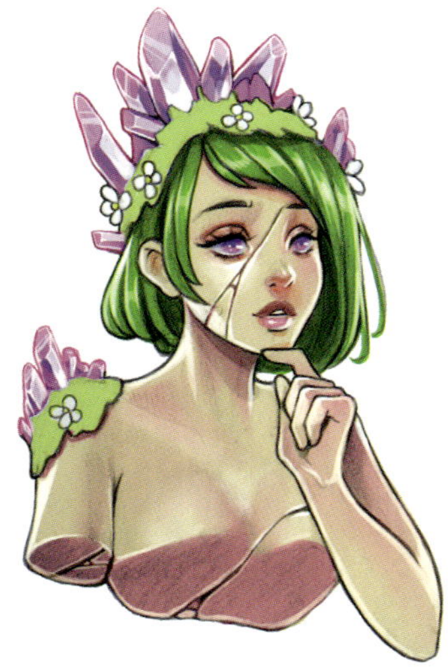

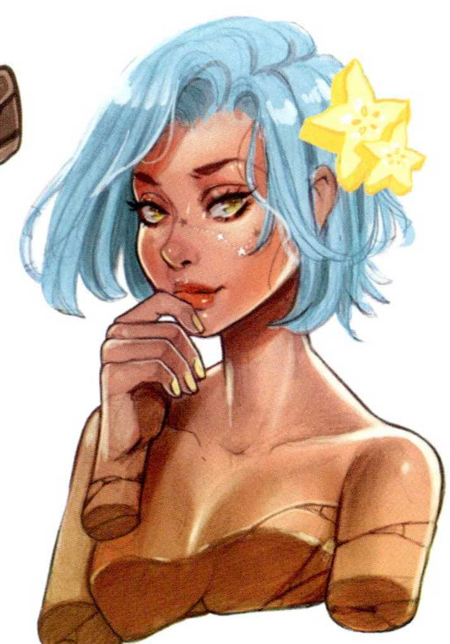

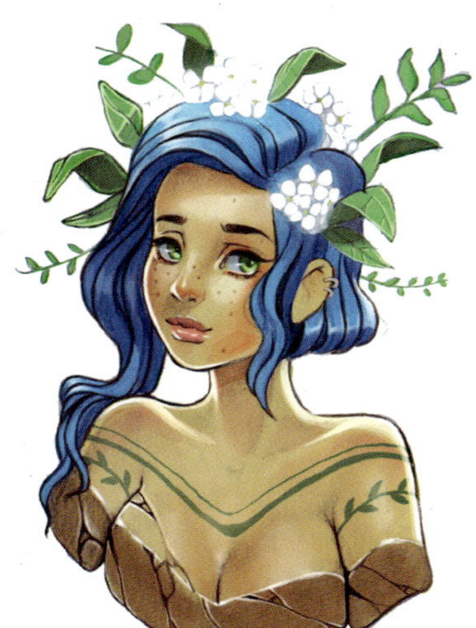

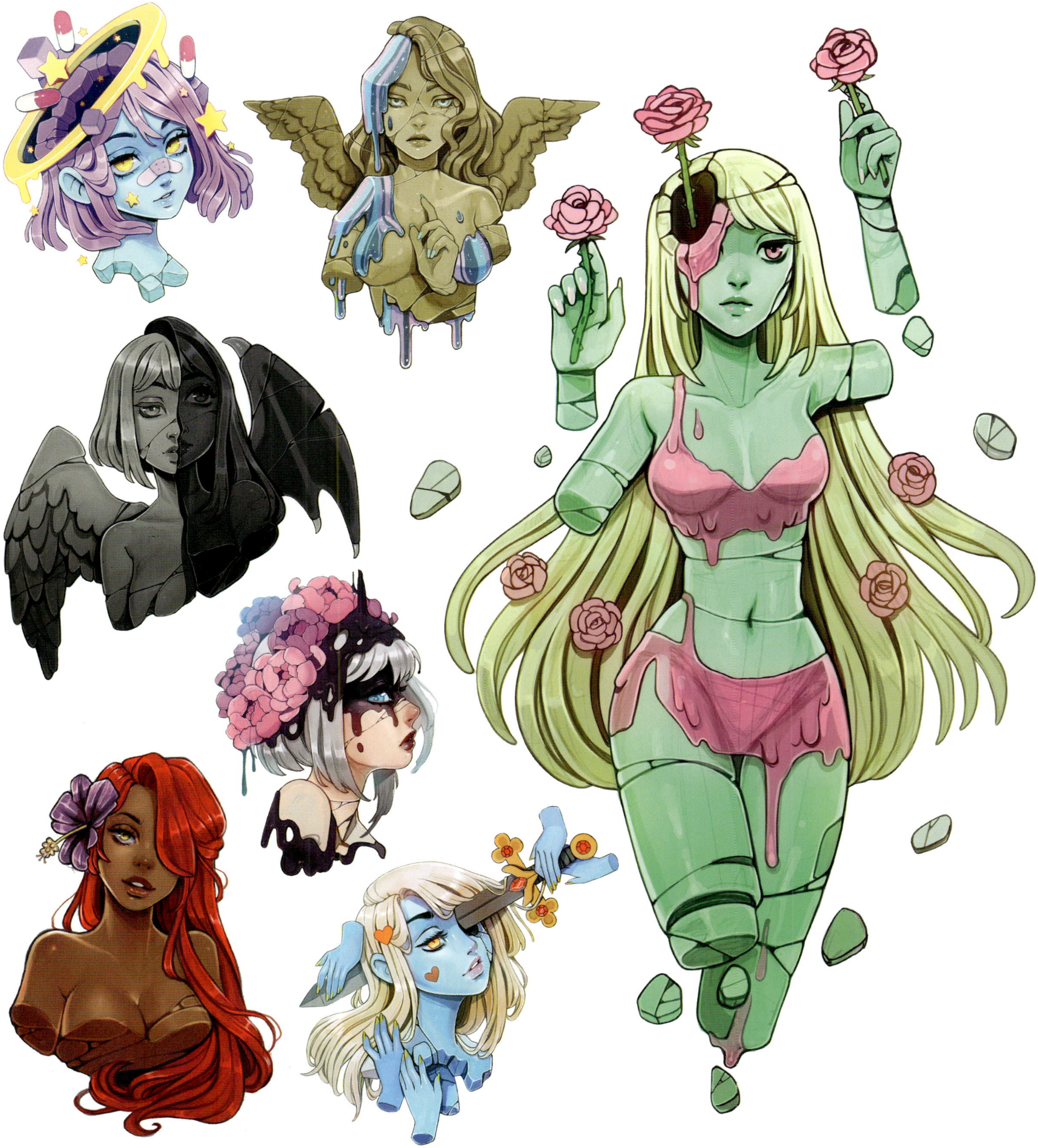

TUTORIAL:

# designing a character

Growing up, my biggest source of inspiration was concept art for video games. I adored the characters, especially the poses. They were so dynamic and full of energy and motion that I would simply stare at them and contemplate how the artists could have constructed them. Over the years, I've tried my best to learn and wield some of the tricks to create dynamic characters of my own. I'm still learning, but it feels so empowering to see art that inspired me as a child and think that I might be able to make something similar now. In this tutorial, I put into practice some of the character-design techniques I have picked up along the way.

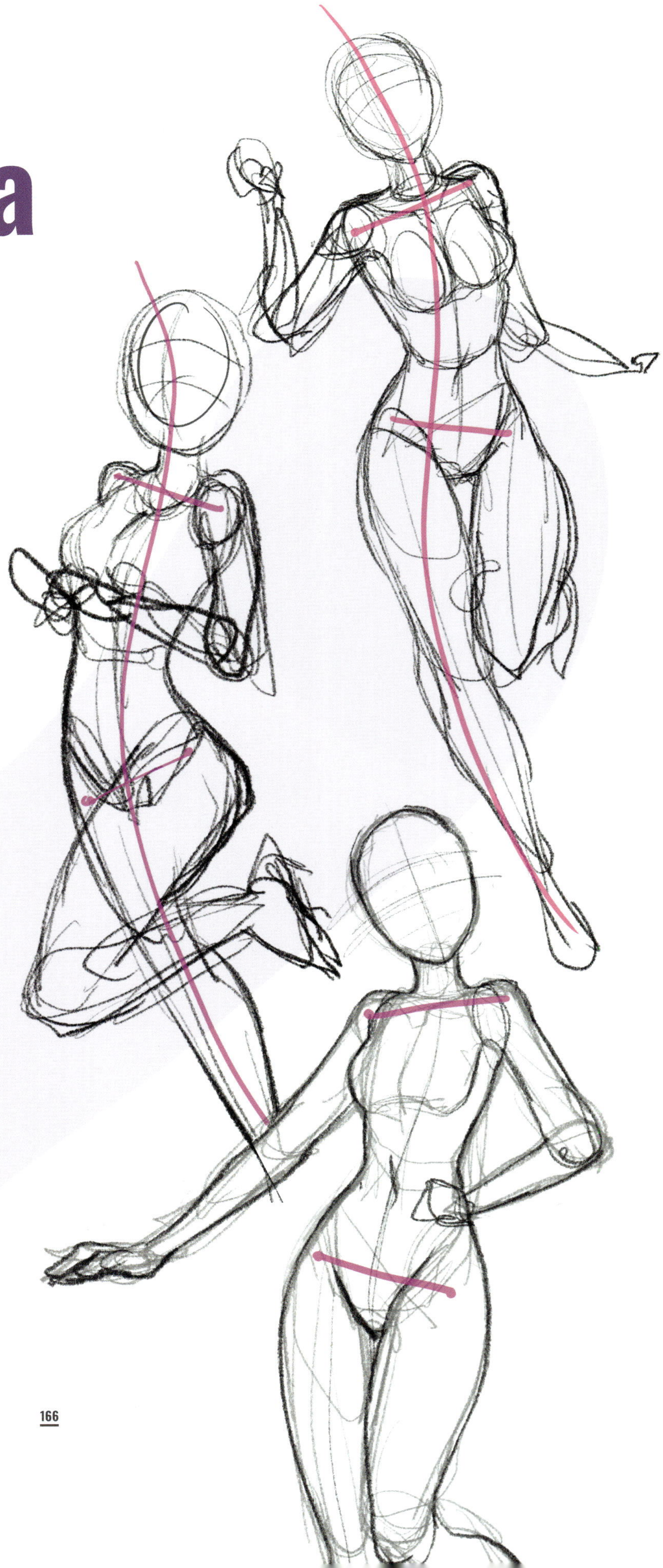

## 1 referencing and thumbnailing

When it comes to the human body, I never draw anything without a reference photo. The human form is so complex and it can be a challenge to master a pose if you don't have anything to base it on. There are many amazing resources for finding poses to reference. Simply pose yourself or a friend and take photos, or use the plethora of free stock photos online. Although, if you want more fantastical poses, they can be a little harder to capture with a gravity-bound human body. Many artists rely on a poseable figurine, and there are even free 3D poseable figures online, so there are many options for reference when tackling a pose.

Once I have chosen a pose, I create a thumbnail. Sometimes an idea feels like it makes sense but when translated to paper it doesn't work out. Thumbnail sketches help to weed out any ideas that don't work before you get too far into the character-design process.

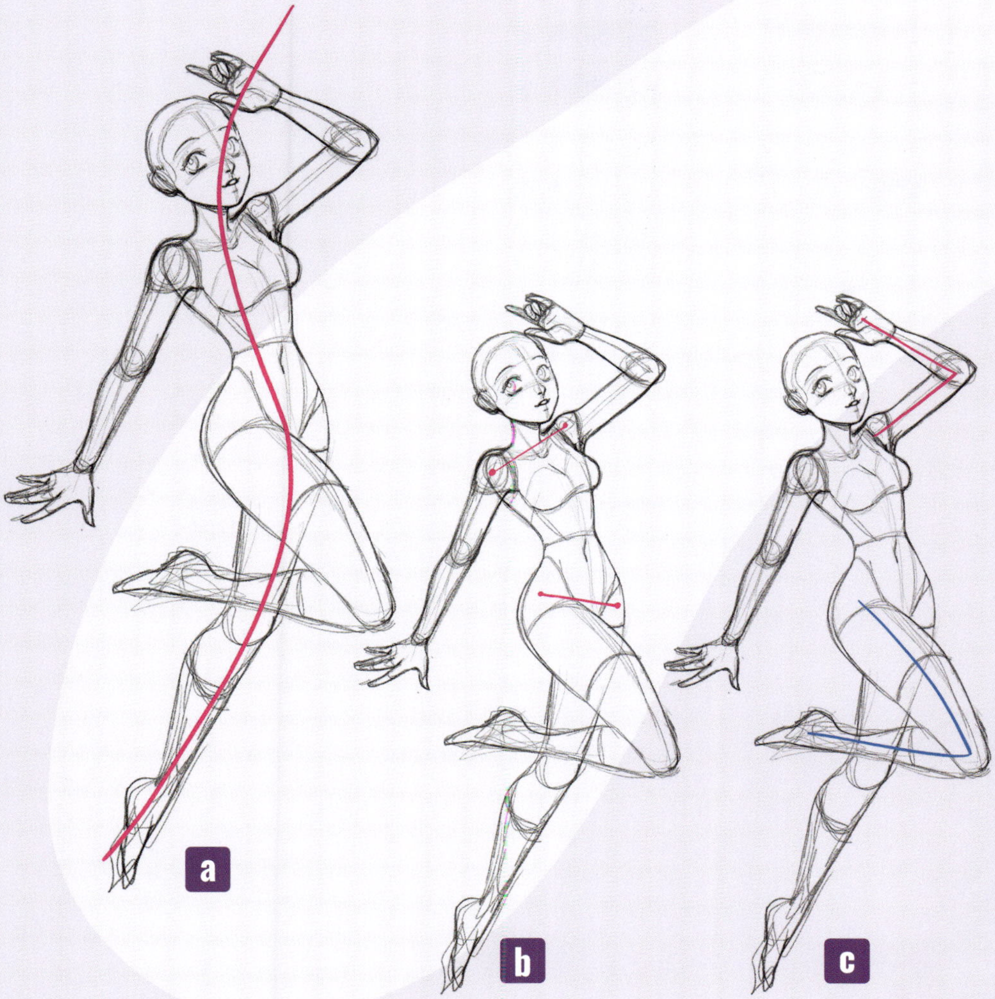


## 2 designing a pose

When designing a pose my top priority is to create "flow" in the image. The human eye is naturally drawn to "S" shapes as they help to guide the eye comfortably around the image, so I look for poses that encompass a natural serpentine flow in the posture. In this pose, that flow is created by the left arm and head facing forward and the left leg going backward **(a)**. Think about how all the parts of the character work together and utilize them to create flow in your own image.

As a general rule of thumb, when trying to create natural-looking poses, the hips and shoulders move in opposite directions: if the left shoulder is raised, the left hip will be lowered down, and vice versa **(b)**. Similarly, the opposite arms and legs move together **(c)**. There are always outliers, but these concepts are generally true.

As I begin to sketch my character, I tackle the basics of the pose before adding anything else such as hair, clothes, prop, and so on. Work as lightly and loosely as possible – don't try to create outlines yet. Instead, try to break the figure down into simple shapes and volumes, such as circles, cylinders, and triangles **(d)**.

I also map out all the joints and conjunctions of the character, including where the arms, neck, and legs meet the torso. This under-sketch will help you place clothes and other elements later on **(e)** so don't skip this step!

### locating joints

When adding mechanical elements to a character, the joints mapped out earlier in the under-sketch are hugely beneficial to help determine where these areas of your character might appear.

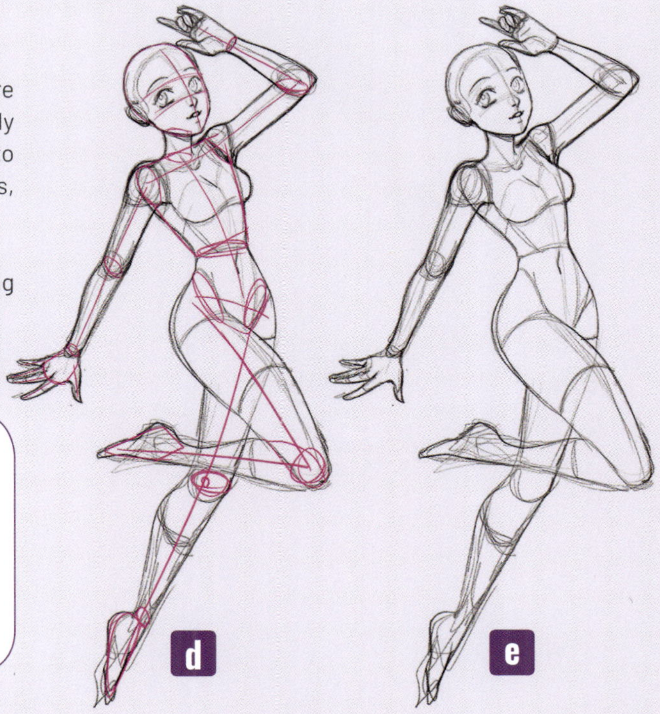

## 3 adding character elements

As you begin to add elements to your character, consider the S-shaped flow that you're trying to create. In this design, I try to make all additional elements move along the established serpentine shape **(a)**. The ribbon in the upper right of the image helps to direct the eye toward the wings, which then guide it downward to the hair, and finally the sword and ribbon complete the "S" as they move toward the lower left corner **(b)**.

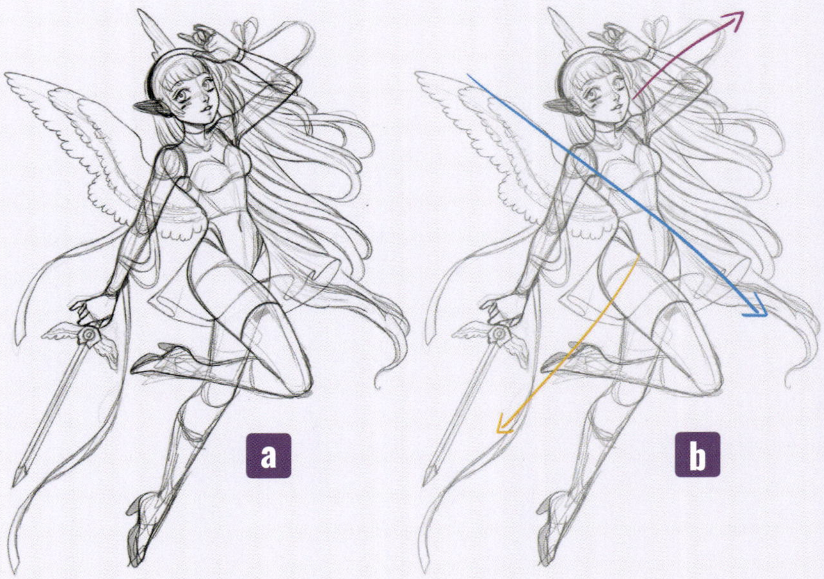

## 4 considering silhouette

When adding character elements, something that can be helpful to think about is the overall silhouette of your drawing. If your character were completely blacked out, is it a distinguishable, elegant, readable shape? If you're struggling with composition, creating the silhouette of your character can help you to discover what's missing. I like to include a mix of bulky shapes as well as light, elegant shapes breaking away from the character. Ribbons, hair, belts, and other decorative elements can work well as smaller, daintier additions.

## 5 Inking

Once you feel happy with the overall sketch, it's time to add the outlines. When introducing the final outlines, I lower the opacity of the original sketch and ink over it. For interest, I vary the line width — not everything needs to be the same thickness! Typically, I create thicker lines on the outlines of objects, and thinner lines on fine details. I never remove the sketch layer — there is a lot of life in the sketch that can get lost during the inking phase. I simply lower the sketch layer's opacity and clean up any outlier lines, but ultimately leave it intact.

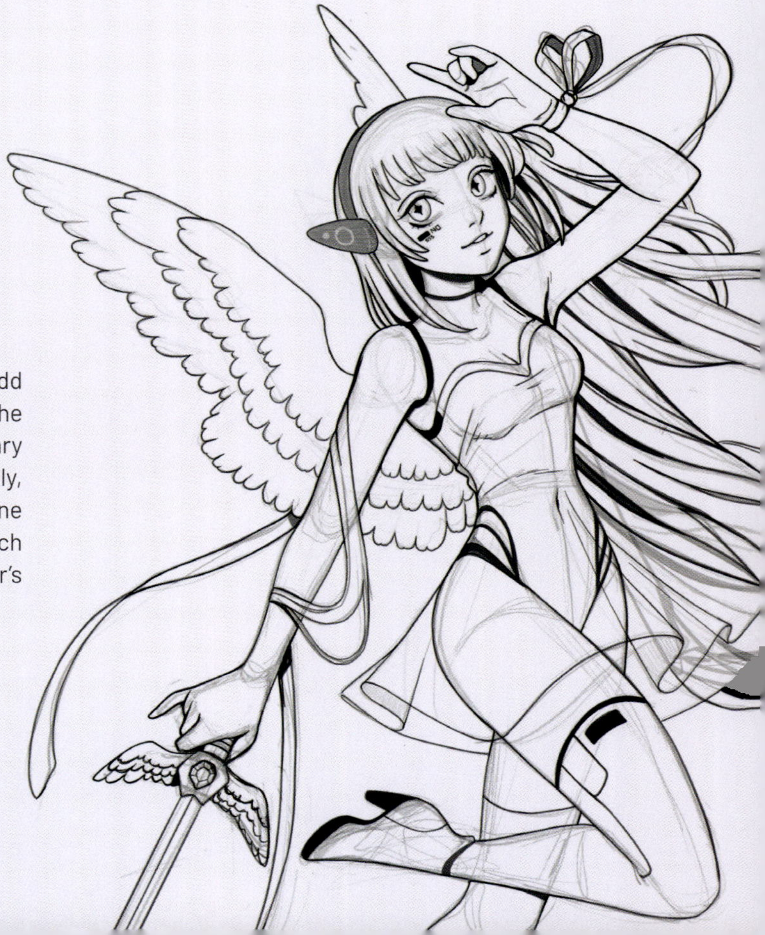

## 6 selecting colors

When choosing colors for characters, I consider two things: complementary colors and warm/cool contrasts. Complementary colors are opposite each other on the color wheel — some common combos are red/green, orange/blue, and yellow/purple. When paired, they can make each other really pop. Similarly, warm colors paired with cool colors can have a lovely synergy.

Here, I want to create a yellow/purple complementary palette with blue accents to offset the warm tones of the piece. The blue will be added later during the detailing phase, but here you can see the yellow tones chosen for the skin and the pink/purple hues for the outfit.

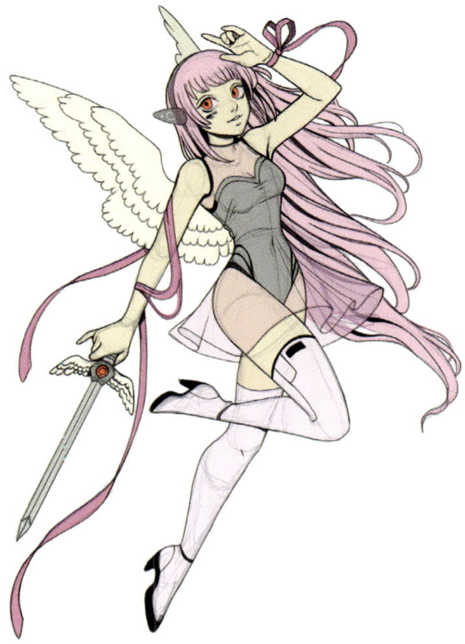

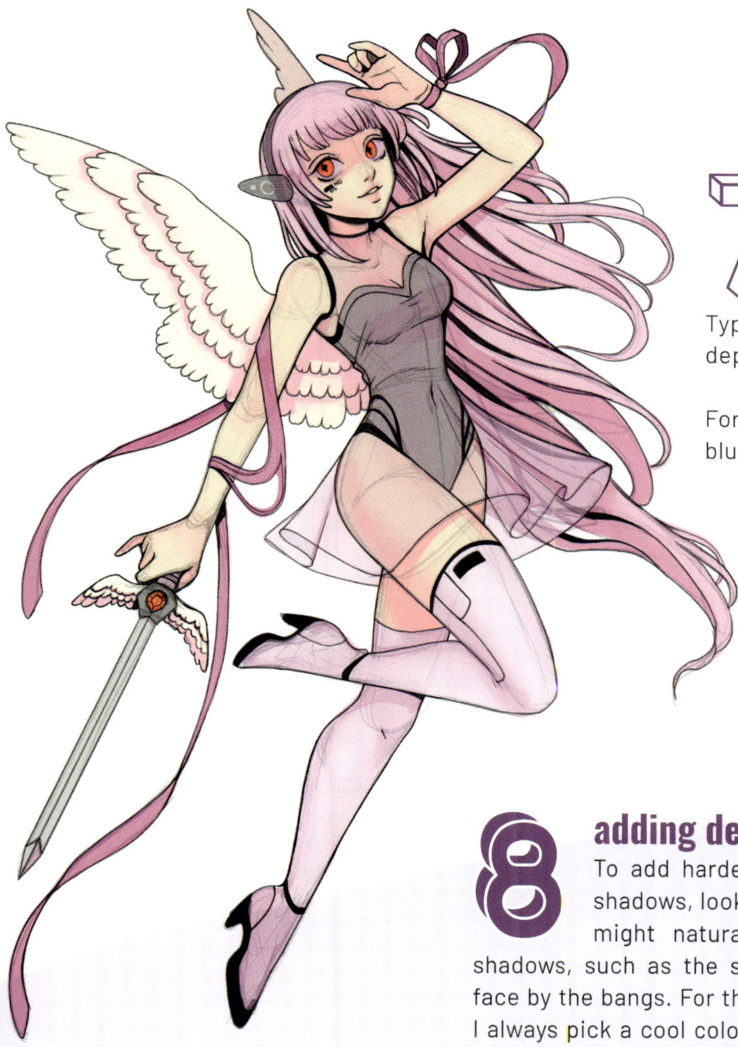

## 7 introducing soft shadows

After adding the base colors, I add the soft shadows. These shadows round out the shapes of the character; they are not harsh cast shadows, but soft, diffused contour shadows. Typically, I use a warm color for this: either a red, an orange, or a pink depending on my overall color palette.

For this particular piece, I use pink because my harder shadows will be blue, creating a lovely purple color when they overlap.

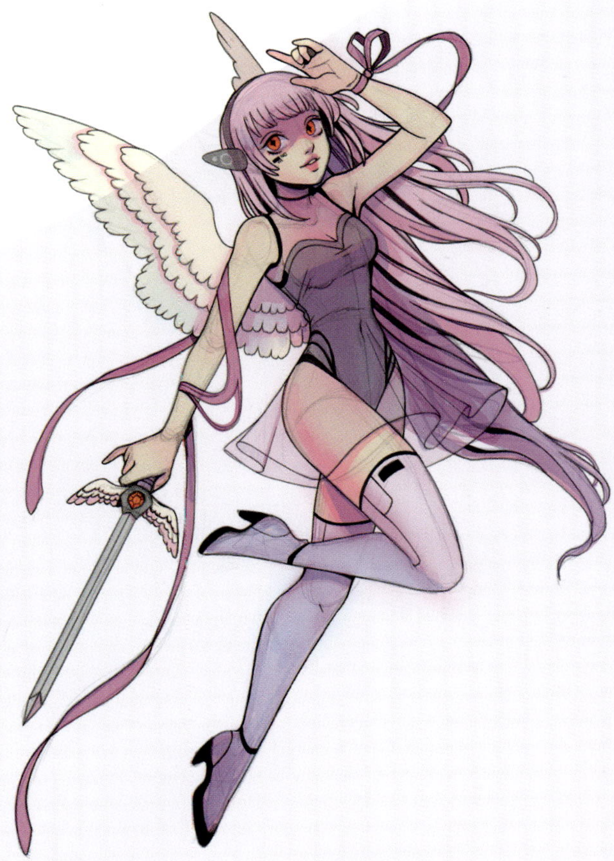

## 8 adding deep shadows

To add harder, more pronounced shadows, look for areas where you might naturally find harsh cast shadows, such as the shadows cast on the face by the bangs. For these darker shadows, I always pick a cool color: either green, blue, or indigo. The areas where I add blue shadows create a purple color where it reacts with the pink area and this accentuates the purple/yellow complementary color palette I chose.

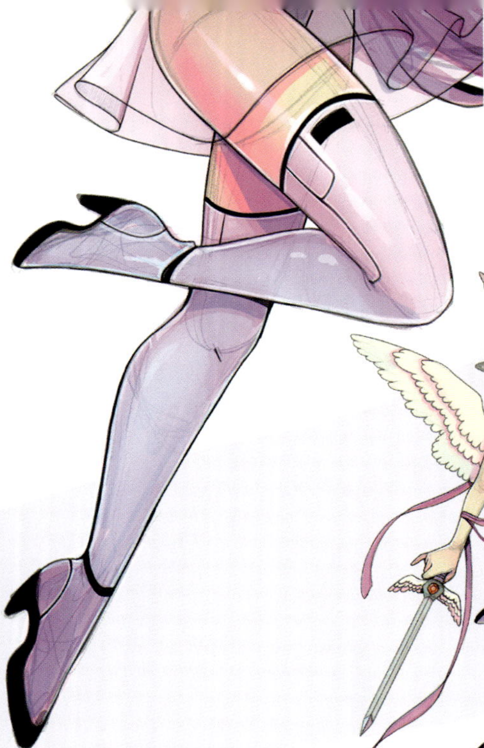

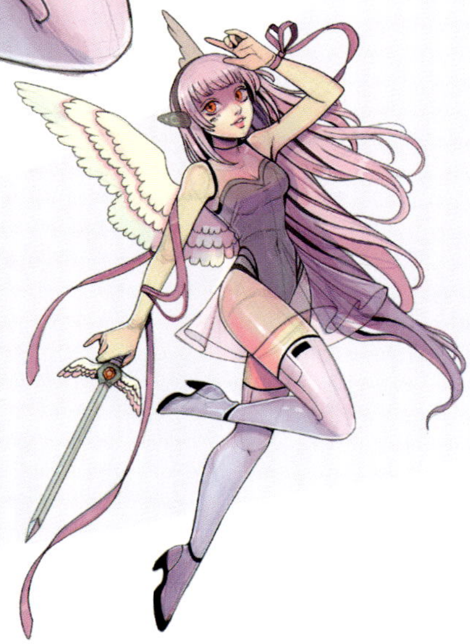

## 9 highlighting

When adding highlights, I often add rim lighting, which illuminates the contours of the shape and helps make my line art stand out. I almost never use true white, choosing instead a pastel version of the color I'm highlighting. On the hair, for example, I use a soft pink. Most of my highlights are very soft and blended — they don't have hard edges. I save my hard, white highlights only for areas I want to appear very shiny, such as the eyes, the lips, the bridge of the nose, and so on. Here, I wanted her legs and boots to have a sort of vinyl plastic feel to them, so they receive a highlight with a very hard edge, whereas other highlights on the image are more subtle and blended.

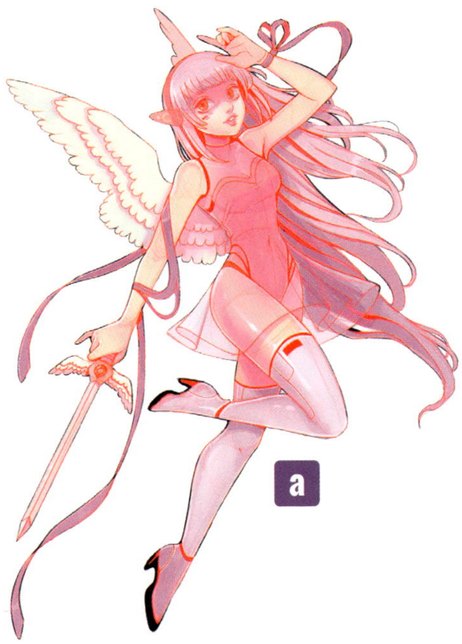

a

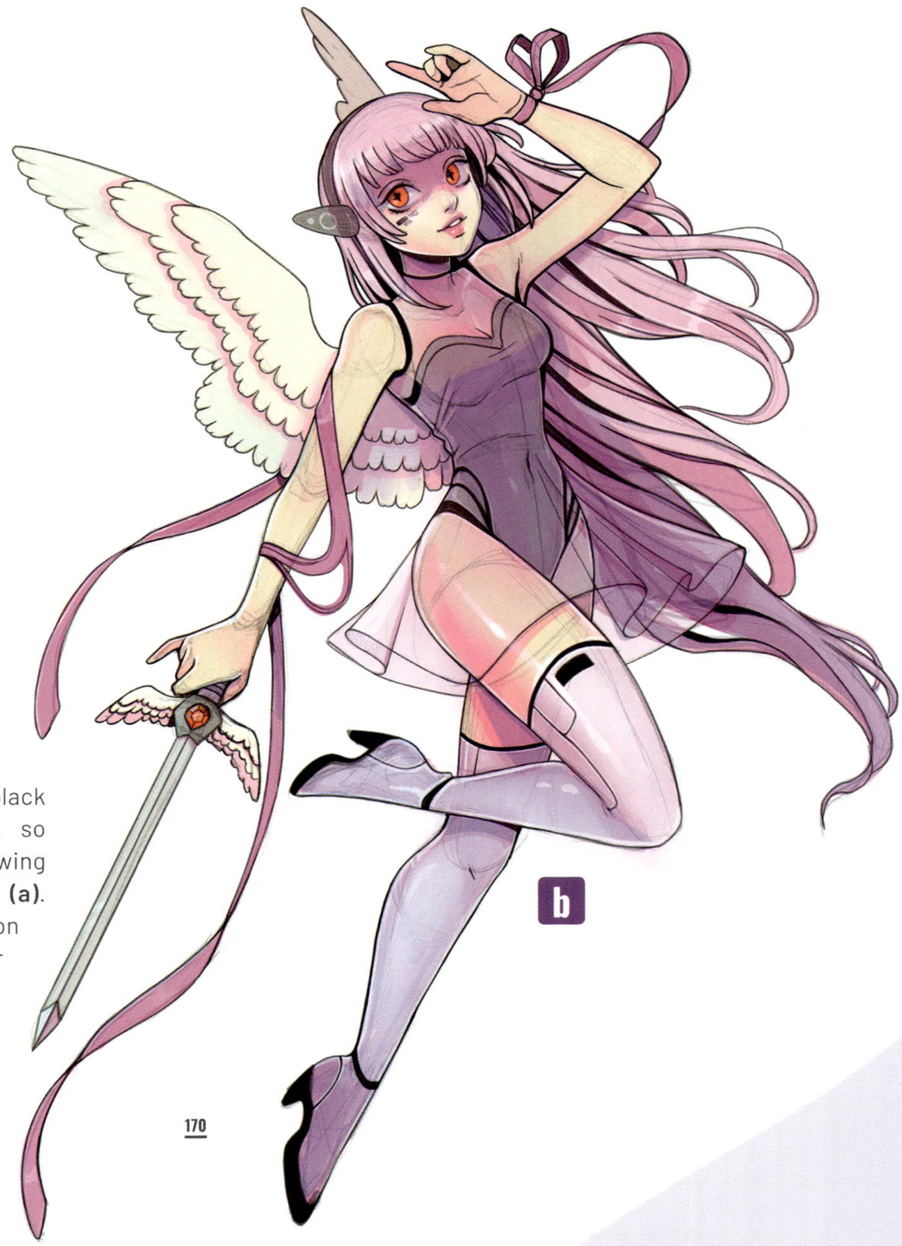

b

## 10 softening

I don't like to use a lot of black outlines in my drawings, so I always soften the drawing with an additional colored Screen layer **(a)**. Find out more about using a Screen layer on page 85. Not only will the new Screen layer help to soften the hard blacks, but it will also give the image an overall cohesive color composition **(b)**.

## 11 adding a gradient

A gradient is a great tool for creating movement and fluidity in a character design because the eye will be drawn first to the brightest part of your image (the focal point), then guided across the figure. To apply a gradient, map out the character's silhouette, set the layer to Alpha Lock, and create a gradient within the shape of your character using various shades of gray **(a)**. I always reduce the opacity of this layer until it looks right **(b)**.

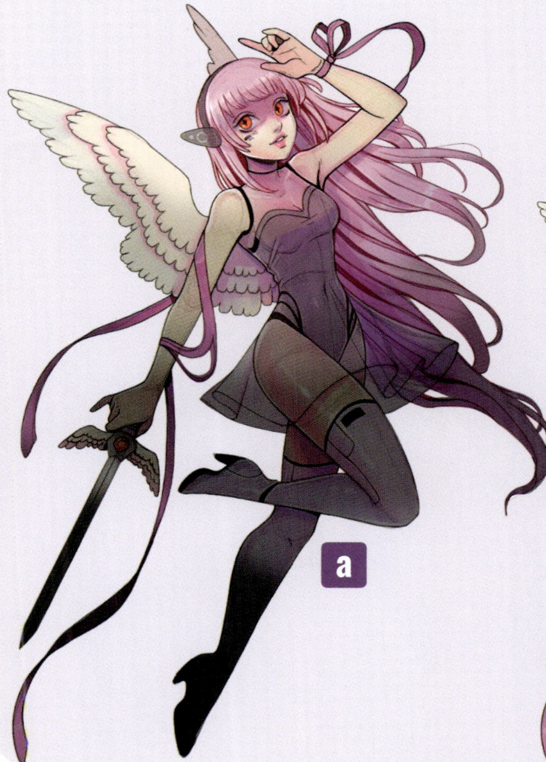

a

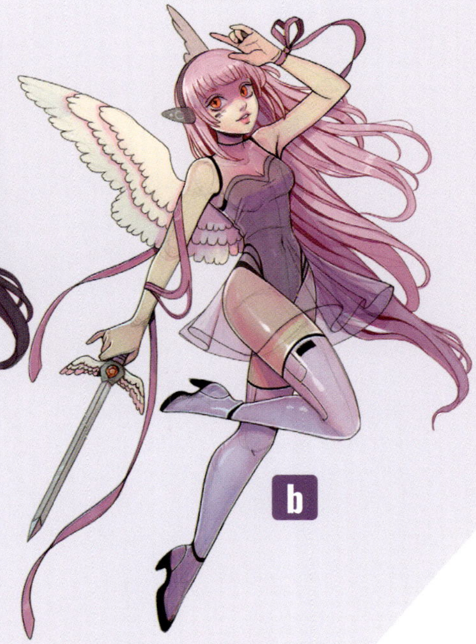

b

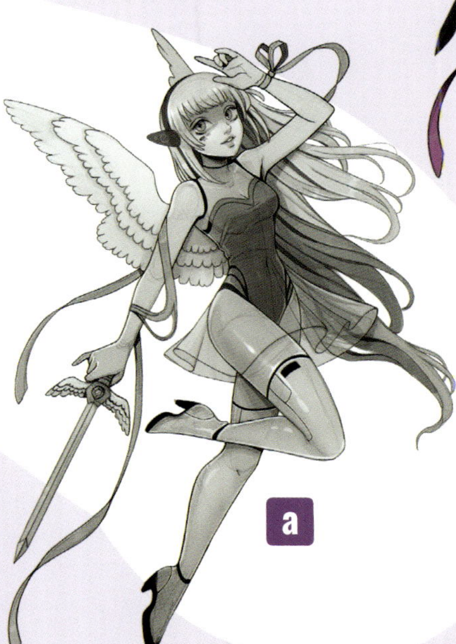

a

## 12 considering value

When designing an eye-catching character, think about using differing values to create contrast. The best way to identify value is to turn the character temporarily grayscale **(a)**. When seen in grayscale, are all elements of the character the same shade of gray, or are there distinctly different areas of lights and darks? Sometimes it can be easy to make everything all the same value even though you're using lots of different colors, so try turning your piece to grayscale every once in a while, to check. In this piece, I add some darkness to the torso and hair to break up the monotony **(b)**.

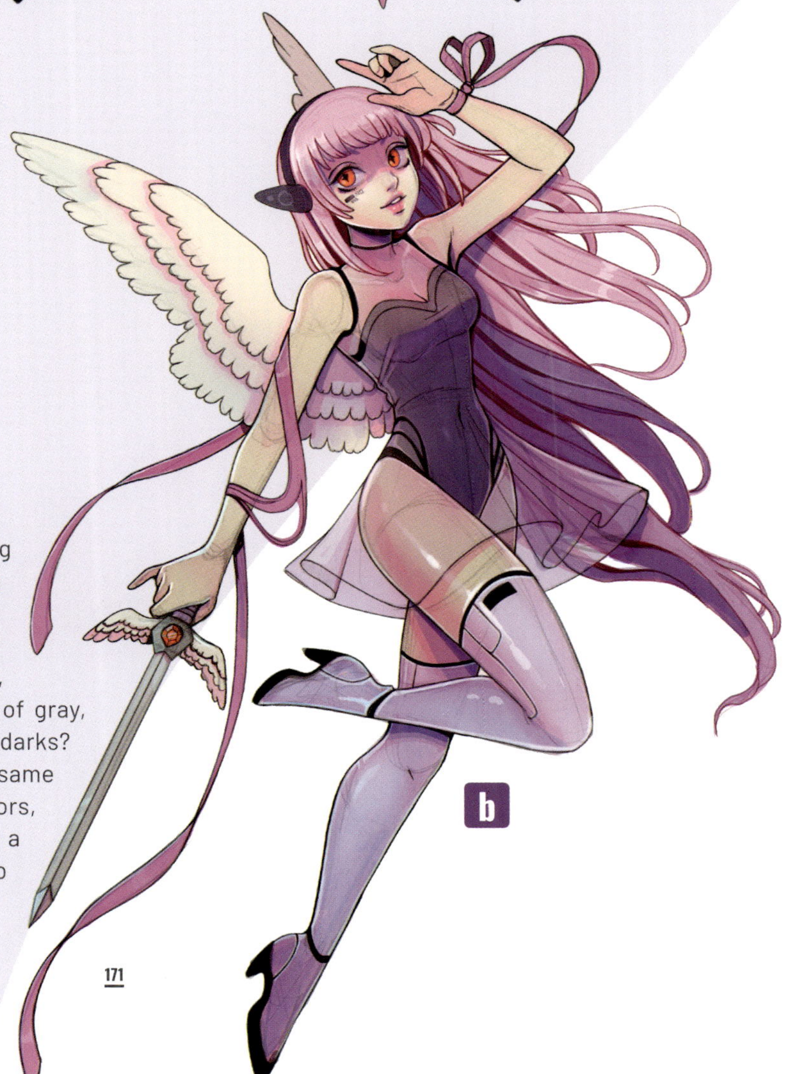

b

## 13 adding ambiance

The addition on a an ambient backlit effect is a core component of my art style, so I choose a bright blue light to work with my cool/warm color contrast **(a)**. Not only does this create a pretty lighting effect, but it can also help add flow to the image (always my number-one priority). Areas that are absorbed by the atmospheric perspective will be pushed further into the background, taking the focus off them and guiding the viewer's eye to the focal point instead **(b)**. If a particular area on the edge of your piece is distracting from your focal point, this can be a useful trick to push it into obscurity.

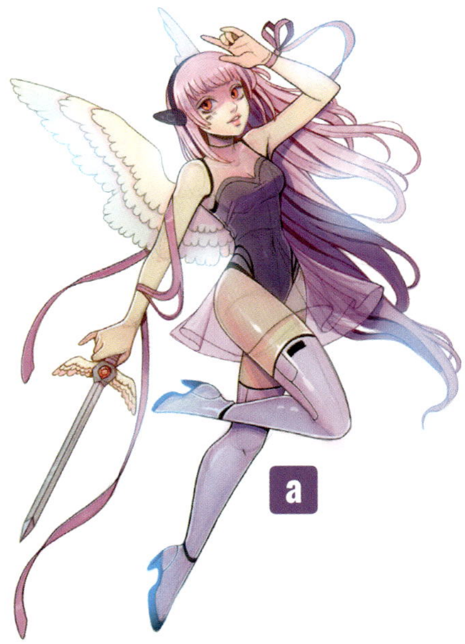

a

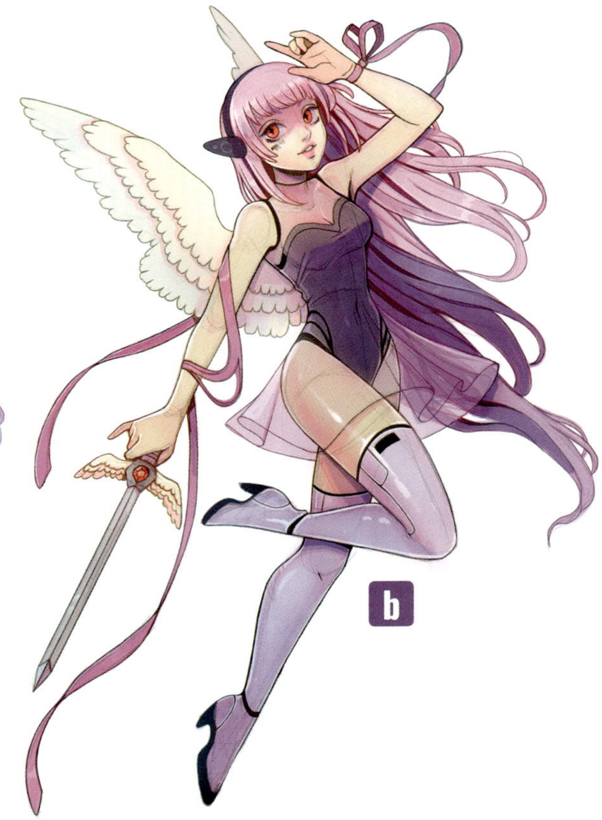

b

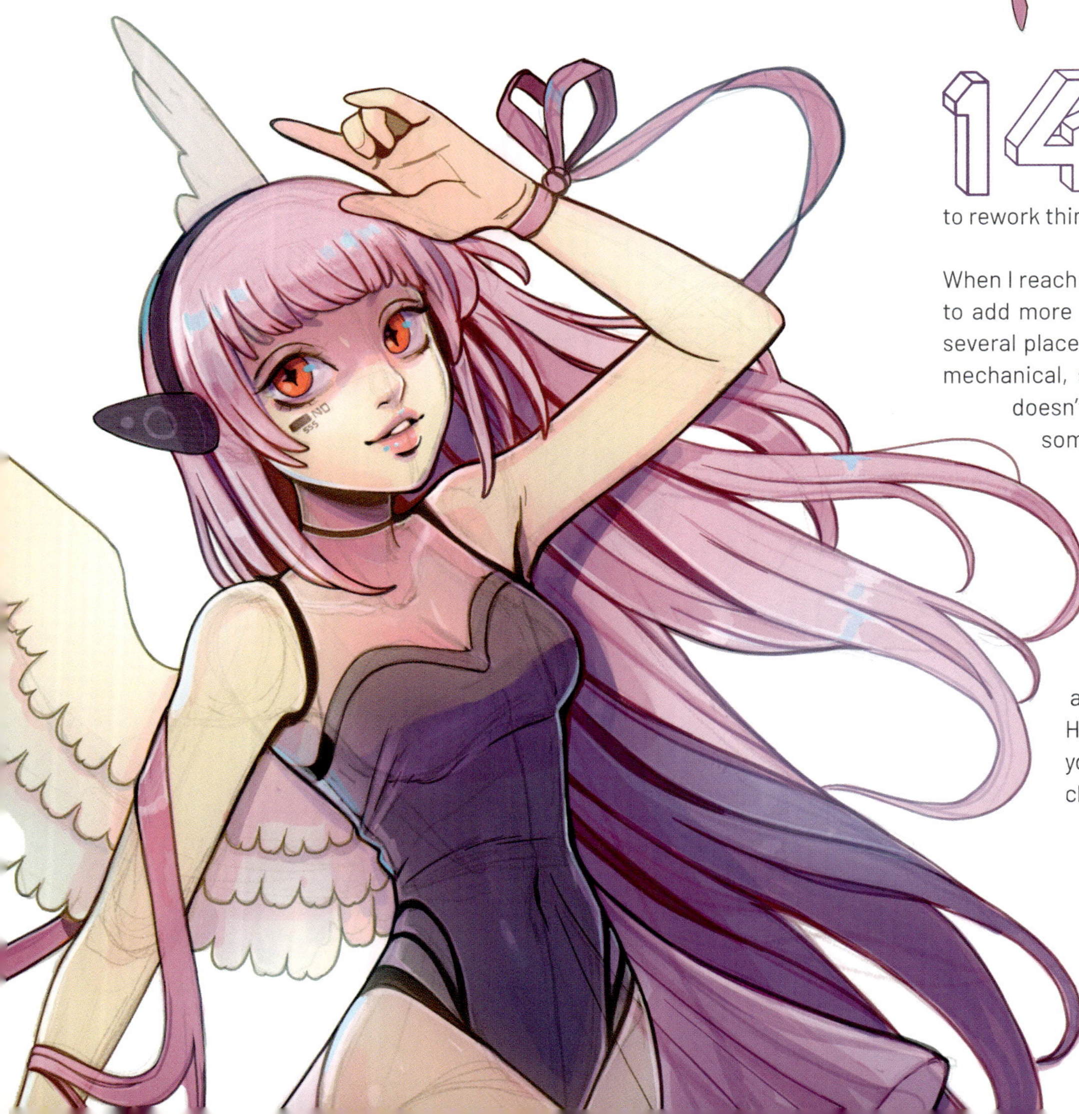

## 14 detailing and finessing

No piece is ever perfect from the beginning. There is always a point in my process where I have new ideas or need to rework things – great ideas evolve during progression!

When I reach the final stages of this piece, I decide I want to add more blue, so use a bright aqua as a highlight in several places. I also want the boots to look a little more mechanical, so add cap details to the knees. This step doesn't always happen at the end for me, but sometimes in the very middle.

Never feel bad for making alterations. These tutorials make it seem like I work in a very orderly fashion but honestly, it's much messier than this! I usually skip back and forth between these steps as I explore different ideas, colors, compositions, and lighting effects – that's totally normal. Hopefully you should have a few new tools under your belt after exploring how to design your own characters and poses!

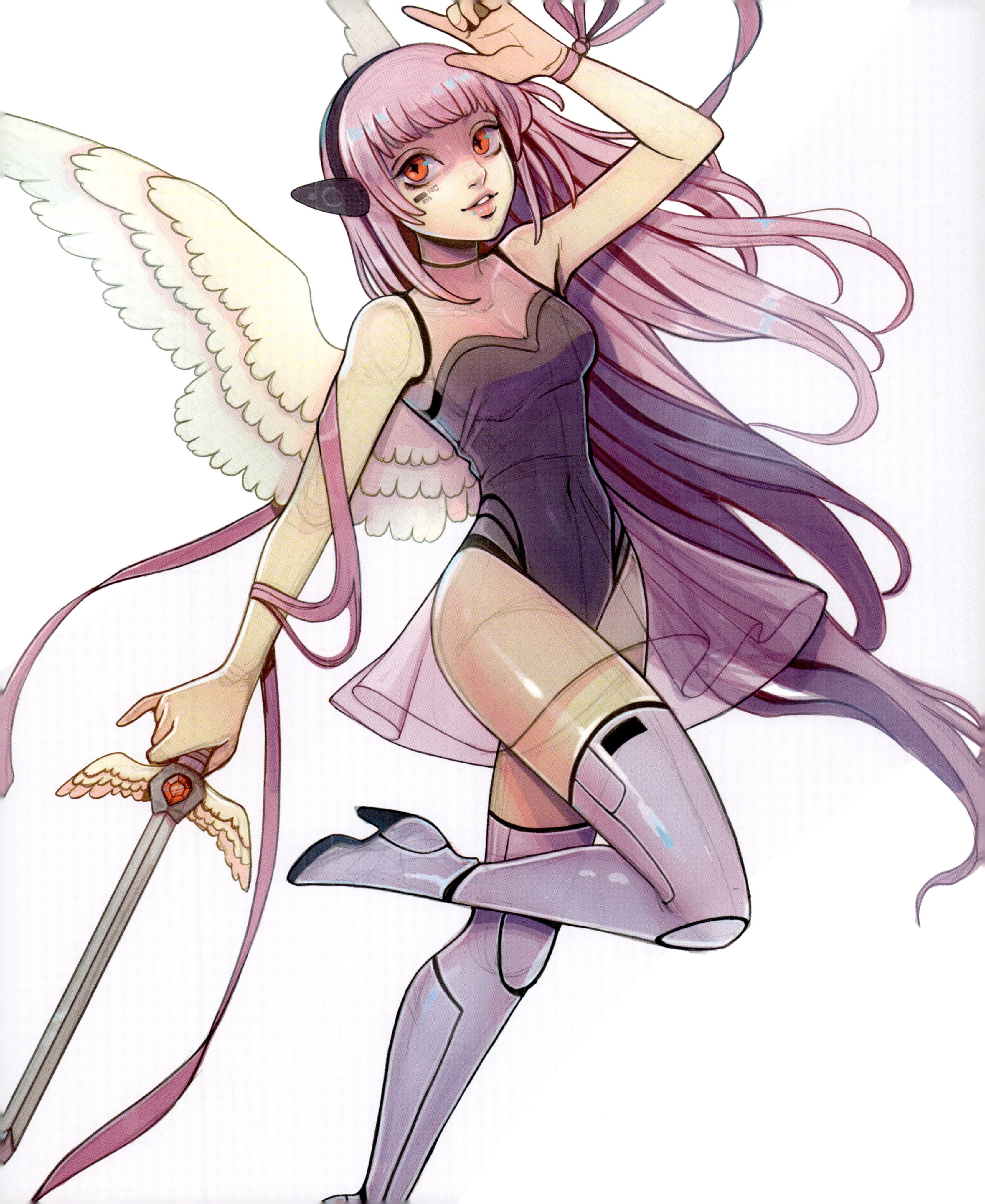

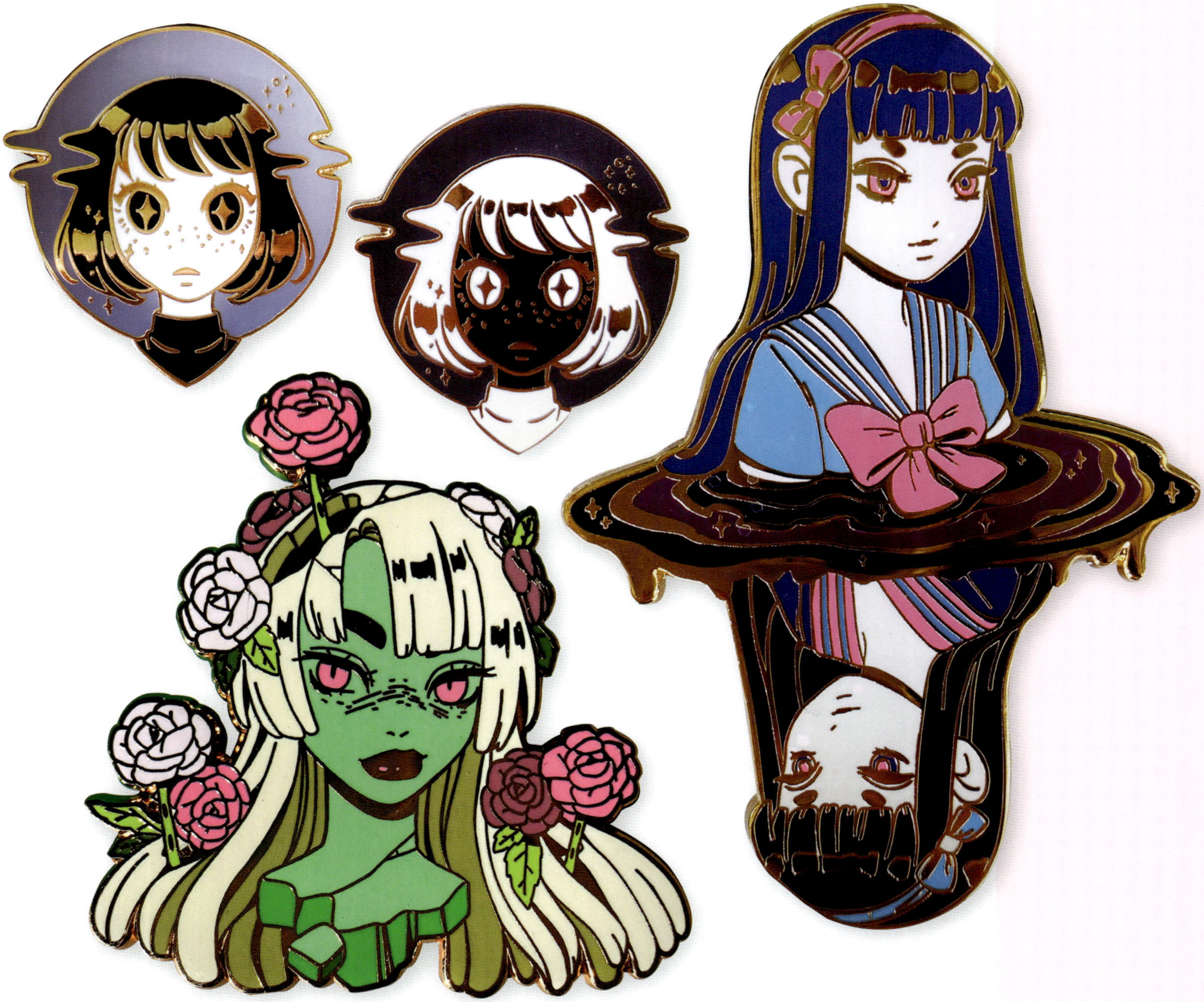

# Turning your art into a career

When I first started making products using my artwork, it was 2017 and I was behind on rent and without a working car. I had maybe 30,000 followers on Instagram at the time, which meant people thought I was totally rich. I had no idea what I was doing and nobody to ask. Being a social media artist is an awkward thing because it's so new, with no "Old Masters" who have been doing it for decades that we can turn to for advice. Much of it was just flying by the seat of my pants, guessing, and failing, then trying again. Google and Facebook groups became my best friends – they were places where I could ask constant inane questions about how to do things. Sometimes people knew the answers, sometimes they didn't.

## Trial and error (a.k.a. Sticking at it)

The first products I ever made were stickers. I didn't have any spare money to buy products in bulk from manufacturers, but I did have a working printer at home and figured I could make them myself as people bought them. I purchased a small amount of cheap sticker paper and some glossy adhesive overlay, then whenever someone bought a sticker I printed it out, added the overlay and cut it out by hand. It was a very tedious process. Just about anything could go wrong — the printer would jam or get streaky, leave a blob on the print, or run out of a specific cartridge and start printing the stickers in all the wrong colors. The adhesive overlay had to be placed perfectly, otherwise it left a crease or bubble that would ruin the page of stickers. If it didn't land perfectly straight, a sticker on the page wouldn't get covered and was thus wasted. Hand-cutting had to be precise, which meant it was very slow, and quickly started to hurt my hands and wrists. Every time any of these things went wrong, entire stickers, or whole pages of stickers, were thrown in the trash. What was supposed to be a cheap way to produce stickers started adding up each time I made a mistake and had to, yet again, throw away another batch of stickers.

Eventually, as a sale event, I offered a free unique sketch to anyone who spent $20 in my store. I was stupid enough to not set any limit on how many sketches I would make and got a huge influx of orders in my store. Because I sold my stickers for $1–2 each, a lot of orders didn't mean a lot of money, but it *did* mean a lot of work. I remember sitting in a very hot room (I had no air conditioning) in a sea of paper trimmings trying to deal with printer jams and streaky lines. At the same time I was meticulously cutting out hundreds of stickers and making a massive pile of original drawings to go with them. My hands were screaming from pain by the end of the week and I stayed up all night drawing sketch after sketch. I vowed to never offer something like this again, and even more so, that I would never cut stickers by hand again. I thought my problems were over with a Cricut machine that would do the cutting for me. But the machine ended up being so particular and finicky that it was more time-consuming and frustrating than cutting out the stickers myself, and I *still* had major printer issues to deal with on top of it.

After about a year-and-a-half of trying to make the product myself, it became abundantly clear that the one way to not go crazy was to start ordering from

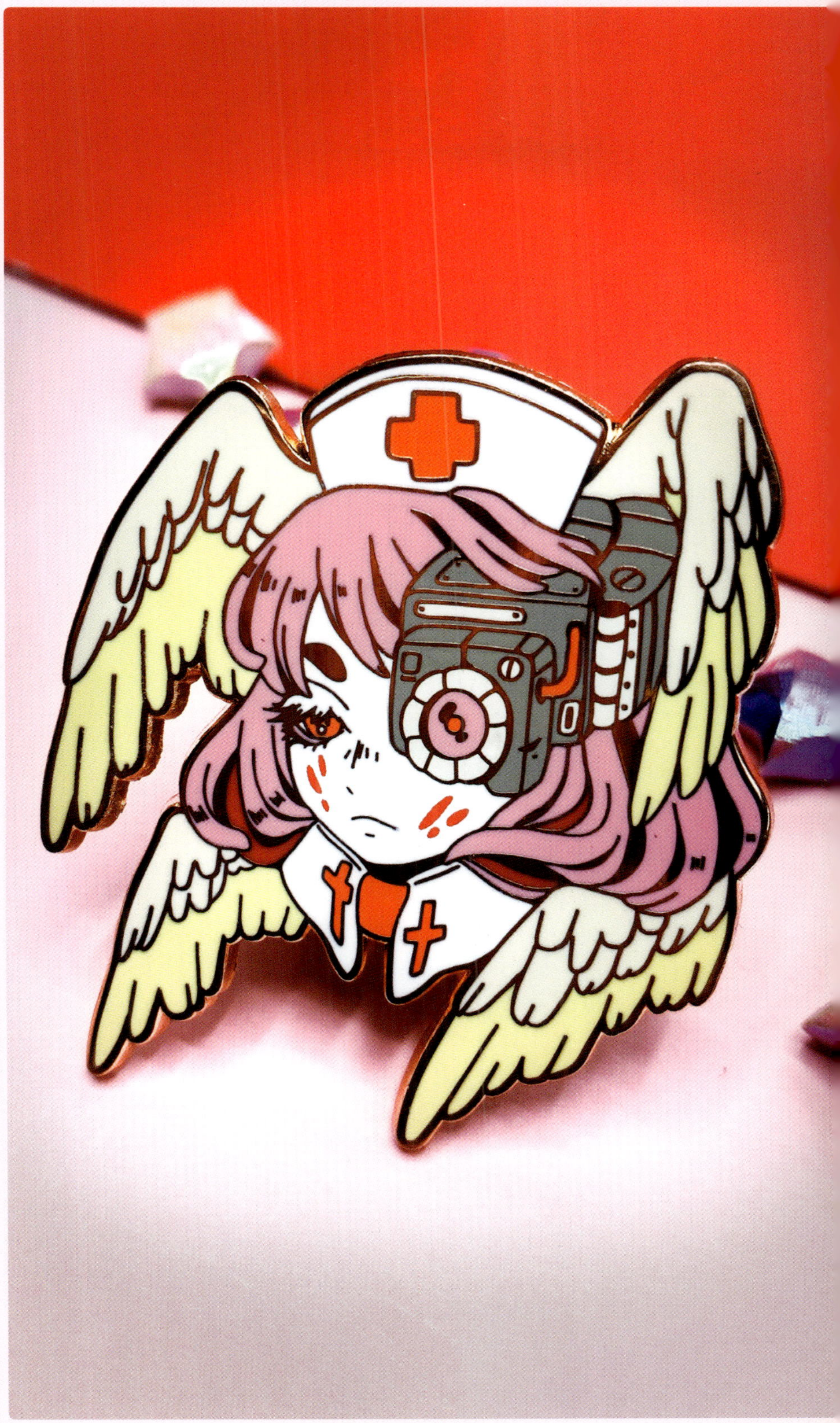

Eventually, I started to make stickers that were pretty cool. As I kept going, I realized that was just how these things went.

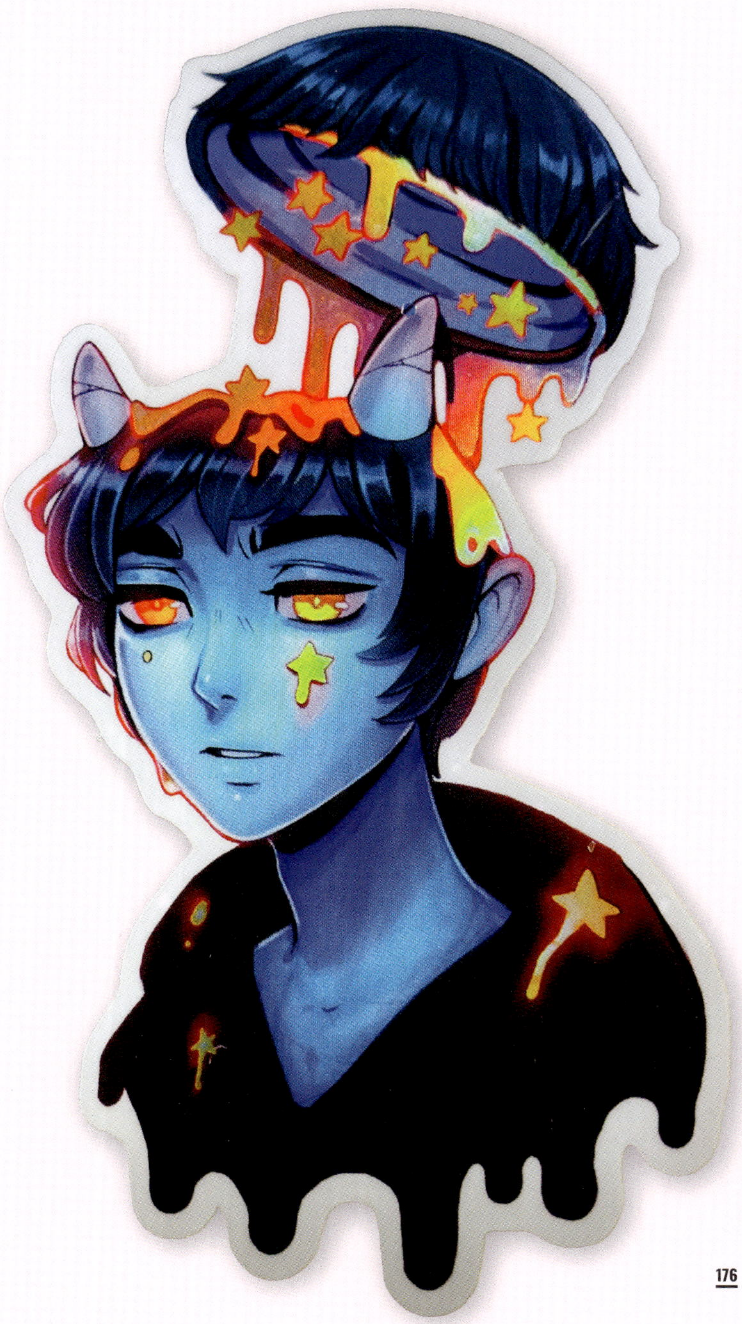

actual companies. I stuck with the Cricut until I finally saved up enough that I could afford to order a batch of stickers from a manufacturer. I was so excited. I found a manufacturer that worked for my budget, and made an order. The stickers from this company were significantly cheaper than the other companies I was looking into but, to my dismay, I quickly discovered why. Normally stickers are coated with some kind of clear overlay that protects the ink, but the stickers I had purchased printed the ink directly onto a piece of vinyl with no protective seal over the top. This meant that after a month or two the design rubbed off them entirely, leaving people with a blank white piece of vinyl. It was terrible. I remember feeling stupid and disheartened that I'd wasted my money on such a bad product. But all I could do was learn from my mistake and try again with a new company, and again with a new company, over and over until I found one I liked.

There were many times that I said out loud, "I wish I had someone to ask about this." It was like feeling out a maze in the dark. But I started to learn the sticker lingo, about the different types of materials and finishes, about which sizes were too big or too small for my designs (usually by ordering a whole batch of stickers in a particular size, only to realize I absolutely hated how they looked). Eventually, I started to make stickers that were pretty cool. As I kept going, I realized that was just how these things went.

In fact, every product I made was trial and error, trial and error, until eventually I figured it out. The first time I ordered artwork prints, I didn't clean the file properly and ended up with a whole batch of prints that had a glaring error on them that I couldn't sell. The first time I ordered key-chains, I accidentally ordered them single-sided with no protective coat over the ink, so they scratched and faded. The first time I ordered tote bags, I asked for the wrong kind of printing and the ink was absorbed into the fabric color, making the print impossible to see. The first time I ordered enamel pins, I used a manufacturer who didn't gold plate the front of the pins and wouldn't reimburse me for the half-gold, half-silver pins they sent me.

When these things happened, I felt frustrated, but now I just laugh. I've accepted that failure is a huge part of the process — anytime you do something new it probably isn't going to go the way you intended. But when I look at what I'm able to make now and how I'm able to make it with ease, I feel so proud that I felt my way out of that dark maze. In many ways I think fondly back to those days, when I made humble little paper stickers at home — it was such an exciting time, wondering where things would go and if they'd work out. I keep some of those original handmade stickers in a frame at my studio to remind me not only of where I started, but also of how far failing over and over again has taken me.

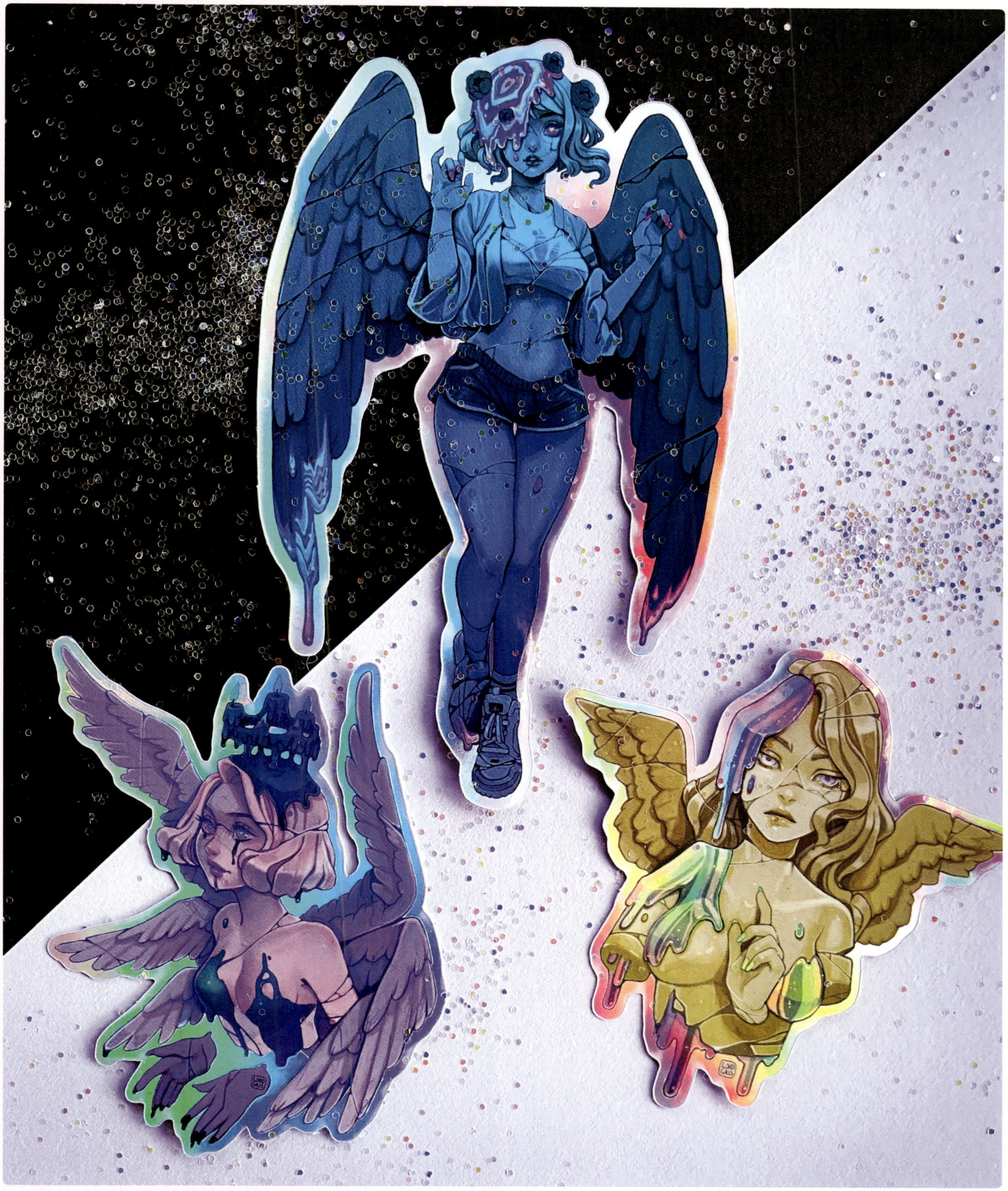

I like being in charge of my own schedule and artistic direction, and this means making products has been the best path for me.

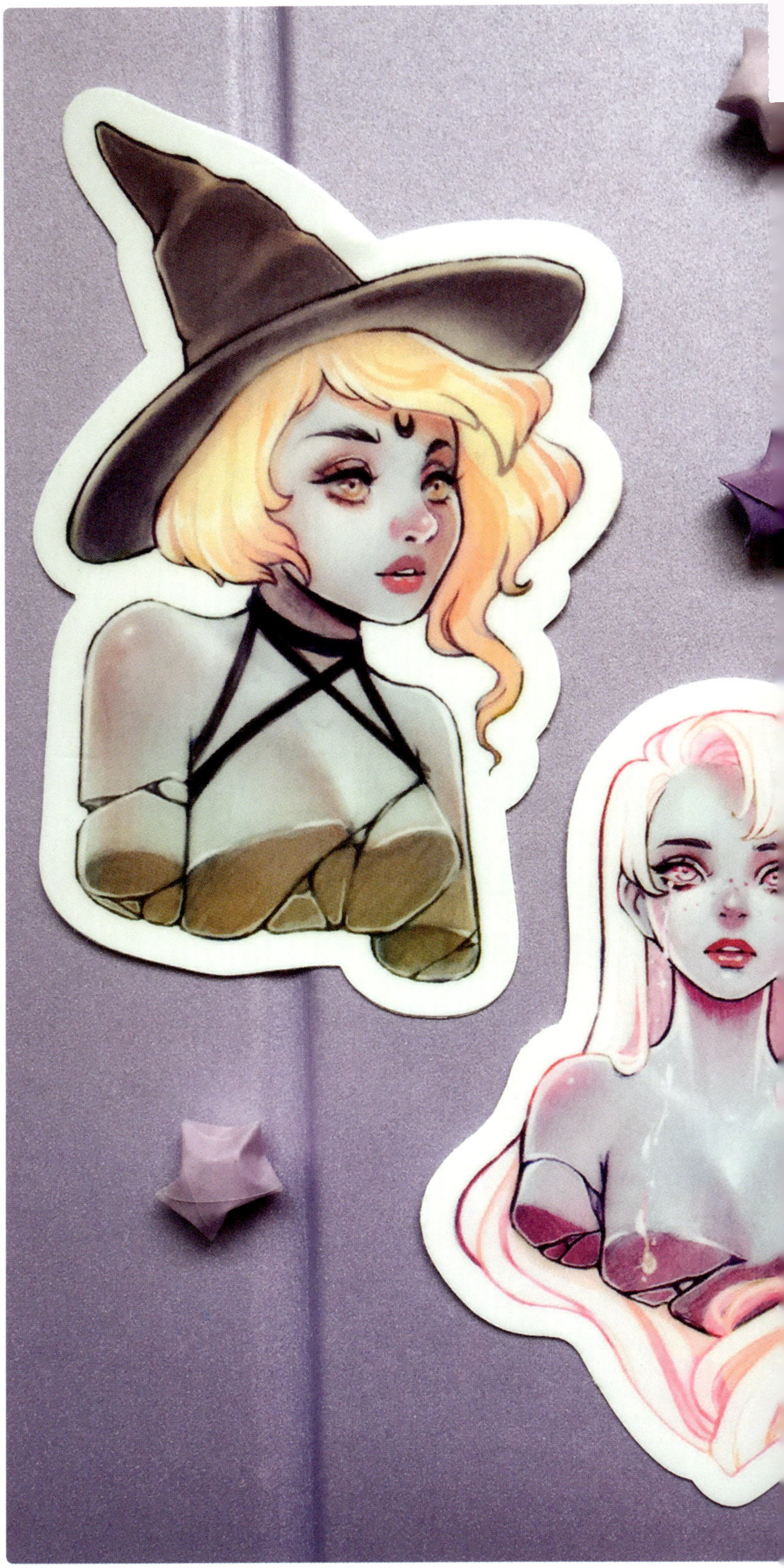

## Making money as an artist

A big question I am asked by younger artists is, "How do you make money from your art?" The great news is there are many ways to make money as an artist, and I'm lucky enough to know people from all across the artistic profession who are thriving through the monetization of their art. The trope of the "starving artist" is an outdated myth. I'm not saying it's an easy path to forge, but it's not impossible to make a living doing what you love – many people do it. Different business models work for different people – what works for someone else may not work for you. Some people work for games companies, advertising agencies, or animation studios. Some are freelance and pick up different gigs when it suits them. Others prefer to be their own boss, working at their own pace, with their own online stores or Patreon to sell the content they produce. There are artists who work exclusively with art galleries, artists who travel the convention circuit selling their products in booths, and artists who teach or work on commissions, creating custom art for paying clients. Sometimes these people have online followings and sometimes they have no social media at all – it just depends on how they enjoy working.

I've dabbled in a lot of things at this point: I've worked on games, I've created concept art for toys, taken commissions, and shown in galleries. Every now and then I take a table at a convention (although it's more to meet people face to face than to sell products). But in the end, I always come back to just enjoying doing things on my own terms. I like being in charge of my own schedule and artistic direction, and this means making products has been the best path for me. But I didn't start out knowing that.

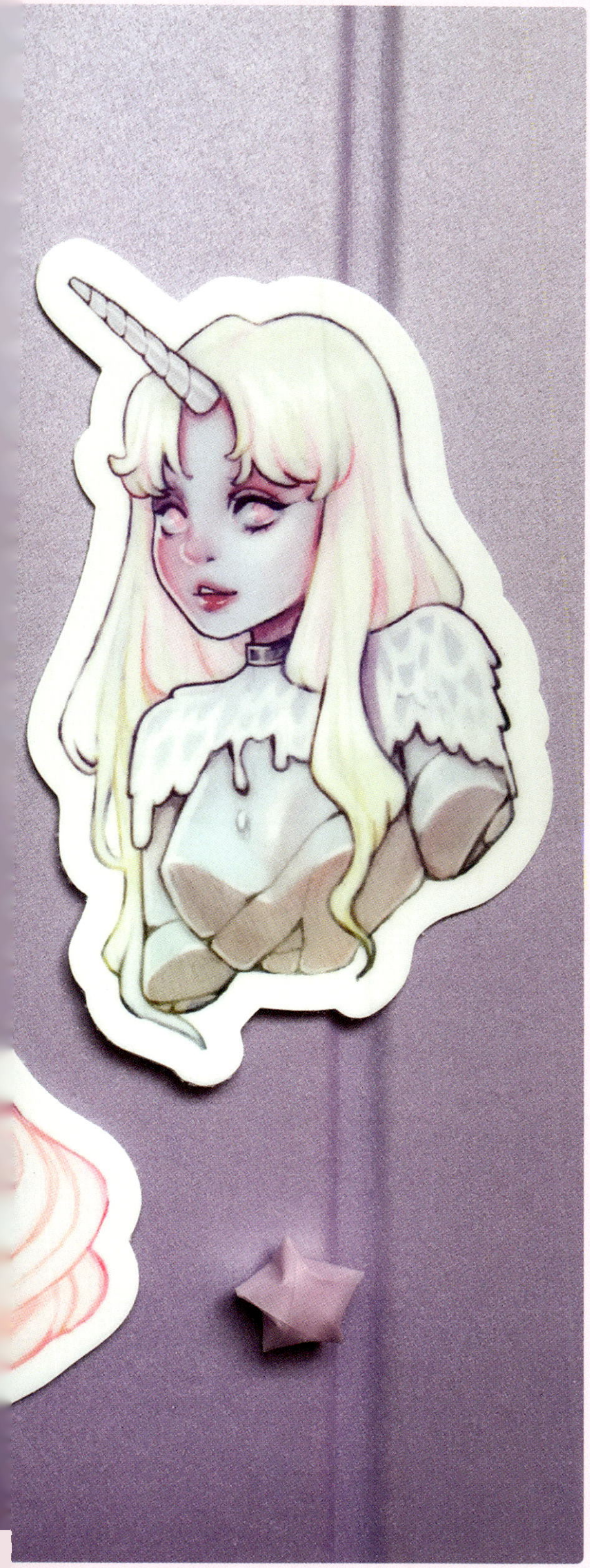

## Experiment and connect

So, the best advice I can give is twofold. Experiment — try different things and figure out what you love. If you really like structured environments and assignments, then working at a company might be for you. If you like making fan art and traveling the world, selling your work at conventions might be the answer. If you enjoy working directly with customers, commissioned work might be for you. If you like staying home and making cute products, running an online store might be for you! You never know until you try.

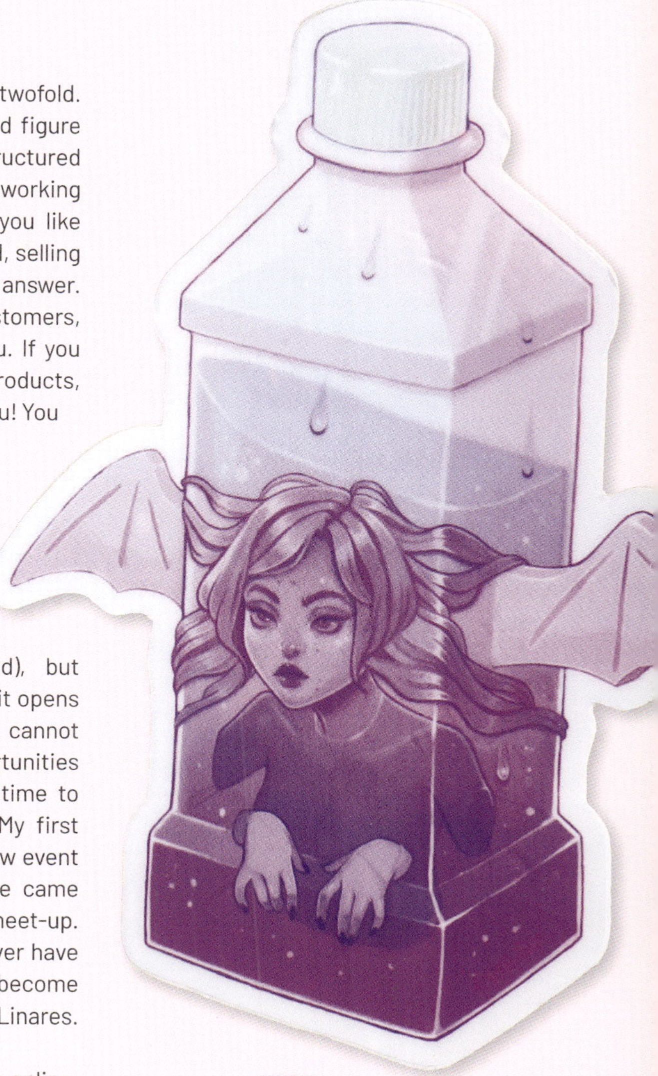

The second most important piece of advice I have is not very popular, but is honestly so valuable, and that is to connect with people. I know as artists, many of us tend to be introverted (myself included), but connecting to people is everything — it opens the doors to what you want to do. I cannot stress enough how so many opportunities fell into my lap because I took the time to leave the house and meet people. My first gallery show came from a Drink & Draw event and working on my first video game came from attending a local game dev meet-up. Even how I learned to paint would never have happened if I hadn't taken the time to become friends with my studio mate, Matt Linares.

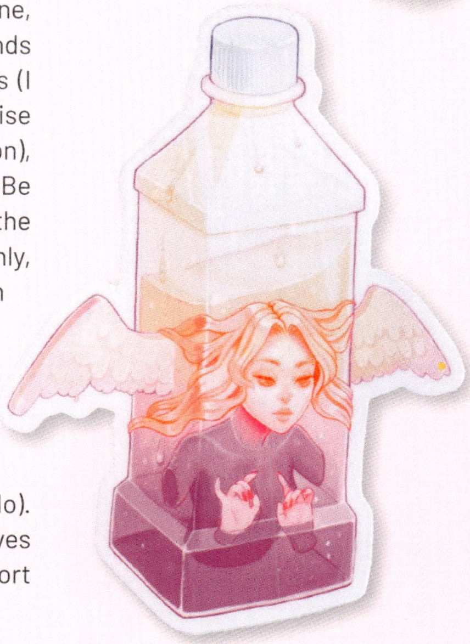

So go out, connect with fellow artists online, go to local art meet-up groups, make friends with your booth neighbors at conventions (I don't mean be a sales person and advertise yourself — I just mean be a normal person), and make some friends in your industry. Be kind, giving, genuine, and generous — be the person you would want to meet. Suddenly, you'll find yourself a little less alone in the art process, able to ask each other questions or pass opportunities along to each other that aren't quite for you (I don't take commissions anymore, but if approached for one, I pass the job onto one of my talented art friends who do). Nobody can do everything all by themselves — it's torture — so giving yourself a support network will do wonders for you.

# remember this...

You have been given a gift to create and to breathe life into the things you touch – that is something that makes you beautiful. Remember to never let anyone take your art from you: not a teacher, a parent, a friend, negative comments online, and especially not yourself. Remember that there is not as much pressure as you perceive, and you don't need to be the most incredible artist to be a successful artist – you only need to make what you love, and love what you make. Remember to be kind, giving, and uplifting as much as you can, to share the creative space with other artists, and embrace the dazzling array of diverse styles all around you. Remember that you have something within you that only you can make; it may take time to pull it out, but the time spent is always worth it. Remember that the first time you do something, it is always messy and full of mistakes, but the second time, it goes better. Remember to love those mistakes because of that.

Thank you for taking the time to read this book. I hope it helps you on your own creative journey, and I truly look forward to what you will make.

# thank you

A huge thank you to my family, who never discouraged my art or my strangeness. For my mother especially, for raising me with the joy of crafts and being my supportive collaborator on all my projects, and for helping me tirelessly in times of need. Thank you for all the hours you spent packaging and writing addresses on so many envelopes for me when I first started out. You have been ceaselessly supportive and I have loved every minute of our time creating together. Thank you to all of those who support me online, be it by leaving kind comments, sending me inspiring messages, sharing your art and your journeys with me, or supporting my store and Patreon – I could not be here without you, and I feel so grateful every day. Thank you to those who backed the Kickstarter for this book to make it a reality. And thank you to the 3dtotal team for reaching out to me to make a book in the first place, and for working so hard to put it all together.